NATIVE AMERICANS

INTERDISCIPLINARY PERSPECTIVES

Edited by
JOHN R. WUNDER
CYNTHIA WILLIS ESQUEDA
University of Nebraska-Lincoln

A ROUTLEDGE SERIES

OTHER BOOKS IN THIS SERIES:

POLITICAL PRINCIPLES AND INDIAN
SOVEREIGNTY
Thurman Lee Hester, Jr.

DANCE LODGES OF THE OMAHA PEOPLE
Building From Memory
Mark Awakuni-Swetland

BLOOD MATTERS
*The Five Civilized Tribes and the Search
for Unity in the 20th Century*
Erik March Zissu

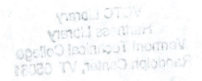

The Power of the Land

Identity, Ethnicity, and Class Among the
Oglala Lakota

Paul Robertson

ROUTLEDGE
NEW YORK & LONDON

Published in 2002 by
Routledge
29 West 35th Street
New York, NY 10001

Published in Great Britain by
Routledge
11 New Fetter Lane
London EC4P 4EE

Routledge is an imprint of the Taylor & Francis Group.

10 9 8 7 6 5 4 3 2 1

Library of Congress Cataloging-in-Publication Data

Robertson, Paul (Paul M.), 1944–
    The power of the land : identity, ethnicity, and class among the Oglala Lakota / Paul
Robertson.
        p. cm. — (Native Americans)
    Includes bibliographical references and index.
    ISBN 0-8153-3591-1
    1. Oglala Indians—Ethnic identity. 2. Oglala Indians—Land tenure. 3. Oglala
Indians—Government relations. 4. Land tenure—Government policy—South Dakota—
Pine Ridge Indian Reservation. 5. Pine Ridge Indian Reservation (S.D.)—History. I. Title.
II. Series.

E99.O3 R63 2001
978'.0049752—dc21

                                                                    2001034875

Printed on acid-free, 250 year-life paper
Manufactured in the United States of America

This book is dedicated to my parents Paul and Rachael Robertson and to my father-in-law and mother-in-law Edward Iron Cloud, Jr. and Mary Locke Iron Cloud for their belief that people who struggle together can make a better world for the future generations.

Contents

Preface and Acknowledgements

The overriding theme of this study is the land and conflicts that have swirled around it for the past 130 years of Oglala history. My interest in the land, particularly in what the Oglala Lakota people generally refer to as their "land base," was piqued shortly after I arrived on Pine Ridge Indian Reservation in 1980. Particularly striking was the divergence in elders' stories about earlier uses of the land and some of the accounts of historians and anthropologists. Elders spoke of a time when the people had control of the land and were able to use it toward a measure of self-sufficiency in the colonial context of the reservation while some written accounts had the Oglala settling back to live on the government dole. The late Severt Young Bear, Sr. told stories of hardship and deprivation, but also of people's ingenuity in dealing with those circumstances. Oglala elder, and former Oglala Sioux Tribal President Johnson Holy Rock, spoke of a viable economy centered around grazing in the early reservation years, and emphasized that the people knew how to get a good bargain when they did business with merchants in nearby border towns.

This study started off as an attempt to weigh in on the different interpretations of Oglala land tenure but those concerns led directly to questions about the development of the colonial situation on the reservation. What were the factors that denied the majority of Oglala people access to their own land? What was the role of the U.S. government's colonial administration? What was the role of the market, of the integration of the reservation and the Oglala people into the broader economic system? Did those factors relate to internal differentiation? How had "mixed blood" and "full blood" differences become so important among the Oglala when they were less so in some other reservations? People regularly invoked such differences to explain political and economic conflicts and differences. How had those differences developed and why had they become such integral parts of the explanations people gave for their history? By providing

ix

some answers to questions like those this study provides a vantage point on the development of the colonial situation on Pine Ridge Indian Reservation during the past 120 years.

There are many people I want to thank for the knowledge they have shared and for the guidance and support they have extended me during the course of this study. Among them are the late Severt Young Bear, Sr. and his wife Myrna White Face Young Bear. We spent many late nights talking about reservation history and the legacy of colonial control. I want to thank Lakota historian Robert Gay, Denny Pilcher, George Iron Cloud, Steven Red Elk, Louis Whirlwind Horse, James Bad Wound, Lucille Fire Thunder, and Royal Bull Bear, all of whom have passed on to the spirit world. I particularly want to acknowledge Johnson Holy Rock, Gerald One Feather, Guy White Thunder, and Oliver Red Cloud, who were patient enough to talk with me and with whom I have been fortunate enough to work alongside of on different issues over the years. I also want to thank Mary White Thunder, JoAnn Tall, George Tall, Doris Respects Nothing, Woodrow Respects Nothing, Alberta Iron Cloud-Miller, Jim Miller, Emily Iron Cloud-Koenen and Bill Koenen, Debbie and Alex White Plume, Calvin Jumping Bull, Billy Quijas, Shirley Murphy, Cordelia and Charlie White Elk, Cecelia Fire Thunder, Marie Randall, Francis and Freda Apple, Edward Starr, Lucille Bull Bear, Manuel Iron Cloud, Bluch Fire Thunder, Leona Young Bull Bear, Anthony Black Feather, Ardis Iron Cloud Hamilton, Wendell Yellow Bull, Bennett "Tuffy" Sierra, Selo Black Crow, Ted Means, Leta Hare, and Russell Loud Hawk.

Nancy Owens, Colin Greer, Richmond Clow, Reginald Witherspoon, Molly Lynn Watt, and the late Alfonso Ortiz were my graduate committee at Union Institute. They provided critical guidance, editorial assistance, and much useful commentary on the earlier version of this study that was my doctoral dissertation. For similar support, and for inspiration to persevere, I want to thank my long time colleagues from Oglala Lakota College, the late Jeanne Smith and her husband Dowell Caselli-Smith. George Salzman's enthusiasm for telling this story, and his contagious commitment to social justice have been inspirational. Samuel Saunders' and John Bandy graciously provided useful comments on one of the chapters. Ted Hamilton and Edward "Buzz" Iron Cloud III's discussions over coffee were very helpful, as was Jeff Iron Cloud's quiet support.

I was fortunate to be able to do archival work at the National Archives in Kansas City, Missouri, and in Washington D.C. Alan Perry, who spent eight years organizing the Pine Ridge Collection in Kansas City, was very gracious and helpful. My stay in Kansas City would not have been possible without the support of Elliot Moore and his wife Virginia Moore, and I owe them a sincere debt of thanks. I also want to thank Fred Hoxie of the Newberry Library, who was kind enough to read an early draft outline of this study and to give me some sound advice that I have tried to follow.

While I was at the Newberry, I was also fortunate to meet Henry Dobyns and he was kind enough to read that early draft and comment on it. John Aubrey was very helpful. He patiently explained the rich collection at the Newberry, and took pains to point me in helpful directions. Julie Lakota, archivist at Oglala Lakota College, provided useful assistance and suggestions.

I would have been hard pressed to complete this project without the support of the United Negro College Fund/Carnegie Mellon Foundation. I am very grateful for their grant, which enabled me to take a year's leave from my teaching post at Oglala Lakota College.

My wife, Eileen Iron Cloud, has been very patient and supportive throughout this process, as has my daughter Willow Grace Iron Cloud Robertson. Willow is ten years old now but she was four when I finished the dissertation the book is based on. Just before I finished it, she told her grandmother Mary Iron Cloud that she wanted to break my computer. Her older brother Chaske and her sister Laurel were remarkably understanding. My wife has patiently listened to my accounts of stories and one piece of data or another, and has provided helpful and patient guidance. Her experience as an elected official of Oglala Sioux Tribal government, as co-founder of the Oglala Lakota Women's Society, and as a member of a *tiospaye* in Porcupine District makes her an excellent critic. I particularly want to thank the late Edward Iron Cloud II and his late wife Mary Iron Cloud for sharing their wisdom and their knowledge with me. I also owe a special debt of thanks to Richard Two Dogs, and his wife, Ethleen Two Dogs. Lastly, I want to thank my late father Paul and my mother Rachael Robertson, for their belief in me and their enthusiasm for this work.

Though this study draws on many voices, the responsibility for the choice and presentation of data and texts, for interpretations made, analyses proffered, and conclusions reached, is mine alone.

Paul M. Robertson
Porcupine, South Dakota
Pine Ridge Indian Reservation
April, 2001

List of Maps and Plates

Maps

Plates

List of Tables and Figures

Tables

Figures

The Power of the Land

CHAPTER I

Makoce Ta Wowasake:
The Power of the Land

Fault lines that have developed in Oglala society during more than a century of U.S. colonial rule over the Pine Ridge Indian Reservation were
readily apparent at a February 1995 meeting at Our Lady of Lourdes
Catholic Mission in Porcupine. Oglala, Minniconjou, Brulé, Sicangu, and
Hunkpapa elders and headsmen had traveled there to oppose a Bureau of
Indian Affairs (BIA) proposal that threatened to take some of the small
amount of land they had left away from them.[1] They wanted no part of a
plan that bureaucrats in Washington D.C. were advancing to solve problems that the colonial system had created in the first place. They talked
long, in strong voices, emotional voices. They spoke eloquently in Lakota,
their mother tongue, and used gestures they do not use when they speak
their second language.

Lakota elder Lucille Fire Thunder from Wounded Knee District gave a
fiery speech in Lakota that day. She lambasted the Bureau for not allowing
the people adequate time to review and respond to the proposal that would
take Lakota land away from landowners – the deadline for input was a
week away. Was she concerned that the officials from the Bureau could not
understand what she said? "No," she laughed, "It wouldn't make any difference if they did. We heard what they had to say." The point of the meeting, she said, was to educate each other, to decide what to do, and to find
a way to stop the Bureau of Indian Affairs from taking their land.

Superintendent Delbert Brewer, Realty Director Frieda Brewer, and Land
Operations Director Jim Glade represented the BIA's Pine Ridge Agency
office. They explained the proposal that had come from then Assistant
Secretary for Indian Affairs Ada Deer, and recorded the people's testimony.
After their opening remarks, they sat back and listened. Ms. Brewer
changed the tapes in the recorder as the hours passed. An interpreter from
the BIA whispered to them occasionally. Some, especially younger people,
gave their testimony in English. The officials were patient, prepared to let

each person have their say. The Superintendent and the Realty Director are Oglala Sioux Tribal members and they know that these things take a long time.

Lakota elders Royal Bull Bear and Joe Swift Bird of the Grey Eagle Society, Chief Oliver Red Cloud, great-grandson of the famous chief, and Reginald Cedar Face, Secretary of the Black Hills Sioux Nation Treaty Council, sat behind a table alongside the Bureau officials.[2] The officials were twenty to thirty years younger than they were. Their relative youth, fancy dress and exclusive use of English set them off from the elders and from the majority of those who testified that day.

All four Lakota elders at the table were "treaty men," descended from chiefs and treaty signers. In their view, the 1851 and 1868 Treaties their ancestors negotiated at Fort Laramie are sacred agreements that were sealed by the *cannupa* (sacred pipe), and are the legal and moral basis for Lakota sovereignty. "Treaty people" are quick to point out that Article VI of the U.S. Constitution says that "all treaties made, or which shall be made, under the authority of the United States, shall be the supreme law of the land." To them, the treaties are a basis for sovereignty and for a Lakota form of government – something the Oglala Sioux Tribal government (OST) organized under the Indian Reorganization Act of 1934 (IRA) lacks. But the IRA government is a factor in their lives and they regularly provide their advice, criticism, and support to elected leaders. The treaty people had helped put a war bonnet on OST President Wilbur Between Lodges when he was inaugurated in 1994; he was at the Porcupine meeting too.

Edward Starr, Lakota Landowner Association Secretary and recent recipient of a Master's Degree in Tribal Leadership and Management from Oglala Lakota College, used an overhead projector to explain four stages of colonialism. Since he wanted to make sure everyone understood what he had to say, he spoke in Lakota and English and distributed a flyer listing the four stages: "1, Military force is used to control the people. 2, The land is taken away. 3, A colonial administration is established to divide and conquer the people. 4, A native elite is created."[3]

Lakota Landowner Association members had occasion to discuss the Porcupine meeting several days later. They expressed doubt about whether the OST would do anything to protect their rights – the OST had known about the proposal for over three months but had not taken any action. They figured that the taking of testimony was a sham, an action taken to cover the Bureau and not a good faith effort to take the wishes of the people into account.[4] They decided they would have to act to protect their interests because they could not depend on their elected officials or the Bureau. They felt Starr's outline of colonialism was accurate: Yes the government had taken away land and now seemed bent on taking away what little they had left; yes, the colonial administration that was the BIA does oppress them, and the fact that it was staffed at the level of the Pine Ridge

Agency with many of their fellow tribal members shows how the people are divided; and yes a native elite had grown up, as evidenced by OST and BIA officials who, they said, did not support the interests of the 80% who are unemployed.[5]

Meetings like that in Porcupine are opportunities for the people to come together and conduct business in the Lakota language, and to address the issues of land, treaty rights, and culture that they hold dear. Lakota people do not leave those issues and traditions to the elected representatives of tribal government. They regularly engage in grassroots action to support their own agendas. They support Treaty Councils, Lakota Landowner Associations, and Grey Eagle Societies that share their goals. It is through their work and commitment that a dream of unity among the bands, a collectivity that the Lakota today call the *oceti sakowin* (seven council fires) is kept alive. It is largely through their work that the importance of land, culture, and treaty rights are continually reaffirmed. They are part of a long unbroken tradition of affirmation of things that are Lakota, and of resistance to the assimilative thrust of U.S. policy and colonial domination.

The themes that emerged at the Porcupine meeting come up endlessly in discussions and countless public meetings on the reservation and have, with some variation, been a focus of concern for more than 100 years. Land, treaties, culture, language, federal legislation, IRA government, mixed bloods, full bloods – all those themes came together that day in Porcupine, as they invariably do at such gatherings. Some Oglalas, especially elders, sum it all up in a phrase: "It all goes back to the land."

For many, the land is a sine qua non of Lakota culture. Looking out over his own land in Porcupine, the late Severt Young Bear Sr. reflected that "This land is my last stand. Custer had his last stand and this is mine." His grandmother had lived in an adjacent one-room log cabin that was still standing. "She lived there and she refused electricity, she told the stories, and she kept the language alive," Young Bear remembered.[6] As past OST President and Lakota elder Johnson Holy Rock puts it, the "land base is a place set aside for us, a place to live, our homeland."[7]

The diminishment of the homeland – both the treaty territory and the reservation land base – and the progressive disenfranchisement of the majority of Oglala people from it is a source of much pain and sadness. "The history of Native America" Vine Deloria, Jr. once remarked "is the history of the land."[8] Much of that history is a history of land theft and of outside interests taking control over the people's lands and resources. It is also a history of resistance, of attempts to hold onto and take back the land.

Land and the conflicts that have swirled around it during the past century on the Pine Ridge Reservation are the unifying themes of this study. The overriding argument is that ethnic, economic, and political differences that are central to Oglala society today are intimately connected to the extension and administration of U.S. colonial rule and to the integration of the land base into the market system. The period covered runs from the Fort Laramie Treaty of 1868 to the imposition of the IRA government in the 1930s, to the conflict over a tribal grazing ordinance in 1995, and finally to the takeover of OST Tribal Headquarters in January 2000. The raw materials for the events and case studies that are presented were gathered through ethnographic and participatory research on Pine Ridge Reservation and through expeditions to the mother lodes of archival materials at the National Archives in Washington, D.C. and Kansas City, Missouri.[9]

This study is an "ethnohistory," an enterprise wherein "'their' history and 'our' history emerge as part of the same history."[10] That recognition is basic. Any examination of a history that so clearly bears the marks of colonial domination and the consequent struggle for dignity and decolonization must come to grips with the central importance of those intertwined strands.[11] Georges Balandier pointed that out forty years ago when he argued that understanding the history and culture of colonized peoples presupposes that we examine the "colonial situation."[12] Vine Deloria, Jr. did the same a decade later in *Custer Died for Your Sins*. His satirical account of anthropologists challenged them to look beyond abstractions like the "caught between two worlds" notion and to explore systematic exploitation of resources and continued white control of reservation lands and resources.[13] The resultant of that exploitation was not a simple product of imposition. In history as in life, outcomes rarely match intent.

The metaphor of a dance and the notion of dialectic are useful guides for examining histories marked by asymmetrical relations of domination. Despite gross inequities in power, the history of colonized peoples is not and should not be victim-history. As Peter Worsley phrased it, ". . . each colony was the product of a dialectic, a synthesis, not just a simple imposition, in which the social institutions and cultural values of the conquered was one of the terms of the dialectic."[14] Another term of that dialectic was resistance to it. Yet another is the creative use that those caught up in the colonial situation make of its characteristics in order to fashion their own futures. Propositions about the colonial situation and relations of domination are guideposts to inquiry and tools for analysis that help inform the effort to expose the sometimes hidden workings of local and extra-local forces that have jointly shaped current political and economic realities on Pine Ridge Reservation.

CHAPTER OVERVIEW

Chapter two, "Roots of Ethnic Difference," explores terms Oglalas routinely use to mark intra-ethnic differences among themselves. The categories "mixed blood" and "full blood" have been in use for at least 150 years. Their differing values, interests, and agendas have been a significant factor in recent Oglala history. Important differences were already apparent before the Fort Laramie Treaty of 1868 was signed.[15] Colonizers seized upon those intra-ethnic differences and used them for their own ends; their actions created further differentiation in Oglala society.

Oglala elders argue that the people were relatively self-sufficient in the early years of the twentieth century, a view at odds with many published accounts which suggest they were dependent on the largesse of the federal government. Chapter three, "Cattle, Grass, and Ethnic Conflict at the Grassroots," follows the lead of Oglala oral history to written accounts of government agents, Indian Rights Association workers, visitors to the reservation, and of Oglalas themselves to develop a picture of the reservation economy between 1879 and 1915. The chapter concludes that Oglalas made productive use of what they had in a mixed economy of subsistence and wage-labor pursuits and that the thesis of ration dependency is a myth.

Chapter four, "The Oglala Omniciye and the Struggle for the Land," describes the effects of regional political and economic influences on the early reservation economy. The struggle of the Oglala Omniciye, (Oglala Council), and its remarkable ability to support Oglala interests against those of the OIA and outside ranching interests contradicts the notion that the Oglala lacked effective leadership in the early reservation era. Differences between mixed blood and full blood Oglala were growing during those years of increasing mixed blood immigration from other states, and were evident in disagreement over the General Allotment Act and the organization of Bennett County. Actions of the OIA and outside cattle interests were instrumental in the decline of subsistence cattle herds the people depended on and migrant labor became increasingly important.

Chapter five, "Doing Their Patriotic Duty," graphically illustrates the oppression Oglalas experienced at the hands of the colonizers and the outside interests they supported. It provides insight into the collaboration of the U.S. colonial regime with those interests at the expense of the Oglala people and their land. The impact the takeover had on the people, the economy, and the environment is described through the voices of the people and through reports of colonial officials. Individual and collective acts of resistance to the government-corporate takeover are described in detail.

Chapter six explores the significance of the advent of representative government on the reservation. The opportunity that imposed western style governments provided to a small group of mixed blood Oglalas was unprecedented. At that juncture they came forward for the first time to challenge the older full blood leadership for political control over tribal affairs. "Representative Government and the Politics of Exclusion" argues that the Indian Reorganization Act of 1934 (IRA) and the short-lived "21 Council" that preceded it ushered in novel developments that gave rise to long-term conflicts over land and politics.

"Land and Power in the era of the IRA" tracks shifting patterns of control over reservation land and assesses the implications of that change for
the future. Chapter seven includes a case study of the recent campaign by
grassroots people to reestablish their ties with the land and describes the
obstacles they faced from their IRA government representatives and the
Bureau of Indian Affairs. Recurrent conflict and crises of legitimacy that
have plagued IRA government on the reservation since the 1930s are interpreted in relation to the growth of a local elite and the development of an
incipient class structure.

The epilogue, "A nation in crisis, poised for change," offers a brief expo-
sition on the January 2000 takeover of Oglala Sioux Tribal Headquarters
and summary comments and analysis.[16]

NOTES ABOUT METHODS

This study has already been described as an ethnohistory. It can also use-
fully be seen as an example of what Michael Burawoy has dubbed the
"extended case method." The method has four dimensions, each of which
is "limited by a corresponding face of power."[17]

The first dimension is participant observation, a technique limited by the
distortion that arises out of the domination inherent in the relation of the
observer and the observed. The author has lived on Pine Ridge Reservation
for the past twenty years and did three years of focused ethnographic
research for this study. This observer's bias is to adopt what Gerrit Huizer
calls the "view from below."[18] That lends itself to learning from the views
of the oppressed who are particularly knowledgeable about the effects of
the relations of domination on their lives and about the deployment of
power. It shifts the object of study from the people to power relations that
they know a good deal about and that they want to change. Some of the
information for this study was gathered through joint action for change.
The description of the Lakota Landowner Association struggle in chapter
seven derives from the author's participation in what academic observers
might call an example of Participatory Action Research (PAR). PAR seeks
to negate the subject-object dilemma by engaging the researcher with the
people in a common project of research, analysis, and action aimed at alter-
ing unjust social arrangements.[19]

The second dimension of the extended case method extends research
"over time and space." This study represents the outcome of extended periods of participation and observation on Pine Ridge Reservation and
achieves historical depth through the use of oral history and extensive use
of written records. The limitation of the second dimension is "silencing."
Voices of some actors will be muted and some events slighted when
observers attempt to understand the flow of social life as process. This
study presents a significant amount of raw data in the form of descriptions
and quotes from many historical actors. Although silencing cannot be

avoided, the method of presentation does afford the reader some opportunity to draw his or her own interpretations.

The third dimension links local processes with extra-local forces. Micro processes that are locally observable are linked to macro processes that are less amenable to observation but nonetheless possess force and help shape local outcomes. The limiting factor is "objectification," i.e., "forces" like colonial control, which are after all made by human beings, can take on the false appearance of permanence or inevitability. This study links events and processes on Pine Ridge Reservation to external forces, especially to the broader economy, colonial control, and federal policy. The ongoing struggle of the people against oppression in the colonial context of the reservation is an indicator of sustained hope and steadfast refusal to give credence to the proposition of inevitability.

The fourth dimension invokes theory to guide research and analysis. The danger is "normalization" – theory can straitjacket interpretation.[20] This study uses theories of colonialism and dependency to help set the research agenda: the colonial situation, land, economic integration, ethnic conflict, relations of domination, people's strategies, and people's history.

Notes

1. The account of the February 9, 1995 meeting in Porcupine is based on the author's notes. The BIA's proposal was another in a series of proposals aimed at solving the problem of fractionated heirship. In the generations since allotment, allotted land has become incredibly fractionated as owners die intestate, i.e., without wills, leaving shares to a number of descendants. Over the course of several generations, many tracts of allotted land have hundreds, or even thousands, of heirs. The BIA plan would have provided that parcels that made up 2% or less of a given tract of land could be purchased when an owner died intestate, and transferred to tribes. Earlier versions of the BIA solution were enacted into law in 1983 and 1984 but were declared unconstitutional because they constituted an illegal taking under the Fifth Amendment to the U.S. Constitution. Nevertheless, as of 2001, many parcels that were taken by the BIA for transfer to tribes before the Indian Land Consolidation Act was declared unconstitutional are still tied up in local BIA offices around the country.

2. Note that the terms Lakota, Oglala, and Oglala Lakota are used interchangeably. That practice, and the use of "s" to indicate the plural of Oglala and other terms of reference, (e.g., Oglalas, Lakotas), is in keeping with the practice that Oglala people themselves use when speaking in English. They often identify themselves as Lakota, and sometimes as Oglala, or as Oglala Lakota, and often refer to other tribal members as Lakotas, Oglalas, etc. The term Oglala refers to a particular Lakota band, the group that is identified with the Pine Ridge Reservation.

Today, the word "Lakota" is used to refer to several bands, including the Sicangu Lakota of Rosebud Reservation. It is also the name for the language that Lakota people use. The terms "Nakota" and "Dakota" refer to other groups of "Sioux" and to the dialects that they speak.

3. Starr, Edward, "Four Stages of Colonialism," February, 1995, Copy in possession of the author.

4. At a subsequent meeting, one week before the deadline for submitting testimony on the fractionated heirship issue, Lakota Landowner's Association member Lucy Bull Bear asked BIA Realty Director Frieda Brewer what she planned on doing with all of the tape recorded testimony from Pine Ridge Reservation. She said the tapes would be mailed to BIA Headquarters in Washington, D.C. But the BIA office there had already indicated it had no capability for handling taped testimony, Bull Bear informed her. "Well, we'll transcribe them then," was the quick response. The local BIA office in Pine Ridge Village, of course, did not have resources for translating and transcribing the many hours of tapes, from meetings all across the reservation, in the one week remaining for input. Later on it was discovered that none of the testimony ever made it to Washington, D.C., a situation discussed more fully in Chapter 7).

5. A rate of 70-90% unemployment is regularly cited on Pine Ridge Reservation The 80% unemployment figure is often given by the Oglala Sioux Tribe. The U.S. Department of the Interior, Bureau of Indian Affairs, 1997 Labor Market Information on the Indian Labor Force put unemployment at 73% in 1997.

6. Author's notes.

7. Johnson Holy Rock, April 7, 1995, Piya Wiconi, Oglala Lakota College, during a presentation called "From Little Big Horn, to Wounded Knee, to the Present: Know your past in order to chart your future."

8. Keynote address, January 27, 1989, at the conference "Who Owns the Land?," Omaha, Nebraska.

9. Alan Perry, archivist at the National Archives in Kansas City, Missouri, spent over eight years organizing and cataloguing over 800 linear feet of archival materials on Pine Ridge Reservation.

10. Wolf, Eric 1982, p. 19.

11. Cf. Said, Edward W. 1993 ; Cf. also Comaroff, Jean 1985.

12. Balandier, Georges 1961, p. 34.

13. Deloria, Vine, Jr. 1970, p. 90–91.

14. Worsley, Peter 1984, p. 4.

15. The land within the Treaty boundaries, the Great Sioux Reservation, included portions of what are today five states. The Sioux Act reduced the Great Sioux Reservation, creating six separate reservations, including the Pine Ridge Reservation. See chapter 2.

16. Topics not covered in any detail in this book include the Black Hills Claim, the Wounded Knee Massacre, and the Wounded Knee Occupation of 1973, though events related to the latter do figure in Chapter 7. Some useful references on the Wounded Knee Occupation of 1973 and events surrounding it are Messerschmidt, Jim 1983; Matthiessen, Peter 1983; Talbot, Steve 1979; Cornell, Stephen 1988. Cf.

Pommersheim, Frank 1993 for a provocative article that includes a review of *Black Hills/ White Justice* by Edward Lazarus and makes the case that lawyers on the Black Hills Claims case failed violated the trust in the attorney-client relationship with their Sioux clients. See also Gonzales, Mario and Elizabeth Cook-Lynn, 1999.
17. Burawoy, Michael 2000, p. 26–28. The references to the extended case method that follow in the paragraphs following are also from Burawoy.
18. Huizer, Gerrit 1979, p. 407.
19. Fals-Borda, Orlando 1991, p. 5.
20. Burawoy, Michael 2000, p. 28.

CHAPTER 2

Roots of Ethnic Difference

"I'm an Indian. I was born here and lived here all my life. I may not know the language or the culture, but I'm Indian."
                    Mixed blood Oglala, 1995

"To be Lakota you have to speak Lakota, and you have to know the ways."
                              Full blood Oglala, 1995

MIXED BLOOD, FULL BLOOD, IESKA, OR LAKOTA?

The notion of "mixed blood" and "full blood" difference is a sensitive one among the Oglala Lakota of Pine Ridge Indian Reservation. Some Oglalas avoid it, some deny it exists, and others take every opportunity to raise it. Ben Riefel, a mixed blood employee of the BIA, and a member of the Rosebud Sioux Tribe who campaigned on Pine Ridge Reservation for the adoption of the Indian Reorganization Act of 1934, labeled the issue "superficial politics."[1] Fifty years later, a former high ranking BIA official and mixed blood Oglala Sioux Tribal member claimed the issue was meaningless, and refused to discuss it.[2] At a recent public gathering, one young mixed blood man wore a tee shirt emblazoned "Half-breeds aren't half-bad" across the front, and "Iyeska" (mixed blood) on the back. Until recently, one mixed blood rancher drove a pickup with the word "Half-Breed," professionally painted, in large letters, on the hood. The issue does not go away, much as some people wish it would.

The terms mixed blood, ieska, Lakota, and full blood, were sprinkled throughout a series of meetings on traditional government held at Oglala Lakota College in 1991. This full blood Lakota elders' statement was typical: "Ieska's have no rights under treaty law, and to be recognized you have to be one-half or more Lakota." Robert Grey Eagle, one of the moderators, and then Vice-President for Community Services at the college, responded:[3]

> We have been subjected too long to the divide and conquer strategy of the non-Indian. When we are divided we will be conquered. . . . How are we going to achieve true sovereignty? We are going to have to start defining Lakota in positive, and not in negative terms. 'Oh, you're not a Lakota because you married so-and-so. Oh, you're not a Lakota because you live in Rapid City. You're a Lakota because you come

from a certain family.' If we are so Lakota, then we have to obey the commandments of the Lakota, and that is to love one another. . . . We are going to have to discuss the areas that bring us together and I had hoped that traditional government would be one of those areas. Speaking Lakota, acting Lakota, being Lakota. . . . We have to give each other time and stop condemning each other. It is my dream some-day that our Lakota people will become one nation. We are divided – an old white-man's trick, and we have fallen for it every time.[4]

In Grey Eagle's view, blood degree, which he referred to obliquely in his reference to the family one comes from, should not be used to assign trib-al members to the categories "ieska" or "Lakota." Nor, he intimated, should cultural competencies like speaking Lakota be used as ethnic mark-ers that serve to divide the people. But it is precisely those things, blood degree and notions of cultural competency, that many Oglalas routinely use to differentiate between ieska and Lakota, or in the common English expression, between mixed blood and full blood.

The Lakota term "ieska," which translates literally as "interpreter," was formerly applied to those individuals who, because of their bilingual skills, acted as go-betweens with the whites. The term is also generally used to refer to persons of mixed ancestry, especially when those persons appear to be phenotypically more white, and when they act in ways that are felt to be non-Lakota, i.e., white. The term "Lakota" refers to the Lakota lan-guage, one of the three dialects spoken by the groups historically labeled as Sioux, and, generally, to the people of the tribes where that dialect is spo-ken. Its other common use is as an ethnic marker to differentiate between those who are considered ieska, or mixed bloods, and those who are con-sidered Lakota, or full blood. As Grey Eagles' comments show, usage is sometimes contested and that contest takes various forms. Differences between mixed blood and full blood Oglalas are regularly announced by linguistic markers, behavioral differences, and recurring conflict between the two. Grey Eagle's point, that blood quantum and the question "who is a Lakota" (or Indian) have been used to divide people up, is often made by others who seek unity in a society that has been sorely divided by colo-nialism.

The dream of unity that Grey Eagle and many others profess remains just that. The notion that a forum on traditional government might be a forcing ground for unity seems far from the mark. In fact, the traditional government forums at the college were really an extension of the Treaty Council meetings into an institutional setting. Treaty Councils, which have been a regular feature of reservation life since the creation of the Indian Reorganization Act government (IRA government, Oglala Sioux Tribal Government, or OST) on Pine Ridge Reservation in 1936, are almost exclusively the haunts of full blood Lakota people, who preferentially speak Lakota, reject the IRA government, trace their lineage back to the signatories of the 1868 Fort Laramie Treaty, and who believe that the mixed bloods, the ieska, are synonymous with the agency town of Pine Ridge Village, and with cultural assimilation. The fact that the issue of Lakota versus ieska figured so large in the traditional government forums is a clue to the existence of persistent ethnic differences on the reservation, differences linked to history and structure.

Like the Oglala people themselves, anthropologists comparing mixed blood and full blood Oglalas consistently cite significant differences in values and behavior. Mixed bloods are consistently depicted as having a better understanding of white culture and institutions than full bloods. They are described as progressive, bureaucratic, individualistic and competitive, and as emulators of the cowboy culture of the west. Many of them, wrote Mekeel, ". . . out-white the whites." Mixed bloods are also said to be more highly educated and materially successful, and to control the tribal council.[5]

Full bloods are generally characterized as less acculturated than mixed bloods. Words frequently used to describe them are "traditional" and "conservative." They are more likely than mixed bloods to be bilingual, speaking both Lakota and English. Full bloods have shown a preference for cooperative economic enterprise, in contrast to the individualistic organization favored by mixed bloods.[6]

Similar differences are said to exist between mixed bloods and full bloods among the Flathead, Sicangu, and Cherokee.[7] Fowler points out that factionalism described for many of the northern plains tribes involves conflicts between mixed bloods and full bloods. More generally, Taylor refers to a ". . . basic division characteristic of all the Indians of the Northern Plains and Northwest, between mixed bloods and full bloods."[8]

What are the roots of that basic division, and why is it marked by conflict? What historical processes are associated with its rise? What are the interests involved in the conflict that characterizes the division? What are the ideologies associated with it?

THE SLAUGHTER OF THE BUFFALO AND THE CREATION OF RESERVATIONS

By the mid-nineteenth century, the vast herds of buffalo on the northern plains were doomed. Buffalo meat and hides had become a major resource for the industrializing east; immigrants traveling west took buffalo; professional hunters took a huge toll and there was a conscious effort to exterminate the buffalo in order to deny the plains tribes the game they depended on. Even by the early 1850s there had been a noticeable decline, presaging the collapse of the hide trade on the northern plains. Fort Pierre Chouteau, the center of a vast trading network that once included over 100 trading posts on both sides of the Missouri between the James River and the Black Hills, and which had shipped an average of 17,000 buffalo hides down the Missouri annually for over two decades, was abandoned in 1857.[9]

By the 1860s the herds were reduced to a fraction of what they had been just thirty years earlier, but even then the pressure on the buffalo did not let up.[10] A combination of entrepreneurial greed, the scorched earth policy of the U.S. government, and a lust for blood, pushed the buffalo to the edge of extinction.[11] "In 1867, when Colonel R. I. Dodge received the regrets of Sir W.F. Butler that his party had killed thirty bulls in a hunt at Fort McPherson below the forks of the Platte, Dodge replied, 'Kill every buffalo you can. Every buffalo dead is an Indian gone.'"[12]

The westward movement of gold seekers and homesteaders intensified pressures on the buffalo, and on the tribes that depended on them. By 1842, Farley Mowat records, the ". . . kill had reached 2.5 million buffalo a year and the great western herds were melting like their own tallow in an incandescent fury of destruction." More than 75 million buffalo hides were handled by U.S. dealers between 1850 and 1885. "The brutal truth is that one of the most magnificent and vital forms of life on this planet was destroyed for no better reasons than our desire to eradicate the Plains Indians and an insatiable lust for booty . . . and for blood."[13] The remaining herds were further depleted and their movements disrupted by the presence of the U.S. Army, and by immigrants traveling to the gold fields of Montana. In the 1860s, Lakota and Dakota bands carried out a series of military actions aimed at dislodging the U.S. Army and stopping the westward movement through the 1851 Treaty territory. The "Red Cloud Wars" of the 1860s, named after the famous Oglala chief, were wars of survival, waged to protect the land and the buffalo from the invading whites.[14]

In July, 1867, the U.S. established a Peace Commission to treat with the western bands of Oglala, Brulé, Hunkpapa, Blackfeet, Minneconjou, and Sans Arcs that had complete control over the Powder River Country and that had effectively closed off the Bozeman Trail to white travel (Map 1). The territory and the game that those bands had secured for themselves, plus the powder and ammunition they were able to secure through their trading links, enabled them to continue a free way of life. Overtures by the Peace Commission were ignored. But in January 1868, Red Cloud indicated he would make peace if the U.S. abandoned its three forts on the Bozeman Trail.

In April, the U.S. dispatched the so-called "Great Peace Commission" to Fort Laramie, on the North Platte River. The leaders of various bands touched the pen between April and November, 1868. Red Cloud, Oglala leader of the Ite Sica (Bad Face band), refused to come in until after the U.S. made good on its promise to remove the troops intended to provide security for immigrant whites from the three forts. The forts were finally abandoned in August and after Red Cloud witnessed the withdrawal of the troops he sent word that he would travel to Fort Laramie only after he had

Map 1. Treaty Lands: Areas recognized by the 1851 and 1868 Fort Laramie Treaties, and showing the Black Hills area that was stolen by the Illegal Act of 1877. Map from Harry H. Anderson.

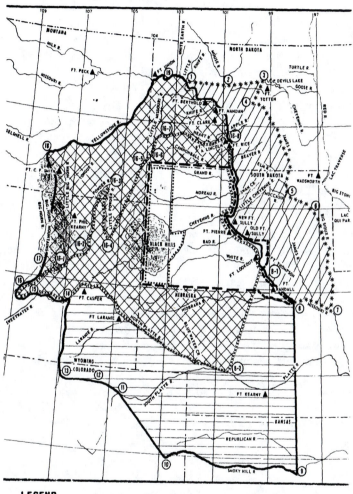

LEGEND

1851 TREATY

1. XXXXXXX   Land recognized by the United States as Sioux country under Fort Laramie Treaty of 1851.

1868 TREATY

2. ▬ ▬ ▬ ▬   Great Sioux Reservation defined in Article 2, 1868 Treaty.

3. /////////   Lands east of the Missouri R. and outside of the Great Sioux Reservation as to which the entire interest ceded by Article 2, 1868 Treaty.

4. ▬▬▬▬   Lands outside of Great Sioux Reservation, as to which the right to occupy permanently was ceded by Article 11, 1868 Treaty.

5. ⬙⬙⬙⬙   Lands within those identified in Item 4 above, established as "unceded Indian territory" by Article 16, 1868 Treaty.

6. ▤▤▤▤   Lands within those identified in Item 4 above, excluded from Article 16, "unceded Indian territory". Includes Article 11 hunting rights.

7. ••••••••   Black Hills portion of Great Sioux Reservation acquired by United States by Article 1 in 1877 Act.

8.   *NOTE:* The rights in lands identified in Items 5 and 6 above, were extinguished by Article 1 in 1877 Act.

"made his meat" in the Powder River country, one of the few remaining places where significant numbers of buffalo remained, underscoring the interests they had been fighting for. Along with 125 other leaders, he came to Fort Laramie in November, 1868, placing his mark on the Treaty on November 20.[15]

Lakota and Dakota leaders of those bands that were still making their living in their accustomed way made it clear to delegates of the Great Peace Commission that the economy their way of life was organized around was at stake. The Brulé leader Spotted Tail said "the cause of all our troubles" was that the whites on the Powder River and Smokey Hill Roads were driving away all the game. The Oglala, American Horse, emphasized that his people did not want any treaty goods. The problem was that "These whites that you have put in my buffalo country I despise, and I want to see them away." Pawnee Killer, another Oglala, told the commissioners that "What little space of country is over there [i.e., the Powder River Country] is all we have left to find game." Man That Walks Under The Ground, also an Oglala, pointed out the havoc that railways were causing: "All my people and myself have been used to hunting for our living. . . . These iron roads have scared off all our game." Red Cloud was adamant that the people wanted to continue to hunt buffalo in their own country. They neither wanted to farm, nor to learn how to farm, as long as there was game to hunt.[16]

The goal of the Peace Commissioners was to move the tribes to the east, away from their hunting territories in the Powder River country, to agencies on the Missouri River. But the Missouri River country to the east was nearly devoid of game, and with the exception of some of the mixed bloods and white men married to Indian women, the people wanted to remain where they were and they wanted Fort Laramie to continue operations. Big Mouth, who was among the first to meet with the commissioners, announced on April 29, 1868, that

> These are my relations staying around here. We loafers here have worked very hard to bring them in. There are about a hundred lodges here alone, with the whites of the country camped with us. I am the chief of that band . . . I do not move from the post, and got any robes or anything to trade, and I am poor and in need of goods . . . This land belongs to me at the mouth of Horse and Bear Creek. I want to settle there.[17]

Besides his band of loafers, and the whites Big Mouth referenced, there were many others, plus a sizeable population of mixed bloods, who were living a settled existence along the North Platte and the Missouri Rivers.[18] Those people were more dependent on the government than the bands to the west. Fire Thunder, for example, who said he had grown up among the whites, complained to the commissioners that annuity agreements in the 1851 Fort Laramie Treaty had not been fulfilled for over five years.[19] The

predicament of the settled groups was an issue during the talks at Fort
Laramie in May of 1868.

Man Afraid of His Horses, one of the Oglala leaders who was allied
with Red Cloud, wanted those who had settled along the North Platte to
remain there.

> I want you to listen to what I tell you now. All these old mountaineers
> are our children. I consider them all as part of ourselves. Strangers
> come amongst us and afterwards go away and leave families, and I
> have taken care of them. . . . The military posts on the Platte I want
> you to have moved. I want the half-breeds to remain on the Platte . . .
> I want no white men from the Missouri to come through here. I want
> the half-breeds to take care of this land. Whether the half-breeds want
> to stay they will state themselves. They want an answer from the com-
> mission.[20]

The mixed blood, John Richard, Jr., agreed with Man Afraid. "I was
raised here. I do not want to go to the Missouri reservation. On the part of
the half-breeds I come forward to say this."[21] When Joseph Bissonette and
some of the other mixed bloods declared they did not share in those sentiments, and wanted to go to the Missouri, General Sanborn declared that
"Any of the half-breeds that desire to remain here can do so and get titles
to the soil. But if any of them think that by going to the Missouri they will
be better off, let them go and they will be assisted."[22] Man Afraid reiterat-
ed his position: "I don't like to be deprived of the half-breeds leaving the
country." Black Hawk concurred, saying "I should like the interpreters and
old traders to remain here where they were raised." High Wolf expressed
a related concern about U.S. interference with trading at Fort Laramie.
Man Afraid specifically mentioned that he wanted trader "Bullock" to
remain at Fort Laramie. Colonel Bullock was a white man who, judging
from his substantial home, must have been quite a successful trader.[23]

The needs that the various bands expressed to the Peace Commissioners
differed in accord with their economic pursuits. The bands in the Powder
River country needed a territory secure from outside incursion by immigrants or soldiers that would threaten the game, and they needed traders so
they could access powder and ammunition; the settled bands wanted access
to game too, and did not want to go to the relatively empty prairies on the
Missouri, but they were also dependent on their relations with settled
whites and mixed bloods, and with the U.S. government; some of the
mixed bloods wanted title to land on the North Platte, and others wanted
what they must have considered the relative security of a reservation on the
Missouri River to the east.

In fact, some of them proposed just that to the U.S. government, inde-
pendently of Sioux or other tribal leaders, nearly five months before the
Great Peace Commission reached Fort Laramie. On November 16, 1867,
132 mixed bloods and white men married to Indian women, living in the

vicinity of Fort Laramie, petitioned the U.S. Congress, and the Commissioner of Indian Affairs, asking for allotments of land and a separate reservation for themselves. The petition starkly illustrates the profoundly different aspirations of the signatories from those of the Sioux leaders, who were doing everything in their power to protect the land and the remaining herds of buffalo from being over-run by whites.

> The undersigned petitioners respectfully represent that they are residents of Dakota Territory in the vicinity of Fort Laramie and are each and all heads or members of Indian families, that they have resided in said Country many years, and came to it originally under the auspices of the old Northwestern Fur Company and for many years depended solely upon said Company for support, that after this Company ceased to do business they, the undersigned, obtained their subsistence by accommodating the Overland trail to the mining regions West, That said families and their half-breed children now number on the Platte and Missouri Rivers more than Two thousand (2000) souls, That the construction of the Rail Road across the Plains has so changed business and travel that all ostensible means of support along the North Platte are destroyed, that they are anxious to locate with their families upon some good agricultural land in the Indian Country and commence farming, and that their settlement in any country would draw about them their Indian Relatives and friends and would aid much in locating and civilizing the Indians. They therefor respectfully petition that a tract of country be set aside to be occupied by themselves, their Indian relatives and friends exclusively & forever located on the Missouri and White Earth Rivers described as follows. . . . And that provision be made by law for them to enter said land or such portions of the same as they may desire in severalty for themselves and their heirs forever. And that each of said petitioners and said half-breeds be allowed to enter three hundred and twenty acres of the same for a permanent home for themselves and their heirs [copied as it appears].[24]

The desire for private property in land, the desire to farm, and the desire for permanent settlement, were a mirror image of the desires of U.S. policy makers and of westering white immigrants, and opposite those of the Sioux bands with which the U.S. sought to effect a treaty of peace. The notion of civilizing the Indians was perhaps a ploy, but it is remarkable just how well the notion would fit with the needs of the U.S. colonial government in the years to come, something taken up in detail later in this chapter. It is worth noting, too, that Article 7 of the 1868 Treaty provides for education "In order to insure the civilization of the Indians entering into this treaty. . . ." In addition, Article 6 provides for 320 acre allotments, a direct reflection of the desire of the mixed bloods and the white men married to Indian women, certainly not an objective that Sioux leaders had in mind for themselves.[25]

Interestingly, both "J. Bissonnette," probably the Joseph Bissonette [sic] who disagreed with Man Afraid and John Richard Jr. about remaining on the North Platte, and "John Richard Sen.," perhaps the father of John Richard Jr., who agreed with Man Afraid, were among the signers of the November, 1867 petition. There was no separate reservation created for the signatories of the 1867 petition, and they, and many others like them, who had settled along the Platte and Missouri Rivers, eventually settled down in areas near the various Sioux Agencies, areas that became reservations after the enactment of the Sioux Act of 1889. Among the names on the petition are Jules Ecoffey, Jacob Herman, John Hunter, Frank Salouway, Nic Janis, Frank Marishalle, Jock Palmer, R. Garnette, Medan Provost, T.S. Twiss, and Thomas Conroy. The surnames of those men, and of others on the petition, are common on Pine Ridge Reservation today. Their names, and their ties with the Northwestern Fur Company, link them to their French ancestors. The involvement of the various Sioux groups in the fur and hide trades with the French began in the 1680s. The weaponry and ammunition that their position in the trade helped them secure was a factor in their dominance on the northern plains from around the 1750s onward.[26] Sioux involvement with the French was thus longstanding and mutually beneficial, at least until the herds of buffalo began to decline markedly. At that point the interests of the western Sioux and those of some of the French who had married into Sioux families diverged. Mixed bloods and full bloods dressed differently as well. The differences are apparent in the remarkable photographs that were taken by Alexander Gardiner at Fort Laramie in 1868 (Plates 1–4).

Although the 1868 Treaty did not provide separate reservations for the mixed bloods and whites, it did make separate reference to them. Article 6 provides for allotments both for individuals ". . . belonging to said tribes of Indians, or legally incorporated with them . . ." if they were heads of families.[27] Later, the governing body of the Oglala on the Pine Ridge Reservation, the Oglala Council, would made specific reference to the issue of incorporation as of the 1868 Treaty in making its determinations about the eligibility of mixed bloods and white men married to Indian women for allotments of land. Oglala Council minutes of November 9, 1910, note that five applicants for allotment were approved, including one who was a ". . . full blood white man married to a full blood Oglala woman," and who was "Incorporated into the tribe and the Council recognized him as such . . ."[28] The Council met on a similar issue on April 23, 1908. Forty-eight delegates took up the matter of several white men married to Oglala women who had ". . . employed counsel to make a fight at Washington to establish their rights as Indians." The Commissioner of Indian Affairs had turned the matter over to the Oglala Council after he received complaints about the white's initiative. The Councils decision was that the several white men should be allotted and one, who was a mixed blood, should be denied. The issue that arose at such meetings was affiliation, affiliation as of the 1868 Treaty. [29]

Some of the white men who had married into the tribe, and some of the mixed bloods, were already, or soon became, successful businessmen. In 1905, Pine Ridge Indian Agent John Brennan described George Brown, a mixed blood who owned allotted land on Pine Ridge Reservation, as an educated man, having very little Indian blood, and who, as the proprietor of a large store on neighboring Rosebud Reservation, was "a man of means and fully able to protect his interests." [30] Some of those men, former trappers, guides, U.S. Army interpreters, and traders, had started up cattle ranches along the Platte, capitalizing on the livestock boom that followed the decimation of the buffalo, and when they moved to the area that became the Pine Ridge Reservation, they brought their cattle along with them. [31]

The 1868 Fort Laramie Treaty established boundaries for the Great Sioux Reservation and stipulated that the U.S. would provide rations, annuity payments, and cattle. The U.S. also agreed to use its military power to prevent entry of non-Indians into the Black Hills. It soon became clear, though, that the U.S. had no intention of honoring the Treaty.

Non-Indians continued to enter the Black Hills but the U.S. looked the other way. Meanwhile railroad, mining, ranching, and farming interests were lobbying to open up the remaining Sioux land. They wanted free access through it to the Black Hills and they wanted the land itself for grazing and homesteading. Already in 1870, the Secretary of the Dakota Territory was waxing poetic about the need to develop the "unbounded resources" of the Black Hills and the prairies that were held by the "jealous savage." [32] In 1875 the U.S. ordered the Sioux to vacate their hunting grounds in the Powder River country, in blatant disregard for treaty provisions that guaranteed them rights to the use of that area in perpetuity. The order came in the dead of winter and it would have been nigh unto suicidal for the people to make the long journey even had they wanted to abandon their hunting grounds, but the U.S. prosecuted the war of 1876 because of the lack of compliance with the illegal order. Later that year the U.S. used the threat of sell or starve in order to obtain a few signatures to whitewash the confiscation of the Black Hills. The theft of 7.7 million acres of land was given a legal veneer by the so-called "Agreement of 1876," which was passed by the U.S. Congress as the Black Hills Act of 1877. The Act contravened Article 12 of the 1868 Fort Laramie Treaty, which provides that 3/4 of the signatures of all of the adult males were requisite to any land cessions, and was finally ruled as an illegal taking by the U.S. Supreme Court in 1980. [33]

Even after the illegal taking of the Black Hills the Sioux bands still had a contiguous territory of 43,000 square miles [34] (Maps 2 and 3). But with their subsistence base all but destroyed, and the U.S. government angered by the defeat of Custer at the Little Big Horn in 1876, most of the Lakota bands that had not already done so settled near their kin at the Indian agencies. Others took refuge in Canada, as Sitting Bull and some of his followers did, and some, under the Oglala leader Crazy Horse, resisted further, finally going in to make peace at Fort Robinson in May of 1877.[35]

In 1889, Lieutenant General Crook, or *Wicahpi Yamni* (Three Stars), as some Lakota still refer to him, orchestrated a combination of threats, intimidation, and promises ostensibly obtaining the signatures of three-fourths of the adult males, the fraction required by Article 12 of the 1868 Treaty for any land cessions, in order to "legally" open up of the Great Sioux Reserve.[36] At the Pine Ridge Agency, though, only 516 signatures were obtained from among 1,366 adults. According to Hyde's analysis, 147 of those signatures were from mixed bloods and white men married to Indian women, 83 were from Northern Cheyennes resident near the Pine Ridge Agency, and 273 from full blood Oglala.[37] Using the 1888 Census figures published in Agent Valentine T. McGillycuddy's 1889 Annual Report as a basis for calculation, 63% of the Northern Cheyennes at the agency signed, virtually all of the mixed bloods signed (the figure works out to 128%, most of the difference probably reflecting the fact that the white men married to Oglala women and the mixed bloods were lumped together in Hyde's calculations) while only 25% of Oglala full bloods signed.[38]

On June 17, 1889, when Crook felt he had softened up the opposition enough at Pine Ridge Agency, and he brought out his papers for the signing, "The squawmen and mixed bloods promply [sic] started the parade. . ."[39] The full blood Oglala signatories were mostly from the bands of No Flesh and American Horse. No Flesh was old and infirm. American Horse filibustered against the proposal for three days, but capitulated after Crook's threat that all lands would be lost if the people did not sign. Crook's other tactics included using white men married to Indian women, and mixed bloods, to persuade individual Oglalas to sign. That proved unsuccessful at the Pine Ridge Agency, though it worked well enough at several other Sioux agencies.[40] The striking solidarity of the mixed bloods and white men married to Oglala women, their shared interests in what the Sioux Act offered – private property in land, cattle, agricultural implements, and other aspects of white culture – closely paralleled what they were asking for in their petition of 1867, as did their willingness to act apart from, and against, the expressed interests of the full blood majority.

Plate 1 – Lakota and Cheyenne Leaders at Fort Laramie, 1868

Left to right: Spotted Tail, Brulé; Roman Nose, Cheyenne; Old Man Afraid of His Horses, Oglala; Lone Horn, Sioux; Whistling Elk, Brulé; Pipe-Sioux. Photographer, Alexander Gardiner. Photo courtesy of the Edward E. Ayer Collection, the Newberry Library, Chicago.

Plate 2 – Oglalas at Fort Laramie, 1868

Contrast the clothing and the hairstyles these men wore with that of those in Plate 3. They wore moccasins, as did the leaders shown in Plate 1. Mixed bloods in other photos in the collection wore leather boots. Photographer, Alexander Gardiner. Photo Courtesy of the Edward E. Ayer Collection, the Newberry Library, Chicago.

Plate 3 – Families, including "mixed bloods" at Fort Laramie, 1868

Note the short hair of the men, their topcoats, bowler hats, and vests. The children sported coats and hats as well. The women, who were apparently wives of mixed bloods and whites, wore more colorful blankets and fewer beads than some of the women in Plate 4. Photo Courtesy of the Edward E. Ayer Collection, the Newberry Library, Chicago.

Plate 4 – Women and young children at Fort Laramie, 1868
Note the hair ties and elaborate beadwork that some of these women wore. Photo Courtesy of the Edward E. Ayer Collection, the Newberry Library, Chicago.

Map 2. Land Grabs and Reservations: Shows loss of land suffered by the theft of the Black Hills, and shows the reduction effected by the Sioux Act of 1889. Map from Utley, 1963, p. 43.

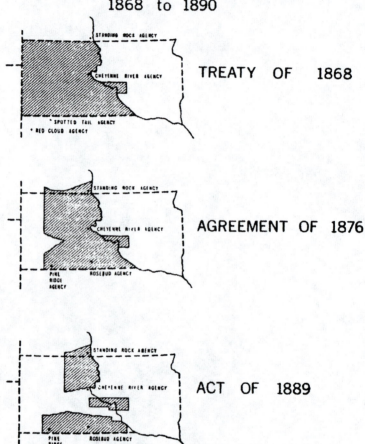

REDUCTION OF THE GREAT SIOUX RESERVATION
1868 to 1890

TREATY OF 1868

AGREEMENT OF 1876

ACT OF 1889

Map 3. Reservation Boundaries: The six reservations established by the
Sioux Act of 1889. Map from Utley, 1963, p.63.

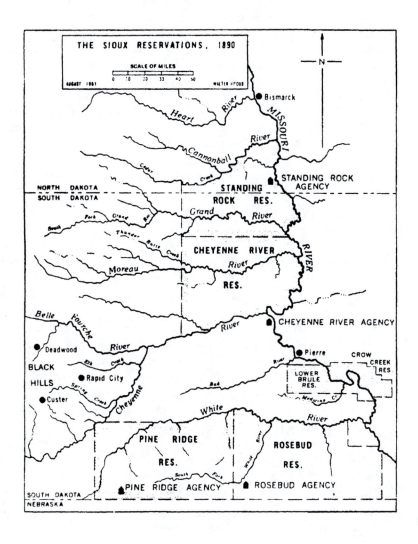

Crook's failure to gather more signatures from Oglala full bloods was a testimony to the continuing strength of the organization of Oglala bands and to the power of the majority of Oglala chiefs, who were strong in their opposition to the proposal to take most of their remaining lands. Though the tactics of what the late Oglala historian Robert Gay referred to as the "Crooked Commission" fell short of the necessary 3/4 of adult male signatures on Pine Ridge Reservation, the U.S. interpreted the 3/4 rule in Article 12 of the Treaty to mean 3/4 of the collective population of adult males from the various signatory tribes of the 1868 Fort Laramie Treaty.[41]

The Sioux Act, signed into law on March 2, 1889, reclassified nine million acres of Sioux land as public land, paving the way for white homesteaders, and creating six separate reservations. The Pine Ridge Reservation, including approximately 2.7 million acres, and numbering 4,549 Oglala full bloods, 503 mixed bloods, and 557 Northern Cheyennes, was the largest in size and population.[42]

THE ETHNIC STRUCTURE OF COLONIAL ADMINISTRATION AT PINE RIDGE

The U.S. colonial administration had a penchant for singling out and separating whole groups of Oglala from their fellows. Sometimes they did it to save money:

> "In your communication on thiS [sic] subject you say that it is a well-known fact that a large number of persons on Pine Ridge Reservation, classed as Indians, and who are on the ration roll, have profited by the assistance they have received from the Government and are now not only beyond want but in many instances are prosperous, and are, therefore, self-supporting. You instruct the agent to go over the ration roll of the agency and erase therefrom all those who are wholly self-supporting. In compliance with instructions in your letter of August 12, I erased from the ration rolls of Pine Ridge Reservation 857 persons, comprised principally of whites and mixed bloods. They are supposed to be all self-supporting, and the withdrawal of their rations is in compliance with spirit of treaty of 1876.[43]

U.S. court decisions further separated people, something that concerned Pine Ridge Indian Agent W.H. Clapp in 1898:

> Under the decision of the Supreme Court in the Draper Case the United States courts hold that jurisdiction, except regarding full-blood Indians, is vested in the State courts. This causes the anomaly of Indians considered as having equal treaty rights, and who are subject to the same control on reservations, being under entirely different jurisdictions according as they are full bloods or mixed bloods . . . It appears to me that Congress should fix the status of these mixed bloods, and provide for them the same jurisdiction as is provided for

> Indians of full blood, or that they should cease to be considered Indians
> in any sense, or for any purpose whatever.[44]

In other cases, the OIA pursued the time-tested tactics of divide and rule,
plain and simple.

Indian Rights Association (I.R.A.) Director Herbert Welsh's 1883 report
notes that teachers in the U.S. government-run Day Schools on Pine Ridge
Reservation were "half-breeds and whites married to Indians."[45] Although
Henry Standing Bear reported that "several returned students," probably
full bloods, were teaching in those schools by 1894,[46] the Superintendent of
Indian Schools could find only one ". . . full-blood Sioux" Day School
teacher among the 31 Day Schools in operation on the reservation in 1903,
and the I.R.A.'s M.K. Sniffen reported that Carlisle graduate Thomas
Three Stars was the only full blood teacher in 1905.[47]

Mixed bloods and whites also filled positions as boss farmers, Agency
clerks, and laborers (full bloods were, in some instances, hired as interpreters for boss farmers).[48] "Indian traders" also tended to come from those
groups.[49] They, in turn, hired mixed bloods and whites. Of seventeen men
employed by the eleven traders on the reservation in 1910, twelve were
mixed bloods and five were white.[50]

There was a pool of qualified full bloods that could have been accessed
to fill such positions; 224 returned students, mostly full bloods, lived on
Pine Ridge Reservation in 1903.[51] Why not hire them for such "positions
of trust?" wondered Charles Turning Hawk in a letter to I.R.A. director
Herbert Welsh. Turning Hawk was a returned student himself. He was also
proprietor of "Chas. T. Hawk and Co., Dealers in General Merchandise"
in Kyle, making him only full blood "Indian Trader" on the reservation.[52]

Mixed bloods and whites were hired over full bloods for administrative,
teaching, and clerical positions, but the pattern was reversed for the Indian
Police and the Court of Indian Offenses. Court judges, and the entire police
force, was manned by full bloods. The police force provided significant
employment, albeit at a rate much lower than that for teaching and clerical positions; 76 Oglala full bloods served on the force in 1882.[53]

When Agent Valentine McGillycuddy established the Indian Police force
on Pine Ridge Reservation in 1879, he bragged that he had ". . . succeeded after encountering much opposition from the chiefs[,] in enlisting a very
efficient police force of fifty members from the best young men of the
tribe."[54]

McGillycuddy was wonderfully pleased with the police force he created.
In 1884, he extolled the Indian Policeman as one who carries

> . . . out his orders to a dot, and, unlike many of his white models East,
> he is no respecter of persons. The Eastern 'philanthropist' or Western
> cowboy, the Indian chief or ordinary 'buck,' is all the same to him in
> the line of his duty. 'Poor Lo,' as a guardian of the peace, feels that the

agent will assume all responsibility. And all of this he does for the munificent allowance of $5 per month (emphasis in original).[55]

McGillycuddy's successor, Agent Gallagher, was quite as laudatory, judging the police force on Pine Ridge Reservation as ". . . probably the best-equipped and most effective of any in the [Indian] service." He attributed that excellence to the full blood leadership, citing ". . .the superior intelligence and soldierly qualities of the commander of the force, Capt. George Sword, assisted by his able lieutenants, Standing Soldier and Fast Horse."[56]

The Court of Indian Offenses also drew high praise. Agent W.H. Clapp wrote that the Court ". . . commands the respect of the Indians and is of great assistance to the agent in dealing with minor cases of wrongdoing."[57] But Clapp, the same man who put his career on the line in his 1897 defense of Oglala economic interests against those of trespassing white stockmen, was a non-progressive when it came to hiring:

> Teachers of Indian blood, no matter how well equipped mentally, fail to obtain the respect and influence among the people to the extent necessary for complete success. They lack in self-reliance, are timid in their dealings with the Indians, and do not command their full confidence. They also, as a rule, are unthrifty, saving nothing of their salaries, usually deeply in debt, and frequently desiring a change, do not make permanent homes and get about them the conveniencies [sic] and comforts usual with white families and desirable as object lessons to the Indians.[58]

Notions like Clapp's were widely shared and expressed. Educated Indian people, in particular, were often singled out for attack. Henry Standing Bear, an 1891 Carlisle graduate, addressed the issue in his 1894 correspondence with Herbert Welsh:

> In the general Indian question the enemies of the Red man often accused him of being incapable of learning and that he was failed to be educated in schools established for him and carry on by heavy expenses, that he goes back from schools to dances and blankets, such is the language of people who are utterly ignorant of our capabilities. . . .[59]

When Welsh brought a May, 1894 attack published in the *Philadelphia Ledger* to Standing Bear's attention, he shot a reply back to the editor:

> In regard to the graduates relapsing into their original condition after they returned to their people, it must be a wrong term used or it is a mistaken idea. The reason – that as far as my knowledge goes I have never knew any graduate of these eastern schools had gone back to Indian life at Rosebud, Cheyenne, and Pine Ridge Agencies where I have been acquainted with them . . . There are only four graduates from those schools have returned to this agency now. Two are now working at their trades and two are clerking in a store. There are sev-

eral other returned students (not graduates) teaching in day schools and several interpreters for district farmers on reservations. Some are raising stock and cultivating land, erecting fences and barns and good houses for themselves and are doing well in their farms. . . . It is unjust and cruel that the fall of one or two returned students in the past, who have been in school one year or a few months were returned to reservations on account of sickness and have returned to Indian life again should be put upon the shoulder of [the majority, who have been] earnest, faithful . . .[60]

Returned students were in a difficult position. Pressures on them were enormous. They were not white enough for the whites, but their experience as boarding school students had changed them, enough so that their own people sometimes held them at arm's length.

On January 7, 1891, in the aftermath of the December 29, 1890 Massacre at Wounded Knee, a young Brulé returned student named Plenty Horses shot and killed Lt. E.W. Casey of the Twenty-second Infantry. A murder charge was lodged against Plenty Horses. In his testimony to the jury, he recounted how U.S. officials had forced him to go to Carlisle Indian School in Pennsylvania, when he was still a boy. At Carlisle they tried their best to make him into a white man. When he was returned to his reservation his own people despised him, because they felt he was too much like a white man; the whites despised him too, because he was still too much an Indian.

George Hyde concluded that Plenty Horse's testimony showed that "He was neither one thing nor the other, and he was very miserable. Being drawn into the ghost dance camp and coming in contact with Lieutenant Casey, it had suddenly entered his mind that here was the opportunity to show his own people that he was as good a Sioux as any of them."[61] Perhaps similar dynamics influenced other returned students to carve out leadership roles as prominent opponents of U.S. government policies.

When Henry Standing Bear defended returned students, he distanced himself from "Indian life" as depicted by racist whites; but he certainly embraced and supported Indian life as it was articulated through the Oglala Council, in opposition to the policies of the OIA. Among other things, he was a founding member of the "Dawes Bill Association" on Pine Ridge Reservation, the group that was likely responsible for devising the petition dated March 26, 1894, and signed by 1,258 Oglala men, that opposed allotment of reservation lands, calling instead for the entire reservation to be fee patented in the name of the Oglala Council, a move that would have facilitated the continuance of communal tenure, something Dawes Act proponents derided as communistic.[62]

Standing Bear and Turning Hawk used what they learned to advance not only their individual well being but also that of their fellow tribesmen. Turning Hawk himself worked diligently for many years on behalf of the

Oglala Council, drafting constitutions, corresponding with allies off the reservation, and assisting in local petition drives.[63] But neither the activism of some returned students, nor racist sentiments about returned students, adequately account for the discriminatory hiring policies followed by the OIA on Pine Ridge Reservation.

When Indian Agent Valentine McGillycuddy assumed his post at the newly created Agency at Pine Ridge, these were his first instructions from the Commissioner of Indian Affairs':

> you must lead and control your Indians; and as occasion requires, you
> must make them understand that you are placed at the agency to rep-
> resent the Government, and, as far as they are concerned, that you are
> to exercise absolute control over them. You will, of course, keep in
> mind that the great object of all your work is to do anything possible
> to promote the civilization of your Indians.[64]

In his drive to "exercise absolute control," McGillycuddy created the Indian Police; to "promote the civilization of [his] Indians" he developed sub-agency complexes in the reservation districts.

Besides reflecting the dual hiring practices of the OIA, the Indian Police drove a wedge between the generations. When Herbert Welsh visited Red Dog's Camp in Wounded Knee District in 1883, tiospaye headman Red Dog explained that he found fault

> with Agent McGillycuddy, because he was permitting young men to
> grow up and become so large as to hide him from the agent's sight,
> referring to the growing importance of the police force, which is com-
> posed of young men, and has thus awakened, in some instances, the
> jealousy of the chiefs. These words seemed to us very suggestive of one
> of the excellent features in Dr. McGillycuddy's administration; he has
> found that a rapid advance toward civilization among the Indians
> could only be accomplished by giving encouragement to active young
> men, who were anxious for improvement and were willing to work,
> and by neglecting tribal theories which existed for the benefit of chiefs
> at the expense of the general welfare of the people.[65]

On December 2, 1890, several weeks before the Massacre at Wounded Knee, Reverend Charles Cook, who was alarmed about the deteriorating situation on the reservation, referred to "The death-struggles of the fast decaying old chieftainship system" and reported that "The non-progres-sives [i.e., those openly opposed to U.S. government policy or activities] have been, pretty much all along, groaning under the weight of the rule of the Indian Police system, enforcing rule and order and work among them."[66] McGillycuddy had hit upon something that Eric Wolf identified as instrumental to breaking the bonds of kinship, specifically of giving young men an alternative path to power, one that freed them from kinship restric-tions.[67] The Indian Police afforded such an avenue on Pine Ridge

Reservation, and they performed their role well, as well indeed, at least in some instances, as McGillycuddy claimed. A few weeks later, when Two Strike led a force of warriors against the Pine Ridge Agency complex following the Massacre of their people at Wounded Knee, General Brooke called out the Indian Police. James Mooney's description shows just how handsomely McGillycuddy's efforts had paid off. In defending the Pine Ridge Agency complex, the "splendidly drilled body of 50 brave men"

> gallantly took their stand in the center of the agency inclosure, [sic] in full view of the hostiles, some of whom were their own relatives, and kept them off, returning the fire of the besiegers with such good effect as to kill two and wound several others.[68]

If the full blood Indian Police were an instrument that could be wielded in support of the "civilizing mission," the mixed bloods and whites, employed as boss farmers, clerks, and teachers, were an instrument designed to carry out that civilizing mission. Their official task was to represent and to promulgate, the plans, values, and ideologies that the colonizer deemed were "in the best interest" of the Indians.[69]

Mixed bloods and whites employed by the U.S. government, plus Indian Traders, and Episcopal, Presbyterian, or Catholic ministers and priests, formed the nucleus of colonial settlements in the reservation farm districts.[70] The logic of the arrangement caught Theodore Roosevelt's attention when he made his fact finding tour in 1893:

> Most of the half-breeds and squaw-men were around the different issue centres, where there were stores, usually a church, and a schoolhouse, etc. Each of these little embryonic towns, where there is a store or a little church with a native clergyman or catechist . . . and two or three families of half-breeds, and squaw-men in neat cabins roundabout, is a small centre of civilizing influence.[71]

The settlements around the Issue Stations in the Districts, the larger Agency complex in Pine Ridge Village, and the reservation boarding schools, were visible expressions of the OIA civilizing mission. Settlements of ethnically distinct groups of mixed bloods and whites, whose wealth and authority obviously flowed from their relationship with the OIA, were juxtaposed physically, symbolically, and structurally to the tiospaye settlements of Oglala full bloods.[72]

The institutionalization of ethnic difference by the colonial administration on Pine Ridge Reservation became a lasting characteristic of Pine Ridge Reservation social organization. The dual discrimination of the OIA's early hiring practices gave some mixed bloods and whites married to Oglala women, on the one hand, and some full bloods on the other, distinct yet complementary projects in the process of colonization. Mixed bloods and whites, with whom the white colonizers felt a certain kinship, were recruited to administer assimilative U.S. policies; full bloods, who had cultural knowledge, and a tradition of policing through the akicita societies, were recruited to effect compliance.[73]

The employment patterns that were set early on in the reservation era have changed somewhat over time, but the shadow of past practices is clearly discernible today.[74] Whites, mixed bloods, and full bloods have numbered among Oglala Sioux Tribal Court judges in the past 25 years on Pine Ridge Reservation, and the police force includes mixed bloods and full bloods, but the latter continue to predominate. Clerical and managerial jobs with the Oglala Sioux Tribe, the State of South Dakota Social Services, the Bureau of Indian Affairs, and the Indian Health Service have been more integrated in the past twenty years, people say, though mixed bloods still predominate over full bloods.

The channeling and manipulation of ethnicity by the OIA, through the skewed hiring pattern adhered to in the early reservation period, and through a number of other mechanisms not touched on here, has produced a legacy of ill feelings, divisive ideologies, struggles over identity, and intra-ethnic conflict.

CONFLICTING ECONOMIC REPRESENTATIONS

In February, 1917, William Spotted Crow and Charles Clifford traveled to Washington D.C. to represent the brief of the Oglala Council to Assistant Commissioner of Indian Affairs, E.B. Meritt. Clifford, a mixed blood, was likely chosen because of his facility with the English language and his knowledge of whites; Spotted Crow, a full blood, was a tiospaye leader, a delegate to the Oglala Council, the governing body that Oglala full bloods had constituted to represent their overall interests after the creation of the reservation.[75] Their mission was to lobby for eleven propositions that the Oglala Council had passed, one of which was to request an expansion of the ration roll.[76]

Clifford spoke first, diplomatically offering Meritt a chance to save some money by offering up ". . . 50 to 60 mixed bloods and squawmen on the reservation who have large numbers of cattle and who should be fee-patented U.S. citizens, but who are not because they want to avoid taxes." Spotted Crow pointed out that other Oglalas were being issued patents to their land, and selling their land for outrageously low sums of from $250-$300 per quarter section (160 acres) to a ring of white land speculators, who operated in concert to keep the price down. "If you do not take care of us we won't have any land. You make an Indian hungry and he will give up anything," he said. Clifford agreed with Spotted Crow that more rations were needed, giving this argument in support:

> An Indian is entirely different from a white person. Look at myself. I
> was raised in Nebraska until I was 13 years old, and I knew that what-
> ever I got I had to pay for, and that I have to hustle and work for my

bread and butter. But an Indian is different. He is placed on a reservation where he is fed and petted, and his self-reliance is lost.[77]

Spotted Crow disagreed:

> To illustrate that my Indians would work if they had the chance take
> the fall when the Nebraska potato fields are ready – whole families of
> Indians go out there and work and they make money during that time.
> During the winter it is very hard for these Indians, and food is so high;
> it is still worse on the reservations. There is no work there for them to
> do. They get together and try to help one another out by dividing what
> they have. Finally they are worse off than they were before. If the
> Indians were like any other nation they would have starved before this.
> They help one another. That is why most of them are alive today. I ask
> the Department to do something for them. People must not rush the
> Indians; they must look into the difficulties and act according to the
> treaties.[78]

Spotted Crow's remarks addressed the interplay of structure and culture.
His description of their interconnections left the dignity of his people, who
were struggling for survival, intact. His people practiced the values of
wacanteognaka (generosity) and okiciyapi (helping each other). They
"helped one another" and took advantages of the meager opportunities
there were, or they would have perished. Clifford put distance between
himself and "Indians," intimating that they, unlike himself and the mixed
bloods he referred to earlier, were passively dependent on government
largesse. They lacked "self-reliance," an argument, to be sure, that Merritt
might have made himself. But prima facie, Clifford's presentation suggests
that his notions about mixed bloods and full bloods sprung from his experience hustling for himself in Nebraska, versus his perception of full bloods
on the dole on the reservation. That experience may have reinforced his
ideas, but an address he read in English to General Crook at the Pine Ridge
Agency in 1889 suggests he, and other mixed bloods, had long held, or
used, those notions. After noting support for the Sioux Act, the prepared
remarks protested the views of those whites who claimed that mixed
bloods and whites married to Indian women were a curse to Indian people.
To the contrary, the statement suggested, they were

> . . . one of the good blessings which God has stored [sic] upon the poor
> red race of North America, because the half-breeds and their fathers
> were the people who have made peace with the red man for you, and
> have helped them more towards civilization than any other class and
> from this fact, the half-breeds and their fathers should be recognised
> [sic] as the helpers of the Indians.[79]

Full bloods and mixed bloods articulate many and varied beliefs about
the values and behavior each group is said to have. A common theme, especially among full bloods, is that mixed bloods put individual gain above the

well being of others, as in the following account by a young full blood woman:

> Full blood people who are poor are more content with their lives than mixed bloods with jobs, who are running people down and are seeking more gain. [Name] is putting his cattle first, putting making money first above the people. He closes off the gates so other people's cattle cannot get a drink in the stream. This is not the Indian value system. It is the white system. In the Indian way you put your people first, and not yourself.[80]

Her full blood husband added that ". . . mixed bloods get ahead of full bloods because the desires of full bloods are not for material gain, [but] the fact of politics, of government, cannot be ignored either."[81]

In analyzing "who gets ahead" he used notions of culture and structure, just as Spotted Crow did in 1917. Their analyses reject the popular notion that culture holds people down economically. But that notion does surface frequently, sometimes in self-deprecating humor and sometimes in a blunt, blame the victim style.

For years the story of two buckets of crabs has been repeated in public forums in Indian Counry. The crabs in one bucket keep climbing out, but the others never make it. They are the Indian crabs – every time one starts to crawl up and out, another one pulls it down. The crab story is a humorous, self-deprecating tale, often told at public meetings and workshops. Sometimes the premise more bluntly put.

Speaking at a the Tatanka Iyacin (In the manner of a Buffalo) Conference on economic development at Oglala Lakota College in 1985, then Pine Ridge Agency Superintendent Ken Fredericks told the crowd and the KILI radio listening audience that "There is a choice between economic development and culture. That's why whites succeed when Indians fail."[82]

Others, with views more in line with those expressed by Charles Clifford in 1917, and the conventional wisdom of political conservatives in the United States today than cynical government bureaucrats, explain poverty by reference to imputed individual characteristics in order to deny the potency of structure. According to one young mixed blood Oglala woman who teaches elementary school on Pine Ridge Reservation, "It's all up to the individual. I'm tired of all of the crying around, of people who are always blaming the BIA, and feeling sorry for each other. If they want to succeed they just have to work at it."[83]

But in the analysis of Spotted Crow, and in the view of many other Oglalas, it is the oppressive weight of the reservation system that holds people down – not their individual characteristics and certainly not their culture. The practice of putting people 's welfare before one's own does not condemn someone to grinding poverty. Certainly, practicing the Lakota virtue of wacanteognaka[84] (often glossed as "generosity" but often interpreted by Lakota people to mean "holding the people in your heart") can and does mean that individuals who are integrated into tightly woven networks of kin, and who "follow the ways," will not accrue significant material wealth because they redistribute it within the network, and more broadly. But "holding the people in your heart" does not keep someone from getting a job, or from accessing enough land to graze a few head of stock for subsistence purposes. That is a matter of "politics, of government."

Mixed blood and full blood Oglalas often forward different explanations for the economic realities on Pine Ridge Reservation. The enduring differences in those explanations correlate with similarly enduring patterns of social relations. Those relations reflect structural differences in the economy, and those differences in turn reflect the political and economic history of the northern plains.

"Once things are named, moreover, power is required to keep the meanings so generated in place – names must, as the Chinese say, be 'rectified.'"
Eric Wolf

Frantz Fanon described the colonial world as a world divided – a Manichean world of settler and native.[85] That world is also frequently divided from within, and the colonized are polarized in ideology and values.[86] Divisions between mixed blood and full blood Oglalas on Pine Ridge Reservation reflect that colonial legacy. Racism, of course, plays a signal role. But the early differential treatment of mixed blood and full blood by the U.S. government owed less to racism than to the pragmatics of divide and rule. Racism served more as a secondary, rationalizing function, than as a cause, as the description of the Office of Indian Affairs' dual hiring strategy for mixed blood and full blood Oglalas shows.

General Crook seized on the desires of mixed bloods and intermarried whites for private property in land, and on their willingness to act against the wishes of Oglala leaders, as an opportunity to advance the Sioux Act of 1889. The Great Peace Commission apparently seized upon similar desires and dispositions when it incorporated the agenda of certain intermarried white men and mixed bloods into the 1868 Fort Laramie Treaty. The crucial point is, as Peter Worsley, Eric Wolf, and Immanuel Wallerstein have pointed out, that whole categories of people, in this case people labeled as mixed blood and full blood, were singled out by powerful others, with real consequences for their relations.[87]

That "singling out" is not a singling out of specific individuals, but of categories. Through the process groups are created, maintained, and changed. Studying the process means studying history. Wanting a historical

perspective, what can be said about ethnic differences is severely circumscribed. Descriptors like the ones cited earlier in the chapter are interesting:
mixed bloods favor bureaucratic organization, full bloods favor cooperative endeavors, and so on. But why do certain ideologies and values prevail
among particular groups? Why do they see the other as they do, and why
do they pursue the courses they do? Discovering that requires an historical
view, a view that can chart the articulations of individual actors against a
background of changing group interests. As Frederick Hoxie puts it, saying
that one side is conservative and the other side is progressive explains nothing.[88]

The interactionist perspective is also problematic. William Powers
asserts, for example, that the ". . . full-blood – mixed-blood distinction is
more profitably analyzed as a continuum . . . in dealing with matters of kin,
it is more profitable to be Oglala; in dealing with matters of economics, one
switches to his 'white' side."[89] While the notion that people use their ethnic
identity to negotiate social life is surely useful, many Oglalas would take
issue with his presumption of the Lakota as "economic man."
Furthermore, kinship and economics are interwoven, not separate, phenomena.[90] The point I want to make, though, is that interactionist notions,
such as the continuum described by Powers, do not in themselves explain
why mixed blood or full blood Oglalas sometimes act in concert with each
other, and sometimes, as when General Crook visited Pine Ridge
Reservation in 1888, against the other. The problem of history goes beg-
ging.[91]

Divisiveness does have its roots in "an old white-man's trick," as Robert
Grey Eagle stressed. One way to fight the legacy of such tricks is to do history, and to do it with the *oyate* , the people, in mind. That means, in
Howard Zinn's words, asking questions that are ". . . important for social
change, questions relating to equality, liberty, peace, justice. . . ."[92] When
you apply that notion to the issue of difference between mixed blood and
full blood Oglalas, you ask questions like "What role might the colonial
context of reservation history have played in shaping inequitable relationships between the two groups?, What about that old white-man's trick?"
The roots of divisiveness need to be dug up and exposed.

But those roots extend beyond the divide and conquer strategies of the
OIA during the reservation period, beyond the Crook Commission and the
Sioux Act of 1889, and beyond the Great Peace Commission and the Fort
Laramie Treaty of 1868. The intra-ethnic split was already in place, a product of the changing economy on the northern plains. The collapse of the
hide trade attendant the slaughter of the buffalo put pressure on Oglalas,
and on their relatives who had been associated with the trade. Oglalas
found it ever more difficult to pursue their way of life because their
resource base was being decimated, and the trade they depended on was
withering; mixed bloods and intermarried whites sloughed off from the

hide trade turned to trading with westering immigrants, and to raising cattle. The Great Peace Commission, the Crook Commission, and the OIA used the existing split for their own ends.

Notes

1. Taylor, Graham 1980.
2. Author's notes, 1985.
3. Traditional government forum at Oglala Lakota College, December 4, 1991, author's notes.
4. Robert Grey Eagle, Traditional government forum at Oglala Lakota College, December 4, 1991, author's notes.
5. Powers, William 1975, p. 118, 119; MacGregor, Gordon 1946, p. 113; DeMallie, Raymond 1978, p. 270; Mekeel, Scudder 1944, p. 215, 216; Bromert, Roger 1980, p. 67; Feraca, Steven 1966, p. 7; Roos and Smith et al. 1980, p. 93.
6. Maynard, Eileen and Gayla Twiss 1970, p. 19; Feraca, Steven 1966, p. 7; MacGregor, Gordon 1946, p. 113; DeMallie, Raymond 1978, p. 307; Powers 1975, William p. 119.
7. Mekeel, Scudder 1944, p. 214; Wahrhaftig, Albert and Robert Thomas, 1972.
8. Taylor 1980, p. 50; Fowler, Loretta 1982, p. 308.
9. Schuler, Harold 1990 p.115, 131, 134.
10. Chittenden, Hiram 1902 p.865–66, NL.
11. Farley Mowat's book, *Sea of Slaughter*, which details the man-caused extinction of species on the northeastern seaboard of Canada and the U.S., makes it clear that economic, political, and psychological factors were involved in those travesties.
12. Weltfish, Gene 1971 p.218.
13. Mowat, 1984, p. 141–143.
14. Doane Robinson, 1904, cites a report by Dakota Territory Lt. Governor K. Warren, recounting his survey of the Black Hills in 1857, in which he describes Indians herding buffalo: "'. . . They were encamped near herds of buffalo whose hair was not yet sufficiently grown to make robes and the Indians were, it may be said, actually herding the animals. No one was permitted to kill any in the large herds for fear of stampeding the others and only such were killed as straggled away from the main bands. Thus the whole range of buffalo was stopped so they could not proceed south which was the point to which they were traveling. The intention of the Indians was to retain the buffalo in their neighborhood until the hair would answer for robes, then to kill the animals by surrounding one band at a time and completely destroying each member of it. In this way no alarm was communicated to the neighboring bands which often remain quiet, almost in sight of the scene of slaughter.'" p. 227–228. Under the circumstances in the 1860s, perhaps herding

was also a necessary response to the conditions on the plains, an activity carried out to protect the remaining herds from wanton destruction.

15. *Proceedings of the Great Peace Commission of 1867–1868*, p. 58, 118, 175; Tanner, Helen 1982, p. 20, 21.

16. *Proceedings of the Great Peace Commission of 1867–1868*, p. 58–59, 175.

17. Ibid, p. 111.

18. The term loafer referred to those Indian people who had become sedentized around a fort or agency. Another equally pejorative term for such groups, whom the whites labeled "friendlies," is "Hang around the forts." There is also a band of Oglala formally known as *Wagluhe*, which is translated as Loafers.

19. *Proceedings of the Great Peace Commission of 1867–1868*, p. 117.

20. Ibid, p. 115.

21. Ibid, p. 115.

22. Ibid, p. 116.

23. Ibid, p. 115–117. Picture of "Colonel Bullock House (Indian Trader) in Ayer Photo, Augur, Box XI, AP2843, NL.

24. Petition "To the Congress of the United States & to the Hon. Commissioner of Indian Affairs, Washington, D.C., November 16, 1867, 132 signatures. OLC Archives. I want to thank Dowell Smith for pointing this petition out to me.

25. Fort Laramie Treaty of 1868.

26. Secoy, Frank 1971, p. 65, 67.

27. Fort Laramie Treaty of 1868.

28. Oglala Council minutes, November 9, 1910. File 064, Box 118, MDF-PR.

29. Proceedings of Council meeting, April 23, 1908. File 064, Box 118, MDF-PR.

30. CIA Leupp to Brennan, September 11, 1905, Box 23, "Land," January 6, 1905 - December 28, 1905, KC.

31. Cf. Gilbert, Hila 1968, p. 34, 69. See also chapter 3 for further discussion of mixed blood cattle operators in the early days on Pine Ridge Reservation.

32. Batchelder, George 1870 p.20,30, NL.

33. Tanner, 1982, p. 26,27; Pommersheim, Frank 1993, p. 339.

34. Utley, Robert 1963, p. 42.

35. Tanner, Helen 1982, p. 26–28.

36. Recent research by Oglala attorney Mario Gonzales, and his assistants Jack Runnels, and the late Robert Gay, proves that over 200 of those signatures were illegal. Mario Gonzales, personal communication.

37. Hyde, George 1956, p. 219.

38. RCIA 1889, p. 152.

39. Hyde, 1956 p. 214.

40. *Ibid*, p. 213–219.

41. Gay, Robert 1984.

42. Sioux Act, March 2, 1889, 25 Statute, 888–899; RCIA 1889, p. 152.

43. J.R. Brennan in RCIA 1901, p. 367. The reference to the "Treaty of 1876" is to the U.S.' illegal taking of the Black Hills under the so-called "Agreement of 1877."

44. RCIA 1898, p. 277.

45. Welsh, Herbert 1883, p. 28, NL.

46. Henry Standing Bear to the Editor of the *Philadelphia Ledger*, May 10, 1894, IRAP Series 1-A, Reel 11.

47. Report of the Superintendent of Indian Schools," RCIA, 1903, p. 415. M.K. Sniffen's report on his visit to Dakota, September, 1905, IRAP Series 1-A, Reel 30.

48. Henry Standing Bear to the Editor of the *Philadelphia Ledger*, May 10, 1894, IRAP Series 1 – A Reel 11

49. Information about mixed bloods and white men married to Oglala women serving as boss farmers is from author's notes. Store owners on the reservation were called "Indian Traders" by the Office of Indian Affairs. Oglala store owners tended to be mixed bloods. Charles Turning Hawk, a full blood who owned a store in the community of Kyle in Medicine Root District was an exception. Some Indian Traders were white men who were not married into the tribe.

50. M1011, 1910.

51. "Report of the Superintendent of Indian Schools," RCIA 1903, p. 373.

52. Charles Turning Hawk to Indian Rights Association, January 3, 1903, IRAP Series 1-A, Reel 16. I was unable to locate a response to Turning Hawk's letter to Welsh. Turning Hawk's troubles with the boss farmers are described in Chapter 4.

53. RCIA 1899, p. 336; "Pay of Police," June 30, 1882, McGillycuddy Collection, OLC Archives.

54. RCIA 1879, p. 40.

55. RCIA 1884, p. 40

56. RCIA 1888, p. 48.

57. RCIA 1898, p. 277.

58. Ibid., p. 276.

59. Henry Standing Bear to Welsh, December 24, 1893, IRAP, Series 1-A, Reel 10.

60. Henry Standing Bear to the editor of the *Philadelphia Ledger*, May 10, 1894, IRAP Series 1-A, Reel 11.

61. Hyde, 1956, p. 311.

62. Henry Standing Bear to Welsh, December 24, 1893, IRAP, Series 1-A, Reel 10; Petition from Oglala to Indian Rights Association, dated March 26, 1894, IRAP Series 1-A, Reel 11. See also chapter 4 regarding Oglala opposition to allotment.

63. Criticism of the education of Indians by late 19th century whites sounds remarkably like modern racist notions, insofar as it suggests that education is wasted on minorities. Paradoxically, returned students were placed in the position of having to defend their use of their enforced education.

64. CIA to McGillycuddy, July 24, 1879, McGillycuddy Collection, OLC Archives.

65. Welsh, Herbert, 1883, p. 30–31.

66. Rev. Charles S. Cook to Welsh, December 2, 1890, IRAP Series 1-A, Reel 5.

67. See discussion of the kin-ordered mode of production in Wolf, Eric, 1982, p. 88–96.

68. Mooney, James 1976, p. 123.

69. The notion of wardship, of Indian wards for whom the U.S. government has a caretaking responsibility, is part of the complex of paternalistic ideas and practices

that rationalized the actions of the colonizing power in Indian Country. In Public Law 103–177, the Native American Resource Protection Act of 1993, the phrase "in the best interest of the Indians" is employed as a rationale for giving the Secretary of the Interior power to determine the length of grazing leases on Indian land.

70. The Episcopals came first, in 1879, followed by the Presbyterians in 1886, and then the Catholics in 1887. Cf. RCIA 1879, p. 40; and "Report of Missionary, Pine Ridge Agency," in RCIA 1888, p. 52–53.

71. Roosevelt, Theodore, 1893, p. 15, NL.

72. See also the discussion of different settlement patterns of Oglala mixed bloods engaged in ranching, and full bloods engaged in pursuits more akin to a subsistence economy, in Chapter three.

73. Other factors naturally entered into hiring for certain positions of authority. Boss farmer selection, for example, surely included calculations of interest. Just as the selection of Pine Ridge Indian Agent John Brennan (1901–1917), was influenced by outside livestock interests, so too may have boss farmer selection reflected a conjunction of interests between themselves and livestock interests, both on and off the reservation. Many boss farmers were, like Agent Brennan, stockmen themselves.

74. Hiring patterns have changed as a result of individual actions and collective struggles. Those stories are yet to be told. The common contention in the literature that mixed bloods predominate in the employment ranks because of educational advantage is only part of the story.

75. Chapter 4 contains an extended discussion of the role of the Oglala Council.

76. Record of Hearing of Pine Ridge Delegates with E.B. Meritt, Assistant CIA, February 26, 1917, 75-33-053 to 80965-22-054, 1907–1939, PR, CCF.

77. Record of Hearing of Pine Ridge Delegates with E.B. Meritt, Assistant CIA, February 26, 1917, 75-33-053 to 80965-22-054, 1907-1939, PR, CCF.

78. Record of Hearing of Pine Ridge Delegates with E.B. Meritt, Assistant CIA, February 26, 1917, 75-33-053 to 80965-22-054, 1907–1939, PR, CCF.

79. Proceedings of the Council of Indians Effecting Agreement of 1889, Legal and Legislative Records, Records of Councils 1875–94, KC.

80. Author's notes.

81. Author's notes.

82. Ken Fredericks, Tatanka Iyacin Conference, Oglala Lakota College, May 9, 1985, author's notes.

83. Personal correspondence with the author. In a later conversation she agreed that employment opportunities are limited.

84. Wacanteognake

85. Fanon, Frantz 1968, p. 41.

86. Van den Berghe, Pierre 1967, p. 144.

87. Wallerstein, Immanuel 1983, p. 76; Wolf 1982, p. 379; Worsley 1984, p. 245.

88. Hoxie, Frederick 1992a, p. 55.

89. Powers 1975, p. 119.

90. Consider in this regard the description of the giveaway in Chapter 3.

91. The interactionist approach could, though, help explain, why some Oglala reject classification as mixed blood or full blood, why some Oglala are not readily classified by others. Somehow, some Oglala have been able to transcend the limitations of a narrow ethnicity, while others struggle mightily to transcend those limitations and fail, phenomena that are touched on in Chapter 6.

92. Zinn, Howard 1993, p. 30.

CHAPTER 3

Cattle, Grass, and Ethnic Conflict at the Grassroots

"The grass was the country as the water is the sea."
Willa Cather

SELF-SUFFICIENCY OR DEPENDENCY?

A small group of about 200 Oglala and non-Indian ranchers control nearly one and one-half million acres of grazing land on Pine Ridge Reservation today. Oglala allottees and their heirs own about 800,000 acres of trust land and the Oglala Sioux Tribe owns about 830,000 acres, but Oglala people overall realize very little from their land. Since the allotment of land on the reservation, which was carried out principally between 1904–1915, land has been fractionated through heirship to the point where today most parcels of trust land are very small and landowners often own several small, widely separated, tracts. As a result lease incomes are often inconsequential, people generally do not even know who the lessee is, and commonly do not even know where the land they inherited is located. This pattern of extreme alienation from the reservation land base is the end result of processes that have been at work since the creation of the Pine Ridge Agency in 1879.[1]

Before the termination era of the 1950s and 1960s, there were a significant number of Oglalas in each of the eight reservation Districts who made their living either partially or principally from the land. Until October 1955, several families in Brotherhood Community in Porcupine District were able to make an independent living by combining subsistence pursuits and wage labor. In Knife Chief Community, also in Porcupine District, Edward Iron Cloud Jr. recalls that hard work and communal grazing afforded his family and others a measure of self-sufficiency until 1958.[2] The situation in the other seven reservation districts was similar. People survived by grazing small herds of cattle in common on parcels that they owned, and sometimes on other parcels that they either leased or otherwise accessed from individual Oglala owners. They also cultivated family gardens, canned vegetables, stored fresh and dried produce in root cellars, collected wild foods, and hunted wild game. They supplemented their

agricultural pursuits on the reservation by working as migrant laborers in
the potato and corn fields of Nebraska, in the beet fields around Belle
Fourche South Dakota, and in Wyoming, and in the apple orchards of
Colorado. It was not a materially rich life, far from it, but Oglala elders
emphasize that they did not need welfare.

The situation changed during the termination era, when the the land
they had run their cattle on in common was consolidated into range units
too large and too expensive for them to rent. Non-Indians and mixed
bloods who had the necessary capital took over the land, forcing the others out of business. The policy aimed at assimilating Native Americans by
relocating them to cities severed, in the main, the remaining economic connection of Oglalas to their land. In the 1960s and early 1970s many
Oglalas also lost their physical ties to the land, moving from homes on their
allotments into the clustered HUD housing projects that were built in every
reservation district.[3] Birgil Kills Straight contrasted the difference between
the earlier state of affairs and current conditions at the *Tatanka Iyacin*
Conference at Oglala Lakota College in 1985.

> What existed in the past on the reservation was farming, ranching, and
> people involved in using the land to make some sort of livelihood. . . .
> Four years ago Shannon County was classified as the poorest county in
> the nation. Yet we have all these people, 20,000 people, living here. We
> also have two and one-half million acres of land, and yet we are clas-
> sified as being poor. Something is terribly wrong when that happens.[4]

The theme of loss of control over the land and consequent loss of self-
sufficiency recurs regularly at Treaty meetings and at other gatherings on
the reservation where people reflect on the currently depressed economic
situation. According to oral histories some of the best times in terms of economic self sufficiency on the reservation were in the early reservation era,
especially in the late 19th and early 20th centuries. Johnson Holy Rock, an
elder and past President of the Oglala Sioux Tribe (1964–1966), put it this
way:

> Going back to the time of pre-allotment period, everyone had livestock
> of some kind [the first allotment on Pine Ridge Reservation was in
> 1904]. Mostly horses, and they had a lot of cattle, and there was no
> fences . . . It was something they could identify with because they
> raised horses while they were still roaming all over this country before
> the treaties . . . Even old Indians that still wore their braids and still
> wore moccasins, wore western clothes . . . had cattle. . . . They were
> pretty self-sufficient. Strange as it may sound, it is possible in those
> days.[5]

Holy Rock's contention that "Even old Indians that still wore their
braids and still wore moccasins . . . were pretty self-sufficient" may indeed
sound strange on a reservation where unemployment ranges between 70

and 80%, and where the land is scarred by erosion and over-grazing. Oglala students in classes at Oglala Lakota College who do not know the oral history are surprised and somewhat skeptical of such stories, perhaps because they seem so out of sync with the current situation. Perhaps it is also because they do not fit with the prevailing ideas about why the economic situation here is so depressed.[6] Popular media accounts exploit the 1980 and 1990 U.S. Census finding that Shannon County, which is wholly on the reservation, is the poorest in the United States. Stories like the recent Emmy-award winning NBC production "Tragedy at Pine Ridge," sensationalize the poverty and attendant social ills and completely ignore the resourcefulness of the people and their struggle to survive, to undo the damage of more than a century of colonial rule, and to free themselves from it.

When what people "know" about Native Americans is based primarily on such media portrayals, what they really know is what Alfonso Ortiz calls "one of the most vicious stereotypes of Native Americans."[7] The racist theme that Native Americans are passive and dependant wards waiting for handouts has been around for a long time. On Pine Ridge Reservation people in power have used it to justify their domination and to blame the people for the colonial situation. Thus on Pine Ridge Reservation in 1913, Agent John Brennan claimed that many Oglalas were ". . . hard up at times and do not make a very good living principally because of the inherent shiftless nature of the average Indian."[8] And in 1925 Agent Ernest Jermark, who was issuing four pounds of meat per month per person wondered if it was too much and if it would be better if he issued none as it was his observation ". . . that the Sioux have been placated about enough, and that the policy pursued in the last 40 years of providing them practically everything they wanted is, in a large measure, responsible for the condition in which we find them at present."[9]

The basic mode of thought does not seem to change much. When asked about the history of Oglala farming and ranching in 1983, L.D. Alderson, then Director of Land Operations in the BIA's Pine Ridge Agency said "Let me tell you about Indians. They used to follow the buffalo around and when they used up what was in one place they moved to the next and used that up. That's why they never did know how to raise crops or cattle and just had to depend on rations."[10] Yet of course it is the Land Operations Division that administers the range unit system that was used to consolidate control over the reservation into the hands of a few whites, whites claiming and receiving Indian preference by virtue of their marriages to Oglala women, and mixed-blood Oglalas.[11]

The notion that Oglalas showed little initiative on their own behalf in the early reservation years sometimes shows up in scholarly research. In his 1958 study of Pine Ridge Reservation family life, Vernon Malan asserts that

> As long as the Pine Ridge families were dependent upon government
> rations and issues, the threat of starvation could be used as an effective
> means of control. In most cases the Indian families passively accepted
> their dependent condition. Since the 'great father' had taken their lands
> from them, he would surely be kind enough to take care of their mate-
> rial needs.[12]

In his more recent 1992 study, Thomas Biolsi, who is writing from a
very different perspective and who emphasizes the role of the oppressive
reservation system in creating dependency, presents a variant of the "He
who feeds leads" theme. While Biolsi emphasizes that Lakotas were not
merely passive, and that there was day to day resistance on Lakota reservations, he maintains that Lakotas challenged neither the presence of colonial agencies nor the practices of surveillance and control that they were
subjected to. He explains that supposed quiescence by reference to the
effectiveness of the Office of Indian Affair's (the OIA, which later became
the Bureau of Indian Affairs, or BIA) "technology of domination." He
argues that through the effective operation of such institutions as reservation police and courts, and especially through the control of ration distribution within the context of an "artificial reservation economy," the OIA
exercised effective domination of the Oglala people. "The Lakota endured
the bureaucratic penetration of their everyday lives by the OIA because the
OIA made their everyday lives possible."[13] Such arguments rest on the conclusion that Oglalas were anything but self-sufficient. Other anthropological and historical accounts of Pine Ridge Reservation's early economy dif-
fer so much from what Malan and Biolsi report that they seem to be
describing another time and place.

In *Warriors Without Weapons*, Gordon Macgregor claimed that largely because of the success of Oglala cattle raising "Rations became so
unnecessary by 1914, that they amounted only to token payments."[14] And
in the *Sioux Chronicle*, George Hyde reported that by 1914 on Pine Ridge
the Oglalas ". . . had large herds and were selling beef cattle in considerable numbers."[15] Biolsi mentioned cattle in his sketch of the reservation
economy but implied that, save for the incomes monopolized by a handful
of mixed blood ranchers who sold cattle to the agencies for redistribution
as rations, they were not a significant factor in the overall economy.[16]

This chapter examines early reservation economic and political arrangements in order to assess conflicting claims about Oglala self-sufficiency,
find historical antecedents to the current pattern of inequity in land ownership and control, and tease out relations between political economy and
differences between mixed blood and full blood Oglalas. How important
was stock raising? How important were rations? How effective was the
OIA at regulating and administering the reservation, and how did the
Oglala people respond to OIA policies and practices? Was the reservation

akin to a "total institution" in the sociological sense, or was there a looser regulatory climate?[17]

CATTLE AND THE EARLY RESERVATION ECONOMY

Pine Ridge Reservation is situated on the short grass plains, and before it was overgrazed by outside interests encouraged by the Office of Indian Affairs, it was a stockman's paradise.[18] BIA Regional Forester George Nyce reminisced about the former richness of the region in an address to the Oglala Tribal Council in Wanblee in 1936.

> I came to this country in 1890. We brought 10,000 head of cattle into this country, not right here but just west of the Standing Rock reservation on Grand River. When we came in here the grass was stirrup deep all over this country. Now what we are trying to do for these grazing lands is to bring them back to you reservation people to what they were at that time. Now we know that we cannot bring it back 100% because this country has been grazed off and your more valuable forage plants have been destroyed. When we came into this country, we considered this Dakota hay worth 10 forks of Texas hay.[19]

The short grass prairie's characteristic grama, buffalo, and slender wheat grasses are especially nutritious. Grama grass cured on the stem still retains its protein content, unlike most forage grasses which lose their value rapidly unless they are cut and stored.[20] In 1905 U.S. government surveyors, surveying the reservation in preparation for allotment, described fine growths of grass of excellent quality for grazing purposes and for haying in townships across the reservation. With the exception of some of the areas in the badlands in the northern portion of the reservation, the land was rich. Some Oglalas today recall their parents' and grandparents' descriptions of the dense prairie sod and of the tall grasses that scraped the bellies of their horses. They made good use of the lush stands of grass.

> The valley along White River is quite thickly settled by Indians. They seem quite prosperous and industrious; most of them having small herds of cattle and horses, for the use of which they cut considerable hay. Beyond a small garden, the settlers have no cultivated land.[21]

Cattle raising had become an important part of the reservation economy as early as 1893. When Theodore Roosevelt visited Pine Ridge Reservation that year, covering 250 miles by horseback and wagon in six days to gather information about day schools and general conditions for the U.S. Civil Service Commission, he reported that "All over the reservation I was struck by seeing herds of cattle guarded by Indians, often boys. They locate their herds right around their own neighborhoods and watch over them carefully." He also noted marked differences among families and saw many that he felt were not doing well and others that appeared to be prospering.[22]

A dozen years later, when Indian Rights Association Secretary M.K. Sniffen visited Pine Ridge Reservation, he found that Oglalas were, in general, making a living from their own efforts. He stayed with several families during his visit and made detailed notes of his observations and interviews. In Pass Creek District he was an overnight guest in the home of Reuben Quick Bear, a full blood married to a mixed blood woman. They owned a five-room, comfortably furnished home, a vegetable garden of five acres or more, and about 30 head of cattle and horses. They were doing fairly well though they had just suffered big losses. Their herd of 75 cattle had been reduced by rustling and severe winter. Eleven head were stolen while Quick Bear was away from home working with an OIA road gang; 45 more perished in the severe winter weather.[23]

In the published account of his travels, Sniffen labeled the work system of the OIA, which mandated that able-bodied Indians had to work for $1.25 per day in lieu of rations, a failure. The system hurt others, as it had the Quick Bears. Work projects were often a considerable distance from people's homes, necessitating camping at the work sites. Wives often went along with their husbands to cook for them, leaving the home, gardens, and stock untended. One objection to the camps was that they seemed to strengthen the customs of dancing and giveaways, which were said to be held every night in the camps.[24]

In spite of any practical problems with the work system, and the alleged evils of the attendant cultural practices, Oglalas were apparently keeping the wolf away from the door largely through their efforts at cattle raising and other uses of the land. Sniffen observed that at Chief Lips Camp in Corn Creek District, "The Indians at this place have more cattle and horses today than they have had for a good while." In Wounded Knee District the people had plenty of hay and stock.[25] Generally, they were doing what they could to make a living and they were not sitting back and waiting for the government to feed them. As Sniffen put it in the colloquial usage of the day, "In all my travels among the Sioux I did not see one blanket Indian."[26] Warren K. Moorehead, an anthropologist employed by the OIA as an inspector, surveyed reservation conditions within thirty miles of the Pine Ridge Agency in the spring of 1909 and came to a similar conclusion. Nearly all of the Oglalas he observed had small herds of cattle and horses, and they were plowing, planting, and "exerting every effort to make some practical use of their allotments."[27]

Judging from the eye-witness accounts at the time, the single most significant factor in the Oglala economy from the early 1890s through about 1915 was stock raising (Numbers of stock owned by Oglalas declined precipitously thereafter). In the decade between 1886 and 1897 Oglala cattle holdings increased nearly nine-fold from 4,618 head to more than 41,000. Their herds peaked at 60,000 head of horses and cattle combined in 1910 (Table 1). The following year, 3,548 Oglalas were reported to be making their living principally by stock raising, and 2,718 partially from stock raising.[28] In 1914, a year of serious drought, when gardens and crops failed, Agent Brennan reported that people had little to support them but cattle.[29] But inequities in cattle ownership were marked. Some individuals had a handful of animals while others had sizeable operations. When the herds reached their zenith in 1910, Brennan reported holdings ranging from five to 1,000 head.[30]

Oglala mixed bloods and white men married to Oglala women generally owned the largest herds, reflecting the fact that they had already been in the cattle business along the North Platte River before they settled near the Pine Ridge Agency.[31] During testimony given at Pine Ridge Agency in 1897, W.D. McGaa, a mixed blood, reported that he had been in the cattle business for 13 years and that he had 700 head near Spring Creek, north of Porcupine. Pass Creek District boss farmer Joseph Rooks, a white man married to an Oglala woman, reported that he owned 200 head. Billy Palmer, a 22 year old mixed blood, living on the White River below the mouth of Porcupine Creek had 600 head. Palmer estimated that four white men married to Oglalas who lived near him had about 2,500 head among them. Medicine Root District boss farmer Smalley estimated that eight mixed bloods and white men married to Oglalas, who lived along the northern border of the reservation, owned around 1,500 head.[32]

Testimony by full bloods at the 1897 meeting shows that they tended to have significantly smaller herds than mixed bloods and whites married to Oglala women. The one exception was Alex Adams of Wounded Knee District who claimed he owned over 500 head. Other full bloods at the meeting owned less than 100 head. Hunts His Horses from Medicine Root District reported that he owned something over 80 head. No Water, from White Clay District, claimed 60 head. Very Good, who lived close to the White Clay issue station, had 50 head. Boss farmer Joseph Rooks estimated that of the 12,000 head of Oglala owned cattle in Pass Creek District full bloods owned between 25 to 50% though they represented by far the majority of the population. Boss farmer Smalley did report that full bloods in Medicine Root District owned somewhat over half of the 6,500 cattle there, but they also represented the majority of the population.[33]

Statistical records for 1900 reveal a pattern of continuing mixed blood predominance in individual cattle ownership. That year in Porcupine District the herds of mixed bloods averaged 84 head while those of full bloods averaged 47, a ratio of 1.8 to 1. The difference was even more pronounced in Medicine Root District, where mixed blood's herds averaged 101 and full blood's herds averaged 26, a ratio of nearly four to one (Table 2).

Table 1: Stock Owned by Oglalas

Year	Horses	Cattle
1886	4,077	4,618
1887	6,553	6,278
1888	7,771	8,889*
1889	9,013	10,968
1891	5,314	7,982
1897	not available.	41,000
1904 (combined horse and cattle)		33,944
1905 (combined horse and cattle)		34,256
1910 (combined horse and cattle)		60,000
1916	8,642	18,113
1917	12,308	15,655
1918	14,302	16,280
1920	not available.	13,460
1925	not available.	7,129
1930	not available.	3,750

Source: Compiled from RCIA and Clapp to Welsh, October 12, 1897, IRAP Series 1-A, Reel 13, NL.

Table 2: Cattle Ownership in Three Reservation Districts*

District/Year	Families	Total cattle owned	Average herd size
Porcupine/1900	56 full blood	2,625	47
	39 mixed blood	3,265	84
Medicine Root/1900	193 full blood	5,077	26
	43 mixed blood	4,355	101
	36 full blood	1,409	39
**Wakpamnee/1900	13 mixed blood	645	50
	6 white men married to Oglala women	497	83

Compiled from Monthly reports of District Farmers and Related lists, Administrative Records, Box 745, KC, and from Miscellaneous Allotment Records, 1907–ca. 1911, Box 867, KC.

*Figures for Pass Creek District not found (The reservation was divided into four districts in 1900; there are nine districts today).

**Wakpamnee figures for those owning less than 25 head not found.

CATTLE, CLASS, AND THE OIA

Mixed bloods and white men married to Oglala women not only tended to have larger cattle herds than full bloods, but they had begun to fence off some of the best land on the reservation to pasture those herds. In July of 1897, Agent W. H. Clapp reported receiving frequent complaints about extensive fencing of large tracts of the reservation, especially by whites married to Oglala women, who had appropriated meadow and grasslands which had been customarily used by Oglala full bloods. In an attempt to curtail the practice, Clapp ordered that no person could have a right to more than one claim, which in that pre-allotment era was apparently 160 acres, the same size as provided for in the Homestead Act. He did rule that in order for a claim to be valid a person would need to live on it or put substantial improvements on it. But the claimant need not live on it – a resident employee was adequate.

Clapp's pronouncements were just that; the OIA was unable to effectively regulate the situation. Two years later, Charles Turning Hawk, a full blood returned student from Medicine Root District, who was active with the Oglala Council, lobbied the Indian Rights Association for help in dealing with the problem. He noted that "The half breeds and squaw men have fenced in all the most fertile lands. . . .," and warned that if that pattern of land holding were to be fixed by ownership through allotment there could be another "outbreak."[34] In 1905, Reverend Johnson, a Presbyterian minister in Pine Ridge Village, told Sniffen that it had become difficult for the Indians to take care of their cattle because "mixed bloods and squawmen had secured the hay flats."[35] Johnson Holy Rock's oral historical account corroborates the written documents. After elaborating on the early economy Holy Rock concluded "When the fences came in, that's when the problems begin."[36]

Oglala full bloods registered their displeasure about the situation with Pine Ridge Agent Jenkins, who was moved to express his concern in an August 1900 letter to the Commissioner of Indian Affairs. Jenkins found ". . . that many of the white men, married to Indians, living on this reservation, have from 300 to 1,000 head of cattle, and are practically monopolizing the best grazing portions of the reservation."[37] A month later the Acting Secretary of the Interior, citing Jenkins' letter, and expressing the intent to keep Pine Ridge Reservation for the "Indians," granted authority for use of the permit system of pasturage there, ostensibly to regulate herd size by exacting an assessment for those Oglala residents with large herds. Under the permit system, heads of Oglala families, including those headed by white men married to Oglala women, were assessed $1.00 per head per annum for any cattle they owned in excess of 100.[38]

Full blood complaints about the fencing practices of mixed bloods and white men married to Oglala women did bring a response, but the remedy applied to them as well. Reverend Amos Ross, the red haired, red bearded

Santee Sioux minister of an Episcopal church in Corn Creek community, said the measure had hurt some full bloods, who then changed their position on the measure from support to opposition.[39] When the tax took effect in 1900, Agent John Brennan downplayed the full blood opposition, estimating that the number of cattle taxed would not exceed 5,000, with two-thirds of that total belonging to "half-breeds, mixed bloods and whites, married to Indians."[40] The lists of cattle owners for three reservation districts contain the names of only five full bloods owning over 100 head. Two were from Medicine Root District and three from Porcupine. Their herds ranged in size from 120 to 150, and though substantial, were much smaller than the herds of a number of mixed bloods in those districts. Significantly, the two men from Medicine Root were Little Wound and American Horse, both of whom were recognized by the government and by the people as chiefs. In Pass Creek District in 1899, the two largest herds owned by Oglalas classified as full blood were those of Young Bad Wound, with 60, and Charging Bear with 50.[41] A few mixed bloods did have very sizeable herds (Table 3).

Table 3: Mixed blood Oglala operators with more than 100 head of cattle in 1900 (3 Districts)*

District	No. operators	No. cattle owned	Range of herd size	Average herd size
Pass Creek	24	5,328	118-600	222
Medicine Root	9	2,478	180-347	275
Porcupine	7	2,550	125-900	364

Compiled from File: Misc. Allotment Records, 1907–ca. 1911, Trust Responsibilities Records, Field Notes of Boundary Surveys 1875–1905, Box 867, KC.

*Data from Wakpamnee District not found.

At any rate, full blood opposition to the tax continued. In 1903, Chief Lip and Charles Turning Hawk, who was by then the President of the Oglala Council, explained their opposition in a letter of protest to the Commissioner of Indian Affairs.

> We do not approve of the grazing system which you have inaugurated for us, for the following reasons. In our past treaties there has never been anything of this sort mentioned. The full-bloods are not yet sufficiently educated, thus they do not make sheds nor fences for their cattle and have never hay their cattle during winters. The squaw men and half-breeds are capable of all these things and we should not be compared with them, as they have by far more cattle and they are utilizing greater more space of grazing land: also they have fenced in more land than full-bloods. They are able to pay $1.00 a head in excess of 100

head of cattle. They should be compelled to comply with this grazing system and exempt all full bloods.[42]

The Commissioner disagreed, claiming that anyone who had more than 100 cattle could certainly afford to pay the tax.[43] Lip and Turning Hawk were surely engaging in a bit of hyperbole in their letter – full bloods did harvest wild hay in order to feed their stock in winter – but their message was clear: Mixed bloods were consolidating their hold over grazing land that full bloods needed. Besides denoting differences in ancestry, the terms "half breed" and "full blood" were associated with differences in education and wealth. Lip and Turning Hawk's emphasis on those factors point to the class distinctions that had arisen between the two groups. The larger commercial operations of some Oglala mixed bloods afforded them the opportunity to consolidate their hold over grazing lands that full bloods needed to maintain and to expand their own herds, leading to the conflicting interests that Lip and Turning Hawk pointed out. The differences between the two groups were class differences, in the classical sense, because each had developed its own common interests in accord with its relationship to the means of production and to the market.[44] One important aspect of that relationship for Oglala mixed bloods involved their role as middlemen.

Persons of mixed ancestry have operated as middlemen in many contexts, and Oglala mixed bloods were no exception. Because they and their ancestors had performed in that role as traders, interpreters, and as voyageurs in the fur trade, it was nothing new for them either.[45] On the reservation some Oglala mixed bloods, and some white men married to Oglala women, served as middlemen by brokering the interests of non-Indians who wanted access to grazing lands on the reservation. In 1896, for example, two white men, Thomas and James Wilson, moved onto the reservation and married mixed blood Oglala women. Having married Oglala women the brothers gained the resources to engage in stock raising, as long as they could prove that those stock belonged to their families.[46] But at the 1898 spring roundup, it was discovered that they had brought in "quite a quantity" of outside stock, an unlawful practice. Clapp expelled them from the reservation.[47] The case of the Wilson brothers is typical, except for the fact that they were caught and that action was taken against them. The practice was widespread and the situation was relatively unregulated. In 1911 J.J. Boesl, boss farmer from Pass Creek District, reported that a delegation of "Indians" (i.e., full bloods) visited his office to protest the actions of mixed bloods and white men who had fenced tribal lands for the purpose of pasturing outside stock. He substantiated their complaint and noted that the same situation characterized other reservation districts as well.[48] Agent Brennan did nothing to interfere. Under the cover of fictitious bills of sale white men married to Oglala women and mixed blood Oglalas continued to bring large numbers of outside stock onto the reservation, pasturing them both in fenced and unfenced tribal lands and on allotments other than their own.

One of the transgressors was the Chief Government Surveyor, Charles Bates, who brought between 1,500 and 1,800 head on in 1911. Later on that year their rightful owner, one William Reynolds, a big cattle operator from Wyoming, turned up to claim them and shipped them to Omaha. Agent Brennan was not overly concerned about his responsibility to uphold the trust responsibility of the OIA and his only action was to write to Bates telling him that "This whole deal, it seems to us, is a rank imposition on the Indians." The cattle had been turned loose to roam on the individually owned allotments of Oglalas and on tribal lands in the Buzzard Basin country.[49] The OIA's unwillingness or inability to regulate the situation kept the door open for further abuse. As a result, certain Oglala mixed bloods, white men married to Oglala women, and outside interests prospered at the expense of the full blood majority. Incentives to continue such illegal practices were high as commercial ranching was a lucrative enterprise in those years and cattlemen were looking to fill up all available range with their stock.

Despite illegal stocking, both mixed blood and full blood Oglalas benefited from the commercial sale of their stock. Both groups sold stock to the OIA, which in turn reissued it over the block as rations, but that was a small matter compared to the commercial outlet. By 1905 Oglalas were shipping substantial numbers of cattle by rail to market in Omaha. The main beneficiaries were of course those with the larger herds, namely certain mixed bloods and white men married to Oglala women.[50] But full bloods shipped some cattle as well. In 1913 Agent Brennan reported that Oglala cattlemen grossed $363,176 from the sale of 5,485 head of cattle and 1,066 head of horses.[51] In 1915 the *Oglala Light* reported that they made numerous shipments of from one to three carloads of cattle and horses. Those shipments were valued from $1,000 to $3,000. A few Oglala mixed bloods made much larger shipments that year. Ben Lessert shipped 450 head, E.B. Ward shipped 360, Louis Pourier shipped 200; Frank Livermont shipped 184, Joe Eccofey shipped 182, William Twiss shipped 175, Thomas O'Rourke shipped 170, Ed Amiotte shipped 120, and Charles Amiotte shipped 119 head.[52] J.D. Corder, a white rancher who owned a business in Pine Ridge Village, shipped 210 head of grass fed three year old steers to Omaha during World War I when cattle prices were high and realized a little over $136 per head, or about $28,560 for the lot. He planned on shipping 125 more soon thereafter.[53]

Mixed bloods and white men married to Oglala women tended to have both bigger herds and more capital than full bloods. Their capital access derived from their roles as brokers for outside interests (which presupposed their willingness to take calculated risks in the quest for profit), and their willingness to use the tribal commons on the reservation for their own individual gain at the expense of the group, brought them a measure of prosperity in the loose regulatory climate of the reservation. In order to be successful they fenced off the most desirable acreage for their own use, brought in outside stock, ignored OIA regulations, and generally committed themselves to the pursuit of profit and individual gain.[54]

Oglala full bloods, on the other hand, grazed their smaller herds in common, with minimal fencing, and had much more limited involvement in the cash economy than many mixed bloods and white men married to Oglala women. Even if they had wanted to fence their herds in during the heyday of the reservation cattle industry, they would have been unable to do so because they could not afford the barbed wire to do the job. They did occasionally sell a few head of stock in order to buy clothing or provisions, but the main use they made of their cattle was for subsistence.

OIA policy was officially aimed at increasing the size of the cattle herds, and to that end they tried to regulate even the subsistence use of cattle. "Legal" sale or slaughter of cattle branded "I.D." required OIA approval (the "I.D." brand stood for Indian Department and indicated that while individual Indians owned the cattle they were held in trust by the U.S., just as in the case of trust land). The procedure was to apply for a permit from the boss farmer. But when Oglalas needed meat for their families, they did not deny them just because the boss farmer would not issue a permit. During the winter of 1908–1909, Medicine Root District boss farmer Ramsey Hawkins complained helplessly of "quite a lot" of unauthorized butchering of I.D. cows. Two months into the winter he had only been able to catch two transgressors, Crooked Eyes and Fool Crow [sic], whom he had arrested and sent to the Agency for punishment. The cows they butchered were their own.[55]

The OIA was no more effective at regulating the subsistence economy of Oglala full bloods than it was at curtailing the excesses of the commercial ranching enterprises of Oglala mixed bloods and white men married to Oglala women. But just because the OIA was not a particularly effective instrument of social control overall, it does not mean that the situation on the reservation was free from oppression.

May Wood captured some of the texture and flavor of that situation in her descriptions of everyday life in her correspondence with Sniffen of the Indian Rights Association. Wood, a white woman who lived with an Oglala family in Manderson in 1913, was impressed by the people but dismayed by the circumstances they had to put up with.

> Grasshoppers are thick when you step. Harriet Bone Necklace: '*She plows* herself and knows a great deal about gardening.' Farmer is Jake Killer but Brennan keeps him busy in office and going on errands for him so he isn't around much. Austin Red Hawk came over today and he is postponing the trip to D.C. A young woman (half sister to my friend Emil Afraid of Hawk, the Chief of Police) was there with her

baby – Si yo ko was dropping in potato pieces fast as the plow turned up the soil. Red Hawk is a keen elderly man. Brennan does not love him. He complained *at Washington* awhile ago (I forgot when) and when the complaints came back to Brennan he 'went for' Red Hawk. He and Chief Eagle good friends . . . The women talk of sending in plea too. I tell them all right, do so. White women 'kick', why should not you. They were talking this morning about the injustice in the matter of 'rations', and how the young women and men are *misrepresented*, and the truth is not told, when the rations are no longer given to them. Some work ('like sailors too) to raise some crops but where it comes to money earnings, what are they to do. To be successful at farming, they must have fences and not these fiendish *barbed* wire ones either.

Wood told Red hawk to write everything down and not go to Washington. Instead, she urged him to hold onto his money instead, as proof that ". . . they are *not* children as Brennan insists they are." She said the prices at Hank Simmon's local store were outrageous. Coal oil, for example, was .30 per gallon there though it could be had for .15 per gallon at the Agency in Pine Ridge Village. And "Simmons weighs groceries (I'm told) in another room – the Indians do not see their articles weighed [emphasis in original]."[56]

High prices, little cash, hard work, OIA failure to honor the ration distribution requirements of the Fort Laramie Treaty of 1868, leaders subjected to harassment by Indian Agents, and the typical mentality of OIA administrators who saw those they administered as childlike, as something less than human, constituted the everyday colonial situation on Pine Ridge Reservation.[57] But the reservation was not a closed system and other forces besides the colonial administration contributed importantly to the context and set the stage for the elaboration and development of economic and cultural practices. The interplay between U.S. governmental regulation and market forces, which underlay the developing horizontal split between Oglala full bloods and mixed bloods, influenced their distinctive economic and cultural repertoire as well.

CULTURAL DIFFERENCES AND THE ECONOMY

Oglala mixed bloods who engaged in commercial ranching operations expressed very different notions about land tenure than Oglala full bloods with their more subsistence oriented operations. W.D. McGaa, who referred to himself as both a mixed blood and as a "quarter breed" at a public hearing at Pine Ridge Agency in 1897, and who owned about 700 head of cattle near Spring Creek, north of Porcupine, made it very clear that he believed that he had the right to exclusive use of the reservation land that he customarily ranged his cattle on: "I claim my range on Cottonwood Creek and Spring Creek."[58] McGaa's claim was being trespassed by cattle owned by an off-reservation white named Kelliher. McGaa said he would have pleasant feelings toward him ". . . as soon as he keeps his cattle off my range." Other mixed bloods at the meeting also cited specific locales where they ranged their herds, and used the term "mixed blood" in reference to themselves and "full blood" in reference to those they distinguished themselves from.

When W.D. McGaa claimed the range on Cottonwood Creek and Spring Creek as his own he was invoking the same unwritten rules that non-Indian ranchers used in the public domain in order to secure their right to claim an area as their range. Such claims would be

> ". . . recognized by his neighbors (but not by law) as range rights. This meant a right to the water which he had appropriated and to the surrounding range . . . if the first ranchman [sic] occupied both sides of the stream, then his recognized range extended backward on both sides to all the land drained by the stream within the limits of his frontage; if he held but one side, then his range (for thus it was called) extended back only on that side. Moreover, it was not good form to try to crowd too much."[59]

As a former member of the South Dakota Stock Grower's Association (SDSGA),[60] a regional protective society, McGaa would have been well aware of those rules as would the SDSGA representative who questioned him about his range at the meeting in Pine Ridge in 1897. Other mixed blood cattlemen were aware of those rules as well, and their dispersed settlement patterns along the waterways on the reservation suggest that they may have used them for self-regulation, just as cattlemen did on lands in the public domain.

Oglala full bloods at the meeting probably used the term "*ieska*" (interpreter) to refer to mixed bloods and simply "Lakota" to refer to themselves, a common practice today. Whatever terms were actually used by full bloods at the 1897 meeting though, the mixed blood interpreters Frank Russell and Andrew Going translated them as "full blood" and "mixed blood." Importantly, full bloods, like the mixed bloods, were using linguistic markers to distinguish between themselves and the others. The way they talked about the land and their use of it further distinguished them from mixed bloods. When Alex Adams, whose herd of 500 cattle was far larger than that of any other full blood at the meeting, was asked to describe his range he replied that it was "Scattered all over the country." No Water, a full blood who owned 60 head of cattle, and who lived on the bank of the White River in White Clay District, made no reference to individually controlled range but instead referred to the "haying grounds." Similarly, Red Shirt referred to the collectivity, noting that "we want to raise some stock" and "we have only a little grass."[61]

Differences between Oglala mixed bloods who engaged in commercial ranching, and full bloods who engaged in a subsistence economy, were also apparent in their distinctive settlement patterns. In the early years of the reservation many of the mixed blood Oglalas owning larger herds of cattle settled near the northern and western boundaries of the Pine Ridge Reservation. Their households tended to be dispersed and they were often settled miles away from the nearest full blood family. Full bloods settlements were mostly from seven to twelve miles away from the exterior boundaries of the reservation and they lived much closer together.[62]

Most Oglala full bloods lived in close proximity to each other in groups of related families called *tiospaye*. *Tiospaye*, classified by anthropologists as cognatic bands, were one of the basic organizational structures of Oglala social and political organization.[63] Each of those flexible residential units of cooperating kin had a recognized leader. Some Indian Agents naturally recognized in them an obstacle to their goals of individualizing the people, and breaking the power of their leaders. Agent Valentine McGillycuddy, still remembered today on the reservation for his tireless commitment to undermine, and to manipulate, Oglala political and social organization, was able to effect some overall dispersal by dividing the reservation into several farm districts, each with its own issue station.

Pushed by the OIA, Oglalas dispersed into the four farm districts, which were delineated along the creeks that flow north into the White and Cheyenne Rivers. Besides the tendency to live in residential units, another part of the problem from McGillycuddy's point of view was that the flexibility of Oglala residence patterns was such that people often moved from one locale to another. Their canvas tipis facilitated that residential flexibility. Because McGillycuddy wanted the people sedentized – it would make them easier to control – he stopped issuing the canvas that Oglalas used to make tipis, substituting doors and the necessary hardware for log cabins. By 1885, over two thirds of Oglala families were living in log cabins.[64]

Log cabins may have reduced residential mobility, but they did not eliminate the Oglala practice of living in close proximity with each other. *Tiospaye*, or perhaps simply extended family clusters, were apparently still the norm in the full blood community. McGillycuddy did not give up his principles easily though, and in his 1885 annual report he boasted that "as a result of an endeavor to break up and scatter the Indians hitherto congregated in villages, several hundred houses have been torn down, removed, and rebuilt on scattered land claims."[65]

But two decades later, the earnest efforts of a skilled colonial agent like McGillycuddy notwithstanding, Chief Allotting Agent Charles Bates was having a difficult time dividing up the land into private parcels in full blood communities along the creeks, because families had settled there in close proximity to each other. Once the allotment process got under way in 1904, one of the biggest problems the government surveyors faced was settling disputes over boundaries in those relatively dense settlements. In many cases groups of between five and ten families were living on one section (i.e., one square mile) of land.[66]

As a result many of the allotments along the Creeks are very small and the balance of the acreage due to the allottee was made elsewhere on the reservation. Some heads of families who lived along the creeks, for example, got as little as 40 acres around their homes and the balance of the 320 or 640 acres they were due elsewhere on the reservation.[67] The creeks were the primary water sources at the time and Oglalas were not inclined to leave a functioning kinship unit in order to imitate the isolated nuclear family living situation of homesteaders on the plains. They stayed on their small parcels along the creeks and continued to graze their stock communally, on both tribal land and on the land of other allottees.

Thus neither the creative repression of a McGillycuddy, nor the assimilative fantasies of the so-called "Friends of the Indians" groups and their congressional allies, could break the back of the Oglala *tiospaye*. Inadvertently and ironically, a result opposite to that intended by policy makers was achieved. The ostensible intent of the General Allotment Act, or Dawes Severalty Act of 1887, was to secure for Indian peoples the fruits of civilization, which their tribalism and communal tenure practices had allegedly denied them; but the advent of private property in land reinforced, for some Oglala full bloods at least, a pattern of *tiospaye* living, especially along the creeks that they depended on for water for themselves and for their stock.[68]

Whites working on and visiting the reservation often referred to the clustered full blood settlements as "camps" and designated them by the name of their leaders. In 1888 Mrs. Charles Cook, wife of a minister on Pine Ridge, referred to "Red Dog's Camp." During his 1905 travels on the reservation, Sniffen commented about passing by "Lip's Camp."[69] Certain rural extended family clusters of full blood Oglalas are still called "camps" today in English and *wicoti* in Lakota. The late Chief Frank Fools Crow's place of residence on Three Mile Creek in Medicine Root District was, for example, referred to as "Fools Crow's Camp."

Those Oglala mixed bloods who raised cattle, and who had settled in a more dispersed pattern along the creeks and rivers, ended up with larger contiguous parcels along those waterways than full bloods. The allotment map for Washington County shows a clearly discernible pattern for Porcupine Creek and Wounded Knee Creek (Map 4).

Map 4: Contrasting Settlement Patterns

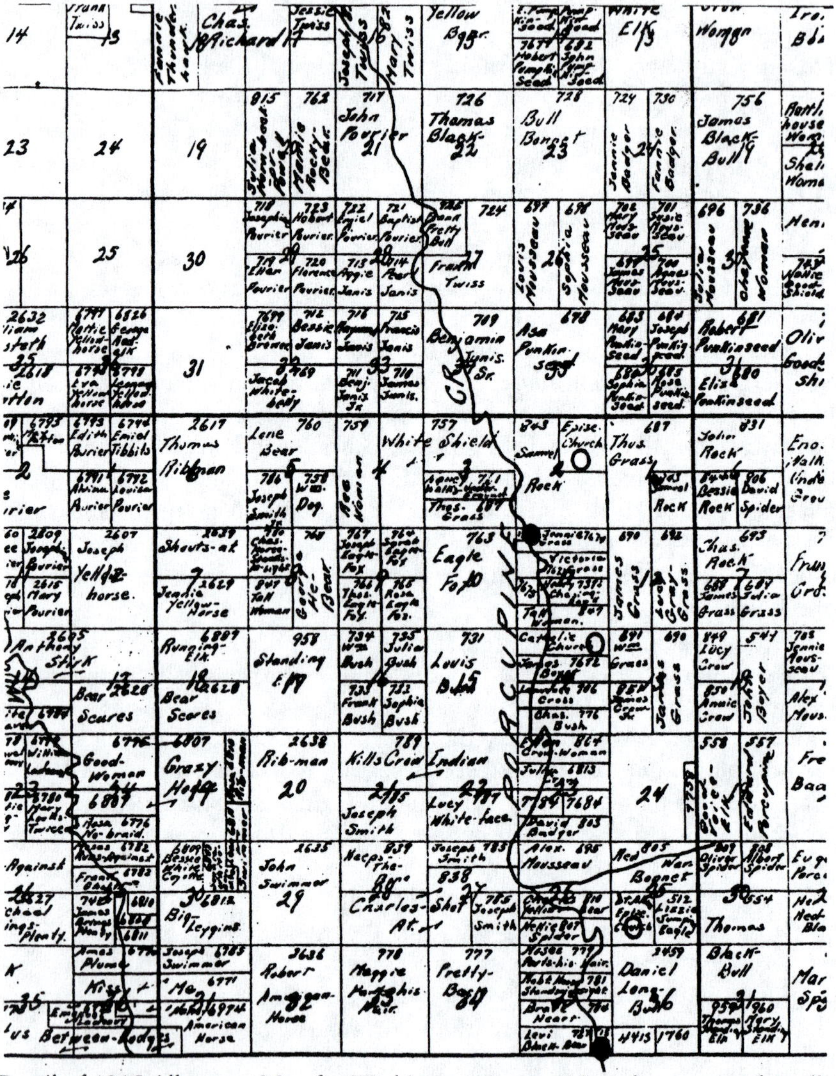

Detail of 1915 Allotment Map for Washington County. Note the pattern of smaller allotments along Porcupine Creek to the south, and the larger allotments to the north. The smaller allotments along the creeks reflect the more closely settled full blood areas, in contrast to the areas of mixed blood settlement. Note also the larger allotments away from the creeks reflecting the comparatively sparse settlement pattern away from the major water sources. Map in Oglala Lakota College Archives.

Mixed blood Oglalas were a relatively small group when the reservation was created, but the proportion of persons counted by the U.S. government as mixed blood Oglalas rose dramatically from 10% of the population in 1888 to 21% in 1901 and 37% in 1925. In the sixteen years from 1888 to 1904 the mixed blood population increased from 503 to 1889, a 375% increase! (Table 4). The increase stemmed from several sources. Mixed blood families were somewhat larger than full blood families. Mixed blood nuclear families averaged 4.2 persons in 1887 while full blood nuclear families averaged 3.6 persons.[70] Mixed marriages added to the increase as well. But by far the most significant factor in the mixed blood population explosion appears to have been immigration.

Table 4. Mixed Blood and Full Blood Population, Pine Ridge Reservation

Year	Full blood	Mixed blood
1888	4549	503
1891	4278	528
1901	5446	1520
1904	5212	1889
1925	4770	2858

Source: RCIA 1888, 1891, 1901, 1904, 1925.

Allotment was a magnet attracting new mixed blood tribal members. Once the allotment work got under way on Pine Ridge Reservation, Chief allotting agent Charles Bates received numerous letters from individuals who wanted land allotments. Inquiries came from Nebraska, Missouri, Kansas, Maryland, Washington, and other states. Bates viewed many of the would be allottees as opportunists who had never been affiliated with Oglala bands but who saw

> a chance to get a large piece of land for nothing, have discovered they are Indians and are asking for rights here, and in some cases are getting them. In looking for a location these people generally go to the south-eastern part of the reservation which is mostly settled by mixed bloods, among whom they discover an uncle, aunt, or cousins to the second or third degree.[71]

Some of the immigrant mixed bloods had never been affiliated with the tribe in the past, their primary link was that of blood. Others had, for various reasons, been out of direct contact with Oglalas on the reservation for some time, but they met the federal government's criterion for affiliation, which stated that "Such as these people as were associated and affiliated with the Sioux March 2, 1889, and their descendants, are entitled to allotment and enrollment."[72] Some of the mixed bloods journeyed to the reservation to claim their allotments in person, others used a power of attorney to claim them by proxy. The influx of mixed bloods dramatically changed the numerical ratio of mixed bloods and full bloods (Table 4), and reinforced and elaborated existing residential differences between the two groups.

The newcomers also played an important role in subsequent political developments on the reservation. Some of those who settled in the southeastern corner of the reservation became active in South Dakota state politics, and were the key local actors in the effort to organize Bennett County, which covers about one million acres in the southeastern corner of the reservation. Despite the opposition of Oglala full bloods, Bennett County was opened to homesteading in 1911, and is defined by the state and federal government as "ceded territory." The county was organized in 1912, paving the way for state jurisdiction (Map 5).[73]

Map 5. The Diminished Reservation

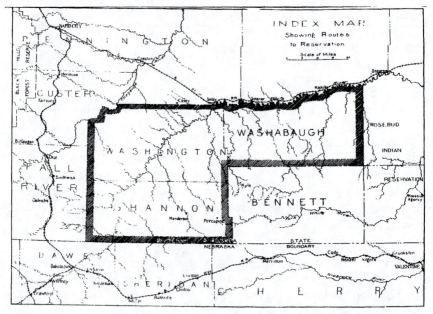

Map showing the four counties that were part of Pine Ridge Reservation. In 1976, Washabaugh merged into Jackson County to the north, with the county seat at Kadoka. Washington County was absorbed into Shannon County in 1942. Bennett County is considered "Ceded" by the U.S. pursuant its opening to homesteading in 1911. It is not considered ceded by the Treaty Councils or the Oglala Sioux Tribe. Approximately one-third of Bennett County is in trust status today, and the Oglala Sioux Tribe continues to exercise jurisdiction in those trust areas. Map is detail from 1914 OIA map of Pine Ridge Reservation. Copy in Oglala Lakota College Archives.

Some of the new mixed blood immigrants became involved in tribal politics as well. The most famous was Frank G. Wilson. When he was approved for an allotment in 1906, he was a resident of Lawrence, Kansas. Though his maternal grandfather was allotted in Porcupine, Wilson settled in Bennett County, where he became involved in state politics.[74] He eventually went on to prominence in tribal politics, becoming the first President of the Oglala Sioux Tribe's Indian Reorganization Act government in 1936.

In addition to differences in kinship, residential patterns, demographic characteristics, economy, views of the land, and politics, important cultural practices distinguished full blood and mixed blood Oglalas. Two such practices were the *wacipi* (dancing to the accompaniment of the drum) and the give-away. Besides being clear markers of difference between the two groups, they became the focus of assimilative efforts by missionaries and Indian Agents because they were linked to the propagation of characteristic Oglala values that those colonizers recognized as antithetical to their purposes. Furthermore, the give-away, which occurred in the same context as the dancing, as well as in other arenas, was a significant redistributive mechanism that served to level out differences among people as it assisted those in need in a culturally appropriate way.

An observant visitor to the reservation in the early years would have seen the many community dance halls that stood out in the clustered camp settlements composed primarily of Oglala full bloods. Oglala dance halls were sometimes substantial octagonal log buildings, but whatever form they took, they were erected by the people, for their public use, in their communities. The Reverend Amos Ross told Sniffen that each camp erected a dance hall in in 1904–1905. There were two in his community of Corn Creek alone. He was keeping a close watch on what was, to him, a dismaying situation that he associated with alcohol and with the give-away. At White Swan missionaries complained that dancing and the give-away interfered with their missionizing efforts. The give-away was singled out in particular as an example of how "The heathen element is trying to destroy the work of the Church."[75]

The U.S. government took a position on Native American social dancing in 1894, issuing a total prohibition and providing for punishment for offenders.[76] That edict was never fully enforced on Pine Ridge Reservation, but it provided a basis for OIA employees to target the dance halls and to limit dancing in them. The rules varied depending on the disposition of the Commissioner of Indian Affairs (CIA) and the Indian Agents. In 1900, Brennan directed the boss farmers to ". . . confine the Indians in your district to two Omaha dances a month, to be held on the first and third Fridays of each month."[77] In 1908, Acting CIA Larabee told Brennan that "The policy of the Office is to place the Indian on the same footing as the white man with respect to his religious, social and other gatherings. The Office believes that the Indians should be allowed to amuse themselves in a reasonable manner and therefore has no objections to permitting dancing of a harmless character."[78] On Standing Rock Reservation, the OIA actually razed a number of dance halls;[79] on Pine Ridge Reservation that apparently did not happen, though on some occasions the halls were closed by the farmers and the rules enforced by the police.

Just as it was with certain aspects of the cattle industry, the OIA was an ineffective apparatus when it came to regulating even such practices as dancing and the give-away. When boss farmers and police did try regulation, Oglala just "went underground," simply moving their dances into people's homes to avoid OIA harassment. Missionaries and others often complained to the Agent about the failure to police Oglala dancing. In 1913, Brennan responded to those complaints by dutifully directing the boss farmers to stop the unauthorized dancing. Instead of following the rules and ". . . holding dances twice a month, first and third Fridays, the Indians in several of the Districts are holding dances two or three times a week and . . . many of these dances are being held at the homes of the Indians."[80] In 1920, complaints about dancing prompted Agent Tidwell's order that dance halls on the Reservation be closed and remain closed, except for the one nearest the issue stations and that that should only be used once per month, on the day before ration issue.[81] The reach of the OIA was not long enough to effectively regulate activities in people's homes, though some of the Agents certainly would have done so if they could have.[82]

Oglala elders remember the dance halls and can still point out their former locations. They equipped the halls with stoves and used them year round for various dances and community activities. Full bloods recall that mixed bloods sometimes visited the dance halls, but the halls were located in the full blood communities and they organized the events and were the primary participants in them.

The government was at least as concerned about the give-away as it was about dancing. The same Acting CIA who talked of putting the Indians on the "same footing as the whiteman [sic]" told Brennan that "The Office is unwilling to sanction this custom of the Indians of making gifts of their property and has prohibited the practice. Neither does it approve of celebrations so elaborate that in providing therefor [sic] the Indians make themselves poor."[83] The OIA's concern with dancing and with the give-away was primarily driven by the notion of individual labor and accumulation. The people should spend time working, not dancing; and they should save what they earned so that they could progress according to the white man's yardstick. Another thing that probably bothered the OIA about Oglala dancing was the opportunity it gave them to collect money to send their representatives to Washington to represent their interests.

OIA personnel were at a loss to understand why Oglalas persisted in giving away their goods. And, even more baffling, they seemed to enjoy it.

Wounded Knee District boss farmer Gleason was at a loss to understand the attitude of Oglalas chosen as "penny holders" at the district's 4th of July dance; penny holders, after all, had to provide the feast for the next Omaha dance. And although "Collections are made at such times . . . no part of the collection is used by the penny holder to pay the cost of the feast. The holder of the penny is quite a looser [sic], but they will not admit it."[84]

The *maza sa yuhapi* (penny keepers) were chosen annually at the fourth of July celebrations in the various reservation districts. During the year leading up to the next celebration their task was to prepare for the *maza sala*, the special honoring of the children, which was an important part of the fourth of July festivities on Pine Ridge Reservation from around 1890 to 1950. During the year they, along with their relatives, saved goods in preparation for the big giveaways that would be held on the next fourth of July to honor the children. The *maza sala* commenced with the gathering of the children, girls and boys from babies to about ten years, into the camp circle. The goods to be given away were laid out on the ground and piled on the backs of horses. Tipis, cash, blankets, and star quilts were given away. They were preferentially distributed to the poor and those who came from other reservations for the celebration. Giving to relatives was, and still is, frowned upon. *Maza sa olowan* (penny songs) encouraged the giving away of horses. Sometimes the horses were turned loose and belonged to whoever caught them. The children being honored were dressed in beautiful outfits, completely beaded vests and pants with striking geometric designs and images of horses and American flags. The *maza sala* was an important learning experience for everyone present, especially the children, who learned through experience the importance of the Lakota virtue of generosity. Parents would often give away the beautiful outfits they had made for their children.[85]

Besides the giving associated with the maza sala at the fourth of July celebration, the "Committee" that organized the overall affair collected giveaway materials for redistribution during the dances. In 1905 Reverend Ross reported that the thirty tipis, horses, cash and sundry articles turned over to the Committee were worth not less than $10,000.[86] Giveaways insured the redistribution of a large amount of goods. Chiefs were expected to give away the most. That marked somewhat of a change from the pre-reservation era when the mercantile relations that Oglalas established with St. Louis earlier, and the local and regional hide trading centers later, had enabled Oglala leaders to break free from the constrictions of kinship ties and thereby accrue relatively large amounts of personal wealth; under the new conditions on the reservation full blood Oglala leaders were known for their willingness to give freely, and sometimes even for their penury.[87]

Okiciyapi (helping each other out) was, and remains, a central feature of life in Oglala communities. Oglala kin and friendship networks provide a kind of social insurance by affording patterned and regular redistribution of resources. *Tiole*, a pattern of regular and extended visiting, was very common until the relocation era. Oglalas would travel long distances, from one community to another by horse and wagon, set up camp and visit for several days at the homes of relatives and friends. In addition to the social benefits, the custom occasioned regular sharing of food and labor. Community feeds, held in conjunction with dances, which were put on by one or more families, were another occasion for food redistribution. Large quantities of soup, bread, and other foods were often prepared and it was expected that people would take *wateca* (food not consumed) home with them.[88]

Cultural and social mechanisms like the give-away served to level out differences among Oglala full bloods and helped insure that they would survive the uncertain economic situation on the reservation. They complemented the subsistence economy of stock raising and of gardening, the vitality of which depended on such unpredictable variables as the Dakota weather. Bad winters sometimes killed many cattle, and dry summers sometimes wiped out gardens entirely. The effects of such setbacks were buffered somewhat by other economic pursuits.

THE MYTH OF RATION DEPENDENCY

Migrant labor was an important component of the Oglala economy from the early part of the century and into the 1950s. In 1915 Oglala Council delegate Joshua Spotted Owl reported that entire families were working in the potato fields of Nebraska.[89] The opening date for reservation schools had been moved from September to October, allowing whole families to work through the harvest season in the potato fields without absenting their children from school.[90] People recall that so many people worked as migrant laborers in some years that "you would find almost no one home in the districts."[91] Indian Agents encouraged the off-reservation work and advertised wage-labor positions through the boss farmers in the Districts (Figure 1). Families would, in addition to their cash earnings, load their wagons up with potatoes and bring those back to the reservation as part of their "stocking up" for the winter. Some of the men found jobs as lumberjacks in the Black Hills. Others, who had been off on extended (six month long) tours with wild west shows in Europe and in the eastern United States, came back with trunks full of food, textiles, shoes, and clothes. "They knew they had to stock up for winter."[92]

Figure 1: OIA Labor Recruitment Notice*

Notice!

Indian-Laborers Wanted.

The C. & N. W. Ry. offers $2.25 per day for laborers at Chadron, Rushville, Gordon, Long Pine and other points and wants Indians *Now.*

Farmers and Police are requested to call the attention of Indians to this work and urge them to accept *at once.* Traders are also asked to call Indians' attention to this notice.

Farmers are requested to ascertain the number of men wanted for fence building in their districts and post rates and names of employers.

This is most important and no one without work should be overlooked.

Pine Ridge Agency, S. D.

July 10, 1917.   C. L. ELLIS,

Special Indian Agent in Charge.

---

*Special Agent in Charge at Pine Ridge Agency, Charles Lee Ellis, was recruiting Oglala labor for off-reservation work on railroads, and for local work making fences, probably for ranchers. Wages for ranch work on the reservation were low. As recently as 1980, some Oglala were being paid as little as $15.00 per day plus meals to work for ranchers on the reservation. A pattern of migrant labor was established early in the reservation era. As recently as the early 1960s , many families regularly left the reservation during harvest time to work in the fields in neighboring states. In those years, many school children enrolled in reservation schools sometime after the fall semester began, reflecting the time of their families' return from the harvest.[93]

Oglalas took advantage of a range of opportunities in order to make a living. They were clearly not sitting back waiting for handouts and they did not simply owe their existence to the largesse of the federal government. The early reservation era Oglala economy was a complex mix of subsistence pursuits, wage labor, commodity production, and entitlements guaranteed by Treaty provisions. But just how important a factor were those entitlements, the rations that the OIA was required by Treaty law to provide, to the Oglala economy?

James Mooney argued that the drastic cuts that the U.S. made in rations subsequent to the so-called "Sioux Act of 1889," precipitated the Ghost Dancing that led up to the Wounded Knee Massacre in 1890 (the relative deprivation hypothesis). The people had been ". . . expressly and repeatedly told" by Three Stars Crook's (Lt. General Crook) Sioux Commission "that their rations would not be affected by their signing the treaty, but immediately on the consummation of the agreement Congress cut down their beef rations by 2,000,000 pounds at Rosebud, 1,000,000 at Pine Ridge, and in less proportion at other agencies."[94] The 20% cut at Pine Ridge continued a downward trend in the beef ration there. In just three years, between 1886 and 1889 the beef ration had been reduced from 8,125,000 pounds to 4,000,000 pounds, a reduction of over 50%. In 1889, Agent Gallagher reported that because of their reduced rations Oglalas had to use 700,000 pounds more of their own beef than they had the previous year.[95] Adverse weather the following year compounded the situation. In his deposition on the Massacre, Bishop William H. Hare wrote that "In 1890 the crops, which promised splendidly early in July, failed entirely later, because of a severe drought. The people were often hungry, and, the physicians in many cases said, died when taken sick, not so much from disease as from want of food."[96] That summer ". . . the Indians at Pine Ridge made the first actual demonstration by refusing to accept the deficient issue and making threats against the agent."[97] There is no doubt that rations were essential to Oglalas in the years before the development of the reservation economy. It could not have been otherwise.

But the reservation economy grew rapidly after the Wounded Knee Massacre. Oglala interest in stock raising was growing; the people knew that the U.S. government would not live up to its treaty obligations by providing sufficient rations in a predictable manner. The unreliability of the ration issue, and the small size of the ration, coupled with the fact that Oglalas were able to fall back on their cattle to provide a significant proportion of their subsistence needs, as they were able to do in 1889 even though their herds were still quite small at that time, would surely have been an incentive to protect and to propagate the growing herds. In 1893, Pine Ridge Agent Penney reported that Oglalas ". . . have done well by the cattle that have been hitherto issued to them."[98] Actually, though, Oglalas husbanded their stock carefully from the beginning. As early as 1879, the year Pine Ridge Agency was founded, Agent McGillycuddy reported that

> "The stock, contrary to predictions of many that they would all be
> 'slain and devoured,' has been well cared for, with a loss so far of not
> over five or six head, and these from natural causes. The increase has

been large, and in addition there has been saved from the beef animals issued to them this summer, about one hundred cows.[99]

The proportion of subsistence that Oglalas provided from their herds increased rapidly and by the fall of 1895 the official records show that they furnished about 2,000,000 pounds of beef for their own consumption, which averages out to about 400 pounds per person per year (on the hoof weight).[100]

Oglala cattle were much more satisfactory than the beef issued at the agency, for several reasons. Most important was the fact that the people could take care of their stock by haying them in winter and were thus able to keep their weight up. The cattle at the herd camp at the Agency, on the other hand, were brought in during the fall of the year, when they were in prime condition. They were weighed upon delivery and that weight was used in calculating the ration issue. The care that they received from OIA personnel was apparently far from satisfactory. A steer weighing in at 1,200 pounds could easily lose several hundred pounds during a winter in the herd camp east of the Agency. In fact, it was possible for the animals to lose 50% of their weight during the winter. When it came time to issue those cattle, they were little but skin and bones, but the people had to eat the losses. In some cases in the spring they were actually receiving only one-half the "on the hoof" weight officially being distributed, though on paper it appeared that full rations were being distributed. Cattle that perished were also accounted for as part of the ration issue.[101] In 1891, Captain Hurst, who was the Post Commander at Fort Bennett, South Dakota, gave the following first-hand account of the failure of the U.S. to provide required treaty rations:

> "The half pound of flour called for by the treaty ration could not be issued in full, and the half pound of corn required has never been issued nor anything in lieu of it. In the item of beef but 1 pound was issued instead of the pound and a half called for in the treaty, and during the early spring months, when the cattle on the range are thin and poor, the pound of beef issued to the Indian is but a fraction of the pound issued to him on the agent's returns, and, under the system of purchase in practice until the present fiscal year, must necessarily be so.[102]

It is with that history and those factors in mind that U.S. government ration distribution figures must be evaluated. The figures in government reports simply cannot be taken at face value. Thus, for example, if we were to take Agent Brennan's 1906 report, which indicates that 5,700 of the 6,700 Oglalas on the reservation were on the ration roll at some point during the year, at face value we would probably conclude that Oglalas were highly ration dependent at that time. His report shows that 4,100 of those 5,700 Oglalas received rations year around. The other 1,600 were removed from the roll for six months during the year while the 500 able-bodied men from the families represented in that group did labor in lieu of rations, under the work system that Sniffen had criticized during his 1905 visit. The laborers in the work system that year were paid $45,000, which works out to $90.00 apiece for each of them over the six month period that they were off the ration roll.[103] That averages out to $15.00 per month, which was was surely a welcome infusion of cash to those families, but even in those days when "a dollar was a dollar" it would not have gone very far to feed a family. That money was placed in Individual Indian Money (IIM) accounts that were administered by the boss farmers in the Districts. People had to make application to the boss farmers to use that money and when they did they were given vouchers in lieu of cash. In that way the boss farmers could play an important role in determining which traders would get the business generated by IIM monies.

In 1903 Charles Turning Hawk asked the Indian Rights Association for help in addressing that problem.[104] That situation, which would have lent itself very nicely to kickbacks to the boss farmers, may have been part of the reason for the high prices charged by traders on the reservation. The amount of money paid out for work projects declined rapidly anyway, and by 1910 the total disbursed for that purpose and for freighting (hauling rations and supplies in to the agency) was $21,895.76, or $15.25 per annum among the 1,238 Oglalas employed that year. In comparison to what the government offered through its projects, even migrant labor paid better. In 1915 Brennan reported that a full blood family of three, a father, mother, and their grown daughter, earned $101.50 picking potatoes in Nebraska between September 22 and October 8.[105] And that money could be used off the reservation where prices were cheaper than in the stores in the reservation.[106]

According to Agent Brennan the rations issued in 1906 were very small, except for beef and flour. The report indicates that each person on the roll was issued 40 pounds of beef and 12 pounds of flour per month. Forty pounds sounds like a substantial amount of meat, until you consider that, besides the flour, it was the main item that people were supposedly subsisting on. But in order to determine just how significant rations were in 1905, a few calculations are in order. The 40 pounds of beef indicated in the report represents "on the hoof" weight, that is, the weight before slaughtering and deboning. Even today, with improved breeding that has produced fleshy cattle, there is a surprisingly small percentage of meat realized from an animal. A good grass fed steer today will dress out at 50% of its "on the hoof" weight. A further 30 to 35% of the dressed weight is bone. The remainder is meat. Thus a 1,200 pound steer will dress out at 600 pounds. Allowing 32% loss in bone leaves 408 pounds of meat. The same calculations, generously applied to the leaner long horn, and other range cattle, that were being issued to the Oglala in 1906, show that the 40 pounds of beef that Oglalas were issued "on the hoof" translated into about 13.6 pounds of beef. Because of shrinkage and other losses at the herd camp, though, for cattle issued in the late fall, winter, or the early spring, that figure would have to be further reduced by anywhere from 10% to 50%.[107]

The amount of rations issued on Pine Ridge declined greatly during the first decade of the century. By 1910 there were no beef rations issued on Pine Ridge at all, though 3,000 persons were carried on the ration rolls in the summer and 4,000 in the winter. The total value of those rations was estimated by Agent Brennan at $21,503.25. Dividing the smaller number of 3,000 persons on the rolls in the summer into that total (even though the total number of recipients was higher) gives an average annual value of $7.16 worth of bacon, beans, coffee, flour, hominy, salt, soap, and sugar that constituted the rations issued on Pine Ridge Reservation that year.[108] That hardly adds up to ration dependence.

Although there was no beef ration in 1910, when Oglala cattle herds had peaked (Table 1), small quantities of beef were issued later on and bacon was sometimes issued in lieu of beef. Agent Tidwell issued bacon in 1920. Besides being issued in small quantities, rations were often of poor quality as well. George Means, an Oglala from Manderson, complained to Tidwell in March of 1920 that the bacon being issued was rancid. Tidwell wrote back to Means agreeing that the bacon was "somewhat rancid" but that

> While the office dislikes very much to have to issue meat that is in this condition, however, it is not unfit to use in view of the fact that it is the only meat on hand, I think it right and proper to issue same to the allottees; as that would be the only course to pursue, unless no meat was issued to them.[109]

Poor quality rations were often issued. That was one of the problems Mooney documented in his study of the Ghost Dance. Even before the reservation economy developed to the point where people were essentially self-sufficient, some rations were perhaps not fit for consumption. In 1886 Agent McGillycuddy discovered that Oglalas were storing spoiling rations for sale to non-Indians at cheap prices. His response was to gradually cut back the amount of rations being issued.[110]

The importance of rations to the Oglala economy declined as the local economy grew. The amount of rations distributed was insufficient to sustain life, even as early as 1889, when the cutback in rations to around one-half of the amount prescribed by Treaty helped create the conditions for the Ghost Dance and the subsequent massacre of about 300 men, women, and children at Wounded Knee in December of 1890.[111] By 1900 the most significant aspect of the ration issue to Oglalas was probably symbolic. By 1910, there can be no doubt of that. The symbolic importance of rations was that they were owed by the United States Government as part of the solemn agreement entered into between Oglala leaders and the United

States. Red Cloud and others who pushed the ration issue must have done so because their own credibility as leaders who had taken part in the negotiations of that Treaty was at stake, and because they viewed the Treaty as a sacred agreement that should not be transgressed. Continual U.S. failure to abide by the terms of the Treaty would have been, and remains, hard to bear.

CLASS, ETHNICITY, AND THE COLONIAL CONTEXT ON PINE RIDGE RESERVATION

The written records of travelers, inspectors, and colonial officials corroborate the contentions of Oglala oral historians, who argue that there was a significant grazing and gardening economy during the early years of the reservation. Thomas Biolsi's notion that the U.S. Government "made the everyday lives of Oglala possible" is too sweeping a generalization, and does not fit with the evidence. The colonial administration of the OIA was one among several factors that helped shape the early reservation economy. The reservation was not a closed system; the conjunction of cultural practices, market relations, and the hard work and initiative of Oglalas within the colonial context of the reservation produced a mixed economy. Wage labor, subsistence pursuits, and commercial production all played a role in that economy.

The U.S. colonial government was largely ineffective at regulating key features of the Oglala economy and culture. The many rules and regulations of the OIA, such as those concerning land claims in the pre-allotment era, and those concerning the consumption of I.D. beef, were not effectively administered by the boss farmers. Those individuals, officially known as Government Farmers, District Farmers, or simply Farmers, were, at any rate so preoccupied with the clerical work involved in making the necessary reports to the OIA bureaucracy and in keeping track of IIM accounts, and so on, that they did not have time to make a serious effort at carrying out such policies very effectively, even when they wanted to. They frequently could not get outside their offices to do the extension work they were supposed to do, let alone regulate dances, suppress illicit trading, and complete other administrative tasks that were being continually laid on them by the Agents. In fact, clerical work took practically all of their time, prompting M.K. Sniffen's remark that "So far as the official title [i.e., Government Farmer] is concerned, it is a misnomer."[112]

In a very important sense, the significance of the OIA role in shaping the early reservation political economy is not to be found so much in its ability to exercise thoroughgoing domination, as in its ineffectiveness in some spheres. That very ineffectiveness, the inability of the OIA to be a totalizing presence, provided an opportunity for the flourishing of mechanisms of redistribution and communal tenure among full blood Oglala, and an opportunity for Oglala mixed bloods to provision individualized commercial ranching operations by requisitioning the commons and brokering outside interests.

Because the reservation was not a closed system, mixed blood Oglalas who came seeking allotments were able to involve themselves in state politics around the Bennett County issue, contributing to the jurisdictional mix on the reservation. The reservation, and all that entailed, was the forcing ground where mixed blood and full blood groups pursued strategies that elaborated and transformed their pre-existing differences. Previously well defined ethnic differences were reinforced; and new political and economic differences, which were sometimes associated with inter-group conflict, emerged.

Notes

1. Oglalas realize less than $3.00 per acre for grazing land, if it is officially leased – sometimes ranchers simply run their cattle on fractionated lands and on tribal lands without bothering to enter into leasing agreements. Landowners have little to say about the land that is legally theirs. Information on land ownership from OST Land Office. Number of Oglala and non-Indian operators comes from lists of permittees for 1977 and 1984, BIA Land Operations Division, Pine Ridge Agency (in possession of the author).

2. Author's notes. An Oglala aphorism that applies to current and past practices of the government, and that is often used in regard to Oglala stock raising is "They don't want to see Mr. Indian get ahead."

3. Information about the general economic situation, the use of the range unit system to move Oglalas off the land, and the significance of HUD housing comes from interviews and conversations with a number of Oglalas, especially with Severt Young Bear, Myrna White Face -Young Bear, Edward Iron Cloud Jr., Steven Red Elk, James Bad Wound, and Charles Apple.

4. Birgil Kills Straight's opening address at the Tatanka Iyacin (in the manner of a buffalo) Conference at Oglala Lakota College on May 9, 1985. Transcription from author's recording.

5. Taped interview conducted by author.

6. Oftentimes ". . . subordinate classes are presented with several different ways of interpreting their underprivileged position in society. They are exposed . . . to the hegemonic ideas of the dominant value-system which justify their inferiority (Worsley, Peter 1984, p. 57)."

7. The common belief of non-natives that Native Americans are "just sitting back and waiting for handouts" is fed by the fact that in the past rations were so visible and different from the transfer payments that non-natives received, and that today federal education and health care for natives are so visible. The fact that those serv-

ices were owed to the people because of the treaties, and that they are and were inadequate does not change the perception (Alfonso Ortiz, personal communication, 1994).

8. Brennan to CIA Burke, August 7, 1913. Box 118, File 064, MDF-PR.

9. Jermark to CIA, October 22, 1925. File 506, MDF-PR.

10. Author's notes.

11. Today 94 percent of the reservation is classified as grazing land. Successful farming is largely limited to the southeast and the northwest portions of the reservation where wheat , corn, and hay are the major crops (One Feather, Vivian 1976, p. 47). During the 1930s substantial acreage was planted to flax and other crops but those enterprising non-Indian farmers were unsuccessful. The eroded landscape they left behind was classified as sub-marginal, and later purchased by the Oglala Sioux Tribe with funds made available by the Indian Reorganization Act. A 1974 BIA report, "Land Use Patterns on the Pine Ridge Reservation, " documents the pattern of control over grazing lands.

12. Malan, Vernon 1958, p.4.

13. Biolsi, Thomas 1992, p. 29–31.

14. Macgregor, Gordon 1946, p.39.

15. Hyde, George 1956, p. ix.

16. Biolsi, Thomas 1992, p. 27, 193 (fn 57).

17. Cf. Goffman, Erving, 1961, p. 1–124, on the "Characteristics of total institutions."

18. The role of the OIA in ushering in destructive outside grazing interests is described in chapter 5.

19. Minutes of Oglala Tribal Council meeting held at Wanblee on January 9, 1936, File 300.9, MDF-PR.

20. See Webb, Walter 1981, p. 29 and Rydberg, Per 1965, p. 104–106, 131, on the short grass plains. Overgrazing came about as a result of the OIA's leasing policies, a subject covered in Chapters 4 and 5.

21. Field notes of survey dated September, 1905. File: Trust Responsibilities, Copies of letters sent by Special Allotting Agent, Charles H. Bates 1904–1914, Volume 1, KC.

22. Roosevelt, Theodore, 1893, p. 4,7, NL.

23. Sniffen's report on his visit to Dakota, September 1905, IRAP Series 1-A, Reel 18.

24. Sniffen, M.K. 1906, p. 28, NL.

25. Sniffen's report on his visit to Dakota, September 1905, IRAP Series 1-A, Reel 18.

26. Sniffen, M.K. 1906, p. 26, NL. The term "blanket Indian" is a derogatory phrase used variously to refer to Native Americans who had clearly not assimilated, and to those who it was felt were not adopting the white man's economic prescriptions. Sniffen seems to be using it in the latter sense. Such terms are, of course, often introjected by the colonized. In recent years some educated full blood Oglala who have worked for the Oglala Sioux Tribal government have been referred to as

"blanket Indians" by some tribal employees. A related phrase that was common in the discourse of OIA personnel and others was "going back to the blanket."

27. Report of W.K. Moorehead, May 2, 1909, Pine Ridge c1909–363 to Pipestone c1909–238, RG 75 BIA Inspector Division – Inspection Reports 1908–1940. Moorehead was also impressed by a series of irrigation dams, of OIA design, that the people had built and were using to irrigate their crops.

28. RCIA 1911, in Johnston, Sr. Mary 1948, p. 115.

29. RCIA 1914.

30. RCIA 1910.

31. Gilbert, Hila 1968, p. 34, 69.

32. Oglalas called the sub-agents, or government farmers, who were assigned to the reservation's farm districts "boss farmers." In speaking about them today they refer to them as boss farmers in English or as "*woju wicasa*" (planter man) in Lakota. Some people also refer to them as "*igmu tanka*" (big cats) with the connotation that they are waiting to pounce, as on an unwary mouse.

33. Report of James McLaughlin, U.S. Indian Inspector, August 19, 1897, RI 1873–1900, Roll 37.

34. Turning Hawk to Welsh, April 29, 1899, IRAP Series 1 - A, Reel 13.

35. Sniffen's report on visit to Dakota, Sept. 1905. IRAP, Series 1 - A, Reel 18.

36. Taped interview conducted by author.

37. Acting Agent Jenkins to CIA, August 7, 1900. Special Case 191, Leasing, Pine Ridge, 1900–1907, RG 75 NA.

38. Acting Secretary of Interior to CIA, September 29, 1900. Special Case 191, Leasing, Pine Ridge, 1900–1907 RG 75 NA.

39. Sniffen's report on visit to Dakota, Sept. 1905. IRAP, Series 1 - A, Reel 18. Information about Ross' tribal affiliation and appearance provided by an Oglala who knew Ross. Ross was a fluent speaker of Dakota, the dialect spoken by the Santee. It is mutually intelligible with the Lakota spoken by Oglalas.

40. Brennan to CIA, December 6, 1900. Special Case 191 Leasing, Pine Ridge, 1900–1907 RG 75 NA.

41. List of "Farming Indians," 1899, Monthly Reports of District Farmers and Related Lists, Box 745, MDF-PR.

42. Turning Hawk to CIA, February 11, 1903, General Records: Land 1/8/1898 – 12/16/1904, RG 75, KC.

43. Acting CIA to Brennan February 20, 1903; Acting CIA to Brennan, March 24, 1903. General Records: Land 1/8/1898 – 12/16/1904, RG 75 KC.

44. Cf. Worsley, 1984, p. 36–37.

45. Cf. Phillips, Paul C., 1961.

46. White men married to Oglala women could raise stock on the reservation but they did so under the cover of the legal fiction that the stock were owned by their Oglala wives. cf. Report of James McLaughlin, U.S. Indian Inspector, August 19, 1897, RI 1873–1900, Roll 37.

47. Commissioner of Indian Affairs to Clapp, June 17, 1898, File 008, MDF-PR.

48. Clapp to Additional Farmers, July 30, 1897; J.J. Boesl to Brennan, June 27, 1911. File 741, MDF-PR It seemed strange to me, at first, to hear some mixed

blood Oglala today, especially older ones, using the referent "Indians," to distinguish full bloods from themselves.

49. John Brennan to C.A. Bates, November 15, 1911, "Trespassing Stock Matters" 1910–1911, File 530, MDF-PR. John Brennan to Boesl, August 4, 1911, "Circulars and letters to Farmers and Employees," Box 743, Volume 9, MDF-PR.

50. Sniffen's report on his visit to Dakota, Sept. 1905, IRAP Series 1 - A, Reel 18.

51. Brennan to CIA Burke, August 7, 1913. Box 118, File 064, MDF-PR.

52. *Oglala Light*, November 16, 1915, No. 3.

53. *Oglala Light*, September, 1917, No. 1.

54. The role of the OIA in the political economy of the early decades of the reservation is developed more fully in chapters 3, 4, and 5.

55. Ramsey Hawkins to Mr. F.E. McIntyre, February 20, 1909. Box 118, File 064, MDF-PR. "Fool Crow" was later changed to "Fools Crow," the surname of the late famous Chief Frank Fools Crow.

56. May Williams Wood to Sniffen, May 19, 1913, IRAP Series 1-A, Reel 27.

57. Cf. Balandier 1961, Georges, and Fanon, Frantz 1966, for discussions of the colonial situation and of the psychology of colonialism.

58. Report of James McLaughlin, U.S. Indian Inspector, August 19, 1897, RI 1873–1900, Roll 37.

59. Webb, 1931, p. 29.

60. Report of James McLaughlin, U.S. Indian Inspector, August 19, 1897, RI 1873–1900, Roll 37.

61. Ibid.

62. Ibid.

63. Tiospaye are sometimes defined as flexible exogamous residential units organized around a core of bilaterally related kin. Cf. DeMallie, Raymond 1978, Hassrick, Royal 1964, or Walker, James 1982 on Oglala kinship.

64. RCIA 1885, p. 35.

65. RCIA 1885, p. 35.

66. Bates to Commissioner of Indian Affairs, January 15, 1906 and August 1, 1912, Letter Books, Volume 1, KC.

67. The formula authorized by the Sioux Act of March 2, 1889 was 320 acres for heads of families, 160 acres for spouses of heads of families, and 80 acres for children under 18. But if the land to be allotted was classified as grazing land, as most of the land on the Pine Ridge Reservation was, the amount was doubled and the formula was 640, 320, and 160 (Sioux Act, March 2, 1889, 25 Stat., 888–899, Sec. 8).

68. A modified pattern of *tiospaye* living, or at least of extended families living in close proximity, continues to a limited extent today, in spite of the fact that many Oglalas moved into clustered housing projects built by U.S. HUD in the 1960s and 1970s. See chapter 6 on the issue of clustered government housing complexes, and of the Relocation era, of the 1950s and 1960s, on residential patterns. See Brophy, William A. and Sophie D. Aberle 1966, Cahn, Edgar S. and David Hearne 1969, Prucha, Francis 1976, and Sutton, Imre 1975, for general treatments of allotment.

See Johnston, Sr. Mary 1948, for a detailed study of the application of allotment
policy among the Sioux.

69. Mrs Charles S. Cook to Welsh, June 20, 1888, IRAP Series 1 - A, Reel 3;
Sniffen's report on his visit to Dakota, September 1905, IRAP Series 1-A, Reel 18.

70. Calculated based on census figures in RCIA 1887.

71. Charles Bates to Commissioner of Indian Affairs, December 18, 1907, Letter
Books, Volume 1, KC.

72. Charles Bates to Commissioner of Indian Affairs, June 5, 1908, Letter Books,
Volume 1, KC. The date of March 2, 1889 refers to the date of passage of the
"Sioux Act," which reduced by about one-half the Great Sioux Reservation set
aside by the Fort Laramie Treaty of 1868, and divided the remainder into six separate reservations (Sioux Act, March 2, 1889, 25 Stat., 888–899, Sec. 1–6).

73. James McLaughlin to Secretary of the Interior, April 19, 1909, Transcript of testimony on the proposed opening of southeastern portion of Pine Ridge Reservation
to settlement." OLC archives. *Bennett County Booster*, April 10, 1912, V. 1, No.
28. See Chapter 4 for more discussion of the Bennett County issue.

74. Charles Bates to F.G. Wilson, April 22, 1908, Letter Books, Volume 1, KC.

75. Sniffen's report on his visit to Dakota, September 1905, IRAP Series 1-A,
Reel 18.

76. CIA to Brennan, November 28, 1900. File: "Land January 3, 1900 to December
19, 1900," Box 22, MDF-PR.

77. Circular from Brennan to Additional Farmers, November 1900. Box 741, KC.

78. Acting CIA Larabee to Brennan, June 26, 1908, File: "Indian Customs and
Picture Writing," Box 127,MDF-PR.

79. Densmore, Francis, 1918.

80. Brennan to Additional Farmers, January 29, 1913. Dorothy Mack Collection,
OLC.

81. Tidwell to Farmers, January 28, 1920, File 155, MDF-PR.

82. When Louis Mousseau, a mixed blood Oglala, complained about the fact that
young people were getting married and then residing with or near the husband's or
the wive's parents, instead of being placed on their own allotments so that they
could make improvements for themselves [as the allotment act intended] Brennan
told him that "The Government cannot camp around the homes of the parents of
these youngsters and supervise the daily life of the family . . . " He said there were
". . . standing orders along this line among the Farmers and other employees all the
time and the Farmers are kept in mind of this order from time to time and urged to
enforce it whenever possible. We would have better success if the parents would do
their part and not harbor the young people." Brennan to Louis P. Mousseau,
March 7, 1917, File 530, Box 634, MDF-PR.

83. Acting CIA Larabee to Brennan, June 30, 1908. File: "Indian Customs and
Picture Writing," Box 127, MDF-PR.

84. Assistant Farmer B. Gleason to Brennan, July 14, 1908. File: "Indian Customs
and Picture Writing," Box 127, MDF-PR.

85. Account of the *maza sala* primarily from Calvin Jumping Bull, Lakota elder and
instructor in Lakota language and culture at Oglala Lakota College. Some details

are from other interviews. Scudder Mekeel gives a different account of the "*maza cala*" [sic] in his article "The Economy of a Modern Teton Dakota Community," 1936, p. 12, but he also emphasizes that the *maza sala* was one of several leveling mechanisms operating in the culture.

86. Sniffen's report on his visit to Dakota, September 1905, IRAP Series 1-A, Reel 18.

87. On the internal differentiation in wealth which occurred among plains groups during the days of the hide trade see Klein, Alan 1983 and Lewis, Oscar 1942. The point about the relation between the status of Oglala leaders and their generosity is regularly made by Oglalas; I have witnessed giveaways where local leaders (informally recognized leaders) give away large quantities of goods, including cars, horses, and land.

88. Taking home *wateca* is still an important practice at the many family and community feeds that are held for various purposes on the reservation. It is commonplace for a family to leave a feed with a gallon or more of soup, and perhaps pie, cake, crackers, bread, macaroni or potato salad, and *wojapi* (berry pudding).

89. Record of Hearing of Pine Ridge Delegates with E.B. Meritt, Assistant CIA, February 26, 1917. 75-33-053 to 80965-22-054, 1907–1939, Pine Ridge, CCF.

90. RCIA 1915, M1011, Roll 106.

91. Author's notes.

92. Author's notes.

93. Ibid.

94. Mooney, James 1976, p. 72.

95. RCIA 1889.

96. Bishop W.H. Hare to Secretary Noble, January 7, 1891. Quoted in Mooney, James 1976, p. 86.

97. Mooney 1976, p. 72, 90.

98. RCIA 1893, p. 287.

99. RCIA 1879.

100. RCIA 1889, 1895. They may have furnished significantly more than what the official records show because those records only record the number of cattle that the OIA authorized Oglalas to butcher. In practice they often butchered stock on their own even though they were supposed to get OIA approval to do it.

101. Mooney 1976, p. 71, 82–83.

102. Report of Captain Hurst to Assistant Adjutant-General, Department of Dakota, St. Paul, Minn., January 9, 1891. Quoted in Mooney 1976, p. 82.

103. RCIA 1906, p. 353.

104. Charles Turning Hawk to Indian Rights Association, January 3, 1903, IRAP Series 1 - A Reel 16.

105. RCIA 1915, M1011, Roll 106.

106. Author's notes.

107. Information on calculating the amount of meat available after slaughter provided to the author by Otte Packing House in Clinton, Nebraska, 1994. Beyond such calculations, there had been a history of government corruption attendant on the issuance of beef. One O.C. Marsh, a Yale University professor contracted to

investigate such matters at the Red Cloud Agency in 1875 found a pattern of systematic fraud. Government reports greatly exaggerated numbers of cattle issued and their weights (Report of the Special Commission Appointed to Investigate the Affairs of the Red Cloud Agency).

108. RCIA 1910, M1011, Roll 106.

109. Tidwell to George Means, March 31, 1920. File 506, MDF-PR.

110. IRA Report 1886, NL. McGillycuddy did not, apparently, have an accurate count of the Oglala and he had overestimated their numbers. His response to the discovery of the spoiling rations was to gradually cut back the amount issued. Thus it could be argued that he simply issued too much for them to consume. But that does not seem very likely in the light of the evidence brought to bear by Mooney in support of his relative deprivation hypothesis.

111. Other factors were of course involved as well. The situation on Pine Ridge Reservation was critical in the aftermath of the Crook Commission and also because of the temporarily increased population as Lakotas from Rosebud and other reserves had come to Pine Ridge. The Rev. Charles S. Cook's account of December 2, 1890 is typical: "The non-progressives have been, pretty much all along, groaning under the weight of the rule of the Indian Police system, enforcing rule and order and work among them. . . . All over the Medicine Root District (Mr. Rofs' Missionary field), up and down the Porcupine Tail Creek, and nearly the whole length of the Wounded Knee Creek, everything has been either plundered or destroyed. *All* the winter's hay has either been entirely demolished by the dancers' hungry horses or burned; every house entered, plundered of its contents, or destroyed – clothing, bedding, provisions, fancy thing's &c. Even the canvas linings of the log houses were torn off and made into Ghost Dancers' *sacred shirts*. Doors, windows, stoves &c. either broken irreparably or scattered everywhere. The Government day school buildings shared the same fate. Our poor people have *absolutely nothing* to go back to when they leave the Agency [emphasis in original]" (Rev. Charles S. Cook to Welsh, December 2, 1890. IRAP Series 1 – A, Reel 5).

112. Sniffen, M.K. 1906, p. 26, NL. Boss farmers had agendas of their own, which they were sometimes pursued more vigorously than their official duties, a subject discussed in chapter 4.

The Oglala Omniciye and the Struggle for the Land

THE "LAST GRASS FRONTIER"[1]

Wanton destruction of the vast herds of buffalo opened up a niche on the Great Plains and capital rushed in headlong to fill it. Cattle raising offered quick profits and a large return on investment in those years, and domestic and foreign capital was quick to seize the opportunity. During the boom times of the 1880s "Easterners, Englishmen, Scotchmen, Canadians, and even Australians flocked to the Plains to become ranchers. . . ."[2] They flooded the plains with millions of cattle and sheep, creating a whole industry that provided meat for distant points like the yards in Omaha, Chicago and other eastern cities, and for growing regional populations like those of the miners and traders who had illegally flooded into the Black Hills after gold was discovered by Custer's 1874 expedition. During the '80s cattle interests bent on expansion tried to gain a legal foothold on the Great Sioux through leasing proposals. Popular sentiment though, favored opening the Great Sioux to homesteaders and to all interests, not just to cattlemen. But cattlemen were impatient and tended not to stand on legal niceties; failure to secure leases did not keep them from exploiting the rich grasslands on the Great Sioux Reservation. By 1884 there were 700,000 to 800,000 head of cattle illegally trespassing on 1868 Fort Laramie Treaty lands from the east bank of the Missouri River west, the area that became the west half of South Dakota in 1889.[3]

The reduction of the Great Sioux Reservation by the Sioux Act in 1889 legalized trespass on the 11,000,000 "ceded" acres that were redefined as public domain, but it did not end illegal trespass on remaining Sioux lands. Cattlemen who were unfettered by government regulation, and who had virtually free reign over the public domain, had the attitude that Native Americans were "foreigners in their own native lands," and that their presence might interfere with their grand industry was a difficult proposition to bear.[4] Widespread illegal trespassing of outside stock on reservation lands was commonplace. Trespassing stock ate up reservation grasslands, threatening the cattle herds of the Lakota and Dakota people. When homesteaders and business interests began to overshadow cattle interests on the plains, cattlemen saw in the reservations the last frontier of the open range. Cattlemen and the Office of Indian Affairs (OIA) joined hands and by the second decade of the twentieth century much of the land on plains reservations was being used to benefit outside interests. But while outside stockmen did trespass and did secure leases of reservation lands, they were not given carte blanche. Tribal leaders and their allies fought to protect their land from corporate and government takeover.

A decisive period in the continuing struggle for control of the grass lands on Pine Ridge Reservation played itself out from about 1897 to 1915. The leading players were cattle interests represented by the Western South Dakota Stock Growers Association, U.S. government officials, and the Oglala Omniciye (Oglala Council). Outside stock interests were intent on accessing grazing lands on the reservation, through legal or illegal means; U.S. officials used their positions to carry out federal mandates and/or to further their own agendas; and the Oglala Omniciye fought to preserve the land base and the tribal cattle economy by standing against land leasing, allotment of land, and the 1910 taking of 1,000,000 million acres of land in the southeastern portion of the reservation. The struggle brought an end to the promising communal cattle economy of Oglala full bloods, and set the stage for corporate takeover of reservation lands.

TRESPASS, CATTLE INTERESTS, AND TRUST RESPONSIBILITY

Trespass by white-owned cattle was a problem for Oglalas who settled around the Pine Ridge Agency even before the reservation was created in 1889. In 1888, Agent Gallagher received reports that there were a large number of white-owned cattle grazing in the vicinity of the Cheyenne River, north of the Pine Ridge Agency, within the confines of the Great Sioux Reservation. He investigated the complaints and found that ". . . these cattle had been placed upon the reserve by their owners for the purposes of securing free grazing."[5] Over the years Oglalas made frequent complaints about trespass to Indian Agents at Pine Ridge but no action was taken until 1897, when complaints from both mixed blood and full blood Oglalas finally prompted officials on Pine Ridge to act.[6]

The first action was directed by Pass Creek District boss farmer Joseph Rooks. In February of 1897, Rooks, acting under the authority of Pine Ridge Indian Agent Major W.H. Clapp, directed Oglalas in Pass Creek District ". . . to drive what foreign cattle they might find ranging on the Reservation across [the] White River, which is the northern boundary line at that point. . . ."[7] Then, on May 17, W.D. McGaa secured a written order from Clapp authorizing him and other mixed bloods and white men married to Oglala women to round-up foreign cattle and bring them to the Agency where they would be impounded and placed in control of the ". . . proper officers of the Court." Both Rooks and McGaa had important personal interests that needed protection from outside stock. Rooks, it may be recalled, was a white man married to an Oglala woman, who owned 200 head of cattle himself, and McGaa, a mixed blood who had a sizeable herd of 700. The other men noted on Clapp's order were also in the cattle business. McGaa claimed that each of them had suffered severe losses the previous winter, losses due in part to the fact that outside cattle were eating the hay that their stock needed.[8] The fact that Clapp's order named mixed bloods and whites married to Oglala women only, may have just reflected McGaa's preference. He may have already had a list of others who felt the same way he did about the situation on the reservation when he went to see Clapp to secure the order. He said he knew each of the men listed on the order and that he had urged them to assist in the round-up, telling them ". . . they ought to fight for their interests as I did."[9] Full bloods too, of course, had interests in keeping outside stock off the reservation and they had taken their own actions. Chief Lip, Chief Red Cloud, He Dog, and others had driven outside stock off the reservation in the past, and the practice was apparently fairly common, though it had provided only temporary relief from the problem.[10]

Clapp's May 17 order brought matters to a head fairly rapidly. Within a few days after the order, McGaa and the others listed on it trailed several hundred head of outside cattle from as far away as forty miles in to Pine Ridge Agency where Chief Herder Henderson impounded them in Agency corrals for about ten days. Then, on Clapp's authority, the brands were recorded, and they were released to the Deputy U.S. Marshal.[11]

The cattle that were impounded belonged to members of the Western South Dakota Stock Growers Association (WSDSGA). That organization reacted strongly on behalf of its members, fearing that Clapp's action might be a precedent that could threaten more general livestock interests in South Dakota. They telegrammed U.S. Senator James H. Kyle (S.D.) on June 19. Senator Kyle notified Interior Secretary Bliss, and on June 25 he ordered U.S. Indian Inspector James McLaughlin to Pine Ridge Agency to investigate ". . . the matter of the impounding of cattle at said agency."[12] McLaughlin finished his business at Fort Gibson in Indian Territory in Oklahoma and was in Pine Ridge on July 7. He set up a hearing at Pine Ridge Agency on July 13, and 44 witnesses were called by Major Clapp and the WSDSGA. The entire stenographer's record of the meeting was transcribed, and the resulting 300 plus pages of verbatim testimony were submitted, along with McLaughlin's conclusions, to the Secretary of the Interior on August 4, 1897.[13]

Clapp proved himself a worthy adversary of the WSDSGA at the July 13 hearing. His role in inviting both full blood and mixed blood Oglalas, whose interests were being threatened by the presence of outside stock, to testify at the hearing was crucial. He did a skillful job of examining and cross-examining witnesses, keeping the testimony largely focused on the issue of trespassing white-owned stock, in spite of attempts by WSDSGA's Washington D.C. based attorney W.W. Anderson, who was a stockgrower himself, to sidetrack it with various arguments intended to justify the presence of white-owned stock on the reservation.[14]

Testimony given by Oglalas, and even by white stockmen at the meeting, proved conclusively that large numbers of outside cattle had been trespassing regularly on reservation lands for years. Oglalas from across the reservation gave similar testimony. Hunts His Horses, who lived on Medicine Root Creek about fifty miles away from Pine Ridge Agency testified that "Down here on Medicine Root, along the whole line along from Medicine Root to Bear Creek, and all over there, the white people's cattle are chock full there. They have been there for the last ten years." Chief Red Cloud, living in Red Cloud Community about two miles from the Agency, scolded the Inspector and the white stockmen at the meeting. "Now my friends you all sleep, and what we do is just to wake you up. There has been outside cattle on the reservation around here for the last twenty years, as I understand it." Snake, from Grass Creek west of Manderson, saw white men's cattle in that area for nineteen years, more of them than Oglala-owned cattle, he said.

Some of the witnesses at the hearing estimated numbers of trespassing stock. Charles Clifford, a mixed blood, reported seeing about 4,000 head of outside cattle all of the time around his neighborhood. Joe Rooks, the Pass Creek boss farmer, estimated that 10,000 head of white-owned cattle were trespassing in Pass Creek District alone. McGaa said he had seen as many as 2,000 head of outside cattle in one bunch at one time. That many trespassing stock certainly posed a hardship on Oglala cattle men.

He Dog told the stockmen at the hearing that he wanted them to take their cattle away as ". . . we have got cattle too to eat the grass, and we have nothing else to live off of." Red Shirt attributed the loss of some of his stock during the winter to the fact that outside stock had eaten up so much of the grass. McGaa complained that outside cattle ". . . ate off the range and a good many cattle were lost last winter."

White ranchers at the meeting did not deny that their cattle were trespassing on the reservation but they tried to justify the trespass. First, they claimed that they could not keep their cattle from drifting onto an unenclosed area, and second, that there was so much grass on the reservation anyway that the presence of their cattle could not possibly harm Oglala cattle interests. John D. Stevens, manager of one white-owned cattle company, argued that in order to keep their cattle from drifting onto the reservation a minimum of a 200 mile buffer zone would have to be established. And that would, he said, ". . . result in destroying the range cattle business entirely." William Gardiner, a judge from the Seventh Judicial Circuit of South Dakota, a resident of Rapid City, whose wife was one of Shidley Cattle Company's directors, said that if the federal law against trespass of outside cattle on reservations was to be invoked it could result in ". . . the total destruction of this great industry and the discouragement of all who are engaged in it." Rather than the law be enforced, the judge maintained, ". . . I think it would be better for the people of western South Dakota, if the mouth of the great Homestake mine were to be stopped and that great industry were to be blotted out than this other industry should be similarly annihilated."[15] Like Stevens, the judge argued that "Our cattle are here by reason of no fault of ours and simply through our inability to keep them within the limits of our own range."

Claims by Judge Gardiner and other spokesmen for white cattle interests that they could not help the drifting of their stock onto reservation land did not hold up to scrutiny. Witnesses testified that following the annual spring and summer roundups, when white-owned cattle were rounded up along with Indian-owned stock and removed from the reservation they appeared again, sometimes within hours of their removal. They were clearly not making any attempt to keep their cattle off the reservation and were, in fact, purposefully and illegally using reservation resources for their own benefit. Clapp observed one white owner sitting in the shade of his house while he watched his cattle cross over the reservation line. He also pointed out that when white cattle men came onto the reservation to gather beef steers for shipment, they left behind their other stock undisturbed so that they might graze on reservation land. When their illegal actions were challenged they would react self-righteously, implying that it was somehow their right to use Oglala resources. When 5,600 white-owned cattle were driven off one small section of the reservation in February of 1897 ". . . there was deep indignation and threats of suit for damages because the Indians had presumed to drive the stock off their own land at that season of the year" (a reference to what happened after Pass Creek District boss farmer Joseph Rooks, with the assistance of Oglalas, and acting with Clapp's blessing, drove foreign cattle out of Pass Creek District).[16]

Some of the white-owned cattle operations represented by the WSDSGA were enormous. WSDSGA's Secretary-Treasurer Frank Stewart reported that their 600 members owned 160,000 head of stock, an average of 267 head each. But Shidley Cattle Company alone, the one that Judge Gardiner's wife had an interest in, and that was managed by G.E. Lemmon of Rapid City, owned about 20,000 head. Lemmon said Shidley Cattle shipped 9,000 head to market in 1896. They sold for around $36.00 per head, or $324,000 for the lot. Shidley Cattle Companies' range was 200 miles long from north to south. Operations of that size were big business in South Dakota in 1897.

The comments of Judge Gardiner and other WSDSGA members at the Pine Ridge hearing showed the arrogance, self-assurance, and disrespect for the rule of law that characterized the big cattle interests of the day. One tactic they may have used in order to secure the use of Oglala land for feed and water for their cattle was bribery. Oglala full blood John Logan testified at the hearing that white stockmen had offered him beef cattle and money if he would refrain from driving their cattle off the reservation. Cattle interests were also adept at playing both ends against the middle. Cattlemen in Fall River, Custer, and Pennington Counties, which are adjacent the Pine Ridge Reservation, argued to County Treasurers there that they should not have to pay taxes on their thousands of head of range stock because they grazed them not in those counties but on the Pine Ridge Reservation.[17]

Cattlemen seeking to avoid paying their property taxes by claiming that they grazed their herds on the Pine Ridge Reservation would have done well to have used the findings detailed in Inspector James McLaughlin's report of his investigation at Pine Ridge to support their claim. His report to the Commissioner of Indian Affairs (CIA) held that "The testimony of twenty-two witnesses . . . conclusively proves that large numbers of foreign cattle habitually range on Pine Ridge Reservation, except at short intervals following the spring and fall round-ups, and have been so ranging thereon for some years past."[18]

Earlier reports of trespassing had been frequently made but this occasion was special.[19] When the impounded cattle were turned over to the U.S. Marshall, and charges were brought against the owners in federal court (pursuant Section 2117, Revised Statutes U.S.),[20] the stage was set for a showdown between cattle interests and the U.S. government. How would the U.S. Government handle its responsibility to enforce the federal law against trespassing on Indian land, when challenged by organized non-Indian stockgrowers, who claimed that trespassing cattle were an essential aspect of their industry, and that enforcement of the federal law would therefore destroy that industry, and hamstring the economy of South Dakota?

WSDSGA attorney W.W. Anderson lobbied the Secretary of the Interior arguing the righteousness of the stockgrowers cause, and asking for his intervention on behalf of the members whose cattle had been impounded. He specifically requested that the Secretary intervene with the U.S. Attorney General.

> . . . in justice to the stock-owners who had such undeserved loss and hardship put upon them I respectfully ask in the name of the Western South Dakota Stock Growers Association, that you request the Hon. The [sic] Attorney General to have these cases, now pending in the Federal Court of South Dakota against the men who had their stock impounded both at the Pine Ridge and Rosebud Indian Agencies, dismissed.[21]

WSDSGA Vice-President John Stevens assured the Secretary of the just cause of the stockgrowers and reminded him that U.S. Senator James H. Kyle had a "deep interest" in the matter.[22] Perhaps the pressure bore fruit because on September 15, 1897 the U.S. Attorney General instructed the U.S. Attorney for South Dakota to *nolle prosequi* the cases (i.e., to dismiss the indictment for prosecution).[23]

Save for Agent Clapp, though, the OIA handled the case gingerly from the outset. Clapp was something of a wild card in the affair, taking the interest of the Oglalas and the rule of law to heart as he had. His sense of injustice was strong and he viewed stock trespass as part and parcel of the history of Indian-white relations:

> It has always been the case where Indians owned property which white men covet, that the equities have been little observed, and in one way or another the Indian has been robbed or wheedled out of his possessions, or they have been taken from him by force and small compensation afterward awarded. These Indians, once the owners of vast territory, were finally placed on their present reservation, and their occupancy of it solemnly guaranteed by treaty . . . [24]

After the Pine Ridge hearings Clapp toured the reservation with Inspector McLaughlin to examine the damage that had been done by trespassing. What he found appalled him, and he was uncompromising about it in his official report:

> . . . the range has been eaten down by trespassing cattle and horses for a distance varying from 5 to 30 miles. To such an extent has this prevailed that for any further use this season or during the coming winter, this belt has been practically ruined. Not only so, but by reason of being so closely eaten down for many seasons, the native grasses have been killed and the ground taken possession of by cacti and weeds. . . As a consequence of this, Indian cattle owners have been forced back and their ranges greatly injured. But this is not all; the foreign cattle greatly outnumbering the Indian cattle, the latter have been induced to follow and drift off, or worse still, have been driven off, and in this way many have been lost. The owners of Indian cattle have found themselves encroached upon more and more each year, and have become greatly discouraged.[25]

Though Inspector McLaughlin's official report confirmed large scale trespassing on the reservation, neither the tone nor the sense of advocacy that characterize Clapp's report are to be found in his. To begin with, McLaughlin contended that Agent Clapp erred when he issued the order for the rounding up and impounding of outside stock without first warning the cattlemen. The crux of the problem posed by the situation was not the question of the violation of federal law and the damage to Oglala efforts at cattle raising, but the public interest:

Public policy demanding that every honorable industry be fostered rather than retarded and believing that the stock industry of South Dakota, which represents approximately $20,000,000 might be seriously affected should section 2117 of the Revised Statutes be strictly enforced in such instances, and recognizing the importance of the question and interests involved, hope for a just and early settlement of the matter. . . . The question now is, how to best meet existing conditions, so as to do justice to the Indians and not impose too great a hardship upon stockmen who occupy neighboring ranges, and are engaged in the only business enterprise that can be made remunerative in that section of the country.[26]

In the spirit of McLaughlin's pragmatism the OIA decided to avoid enforcing the federal law. On November 22, 1897 Acting Commissioner of Indian Affairs Towner notified the Secretary of the Interior that his office had directed Agent Clapp ". . . to take such peaceable means as his experience and knowledge of the situation might seem to him advisable to remove all trespassing cattle and other stock from the reservation."[27] The Secretary concurred with the arrangement, including the proviso that trespassing cattle would have to be removed without incurring public expense.[28] In the final analysis the evidence of illegal trespass and damage to Oglala stock raisers brought out at the hearings weighed less with the OIA and the Department of the Interior than the influence of the South Dakota cattle interests and their supporters. The Department's position marked a retreat from an earlier directive from the OIA. In May of 1897, shortly after the roundup of foreign stock by McGaa and others acting on Agent Clapp's order, Acting Commissioner of Indian Affairs Thomas P. Smith advised Agent Clapp to release those particular stock, to warn the cattlemen that the law would be enforced, and thereafter to impound trespassing stock for delivery to the U.S. Marshall.[29]

Cattle interests were not satisfied with simply winning the case. They wanted Agent Clapp out, and someone more sympathetic to them in. In October, 1897, former Pine Ridge Agent Valentine T. McGillycuddy wrote to Clapp and to Herbert Welsh, head of the Indian Rights Association (I.R.A.), noting that a determined effort was being made by cattlemen, including Judge William Gardiner (the same who testified at the Pine Ridge hearings and who, along with his wife had an interest in the Shidley Cattle Company) and C.J. Briel, who was an attorney for the WSDSGA, and, according to McGillycuddy, a "'. . . local dispenser' of federal patronage," to secure the appointment of John R. Brennan, a rancher and a resident of Rapid City South Dakota, as Agent at Pine Ridge.[30] The State Central Committee endorsed Brennan for the job.[31]

But Agent Clapp had done nothing that could be officially construed as a cause for removal, and had some considerable support in McGillycuddy and Welsh. After McGillycuddy left the Pine Ridge Agency he became the

President of the State School of Mines in Rapid City, South Dakota. At Pine Ridge he had built a reputation with the establishment as a capable, hard working, honest, no-nonsense Agent, and was well-regarded by the OIA and by the independent Indian Rights Association (I.R.A.). One of that organizations' goals was the placement of honest and capable men as Indian Agents; under Welsh it had become a force to be reckoned with in Washington D.C.

McGillycuddy judged John Brennan, the cattleman's choice, as ". . . in many ways a good man" but warned that "He would in this case be tied up and under the control of the stock association and what that means to the Indians and their stock interests you can appreciate and the Department should."[32] Clapp, he advised Welsh, should stay.[33] Welsh apparently did lobby for Clapp; in January 1898 Clapp thanked Welsh for his "nice letter" and noted that the Secretary of the Interior told him he was pleased with him and anticipated no change in his placement.[34]

Clapp retained his post as Indian Agent at Pine Ridge until 1900, despite WSDSGA claims that he had failed in his ". . . duty to see that Justice and Equity obtain between the Indians and neighboring citizens,"[35] and despite the lack of support from his superiors for his stand on the trespassing issue. But John R. Brennan was finally appointed as Pine Ridge Indian Agent in 1900, and served in that capacity until 1917.

After the OIA decision on the trespass, Agent Clapp did the only thing he could do about the problem, notifying the boss farmers to ask Oglalas to round up foreign stock and expel it from the reservation, being sure to incur no public expense – a remedy which had proven of limited utility in the past.[36] On July 27, 1897, the Oglala Council signaled its concern about the cattle trespass at a special meeting convened four miles west of the Agency. The Council proposed to levy a penalty of $1.00 per head for trespassing stock, the same penalty specified in the federal statute. Inspector McLaughlin, who was attending at the invitation of the Council, estimated that there were 250 Oglalas at the meeting, including Red Cloud, Little Wound, American Horse, George Sword, He Dog, Lip, Big Road, and Turning Bear, all of whom were well known tribal leaders. The Council's proposal did not move McLaughlin to recommend that the federal law against trespassing be enforced, but the tone of the meeting convinced him that something should be done. Otherwise,

> . . . the more lawless Indians may kill enough of them to satisfy what they consider their just dues, such action on their part would create e friction and lead to serious trouble, beside [sic] retarding the progress of the Indians toward civilization, therefore prompt settlement of the questions involved is imperatively demanded in order to remove the causes of discontent.[37]

So that the interests of trespassing cattlemen would not be jeopardized by "the more lawless Indians," McLaughlin recommended construction of a fence on the east side of the Cheyenne River and on the south side of the White River. "This would give the neighboring stockmen the entire White River for watering their stock. . . "[38] Indeed it would – such a project would sanction outside stock interests' use of that portion of reservation land between the Cheyenne and White Rivers and the proposed fence, in addition to securing the water from those rivers, both of which make up a substantial portion of the boundary line of the reservation, for the exclusive use of white ranchers. In subsequent years a fence was built along the northern boundary line but trespassing stock continued to come in along the western and southern boundaries.

The fence did not end trespass. Oglalas still complained about trespassing stock, prompting John Brennan, the cattleman's agent, to order a roundup in 1903. About 600 head of trespassing stock were gathered but Brennan claimed that when he tried to collect for damages the owners:

> contended that they were doing everything possible to keep their stock from comming [sic] over the line, that the cattle drifted over in spite of their best efforts, the the [sic] law of South Dakota recognized a free range, therefore they were not responsible. They also contended that the Department ruled in 1897, that where a free range existed and Indian Reservations were not fenced, that should outside stock drift onto a reservation, the Indians should, at their own expense, drive the stock over the line and without damage to the stock. Judging from the correspondence, the cattle men won the case [i.e., in 1897].[39]

F.M. Stewart, Secretary-Treasurer of the WSDSGA, suggested to Brennan that he should take up the matter of fencing the west line with the Department of the Interior to determine if it could be built at the expense of the government or the Indians. After all, Stewart contended, "We feel that the west line should be fenced the same as the north line and thus give settlers adjacent to the line equal protection. As it is at present we are required to keep our cattle under herd while on the north line the Gov'mt has provided a fence and line riders."[40]

OGLALA OMNICIYE AND THE STRUGGLE FOR THE LAND

Sometime after the Pine Ridge Agency was established the Oglala formed a governing body they called the Oglala Omniciye, or the "Oglala Council" in English. The exact date of the Council's formation is uncertain, but it was evidently formed during the tenure of V.T. McGillycuddy, the first Indian Agent at Pine Ridge. In an 1889 letter to McGillycuddy, George Sword, Captain of Police at Pine Ridge Agency, noted that he was concerned about the activities of the Council that was formed while McGillycuddy was Agent, that is, sometime between 1879–1886.[41]

The Oglala Omniciye marked a departure from pre-reservation Oglala political organization, in that it met regularly on behalf of all Oglala bands. It sought to integrate those bands, which had been autonomous political units for most of the yearly round in the pre-reservation era, into one governing authority that could regularly speak for all Oglalas. The symbolic and legal bases for the Council were the treaties that had been negotiated with the U.S. government. The 1851 and 1868 Fort Laramie Treaties provided a written, legal foundation for a nation-to-nation relationship between the Oglala and the United States. Many of the issues the Oglala Council dealt with, including land claims, rations, annuities, and education, directly involved treaty provisions.

A September 21, and 22, 1903, meeting with U.S. Representative E.W. Martin (S.D.) at Pine Ridge Agency, on the so-called 1876 Treaty, which the U.S. used as a smokescreen for the confiscation of the Black Hills, contains interesting commentary on the Oglala Council by Oglala themselves.[42] Asa Kills A Hundred had this to say about the Council he headed at the time: "We have a council in the Oglala on this reservation, we have something like the Great Father's Council, but here when we decide anything, we vote for it first, and if we decide then, [sic] it is as if we were of one mind."[43] Kills A Hundred's remarks are echoed today on Pine Ridge Reservation where some Oglala who speak Lakota translate Oglala Omniciye as "a meeting of the minds where decisions are made."[44] Several Oglalas at the 1903 meeting discussed honor, prefacing statements with the phrase "If you are a man. . . ." Afraid of Bear, for example, told Congressman Martin that ". . . we talk to you for a man, and if you are a man, help us and try to see all these crooked things and try to straighten them out for us." Thomas Black Bear also emphasized honor, noting that ". . . what we say we mean." None of what the people said had any effect on Representative Martin, who pronounced the Agreement valid, but the meeting does provide insight into the views of the people about their political culture vis-a-vis that of the U.S. At the end of the meeting Council President Kills A Hundred addressed the gathering at length in Lakota. By unanimous vote the people concurred that the 1876 proceedings on the Black Hills were not a treaty, because the requisite three-fourths signatures had not been obtained.

And of those who did sign, maintained Lawrence Bull Bear, "The people did not tell these chiefs before they came that they gave them authority to sign that bill, they didn't say any such thing. Therefore, I think that that wasn't a true treaty, because the people didn't give the chiefs the authority to sign this, so they were telling lies."[45] The legitimacy of leaders hinged on their faithful representation of the expressed interests of the people, as Bull Bear's comments in 1903 made clear, and as Treaty Council members today emphasize.

The Oglala Council represented tiospaye across the reservation. At the Black Hills meeting Chief American Horse pointed that out to Congressman Martin, noting that "All of this Oglala Council has gathered from all over the reservation."[46] Members of the Oglala Council included

Oglala men who were recognized by the people as, and who presented themselves as, "chiefs and headmen" in English.[47] Recognition as a chief or headman came from the tiospaye. Sometime in 1936 or 1937, when William Spotted Crow, who was chosen as "Sergeant at Arms" of the Oglala Council thirty years earlier, defined tiospaye for Pine Ridge Superintendent W.O. Roberts, he said it was a ". . . group of people here that have a chief and over there is another group of people and they have a chief and so on."[48]

The Council elected officers annually, moved its meetings from one district to another, ran meetings in accord with parliamentary procedures, appointed ad hoc groups to work on specific issues, chose delegates to conduct business in Washington D.C., and, at least part of the time, elected a standing "Committee" made up of representatives from each reservation district.[49]

Colonial official's notions about the Oglala Council were mixed. In 1900, Jenkins, the Special Agent in Charge at Pine Ridge, noted that Council meetings had been held a dozen or more times each year before he arrived and recommended that they be allowed to continue. He witnessed a meeting that October and reported that it was peaceable, conducted according to parliamentary rules, and opened with a prayer.[50] In years following, Agent John Brennan had a very different, and more typical, perspective. His 1907 opinion was that

> The Oglala Council, as organized, serves no good purpose that I can see. It is unwieldy, lacking in business methods, a detriment to the Indians' interests and interferes with the proper transaction of Agency business. . . they always make the occasion one of feasting and boasting about the wonderful deeds they did when they were younger and on the war path. These councils last generally from a week to ten days, sometimes longer.[51]

The Council, he claimed, was composed of ". . . older, nonprogressive Indians who shut out the younger element."[52] Members amounted to about 300 mostly ". . . old and non-progressive Indians who call themselves Head Men and Chiefs," he declared in 1909. He impugned the body as "harmless" and recommended against abolishing it.[53] The previous year, in another letter to the Commissioner, Brennan's purple prose was more passionate:

> Turning Hawk still president of the 'Great Oglala Council,' so called . . . As a rule these councils are a farce. A few old and non-progressive Indians get together, secure the services of some worthless returned student Mixed-blood for secretary, and proceed to feast and discuss all sorts of fool questions. Their secretary shapes up the report to fit his own ideas of how affairs on the reservation should be conducted. Eighty per cent of the people on the reservation know nothing about these councils.[54]

Brennan's pejorative characterization of the Oglala Council came on the
heels of efforts of several years duration, efforts that he had made to secure
cheap leases of large portions of the reservation for outside cattlemen.[55]
In addition to opposing Brennan's leasing proposals, the Council

> ... opposed the working system when it was inaugurated on this reser-
> vation, and when they found they could not prevent the men from
> going to work, they undertook to dictate how the working fund should
> be expended – insisted that this money should be paid the Indians for
> working around their own places. . . . When a vacancy occurs in the
> Agency, such as Farmer, Assistant Farmer, Herders, Line Riders, etc.,
> this council tries to dictate who shall and who shall not be appointed
> to fill the vacancy.[56]

What Brennan styled "all sorts of fool questions" were key issues of control over land, labor, and capital – the province of government.

The Council petitioned the Commissioner of Indian Affairs for formal
recognition in 1904 and again several years later. Acting CIA Larrabee's
1907 response held that the OIA viewed the Oglala Council as a political
body that represented the interests of its members only, and not the interests of the whole tribe. More generally, "The practice of the Service has
been to recognize only general councils called for the purpose of transact-
ing such business as may be presented; or in special cases, such as leasing
tribal lands where the office recognizes the action of a smaller Business
Committee appointed by the general council . . . "[57] Recognized or not, the
Oglala Omniciye set itself the tasks of government, and would not be satisfied with being the mere tool of the OIA that Larrabee thought such
councils should be. And as far as leasing matters were concerned, the
Council did not choose to appoint a Business Council, but handled those
questions as a whole.

The Oglala Omniciye was vigilant in its work to protect the reservation
land base from outside encroachment. It repeatedly denied requests by outside cattle operators to establish cattle trails across the reservation for
movement of their stock to shipping points on the Fremont, Elkhorn and
Missouri Valley Railroad, which ran 20 miles south of the reservation.[58]
When, in 1900, the OIA authorized the Indian Agent to permit (i.e., to
lease) reservation land to non-residents, the Council asked the Secretary of
the Interior and the CIA to annul the action. They accompanied their
request with a petition bearing 432 signatures of the "President, Secretary,
and Head men of the Council of the Sioux Tribe of Indians" who were
present at the Council's November 10, 1900 meeting. The cover letter was
signed by Robert American Horse, President, Charley Parke, Secretary, and
George Fire Thunder, Interpreter for the Council. The first name on the
petition is that of Red Cloud, followed by Big Road, Red Dog, Kills A
Hundred, and Kicking Bear, all prominent Oglala leaders.[59]

In support of its November, 1900 petition, the Council cited the reduction of rations issued by the OIA, the consequent dependence of the Oglala
on the cattle industry, and the need of the reservation range for fattening
their cattle. The Council noted that grass had been poor that year, necessi-
tating the movement of stock owners about the reservation in order to
secure better pasturage, and pointed out that ". . . the presence of outside
stock and the owners thereof upon our reservation will mean the destruction of our Range [sic], and [will be] the cause of constant trouble between
us and the whites." The Council also cited the fact that the northern fence
was soon to be supplemented so that the reservation would be fenced
against the trespass of outside stock, implying that the fence would benefit
them because it would secure the land for their use. Lastly, the members
emphasized their understanding that without Oglala approval the
". . . Department has not the right to lease . . . especially so in this case,
where we have made valuable concessions [i.e., the reduction of the Great
Sioux Reserve by the Sioux Act of 1889] to secure title to our reservation."[60] The Oglala Council was clearly aware of the 1891 Leasing Act,
which made leasing of tribal land contingent on tribal approval.[61]

Agent John Brennan, in his first year on the job, seemed supportive of
the Council's position. He reported that as soon as the order authorizing
Agents to issue permits to outsiders was issued, the Oglala held councils at
different points on the reservation to discuss the order, and that 35 of the
leading men of the council had been sent to him to discuss the matter. They
planned a trip to Washington to express their discontent, but Brennan recommended a petition and said he would help them get an answer. He
inspected the range and found that grass was poor and that Oglala-owned
cattle were thin. As a result he said, he was telling outsiders that the reservation could not take care of them.[62] But a few years later Brennan was
singing another tune. In a letter to the CIA in 1905, he railed about the
Council's position against leasing to outsider cattlemen, arguing that "We
might just as well be earning $40,000 or $50,000 a year from grass [i.e., at
$1.00 per head per year] that is and has been for twenty years going to
waste. There are applicants now, good responsible cattle men, asking to put
on some 25,000 head [of cattle]."[63]

Except for the occasion of his first year as Agent (1900), when his
inspection of the reservation range showed that overgrazing posed a threat
to Oglala cattle, Brennan attempted to accommodate requests by outside
stock growers to bring cattle onto the reservation, either under the permit
system of $1.00 per head, or under a system of leasing of specific tracts of
tribal land. Brennan, in fact, had proven himself worthy of the WSDSGA's
endorsement, making strenuous efforts on behalf of stock interests. In 1906
he described his efforts in these remarks to the CIA: "For the past five years
I have labored diligently and used all legitimate means to induce them [i.e.,
the Oglala] to lease their surplus lands for grazing purposes, but each time

the matter is brought up I have a fight on my hands."[64] A few months later he complained that "The question of leasing their surplus lands for grazing purposes was submitted to them for approval nearly every year for the past five years, but the council saw fit to vote against the question when presented."[65] What was "surplus" to Brennan, was not "surplus" to the Oglala. (Since Columbus' arrival whites customarily viewed Indian lands as surplus to Indian needs, as a commodity that needed to be harnessed for white interests.)

Interest in leasing reservation land was growing. Homesteaders had replaced ranchers as the hope of cities and communities dreaming of economic development on the plains. Ranchers fearful of losing out to homesteaders engaged in the illegal practice of fencing tracts falsely claimed under the homestead laws, and often adjacent tracts as well, in order to secure range for their animals. But practices tolerated in the past were now being questioned. In 1902, President Theodore Roosevelt, who admired ranchers on the plains, nevertheless told the ranchers that the fences they had illegally erected must come down. That year a series of arrests of offenders was dubbed the "Roosevelt Round-Up." Settlers were having their day. But the cattlemen were not finished and "It was on the Indian grass that the open range cow industry made its last stand."[66] One of the first signs of the rancher's success was the acquisition of the huge lease on Standing Rock Reservation in 1902.[67]

In 1904 Brennan wrote to Kills a Hundred, President, and Thomas Black Bear, Secretary, of the Oglala Council, asking if the Oglala Council would consider leasing about eight townships in the northeast corner of the reservation and, in addition, allowing 15,000 to 20,000 head of cattle in under the permit system at $1.00 per head. He told them that the "Indian Department has been contacted by a number of stockmen asking for the leases" and tried to sweeten the pot by assuring them that "It will be the means of earning considerable money that you will all share in."[68]

When the Oglala Council rejected Brennan's recommendation to lease about three townships (ca. 69,120 acres) in the northeast portion of the reservation in 1902, he asked the CIA for permission to go ahead and lease anyway. But the CIA responded that ". . . at present it [i.e., the OIA] does not feel like ignoring their expressed wishes in the matter."[69] Again, after the Council rejected his 1904 proposal, Brennan recommended bringing on 20,000 to 30,000 head of outside cattle; and again the OIA responded that "It is deemed impolitic to force the system upon them," even though Brennan had circulated petitions in favor of leasing and had garnered around 500 signatures of "Indians and mixed-bloods," and had a document bearing the signatures of six persons including those of John Kills A Hundred (not, as Brennan said, the Council President, who was Asa Kills A Hundred), Thomas Black Bear, and four others, three of whom identified themselves as "Judge of the Indian Court."[70]

Brennan did note that there was strong opposition to leasing and that Kills A Hundred himself had come to his office with one of several delegations to protest the proposed leasing and to ask that the petitions bearing the 500 or so names not be sent in to the CIA.[71] No mention of the law requiring tribal consent for leasing was made. But the Acting Commissioner advised Brennan to take the matter up again in the fall ". . . with a view to securing the consent of a majority of the male adults for the inauguration of the permit system to commence May 1, 1905."[72] Though the OIA refused to sanction arbitrary and illegal leasing of tribal land, it would encourage going around the Oglala Council, which they would not officially recognize, in an attempt to secure majority support for leasing. So Brennan put his colonial system to work in an effort to garner the needed support.

Boss farmers in the reservation districts were directed to gather signatures on petitions in support of leasing. In Pass Creek District Boss farmer John Boesl got 121 signatures of what he styled the ". . . progressive Indians of the better Class." But not all of those Boesl deemed progressive signed. He regretted, he said, that ". . . the petition was aposed [sic] by Some [sic] of the more progressive Indians, and by a few living along the line of the reservation, who permit stock to come on the reservation for pay which they appropriate to their own use."[73]

There is good reason to believe that the tactics Brennan and the boss farmers used in order to get signatures on the pro-leasing petitions involved coercion and misrepresentation. A couple of years before Brennan's 1905 effort to get signatures reservation wide, the boss farmer in Medicine Root District was allegedly using his office to pressure tribal members to sign a petition for leasing of land in the district. Charles Turning Hawk, then president of the Oglala Council, wrote the Indian Rights Association noting that it had been alleged that the boss farmer compelled one or two young men to sign their names to the petition before he would let them access money they had in his office [probably IIM (Individual Indian Money Account) funds].[74] According to George Fire Thunder, writing to M.K. Sniffen of the I.R.A. for the Committee of the Oglala Council, both Brennan and the boss farmers were using illicit tactics in their 1905 effort to garner signatures in support of the permitting system. "The Farmers and Agent are working and pressing the leasing scheme. Their schemes are to promise the Indians all their old time dances, if they will sign. They also promise them anything that the Indian wants just to secure his name . . . if an Indian refuses to sign he is in a position equal to a prison."[75]

The petitions in support of cattle permits that the the boss farmers circulated in the districts were written in English and in Lakota. The assessment of the Committee of the Oglala Council was that "The petitions are written in such form so as to make it look as if the Indians were the ones that have gotten it up, but the truth is, they have made up these petitions in this form so as to make it look strong and at the same time shield themselves."[76] It was unusual to have anything distributed by the OIA or the boss farmers in the Lakota language, even though many of the people spoke only Lakota. The practice was that postings at the boss farmer's offices in the districts were in English only.[77]

The wording that was used suggested that the signers were supporting permitting of outside cattle so long as the ". . . number of such cattle shall not exceed the number that can graze without detriment to the cattle belonging to the Indians and provided that such permits shall not lease the land [sic], and s [sic] shall not interfere with any right ot [sic] privilege now belonging to the Indians on the reservation." In addition to wording that would appear to protect Oglala resources, the petition included a section that suggested that those persons who were illegally grazing on the reservation would be subject to penalties:

> We, the undersigned Indians belonging on the Pine Ridge U.S. Indian Reservation, South Dakota, hereby petition the Hon. Commissioner of Indian Affairs to collect each year not less than one dollar per head for each animal grazing on this reservation and that belongs to any person not having treaty rights on this reservation, and to pay all money so collected to Indians belonging on this reservation.[78]

Thus the petition grossly misrepresented and obscured the true intentions of Agent Brennan. Brennan's desire to pasture 40,000 to 50,000 head of outside stock on the reservation under the permit system, was obscured by the promise to allow only so many cattle as could graze on the reservation without harming Oglala cattle raising. Further, the suggestion that the signers were in support of assessing $1.00 per head for stock belonging to persons not having treaty rights on the reservation, i.e., in support of collecting the trespass fee stipulated by the Federal Statute 2117 that the U.S. had turned its back on in 1897 and later under Brennan's tenure as Agent, was blatant and cynical manipulation.

In February 7 and 8, 1905, the Oglala Council met in Wounded Knee to work out a strategy for fighting the leasing of reservation land. They decided to send a petition against leasing and they appointed a committee ". . . consisting of twelve men to fight the 'Leasing Scheme.' George Sword, Red Hawk, Short Bull, Red Shirt, He Dog, Howard Bad Wound, Moses Red Kettle, Lawrence Bull Bear, Thomas Black Bear, Running Hawk, Black Elk and William Iron Crow were selected. Those men, who represented the various reservation districts, met with Agent Brennan in an effort to dissuade him from circulating the pro-leasing petitions and to lodge a complaint about the manner in which the boss farmers and other government employees were conducting the pro-leasing petition drive. This according to George Fire Thunder, in detailed letters about the leasing question that he sent to the Indian Rights Association's M.K. Sniffen on behalf of the committee of 12. Brennan intimated that he was only taking orders, telling the committee only that ". . . he had a letter from the Commissioner instructing him to have the Farmers take up this 'Leasing Scheme.'" In addition, Brennan told them, pro-leasing signatures gathered the previous year were still in the possession of the Department. Fire Thunder asked Sniffen to notify the Commissioner that those names were not valid for the current leasing battle. In his February 21 letter he reported that the Oglala Council already had 751 names on a petition against leasing and more were coming in every day.[79]

Fire Thunder pointed out several practical problems that the Council had in doing their petition. Most of the signers who could write signed their names in Lakota. "Some think that if we send them in as they are that the Dept. will give us the (Horse Laugh) because they can't read Indian, and that they will think that we are writing anything. Others think that if we rewrite the names in one hand that it won't be genuine." Another problem was that they could not insure that the signatures they gathered would be recognized as official. "You see the other party had the Census Roll by which to make the signers sign their correct *Census name*."[80] In the end they re-wrote some of the names in English, had those witnessed by two parties, submitted a typed list of the other names having had it certified as a true copy of the original, and notarized by the Shannon County Notary Public.[81] They were clearly very shrewd, and they understood the political process.

The Oglala Council collected a total of 981 signatures against the leasing of reservation land and forwarded their petition to the CIA on March 18, 1905. A combination of dishonest wording on the pro-leasing petition and strong-arm tactics netted Agent Brennan 748 signatures, and he forwarded those to the CIA in April 1905. He attributed his inability to secure more signatures to the "Great Oglala Council, as they style themselves." Though he failed to get the majority of Oglala signatures, he maintained that the majority of Oglala were in favor of leasing or taking in outside cattle under a permit system ". . . but the old coffee coolers, squaw men and non-progressive Indians, bull-dozed them and prevented, as far as they could, the signing of the petitions."[82]

The leaders of the Oglala Council were not working in isolation. Throughout the push for leasing they kept in touch with the Indian Rights Association (I.R.A.), which lobbied on their behalf. Their connection with the I.R.A. enabled them to bring their story to the attention of politicians in Washington D.C., and to keep abreast of developments there. When they heard that CIA Leupp planned to visit Pine Ridge Reservation in the spring of 1905, they decided to present him with a copy of their anti-leasing petition in person. But Leupp made it only as far as neighboring Rosebud Reservation. George Fire Thunder forwarded the copy to Sniffen of the I.R.A. on May 1, 1905, with instructions to send their previous letters, in which they detailed the ongoing graft on Pine Ridge Reservation for the

CIA. Fire Thunder's comments show that the Council also had information about what was happening on other reservations. "It appears that Mr. Leupp is looking up the affairs at some of the other reservations. We believe that if you will forward our letters explaining the schemes of Leasing Promoters that he will give this Agency a shake up. We want the Gov to give us as much protection as the Cattle men are afforded."[83] Samuel Brosius, an I.R.A. attorney, wrote back to Fire Thunder on May 9 noting that "A few weeks ago I was advised by the Honorable Commr. Indian Affairs that there was no intention of leasing the lands of the Pine Ridge Reservation the present season for the use of outside cattle."[84] Thus, for the moment at least, yet another attempt to deliver the reservation into the hands of outside cattle interests had been defeated.

The Oglala Council was very clear about why it took a stand against leasing. In the letter that accompanied the Council's petition to the CIA, William Iron Crow, Red Shirt, Red Hawk, George Sword and Howard Bad Wound, members of the Committee of the Oglala Council laid out their reasons:

> Do not think that we are opposed to the leasing, simply because we say 'no'. We have reasons for opposing such a scheme. We are certain that if our land is leased that we will suffer from its effect, like the Indians on the other reservations. It will take from five to ten years to get over its effect, if cattle are allowed to graze on our land. Our fathers and grandfathers made treaties with the Government. In these treaties, they framed laws by which we were to be governed. In Sec. (11) of the Crook treaty of 1889 [AKA Sioux Act of 1889], it states . . . It requires a 3/4 majority to carry any agreement . . . Who, or what man has made a law by procuring a 3/4 majority of the Indians to agree to leasing their lands? . . . Our white brothers should be satisfied with what land they have taken from us. We will soon get our allotments, and we think that it would be better for them not to disturb us with their leasing schemes . . . If we are to be bothered by these grafters all the time, we never will reach the stage of self supporting. We, the Committee of the Oglala Council, address this petition to you, and respectfully ask that you will look into our requests without delay.[85]

Perhaps the Committee was anticipating the paternalistic and racist attitudes of OIA bureaucrats who regularly applied such labels as "non-progressive" to them by prefacing their remarks by the statement "Do not think that we are opposed to the leasing, simply because we say 'no.'"[86] The main emphasis of the text, on the importance of maintaining control over the land in order to be self-sufficient, was the same as that the Council outlined in 1900, in its earlier petition against outside grazing.

Communal ownership of the reservation land base was crucial to the success of the Oglala Omniciye's fight to stop large scale leasing on Pine Ridge Reservation. Because of the federal statute regulating the lease of tribal land, (i.e., land held in common), the U.S. government was legally enjoined from unilateral leasing; and as long as the land was held in common, there was no threat that outsiders could gain legal footholds on the reservation land base through individuals who might have favored leasing. But once the land was divided into private tracts by allotment, leasing could, and did begin on Pine Ridge Reservation. Some individuals began to lease their land, with the Agent's approval, and tracts held by minors were leased at the discretion of the Agent, even above the protest of the parents.[87] But the amount of land leased was relatively small for some years, as cattle men favored large, contiguous tracts for their stock. In 1913, there were 50,000 acres of allotted land leased for grazing, and none for farming – less than 3% of the approximately 2,000,000 allotted acres on the reservation.[88] And although the Oglala Council had held the line on leasing of tribal land at least until 1910, when Agent John Brennan reported that no tribal lands were under lease, by 1913, 80,000 acres of tribal land in the sandhill country adjacent the southern boundary of the reservation had been leased.[89] Thus the allotment era coincided with increased leasing of land by outside interests, and although the amount of acreage under lease was relatively small, the stage had been set for further incursions of outside grazing and farming interests onto the reservation.[90]

THE "CATTLE RING" AND THE RESERVATION ECONOMY

There were other factors besides leasing though, that were a threat to the interests of Oglala stock raisers. George Fire Thunder, one of the leading figures in the Oglala Council's fight against what he called the "leasing scheme," argued that a "Cattle Ring," was operating on Pine Ridge Reservation, enriching its members at Oglala expense. The ring included Agent Brennan and his boss farmers, white traders, white men married to Oglala women, and one H.A. Dawson, Vice-President of the Western South Dakota Stock Growers Association.[91]

Traders, Fire Thunder maintained, capitalized on the OIA's forced work system by extending credit on the strength of the work and charging exorbitant prices, with the result that Oglalas had little to show for the work they did.[92] People were encouraged to accumulate debts, and sometimes, when the work was done nothing was left over, and at other times, there were not even enough earnings to pay the debt incurred. In addition to their linkage with the work system, traders on Pine Ridge Reservation were tied to the colonial system in another important way. The relationship between boss farmers and traders, as noted in the previous chapter, was closely akin to that of the classic model of a company store. Charles Turning Hawk, who, like Fire Thunder, was a returned student and a leader of the Oglala Council, and who was himself a trader in Medicine Root District – his letterhead read "Chas. T. Hawk & Co., Dealers in General Merchandise"[93] – described the operation of traders in some detail.

Whenever the Indians wish to trade with the Indian trader, the Farmer gives them an order to the store, saying that the Indian has his permission to trade. This is done, or otherwise the Indian cannot do business with the trader. Where any money comes to the Indian through the Farmer, the trader presents his bill against the Indian and the Farmer collects the bill from the Indian in his office. Thus the Indian is forced to pay his bill in the Farmer's office instead of going to the trader's store, where the debt had been incurred. . . . The Indian is encouraged to accumulate debt, so that when he is paid for the work he does not have a cent left over at times after paying his debts[94]

Besides favoritism, in this case probably of Indian traders who were white or mixed blood over the full blood Turning Hawk, the situation would have enabled the traders to keep their prices at exorbitant levels, enriching both themselves and cooperating boss farmers. The relationship of boss farmers with traders was one important basis for making them a significant factor in reservation economic life; another was their control over the issuance of permits to sell cattle.

Turning Hawk claimed that boss farmers and cattle buyers interested in Oglala-owned cattle sided together, obliging sellers to take whatever price the buyer would name.[95] By 1905, fair numbers of Oglala stock were being sold. During his September 1905 interview with Sniffen, Fire Thunder ". . . stated that the Indians (some of them) are selling one year calves [i.e., yearlings] to H.A. Dawson; that this is being done constantly; that the farmers buy horses from the Indians, especially Smoot."[96] Reverend Johnson, a Presbyterian minister in Pine Ridge, told Sniffen that "Last week a lot of cattle belonging to the Indians was sold for $16 and $18 a head." Johnson's assessment of the local power structure was similar to that of Fire Thunder. Boss farmers, he felt, were ". . . in league with the clique that wants the money the Indians get. This clique is a traders' combination. . . ."[97] Fire Thunder said of the boss farmers, "they pretend to help us when they are doing their best to hurt our main source of self support, *that of raising stock* [emphasis in original]."[98] The siphoning off of Oglala cattle would, of course, reduce the need of Oglalas to access the range for their own herds. Some of the boss farmers were apparently beneficiaries of the situation, and had taken advantage of their positions to enrich themselves at Oglala expense.

One of the worst offenders, contended Fire Thunder, was Boss farmer W.C. Smoot, who had a large herd of cattle and horses on the extension just south of the reservation line in Nebraska. In December 1905, Smoot was arrested in Nebraska for land fraud. He was charged with having "induced some 75 Indians to file for the cattle kings" under the Kinkaid law. Smoot was later cleared of charges in an Omaha court, but a petition against his reinstatement was circulated on Pine Ridge. Besides buying horses from the Oglala, Smoot was, Fire Thunder believed, working with

Henry A. Dawson, Vice-President of the WSDSGA, as part of the cattle ring.[99] Significantly, perhaps, Smoot and fellow boss farmer James Smalley were brand inspectors for the WSDSGA during the push for leasing on Pine Ridge in 1905.[100]

But Fire Thunder was convinced an even bigger player in the "trader's combination" than the boss farmers was Henry A. Dawson. In 1905, Fire Thunder wrote the Indian Rights Association's M.K. Sniffen charging that the

> . . . main person back of the 'Leasing Scheme' is H.A. Dawson. This man controls all the reservation stores. He keeps back and has for his Agent Dr. Jas. R. Walker the Agency physician. How can we help ourselves when the Government will allow a man of this sort to be among us who is the Vice Pres. of the S.D. stk. Asso and one of the largest cattle owners in this section of the country. With this power he has influence over every one on the Reservation – and through it will cripple us [emphasis in original].[101]

Dawson was in the U.S. Postal Service in Maryland before he transferred to the Indian Department, and he came to the Pine Ridge Agency as a clerk in 1882, but his fortunes rose rapidly at Pine Ridge. He bought the trader's store in Pine Ridge Village in 1884. Other members of his family relocated to Pine Ridge Reservation too. One became a boss farmer in Porcupine, and another, who had come to the reservation with nothing, opened up a store in Medicine Root District a month later.[102]

Dawson was a phenomenally successful individual and an opportunist. In 1891, he earned $1,250 by contracting with the U.S. government to inter the victims of the December 29, 1890 Wounded Knee Massacre in a mass grave. By 1892 he had acquired significant capital, and that year he invested $20,000 of his own money in the cattle business. Among the cattle he bought that year were 450 two-year olds that he purchased from "his Indian friends" on Pine Ridge Reservation.[103] Years later his foreman, Will Hughes, recalled that the outfit enjoyed "Free grass, no income tax, no county tax, only a small state tax, no feed bills . . . "[104] In the first decade of the twentieth century, when the public domain lands were filling up with homesteaders, Dawson ran cattle on leases on several reservations in South Dakota. By 1910, he was the biggest operator in the state, when he shipped 16,000 head of cattle to market.[105] Dawson was Vice-President of the WSDSGA from 1898 to 1908, and President of the organization from 1908–1912. His rise in the organization began with his election to the WSDSGA's executive committee in 1895, 1896, and 1897. He was one of the witnesses who testified on behalf of the WSDSGA at the 1897 hearings in Pine Ridge. Some of the cattle Agent Clapp ordered impounded belonged to Dawson. During the hearing Clapp produced the S.D. brand book, which listed Dawson's range as Pine Ridge Reservation, but Dawson claimed that the book was wrong, that he ranged his cattle north of the reservation boundary, and that his impounded stock had just drifted across the reservation line.[106]

Brennan, of course, had been supported by the WSDSGA for the position of Agent in the first place, and he was active with that organization during his tenure as Agent. From 1915 to 1918, in fact, he was on the WSDSGA's Executive Committee (Brennan was Indian Agent at Pine Ridge from 1900 to 1917).[107] Brennan himself was a cattle man, and owned a ranch two miles east of Rapid City, South Dakota. Brennan's ranch was a modest 540 acres when he sold it in 1917, but it brought $40,000, and was described as "one of the most valuable places in the [Black] Hills."[108]

But Brennan was not just narrowly a supporter of the stock interests. He was a rancher, but he was also a businessman, and was among the founders of Rapid City. In 1882, well before he became the darling of the WSDSGA, when stock interests in Dakota Territory were making efforts to obtain a legal foothold on the Great Sioux Reservation by procuring leases on it, it was Brennan who drafted a resolution to Washington pursuant a mass meeting of concerned citizens in Rapid City, arguing that the Great Sioux Reservation should be opened not just for stockmen but opened "for all." The Great Sioux Reservation was, he wrote, "'of no value'" to the Sioux and it was "'only a question of time when the Indian title will be extinguished to a greater portion of the reservation, which serves no useful purpose in its present condition either to the Indians or to the country at large but is a clog in the wheels of progress.'"[109] Brennan's argument was common currency in western Dakota Territory at the time, offering a rationale and a plan to unite lands to the east and west of the Missouri, and insure statehood.[110]

The reduction of the Great Sioux Reservation did nothing to change Brennan's mind about land held by the Sioux. Judging from his activities as Agent he must have believed that all land that belonged to Native Americans was a "clog in the wheels of progress." He worked assiduously on behalf of stock interests and homesteaders alike. After allotments were made Brennan worked hard to encourage the sale of Oglala lands to whites, so that the Oglala would have the benefit of their example, he wrote.[111] The Oglala Council's interests were directly opposite his own, and he knew it. When he avoided the name calling his analysis seemed to be much more acute. He argued that the Council's position against ". . . the sale of heirship lands is for the purpose of holding the reservation intact to be controlled in a tribal way as heretofore, also to keep whites from settling or securing a foothold on the reservation."[112]

George Fire Thunder's analysis of the power structure is supported by the reports of other influential Oglalas. In 1902, George Little Wound, son of the famous Chief Little Wound, claimed that boss farmer James Smalley was harassing prominent Oglalas from Medicine Root District.[113] In 1906, Lawrence Bull Bear noted that the Agent had been ". . . trying for some years to force leasing of land to the Ranchmen."[114] In 1913, Henry Standing Bear, who was long active with the Oglala Council, and who, after the implementation of the IRA government on Pine Ridge Reservation, was an elected representative on the Oglala Sioux Tribal Council, argued that Agent Brennan was one of the "worst enemies" the Oglala had during the past ten years. Standing Bear believed that Brennan and other government workers had backing from U.S. Congressmen from South Dakota and that they should be removed.[115] Charles Turning Hawk, of course, had earlier decried the self-interested relations between non-Indian traders and boss farmers, and he had also taken U.S. officials to task for trampling on Oglala rights. Still a voice for his people in 1915, he contended that Brennan was "from the stock association so if Brennan be removed we will be all right. Brennan has been here as Agent for fifteen years holding a job. Therefore quite a number of this people has no cattle and just few of them have cattle. . . ." Echoing George Fire Thunder's characterization of the cattle ring, Turning Hawk concluded that "They are all one Association in this reservation."[116] In 1913, Standing Bear called for a "cleanup" in reservation personnel just as Fire Thunder had in 1906, when he argued that the ". . . whole set of officers on the Reservation . . . are all corrupt and need a thorough cleaning up."[117]

Over the years remedies had been sought through the Inspection Division of the OIA, but Oglalas were not confident in that avenue, having found as in 1897, that bringing out the facts of their situation to the OIA would not alter the situation. Their preferred channels for lobbying were the Indian Rights Association and Congressmen. George Fire Thunder summed up the sentiments in a letter to Sniffen: "You know that for a long time we have been hoping to convince the Department of the corruption of the officials in charge of this Reservation – but on account of the same conditions existing in the Inspecting Division of the Department we have been unable to prove our cases."[118] Whether or not the various players, including U.S. government employees on the reservation, the WSDSGA, and the traders constituted a "cattle ring" in the sense of a conspiracy, it seems clear that their interests overlapped, and that those interests were not those of the majority of the Oglala, those which were being defended by the Oglala Council.

The overgrazed belt of land along the reservation's borders that Clapp found during his trip around the reservation a few days after the 1897 trespass hearings showed how apt the metaphor of a ring, of a surrounded reservation, was. When G.E. Lemmon, a WSDSGA witness at the trespass hearing in Pine Ridge, claimed that the stock interests in Dakota were surrounded by reservations, Agent Clapp took issue and asked if it was ". . . not a little the other way, and is not the reservation surrounded by the ranges?"[119] Even today on Pine Ridge Reservation some Oglalas describe the forces that control the reservation land base as a "ring."[120] The various

interests referred to as the "cattle ring," the pressure on Oglala stock raisers arising from the trespass of outside stock, the control of capital by the
Agent and the boss farmers, the impact of allotment and the increased leasing that went along with it, mixed blood control over the hay lands, and
the probable use of debt as a lever to force sale of cattle at reduced prices
were the political and economic factors surrounding the decline in the cattle economy of full blood Oglalas.

In 1913 Agent Brennan took official note that something was happening to Oglala stock. In a letter to his boss farmers, it appears as though it
had just come to his attention that they had ". . . issued a large number of
permits to Indians to traffic among selves in ID [i.e., Indian Department
brand] cattle and these purchased by well-to-do mixed-bloods and whites
married to Indians in such numbers as to almost deplete the herds in certain localities of this class of stock." He warned that "No permits to be
issued for sale or barter of this stock among the Indians for sale outside and
if transgressed vigorous prosecution will follow."[121] But in a 1915 letter in
the *Oglala Light*, defending himself from criticism about economic conditions on the reservation, Brennan made no reference to such problems,
blaming instead the Oglala themselves: "As a general proposition, the
Sioux have no sense of the value of money and the great problem of the
Superintendent is to keep the Indian from mismanaging his own affairs and
spoiling himself."[122]

Rose Bernhardt's 1913 letter to I.R.A. attorney Samuel Brosius provides
an interesting outsider's account of Agency officials, and of Oglala feelings
toward them:

> . . . by close observing one can detect the fear and hatred the Indians
> have for their head officials. Again it tends to cultivate a mean dispo-
> sition with the Indians which they resent in silent contempt. If I could
> relate every incident that transpires here, You [sic] in your great sym-
> pathy would find some way to put an end to these cruel despicable
> grafters and hypocrites.[123]

MIXED BLOOD AND FULL BLOOD DIVIDED ON ALLOTMENT

During the visit of General Crook's Commission in 1889, Spotted Elk
expressed the general sentiment about allotment on Pine Ridge
Reservation: "I dont [sic] want to take land in severalty, and my people
dont [sic] want it that way (applause)."[124] There was, however, some organized effort to gain support for the measure among the Oglala. One early
effort was made by an Oglala officer on the Agency police force. Second
Lieutenant of Police Joseph Fast Horse wrote to the I.R.A.'s Herbert Welsh
in 1888 saying that he was ". . . much interested in the matter of the *Land
in Severalty*, taking the names of all who are friendly to that scheme. I now

secured altogether 136 names – and I intend to go about on the same errand." Fast Horse's rationale was that "We must live on our pieces of land, cultivating and improving the same, and accustoming ourselves to all kinds of manual labor, so when the whites should [word unclear] among us as neighbors, the advance we will have made in the meantime will be of advantage to us . . . in the race for existence."[125] The Reverend Charles Cook of Pine Ridge, a strong supporter of allotment, wrote the I.R.A.'s Welsh that George Sword, the Captain of Police at the time, had indicated to him that First Lieutenant Standing Soldier was also supporting the allotment idea, though Sword himself opposed it. Cook felt that overall "The feeling against the bill is strong and is getting stronger, judging from the number of meetings held."[126] The strongest supporters of allotment were mixed bloods and white men married to Oglala women, who were the first to sign the Sioux Act that General Crook was pushing in 1889.[127]

But by far the majority of Oglalas actively opposed allotment. In 1894, 1,258 Oglalas males, over 80% of all adult male Oglalas, petitioned against the measure. The text of the extraordinary document is reproduced in full below:

> The signers of this petition, being a large majority of the Ogalalla Indians, males, of lawful age, of the Pine Ridge Agency, respectfully and earnestly petition and request that you will cause this, their prayer, to be brought before the President, to the end that he may obtain from Congress the enactment of such laws as will secure to us, as a people, the title in fee simple to our present reservation, in perpetuity. We are not in favor of taking land in severalty, having before us the disastrous results of that policy, as shown in the case of our brothers, the Cheyennes and Arapahoes. We believe that if our land can be given to us as a people, that we will in time become civilized, according to the white man's standard, and develop into an orderly, intelligent, loyal, self-supporting people. Our land is at present secured to us only by treaty stipulations. Our experience, and the experience of our fathers, teaches us that such tenure is feeble and unreliable. Without a clear and undisputed title to our land we, and our descendants, can never go forward in development, because we can never have full and complete confidence in our future. If we have a home for ourselves and our children, and children's children, assured to us, we feel that we may then, in time, become a self-governing body of loyal citizens, civilized, enlightened, thrifty, industrious and able to contribute our proper share of the duties, responsibilities and burdens of government. Our homes being assured to us, we feel that we shall go forward in the straight road, as has been done by all peoples who have prospered before us.[128]

The text of the petition shows the continuing importance that the people assigned to maintaining a land base as a foundation for the Oglala nation. The stands they took against allotment and leasing were stands for maintaining a homeland, and for maintaining a basis for an independent economy; those stands had everything to do with future oriented planning, with nation building and nothing to do with rigid, "non-progressive" mind sets.[129]

The Oglala Council also made a very specific economic argument against allotment. In 1904 Oglala Council President Asa Kills A Hundred patiently explained to the Commissioner of Indian Affairs that "Experience shows us that this is not a farming country but is good for stock raising purposes only . . . ".[130] That same year, the year the first allotments were made on Pine Ridge Reservation, Agent Brennan reported that the majority of full blood Oglalas remained opposed to the measure.[131] Three years later Chief Allotment Agent Bates reported that some of the ". . . hardest kickers against the [allotment] work [were] . . . several camps of the old, non-progressive and troublesome full-blood Indians. . . ."[132] One important reason for the continuing opposition of Oglala full bloods to allotment had to have been their commitment to maintaining control over the land base that supported their subsistence-oriented cattle economy. Communal grazing on tribal land, was, after all, the most important factor in the Oglala economy at the time, and dividing up the land with metes and bounds, and with fences, would strike directly at that primary source of Oglala self-sufficiency.[133]

The arguments that Oglalas made against allotment, and against leasing too, were supported by their analyses of situations on other reservations, as in their assessment of the disastrous effects of allotment on the Cheyenne and Arapahoe. Besides watching those situations, they studied policy initiatives, Congressional appropriations, and kept tabs on the changing political winds. By 1894, for example, Henry Standing Bear and six others had formed a "Dawes Bill Association" on the Pine Ridge Reservation, in order to study the allotment question. The Association gathered information on the question and established a reading room in Corn Creek in order to educate themselves and others about it. Standing Bear, like George Fire Thunder, was a returned student, active with the Oglala Council. Besides heading the Dawes Bill Association, Standing Bear was the Chair of a Committee on the allotment issue in 1894, probably a Committee of the Oglala Council. It seems likely that the Committee, along with the Dawes Bill Association, which, according to Standing Bear, included ". . . the most influential and intelligent chiefs, Indians and returned students of our people," played a role in drafting the petition against allotment.[134]

The petition signers were primarily Oglala full bloods.[135] The signatures are grouped according to Camp (i.e., tiospaye) and locale. None of the French, Spanish, Scotch, or other surnames of mixed blood Oglalas appear on the petition. Mixed bloods, and white men married to Oglala women, who supported the Oglala Council's fight against leasing, were at odds with the Council over the allotment question. While both groups had an interest in keeping outside cattle off the reservation, the different land tenure practices of Oglala mixed bloods and full bloods underlay their opposed points of view on the question of allotment. Mixed bloods opted for private property in land, for something that would secure their individual rights to the land, rather than a continuation of communal ownership. It would have been to the advantage of mixed bloods and the white men married to Oglala women, some of whom engaged in commercial, rather than subsistence, ranching, and others of whom were recent arrivals on the reservation who had come seeking land anyway, to own land, and the concept of private property in land was not foreign to them. Another factor had to do with their relationship to the Oglala Council. The Oglala Council, was primarily a body of full blood Oglalas, although mixed bloods were sometimes elected to the office of Secretary.[136] Because mixed bloods had no tiospaye of their own, they had no direct representation on the Oglala Council. Had the petition to acquire title for the Council to the entire reservation succeeded, their position might have been less secure. Neither the larger mixed blood operators, nor the recent arrivals, had a stake in communal ownership. Yet the ability of the Oglala Council to exercise some control over the land base hinged on the continuation of communal ownership.

THE ORGANIZATION OF BENNETT COUNTY AND OGLALA UNITY

In 1908 and 1909 U.S. Senator Gamble (S.D.), introduced legislation to open the southeastern portion of Pine Ridge Reservation to homesteading. The Oglala Council passed resolutions opposing the opening, met with Inspectors on Pine Ridge to make arguments against the opening, and sent delegates to Washington to lobby against the measure. OIA Inspector McLaughlin met twice with the Oglala Council on the reservation in 1909, reported that all speeches at the meetings were in opposition, and that in his other discussions with whites and Oglalas on the reservation, he ". . . did not meet a single person, including agency officials and employees, who were in favor."[137] But in the latter part of April, 1909, after his two meetings with the Oglala Council, he met again with a small group of individuals at Allen, in northwestern Bennett County, and there found support for the proposition. In 1911 U.S. President William Taft signed the bill authorizing the opening and the "cession" of about 1,000,000 acres in Bennett County.[138]

Figure 2: "For the Mixed Blood County Seat"

BENNETT COUNTY BOOSTER.

VOLUME 1   LACREEK, BENNETT COUNTY, SOUTH DAKOTA, FEBRUARY 28, 1912   NUMBER 22

W. C LUSK. Pres. Yankton, S.D.   P. E. SKALINDER. Vice Pres. Lacreek, S.D.   MAURICE W. JENCKS. Sec. & Treas. Sioux City, Ia.

Keep Your Eye on Lacreek, South Dakota

For the Mixed Blood County Seat

IT IS THE CENTER OF THE PRESENT POPULATION AND WE ARE FOR THE PRESENT POPULATION

HENRY C. COTTIER
Western Manager
Lacreek Townsite Company

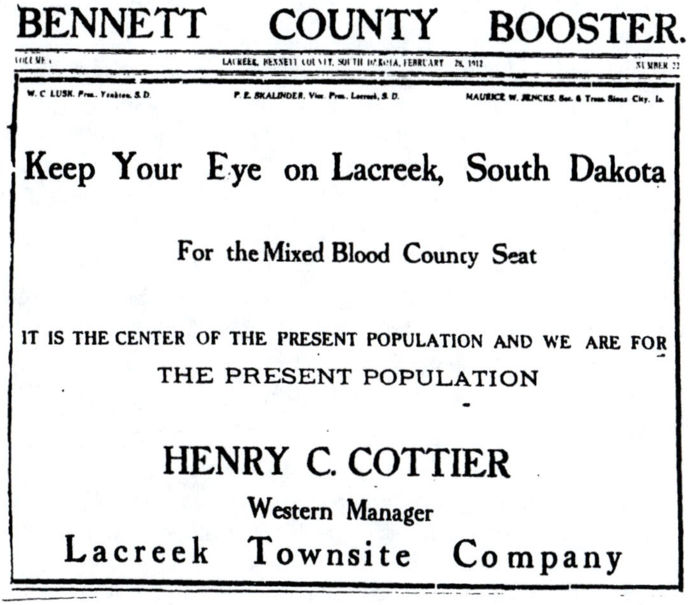

Once the "cession" occurred, land speculators, small businessmen, and settlers in the ceded area set their sights on organizing Bennett County. Oglala mixed bloods were among the leading figures in the push for organization. Henry C. Cottier gathered signatures on the petition calling for an election, and later carried it personally to S.D. Governor Vessey. Cottier got involved in the debate over whether the county seat should be in Martin or Lacreek. As "Western Manager" of the Lacreek Townsite Company, he ran a series of pro-Lacreek ads in the *Bennett County Booster*.[139] The ad for February 28, 1912, (Figure 2) was typical. In an interview for the *Booster,* Cottier said "'I am for a mixed blood organization and a mixed blood county seat and after looking over the townsite location situation in Bennett county have decided that Lacreek is the only town that rightly belongs to the county honors, as it is located in the center of the present population. . . ."[140]

James Ryan, also a mixed blood, supported the organization effort from his home in Valparaiso, Indiana. Ryan, who owned both trust and deeded land in Bennett County, wrote a series of pro-organization articles in the *Booster*. The very first issue of the *Booster* carried a column where he made the case that it was in the interest of himself and "countless other allottees" to boost for county organization.[141] Ryan's rhetoric soared in a subsequent piece, where he invoked images and values that had spurred westward migration for generations:

In Bennett county, in decades gone by, under the unchanging
and changeless order, no newspaper ever appeared to herald an era of
the Caucasian civilization. But the inevitable and escaping years
make changes, and this time the fair land of Bennett county is the
beneficiary. At the present time the county is in the nation's eye; from
thousands of men in rural and urban communities, come inquiries
pertaining to the homesteads which Uncle Sam has told of being
available in the land of opportunity. From every county in the Union
hundreds of earnest men and women are journeying to the registration
points laden with the high hope that they may be fortunate enough get
a quarter section upon which they can build a humble home and thus
better individual destiny . . . they are not only willing and anxious
to enter a new region but are also disposed to make sacrifices, if need
be, to gain a humble acre over which they can be sovereign against
everything but the law.[142]

On April 9, 1912, the people of Bennett County, excluding the "ration
drawing Indians who have not severed their tribal relations," voted in
favor of organization and elected a predominantly mixed blood slate of
candidates to County office. A *Booster* editorial predicted the mixed blood
victory in the first election, citing the fact that most non-Indian
settlers had not yet met their residency requirements. The paper welcomed
the eventuality, noting that "Many of the mixed bloods are more progressive than a majority of white men in pioneer communities and are counted
well-to-do men. It augurs well for the new county and they must take up
the 'white man's burden' of a new form of government."[143]

Some mixed bloods may have been anxious to shoulder the "white
man's burden" but their pre-eminence in local affairs in Bennett County
was short-lived. By the time the next election rolled around, white settlers
did meet the residency requirements for voting, and they elected their
own.[144]

The Oglala Omniciye marked an important change in Oglala political
organization. The Council met the need that Oglalas had, in a reservation
environment, for a national, or tribal government, that could handle the
issues that regularly faced the Oglala people as a whole. The effectiveness
of the Council was demonstrated by its ability to mobilize large numbers
of people, and to carry on extended and sophisticated campaigns in order
to defend the land base and the interests of the Oglala people against the
interests of outside stock growers, despite the corruption of local OIA officials, and despite the failure of the Interior Department to uphold the law.

The Oglala Council's campaign against leasing and allotment demonstrated its strength, and its commitment to serving the interests of the
majority of the Oglala. The Councils' ability to defeat the leasing propos-

als of Agent Brennan and his boss farmers, and the strength of the support it was able to muster against land allotment, show that the Council enjoyed the support of the Oglala people. Oglala Council leaders showed themselves to be impressive figures, who understood the concepts of sovereignty and treaty rights, and who were committed to using Oglala land for the benefit of the Oglala people. Agent John Brennan's contention that the Council was unorganized, lacking in business methods, and non-representative of the people was the rhetoric of a frustrated official.

The existence of effective Oglala leadership in the early days of Pine Ridge Reservation parallels Fred Hoxie's finding that astute leaders, who fought to protect the rights of their people, emerged early on in the history of the Crow Agency in Montana, and at the Cheyenne River Sioux Tribe's reservation in South Dakota. Hoxie's description of the Crow leadership as a "formidable political machine" would fit that of the Oglala Council as well.[145] Assertions like that of Raymond DeMallie, that there is a gap in Oglala leadership from the late nineteenth century to the present,[146] may reflect the fact that, as Richmond Clow has pointed out, scholarly attention to reservation-era political organization has tended to focus on the period beginning with the Indian Reorganization Act of 1934.[147]

Clow's analysis of the constitutions of pre-IRA Councils on Pine Ridge and Rosebud Reservations shows that they reserved more tribal sovereignty than did those of the IRA governments which succeeded them. The IRA constitutions included limiting clauses.[148] Even today, for example, the Oglala Sioux Tribe's constitution gives review authority, over the choice of attorneys to represent the tribe, to the Secretary of the Interior.[149] That provision could have hampered the Oglala Omniciye, perhaps by keeping it from working with Indian Rights Association attorney Brosius on the leasing issue, as he had assisted other tribes in their struggles against leasing. Limiting clauses and the tendency of some IRA governments to concentrate on handling federal programs has led them to be models of self-administration, whereas the Oglala Omniciye approximated a model of self-rule.[150]

Despite a lack of U.S. recognition, and despite the intent of the U.S. government to use the Oglala Omniciye on a "Don't call us, we'll call you" basis, the Oglala Omniciye continued to meet, to work with the Indian Rights Association, to send delegates to Washington, to pressure the Indian Agent at Pine Ridge, and to go around the Agent and official OIA channels in order to be heard. Over and over again the Council held the line in order to protect the reservation land base. The Council frustrated OIA officials, who surely never suspected that the Council could effectively use the 1891 Leasing Act to keep large-scale leasing at bay. The successful organizing efforts of the Oglala Council gave subsistence cattle raising, on a communal basis, a chance – for a while at least. Even though some of the best grazing grounds had been taken up by the mixed bloods with the larger herds, and trespassing by outside stock continued to be a problem, Oglala stockmen were successful for a time.

But large scale trespassing by outside stockmen put continuous pressure on the grasslands that the expanding Oglala cattle industry depended on, and a combination of U.S. officials, traders, and stock interests eventually undermined the self-sufficiency of Oglala cattle raisers. Leasing of allotted lands and the decline of the subsistence cattle raising of Oglala full bloods loosened the control of the Oglala Omniciye over the reservation land base. Some mixed bloods and white men married to Oglala women were apparently beneficiaries of the situation and were able to use their greater capital resources to purchase the cattle of Oglala full bloods at the reduced prices the reservation system made possible.

Although there was a conjunction of interests between Oglala mixed bloods and full bloods on the questions of outside leasing and trespassing stock, differences between them were apparent over the issues of allotment and Bennett County. A key issues seems to have been that the Oglala Omniciye did not integrate mixed bloods, who lacked tiospaye organization, into the polity in any significant way. But the issue was not just one of tiospaye organization. Full blood Oglala leaders like George Fire Thunder and Charles Turning Hawk were themselves integrated into the subsistence economy of communal cattle grazing, and that economy was, as shown in the previous chapter, at odds with the more commercially oriented economy of those mixed bloods with larger herds of cattle. The differences between the two groups were at once cultural, social, economic, and political. Judging from their role in the organization of Bennett County, some mixed bloods, such as Henry Cottier and James Ryan, had embraced values and aspirations very unlike those of the Oglala full bloods. Their behaviors and their values paralleled those of white settlers and were alien to those of Lakota full bloods.

The role of U.S. government officials in the reservation political economy was mixed, partly because of the different individuals that occupied positions of power, but especially because of assessments the OIA made of the influence of those with interests in reservation land. The seemingly contradictory U.S. decisions to refuse to enforce the federal statute against trespassing after the 1897 hearings at Pine Ridge and the subsequent refusal to over-ride the wishes of the Oglala on the leasing question in 1905 were all of a piece. The decision to go ahead with allotment in spite of Oglala opposition was similarly based on assessments of the power equation. The Sioux Act of 1889 authorized allotment, the Indian Rights Association supported it, and regional and Congressional interests advocated for it. Save for Dr. T.A. Bland's Indian Defense Association, which had worked hard to defeat allotment and the Sioux Act of 1889, the Oglala had no influential allies in their struggle.[151]

Apart from rational calculations the OIA and Interior Department made, though, were the irrational elements that influenced outcomes. The obvious racism and greed of officials like Brennan, for example, was not a negligible factor. When white men's cattle and pockets were threatened by the possible fallout from the cattle impoundment in 1897, the U.S. government bureaucracy jumped to deal with the situation; but when Oglala cattle were threatened by trespassing white-owned stock, complaints could be made repeatedly and nothing would be done. Powerful white economic interests, like those represented by the WSDSGA, got quicker and more thorough action than the Oglala ever did. Bald-faced comments made by WSDSGA witnesses like Judge Gardiner at the 1897 Pine Ridge hearing, about the primacy of naked economic interest over the rule of law, evidenced a well-deserved confidence that their government would support them no matter what.

The challenges the Oglala faced before World War I were enormous. Political and economic forces, both national and regional, threatened their land and livelihood. The reservation was not an enclave. The reservation was being integrated into the market economy and the OIA played a supporting role. The Oglala were confronted by the underbelly of that economy, and by OIA complicity, at every turn.

Notes

1. From the book *Last Grass Frontier: The South Dakota Stock Grower Heritage*, Lee, Bob and Dick Williams 1964.
2. Webb, Walter 1931, p. 234.
3. Schell, Herbert S. 1968, p. 244, 247; Utley, Robert 1963, p. 44; Lee and Williams 1964.
4. "Foreigners in their native land" is the title of Chapter 7 from *A Different Mirror*, Takaki, Ronald 1993.
5. RCIA 1888, p. 49.
6. James McLaughlin to CIA, August 19, 1897, RI, Roll 37.
7. Ibid.
8. James McLaughlin to CIA, August 19, 1897, RI, Roll 37; Transcript of hearing "In the Matter of the Investigation of the Impounding and Holding of Certain Cattle by the Agent at the Pine Ridge Indian Agency," July 13, 1897, RI, Roll 37 (hereinafter referred to as "1897 Hearing").
9. 1897 Hearing, RI, Roll 37.
10. James McLaughlin to CIA, August 19, 1897, RI, Roll 37; 1897 Hearing, RI, Roll 37.
11. 1897 Hearing, RI, Roll 37.

12. C.N. Bliss to James McLaughlin, June 25, 1897, RI, Roll 37.

13. James McLaughlin to Secretary of the Interior, August 4, 1897, RI, Roll 37.

14. Ensuing discussion and quotations regarding the trespassing of white-owned cattle on Pine Ridge Reservation is based on testimony given on July 13, 1897 at Pine Ridge Agency, as contained in 1897 Hearing, RI, Roll 37, unless otherwise noted.

15. The law that Judge Gardiner was referring to was Section 2117, Revised Statutes, U.S.

16. Clapp to McLaughlin, July 28, 1897, RI, Roll 37.

17. McGillycuddy to Welsh, October 16, 1897, IRAP Series 1-A, Reel 13.

18. McLaughlin to CIA, August 19, 1897, RI, Roll 37.

19. Five years earlier, in 1892, Inspector Miller noted that cattle were continually straying over the western boundary of the reservation. Miller to CIA, September 24, 1892. Inspection Reports to BIA 1873–1900, Roll 36, OLC. Inspector McLaughlin also noted that frequent reports had been made to former Agents on Pine Ridge. McLaughlin to CIA, August 19, 1897, RI, Roll 37.

20. Section 2117, Revised Statutes U.S. quoted in W.H. Clapp, Notice dated May 22, 1897, RI, Roll 37.

21. W.W. Anderson to Secretary of Interior, July 30, 1897, RI, Roll 37.

22. John D. Stevens to Secretary of Interior, July 27, 1897, RI, Roll 37.

23. Acting CIA to Secretary of Interior, November 22, 1897, RI, Roll 37.

24. W.H. Clapp to McLaughlin, July 28, 1897, RI, Roll 37.

25. Ibid.

26. McLaughlin to CIA, August 19, 1897, RI, Roll 37.

27. Acting CIA Towner to Secretary of Interior, November 22, 1897, RI, Roll 37.

28. Major W.H. Clapp to Additional Farmers, no date, RI, Roll 37.

29. Acting Commissioner Thomas P. Smith to Captain Wm. H. Clapp, May 25, 1897, RI, Roll 37.

30. V.T. McGillycuddy to Clapp, October 2, 1897; V.T. McGillycuddy to Welsh, October 16, 1897; V.T. McGillycuddy to Welsh, October 18, 1897, IRAP Series 1-A, Reel 13.

31. V.T. McGillycuddy to Clapp, October 2, 1897, IRAP, Series 1-A, Reel 13.

32. Ibid.

33. V.T. McGillycuddy to Welsh, October 9, 1897, IRAP Series 1-A, Reel 13.

34. Clapp to Welsh, January 18, 1898, IRAP Series 1-A, Reel 13.

35. W.W. Anderson to Secretary of Interior, July 30, 1897, RI, Roll 37.

36. Major W.H. Clapp to Additional Farmers, no date, RI, Roll 37.

37. McLaughlin to CIA, August 19, 1897, RI, Roll 37.

38. Ibid.

39. John Brennan to CIA, October 19, 1903, Special Case 191 Leasing, Pine Ridge, 1900–1907, RG 75 NA. In response to complaints about trespassing stock in 1903, Secretary-Treasurer Stewart of the WSDSGA recommended a fence be built along the western boundary of the reservation as well or that an arrangement be made so that settlers could pay a grazing fee as they did on neighboring Rosebud

Reservation. Stewart to Brennan, October 15, 1903, Special Case 191 Leasing, Pine Ridge, 1900–1907, RG 75 NA.

40. F.M. Stewart to Brennan, October 15, 1903, Special Case 191 Leasing, 1901–1907, RG 75 NA.

41. George Sword to McGillycuddy, June 6, 1889, McGillycuddy Collection, OLC. Thomas Biolsi, 1992 p. 52, reports that the Council was organized ca. 1891. Dates for McGillycuddy's tenure as Agent from RCIA 1879, p. 37 and RCIA 1886, p. 76.

42. The "sell or starve" threats that the U.S. made induced only a few to sign the so called Agreement of 1876. The "Agreement" was a cover for confiscation; there was no attempt to secure the signatures of the three-fourths of the adult males that Article 12 of the 1868 Fort Laramie Treaty stipulated must agree to any land cession. Cf. Utley 1963, p. 41 regarding "thinly veiled threats of intimidation" that the U.S. used to secure the "Agreement of 1876." Article 12 of the 1868 Fort Laramie Treaty states in part: "No treaty for the cession of any portion or part of the reservation herein described which may be held in common shall be of any validity or force as against the said Indians, unless executed and signed by at least three-fourths of all the adult male Indians, occupying or interested in the same. . . ."

43. Report of proceedings of 1903 Oglala Council meeting.

44. Gerald One Feather at a meeting of the Institutional Development Committee on traditional governance at Oglala Lakota College, March 1994.

45. Report of proceedings of 1903 Oglala Council meeting.

46. Ibid.

47. Author's notes. Cf. also Oglala Council to Secretary of Interior and CIA, November 10, 1900, Special Case 191 Leasing, Pine Ridge, 1900–1907, RG 75 NA.

48. Memorandum of Meeting of the Old Treaty Council, no date (probably 1936), File 062, MDF-PR.

49. Oglala Council to Brennan, May 3, 1915, File 064, MDF-PR; Jermark to Ralph Case, February 24, 1926, File 062, MDF-PR; Acting CIA Larrabee to Brennan, April 21, 1907, File L-Land, Jan-Dec 1906, Box 23, KC; Special Agent in Charge Jenkins to CIA, October 23, 1900, 75-33-053 to 80965-22-054 1907–1939, CCF.

50. Special Agent in Charge Jenkins to CIA, October 23, 1900, 75-33-053 to 80965-22-054 1907–1939, CCF.

51. Brennan To CIA, March 28, 1907, 75-33-053 to 80965-22-054 1907–1939, CCF.

52. Ibid.

53. Brennan to CIA, June 24, 1909, 75-33-053 to 80965-22-054, 1907–1939, CCF.

54. Brennan to CIA, February 20, 1908, 75-33-053 to 80965-22-054, 1907–1939, CCF.

55. Brennan To CIA, March 28, 1907. 75-33-053 to 80965-22-054 1907–1939, CCF.

56. Ibid.

57. Charles Turning Hawk et al. to CIA, March 24, 1904, 75-33-053 to 80965-22-054 1907–1939, CCF. Acting CIA Larrabee to Brennan, April 26, 1907, 75-33-053 to 80965-22-054 1907–1939, CCF.

58. Acting CIA to Brennan, May 23, 1901, General Records, Land 1/8/1898 – 12/16/1904, KC; Acting Commissioner to Clapp, May 10, 1900, General Records, Land 1/8/1898 – 12/16/1904, KC.

59. Oglala Council to Secretary of Interior and CIA, November 10, 1900, Special Case 191 Leasing, Pine Ridge, 1900–1907, RG 75, NA.

60. Ibid.

61. 1891 Leasing Act , 26 U.S. Statute L. 795, discussed in Clow, Richmond 1987a, p. 23–24.

62. Brennan to CIA, December 3, 1900, Special Case 191 Leasing, Pine Ridge, 1900–1907, RG 75, NA.

63. Brennan to CIA, April 14, 1905, Special Case 191 Leasing, Pine Ridge, 1900–1907, RG 75, NA.

64. Brennan to CIA, November 17, 1906, Special Case 191 Leasing, Pine Ridge, 1900–1907, RG 75, NA.

65. Brennan to CIA, March 28, 1907, 75-33-053 to 80965-22-054 1907–1939, CCF.

66. Lee and Williams 1964, p. 223, 224.

67. Cf. Clow, Richmond 1987a.

68. Brennan to Kills A Hundred and Thomas Black Bear, May 24, 1904, Special Case 191 Leasing, Pine Ridge, 1900–1907, RG 75 NA. A township is 36 sections of land. A section is 640 acres.

69. Acting CIA to Brennan, November 15, 1902, General Records, Land 1/8/1898 – 12/16/1904, KC.

70. Petition, dated May 30, 1904, Special Case 191 Leasing, Pine Ridge, 1900–1907, RG 75 NA.

71. Brennan to CIA, July 7, 1904, Special Case 191 Leasing, Pine Ridge, 1900–1907, RG 75 NA.

72. Acting CIA to Brennan, July 16, 1904, General Records, Land 1/8/1898 – 12/16/1904, KC.

73. Boesl to Brennan, March 25, 1905, Special Case 191 Leasing, Pine Ridge, 1900–1907, RG 75 NA.

74. Charles Turning Hawk to Indian Rights Association, January 3, 1903, IRAP Series 1-A, Reel 16.

75. George Fire Thunder to Sniffen, January 30, 1905, IRAP Series 1-A, Reel 18.

76. Committee of the Oglala Council to Herbert Welsh, Indian Rights Association, January 12, 1905, Special Case 191 Leasing, Pine Ridge, 1900–1907, RG 75 NA.

77. Reverend Cleveland in an interview with M.K. Sniffen, Sniffen's report on his visit to Dakota, September 1905, IRAP Series 1-A, Reel 18.

78. Petition in support of permitting on Pine Ridge Reservation, 1905, Special Case 191 Leasing, Pine Ridge, 1900–1907, RG 75 NA. The wording on the petition circulated by the Oglala Council was clear: It was addressed to the Commissioner of Indian Affairs and said, in English, that the signers ". . . being adult males of twenty-one years of age or over, hereby respectfully request and petition that you do not enter into an agreement or agreements for the leasing of our surplus and unused

tribal lands. . . ." Petition against leasing, March 18, 1905, Special Case 191 Leasing, Pine Ridge, 1900–1907, RG 75 NA.

79. George Fire Thunder to Sniffen, January 30, 1905 and February 21, 1905, IRAP Series 1-A, Reel 18.

80. George Fire Thunder to Sniffen, February 21, 1905, IRAP Series 1-A, Reel 18.

81. Petition against leasing, March 18, 1905, Special Case 191 Leasing, Pine Ridge, 1900–1907, RG 75 NA.

82. Brennan to CIA, April 14, 1905, Special Case 191 Leasing, Pine Ridge, 1900–1907, RG 75 NA.

83. George Fire Thunder to Sniffen, May 1, 1905, IRAP, Series 1-A, Reel 18.

84. Brosius to Fire Thunder, May 9, 1905, IRAP Series 1-A, Reel 18.

85. Oglala Council to CIA, March 18, 1905, Special Case 191 Leasing, Pine Ridge, 1900–1907, RG 75 NA.

86. A typical strategy in the colonial field was to belittle the "native" political and legal systems, sometimes even with the conscious attitude that by so doing, confidence in indigenous structures could be eroded. Cf. for example Wallace, Anthony F.C. 1972, p. 197–198.

87. RCIA 1910, M1011, Roll 106.

88. Ibid.

89. RCIA 1910; RCIA 1913, M1011, Roll 106.

90. Chapter 5 details the advent of big leasing on Pine Ridge Reservation.

91. George Fire Thunder to Sniffen, January 30, 1905; February 21, 1905; February 24, 1905; February 25, 1905; March 3, 1905; March 18, 1905; March 27, 1905; May 1, 1905, IRAP Series 1-A, Reel 18. Sniffen's report on his visit to Dakota, September 1905, Entry for September 25, 1905, interview with George Fire Thunder, IRAP Series 1-A, Reel 18.

92. Sniffen's report on his visit to Dakota, September 1905, Entry for September 25, 1905, interview with George Fire Thunder, IRAP Series 1-A, Reel 18.

93. Charles Turning Hawk to Welsh, December 15, 1902, IRAP Series 1-A Reel 16; Charles Turning Hawk to Sniffen, July 16, 1915, IRAP Series 1-A, Reel 30.

94. Charles Turning Hawk to Indian Rights Association, January 3 1903, IRAP Series 1-A, Reel 16.

95. Ibid.

96. Sniffen's report on his visit to Dakota, September 1905, Entry for September 25, 1905, interview with George Fire Thunder, IRAP Series 1-A, Reel 18.

97. Sniffen's report on his visit to Dakota, September 1905, Entry for September 22, 1905, interview with Reverend Johnson, IRAP Series 1-A, Reel 18.

98. George Fire Thunder to Sniffen, January 30, 1905, IRAP, Series 1-A, Reel 18.

99. George Fire Thunder to Sniffen, January 1, 1906, IRAP, Series 1-A, Reel 18. George Fire Thunder to Sniffen, Jan. 26, 1907, IRAP, Series 1-A, Reel 19.

100. Lee and Williams, 1964, p. 236. An interesting commentary on boss farmers is in Sniffen's notes of his interview with Fire Thunder: "According to Fire Thunder, Smoot has been thirty years among the Indians, and is always talking about this. When some bridge work was to be done Smoot said the Indians could not work and he would have white men for it. Fire Thunder said, in effect: 'It does not speak well

for you. You have been among the Indians thirty years teaching them, and they can not work. That don't speak well for you." Sniffen's report on his visit to Dakota, September 1905, Entry for September 25, 1905, interview with George Fire Thunder, IRAP Series 1-A, Reel 18.

101. George Fire Thunder to Sniffen, February 21, 1905, IRAP Series 1-A, Reel 18.

102. Sniffen's report on his visit to Dakota, September 1905, Entry for September 25, 1905, interview with George Fire Thunder, IRAP Series 1-A, Reel 18.

103. Lee and Williams 1964, p. 225, 453.

104. Ibid., p. 246.

105. Ibid,. p. 245–246.

106. 1897 Hearing, RI, Roll 37.

107. Lee and Williams 1964, p. 454.

108. *Oglala Light*, October 1917, No. 2.

109. Quoted in Lee and Williams 1964, p. 137.

110. South Dakota became a state in 1889.

111. Sniffen's report on his visit to Dakota, September 1905, Entry for September 25, 1905, interview with George Fire Thunder, IRAP Series 1-A, Reel 18. Lee and Williams 1964, p. 236.

112. Brennan to CIA, January 8, 1909, 1907–1939, PR 9514-37—54 to 7406-30-056, CCF.

113. George Little Wound to Welsh, December 9, 1902, IRAP Series 1-A, Reel 16.

114. Lawrence Bull Bear to Sniffen, April 18, 1906, IRAP Series 1-A, Reel 18.

115. Henry 'Standing Bear to Sniffen, June 24, 1913, IRAP Series 1-A, Reel 27.

116. Turning Hawk to Welsh, December 15, 1902, IRAP Series 1-A, Reel 16. Charles Turning Hawk to Sniffen, July 16, 1915, IRAP Series 1-A, Reel 30.

117. George Fire Thunder to Sniffen, January 1, 1906, IRAP Series 1-A, Reel 18. Henry Standing Bear to Sniffen, June 24, 1913, IRAP Series 1-A, Reel 27.

118. George Fire Thunder to Sniffen, January 1, 1906, IRAP Series 1-A, Reel 18.

119. 1897 Hearing, RI, Roll 37.

120. Author's fieldnotes.

121. Brennan to Farmers, August 2, 1913, File 530, Box 631, A Bunch of Miscellaneous Stock Stuff 1912–1914, MDF-PR.

122. *Oglala Light*, December 1915, No. 4

123. Rose Bernhardt to Brosius, October 13, 1912, IRAP, Series 1-A, Reel 26.

124. Proceedings of the Council of Indians effecting Agreement of 1889. Chas. Foster, Wm. Warner, And George Crook Commission, Box 779, KC.

125. Joseph Fast Horse to Welsh, February 27, 1888, IRAP Series 1-A, Reel 3.

126. Reverend Charles S. Cook to Welsh, October 26, 1887, IRAP Series 1-A, Reel 2.

127. See discussion in Chapter 2.

128. Petition to the Secretary of the Interior, dated March 26, 1894, Box 780, Legal and Legislative Records, Petitions, KC.

129. Agents reflexively cited non-progressivism as the reason for opposition to government policies they favored. Thus, for example, Agent McGillycuddy ascribed Oglala opposition to allotment provisions in the preposterous "Sioux Land

Agreement" of 1883, to ". . . non-progressives led by Red Cloud and other 'ancients" . . . The Indians opposing the agreement at the Pine Ridge Agency consist most decidedly of the non-progressive element, the ones who cling to the ancient customs, the chiefs and tribal system. . . ." Agent McGillycuddy to James H. Teller, Esq., Dated 1883, McGillycuddy Collection, OLC.

130. Kills A Hundred to CIA, 1904, Special Case 191 Leasing, Pine Ridge, 1900–1907, RG 75 NA.

131. RCIA 1904, p. 330.

132. Bates to Commissioner of Indian Affairs, November 13, 1907 and December 18, 1907, Letter Books, Volume 1, KC. See chapter 3 for more discussion on the allotment issue.

133. George Fire Thunder to Sniffen, January 30, 1905, IRAP, Series 1-A, Reel 18.

134. Henry Standing Bear to Welsh, April 29, 1894, IRAP Series 1-A, Reel 11. Henry Standing Bear to Herbert Welsh, January 31, 1896, IRAP Series 1-A, Reel 12.

135. At the time, 1894, most mixed blood Oglala had European surnames. Today, of course, many of those considered to be mixed blood have Lakota names.

136. See for example, Oglala Council to Secretary of Interior and CIA, November 10, 1900, Special Case 191 Leasing, Pine Ridge, 1900–1907, RG 75 NA.

137. McLaughlin to Secretary of Interior, April 19, 1909, Pine Ridge c1909-363 to Pipestone c1909-238, BIA Inspector Division – Inspection Reports 1908–1940, RG 75 NA; Gay, Robert 1987, p. 3, 6.

138. Gay, Robert 1987, p. 8. The opening rested on the Allotment Act, which provided that reservation land in excess of that needed to supply individual allotments, could be declared "surplus" and thereby "ceded" to the U.S. In addition, the Lone Wolf case held that the U.S. had plenary powers, which included the power to abrogate treaties.

139. *Booster*, Vol. 1, No. 19, Feb. 7, 1912; Vol. 1, No. 21, Feb. 21, 1912; Vol. 1, No. 22, Feb. 28, 1912; Vol. 1, No. 23, March 6, 1912.

140. *Booster*, Vol 1, No. 22, February 28, 1912.

141. *Booster*, Vol 1, No. 1, October 4, 1911.

142. *Booster*, Vol 1, No. 2, 1911.

143. *Booster*, Vol 1, No. 28, April 10, 1912.

144. Ursula Gaertner, personal communication, 1994.

145. Hoxie, Frederick E. 1992a, 1992b.

146. DeMallie, Raymond 1978, p. 297.

147. Clow, Richmond 1987b, p. 125.

148. Ibid.

149. Section 1, paragraph b, under Article IV, "Powers of the Council," of the "Constitution and By-Laws of the Oglala Sioux Tribe of the Pine Ridge Resrvation, South Dakota," reads as follows: To employ legal counsel for the protection and advancement, of the rights of the Oglala Sioux Tribe and its members, the choice of counsel and fixing of fees to be subject to the approval of the Secretary of the Interior" (copy in possession of the author).

150. Cf. Barsh, Russel Lawrence 1991a, and 1991b for discussion of OIA's assimilative, domesticating intent regarding IRA governments.
151. Hyde, George 1956, p. 213.

CHAPTER 5

Doing Their Patriotic Duty:
The World War I Takeover of Oglala lands

"Whatever land-tenure pattern prevails in a given area, it is the landless and the near-landless who are on the bottom."
Erik Eckholm

"It is hard to be a landowner."
Severt Young Bear, Sr.

OUTSIDERS TAKE OVER OGLALA LAND

The Oglala Council successfully beat back attempts to lease the Pine Ridge Reservation in the first decade of the century, but the victory was short-lived. Wholesale leasing was ushered in with a vengeance during World War I. Use of allotted land by outside cattlemen skyrocketed from 50,000 acres in 1913, to 500,000 acres in 1917, to over 2,000,000 acres in 1918. By 1919 the Superintendent reported that ". . . all land has now been leased or applied for." The importance of cattle to Oglala subsistence had declined as dramatically as outside use of the reservation land base rose. Though cattle were the main source of support for the Oglala in 1914, only a few Oglala, mostly mixed bloods, owned cattle by 1920.[1] The number of Oglala making their living principally from stock raising plummeted from 3,548 in 1911, to 368 in 1917; the number depending on stock raising for partial support declined from 2,718 in 1911, to 988 in 1917.[2] The economy of cattle, horses, gardens, and wild hay that had provided a measure of self-sufficiency vanished like ice on a summer day, and almost overnight outside cattlemen gained control over the lands of Oglala allottees.

The sharp rise in leasing of allotted land on Pine Ridge Reservation is explained in two different ways in the literature, and in a third way in the oral history. One view suggests that the Oglala sold cattle herds in order to cash in on the higher World War I meat prices, and then turned to leasing. George Hyde was the first to make that argument:

> most of the Sioux full-bloods lacked the shrewdness of white men. They were like children, ready to sell their cattle at any price when a whim to buy something took them, and spending their money for useless articles that took their fancy. . . For a few years they lived lavishly, spending on every whim. Salesmen tempted them, and the reservation was soon invaded by fleets of new and shiny Fords. . . They had now sold nearly all their cattle and many families were facing starvation.[3]

Besides faulting the Oglala, Hyde blamed the OIA for letting the situation run its course. It was the fault of ". . . the officials that the Indians, having been induced to sell their cattle, leased their lands to white men and sat down to live on their rents."[4] In other words, it was the folly of Oglala landowners, and the failure of OIA paternalism that separated Oglala landowners from control over their allotments. Like Hyde, Raymond DeMallie reported that higher wartime meat prices and a desire for material goods enticed the Oglala into selling their herds, leaving them in a state of dependency.[5] Similarly, Robert Utley concluded that "the high beef prices of World War I lured them into selling their herds and plunging once more into poverty."[6]

Thomas Biolsi recently advanced a different explanation for large-scale leasing. Unlike Hyde, DeMallie, and Utley, he is not concerned with the issue of what happened to Oglala cattle, because his main argument hinges on the dependency of the Oglala within the framework of an artificial reservation economy, an economy that did not, in his view, afford self-sufficiency anyway. Biolsi contends that leasing was a rational response by Lakota allottees who were unable to make good economic use of their lands because allotments were scattered, and the people lacked capital. He accepts the official line, that the OIA considered leasing of allotments "an evil," and explains the fact that most of the Pine Ridge Reservation had been leased to white ranchers by 1918, as an outcome of calculated individual decisions by Oglala allottees.[7] It was, he argued, "more profitable for an allottee to rent land to non-Indian operators than to work it himself."[8]

Oglala oral accounts offer yet another view of the loss of their cattle herds and of the advent of the big lease era. Oglala elder Russell Loud Hawk's view, similar to others often heard, holds that "The cattle herds were forcibly rounded up and sold off in 1916 and 1917. People had no choice in the matter. The old people say this. The reason it was done was that other cattle interests wanted to get the land. The whole history of the land could be boiled down to the fact that white people want it." Some, like William Horn Cloud, recalled that the people resisted the leasing of their land. As for the lease money owed by the big cattle operations, oral accounts like those of Oglala elder Johnson Holy Rock hold that the people never received the lease money they were owed.[9]

Another view of the circumstances surrounding the issue of Oglala-owned cattle, presented in the previous chapter, argues that those cattle declined in the years preceding World War I, a period when the cattle market was relatively depressed, as a result of a cattle ring operating on the reservation. Yet to be examined are the factors that lay behind and surround the large-scale leasing of the reservation land base. Some of the initial questions that need to be answered are: Was the OIA a passive bystander in the affair, as Hyde and Biolsi suggest, or did it play a more active role? Did the Oglala willingly lease their land or were they forced? Was it more profitable for the Oglala to lease their land than to work it? Is there support for Holy Rock's contention that lease monies owed were not even paid? After their lands were leased to white men, did the Oglala "sit down to live on their rents," as Hyde suggested, or did they resist big leasing, as William Horn Cloud maintained? Did the OIA do something along the lines suggested by Russell Loud Hawk, to create an opportunity for "cattle interests [that] wanted to get the land?" Or, was big leasing an outcome of economic processes that incorporated reservations into the capitalist economic system, and federal policies that paved the way for corporations and outside interests to gain control over Indian lands and resources, as Joseph Jorgensen's use of dependency theory to explain underdevelopment on reservations would suggest?[10] Finding out why, when and how outsiders gained control over the reservation land base requires a corrective history of the big lease era on Pine Ridge Reservation.

WHOSE LAND AFTER ALL?

In the spring of 1918 big cattle outfits from Wyoming, South Dakota, and Nebraska took control over 1,000,000 plus acres of allotted land on Pine Ridge Reservation. In May and June their drovers herded between 75,000 to 100,000 head of cattle, horses, and sheep onto the holdings of several thousand Oglala allottees. The bawling of cattle and the trampling of gardens around their homes were probably the first indications that Oglala landowners had that the use of their land had been secured for others (see Map 6). Even though Pine Ridge Indian Superintendent Henry Tidwell signed agreements with the cattle operators in December of 1917,[11] the first notice that the Oglala had about the deal came from the boss farmers in mid-April, two weeks before the big herds were scheduled to be driven onto their allotted land. The only indication of official notification in the records is an April 12, 1918, letter from Superintendent Tidwell to the boss farmers:

> I wish you would give notice to such Indian [sic] of your District as have allotments within the Townships given in the attached sheet that all of the following have been granted proper authority from the Indian Office to turn cattle, sheep or horses on this land for the months of May, June, July, August, September and October, and be charged a trespass fee in lieu of a lease at the same rate per acre as under a grazing lease: Newcastle Live Stock Co., W.D. McKeon, E.E. Mead, Earl Updike, Thomas F. Arnold, Lance Creek Cattle Co. That the reason for this action is on account of lack of sufficient clerical help to turn out all the leases for these people within the time required. Regular leases will commence November 1st, 1918, but in the meantime, these people will be allowed the use of the land under a trespass fee. Such trespass fee will be paid into this office by these different outfits and then

Map 6: The Enclosure of Oglala Land

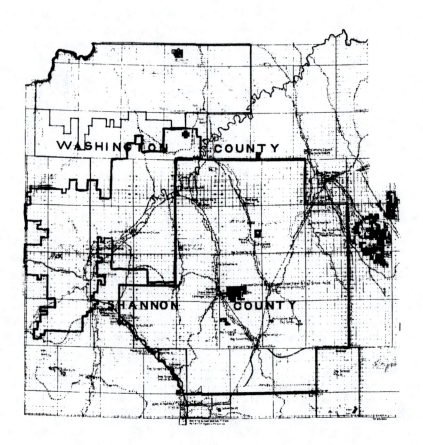

Detail of trespass areas turned over to three outside lessees by the OIA in 1917 and 1918. The enclosed areas included the allotments, the homesites, and the creeks that were the main source of water for Oglala landowners. Thomas F. Arnold's pasture was in the extreme upper left. The Brown and Weare outfit had the pasture below Arnold's. W.D. McKoen's Newcastle Land and Stock Company, the "7L," had the largest tespass area, encompassing over 19 townships, an area of about 438,000 acres of land, land "owned" by Oglala allottees. Detail of map is from 1914 OIA map of Pine Ridge Reservation. Copy in Oglala Lakota College Archives. Areas under trespass reconstructed by the author from the trespass agreements noted in the text of this chapter.

disbursed to the Indians whose lands are being used. Therefore, any cattle, sheep or horses belonging to any of these outfits should be permitted to graze for the above months pending the completion of their leases, and all Indians having allotments within this territory should be advised of this.[12]

The 47 townships, or 1,082,880 acres of land, marked for legalized trespass represented 37% of the area within the original boundaries of the reservation.[13] Such was the "proper authority" of the Indian Department, that it could set aside the property rights of several thousand Oglala allottees in order to secure their lands for the use of six outside cattle concerns – all without executing a single lease.

Wartime conditions had driven the cattle market sharply upward in 1918, and interest in reservation grasslands was high.[14] In addition to the one-million plus acres of allotted land the OIA had designated for legalized trespass, one-million more allotted acres were scheduled to be leased by the end of the year. By 1920, Inspector John Bale reported that outside stock interests had leased most of the reservation. Overall, about 6,000 Oglala allotments had been leased, or, more correctly, secured for the use of outside cattlemen through agreements and legalized trespass arrangements negotiated by OIA officials. Under the circumstances, Bale concluded, the Oglala "had little say so over their lands."[15]

Besides having had absolutely no role in the decision making that turned their allotments over to the large cattle concerns in the first place, Oglala allottees soon found that collection of the trespass and lease fees that had been promised them by the OIA was anything but assured. The Agency claimed that the delay in collections was due to the massive amount of paperwork required for executing 6,000 individual leases.

The Agency, as Tidwell had pointed out in his letter to the boss farmers announcing the imminent arrival of outside cattle, was short on clerical help. That problem had been anticipated even before the agreements that let the outside cattlemen onto the reservation had been signed. As part of the negotiations that led to the trespass agreement for the big outfits that came onto the reservation in 1918, those outfits had ". . . agreed to furnish the necessary help to prepare these separate leases and to pay for same at their own expense."[16] Half a century later, John Glover, who was the manager of the Newcastle Land and Livestock Company's Quarter Circle 7L, the biggest outfit that ever operated on Pine Ridge Reservation, recalled that they did assist in the lease work in the summer of 1918. He and a lease clerk from the Agency spent a day each in the five districts and got so many lease agreements signed that they ". . . had bales of them as big as a bale of hay."[17] The Agency also tapped vacationing "school boys and girls" for the lease work.[18]

But even the joint efforts of school children, cattlemen, and the U.S. government failed to accomplish the task. By September, 1919, only 2,000 of the 6,000 leases needed were in force. Newcastle's 7L outfit, (7L" was Newcastle's brand) had been using about 438,000 acres of allotted land for seventeen months, but only 20% of the lease money had been collected, a situation that reflected the uncompleted lease agreements. Newcastle's director, W.D. McKoen, told Inspector Linnen that he was "perfectly willing to pay" and would, as soon as the lease agreements were executed.[19] There was no mention made of the bales of signed leases Glover remembered.

The U.S. government's inability to handle the leasing situation it had created compounded the problems of Oglala landowners. Outsiders controlled their land and they got precious little in return. In 1919, the Pine Ridge Agency took in about $178,000 in lease money for the 2,000,000 acres of Oglala allotments that were being leased.[20] At the time, lessees submitted lease money directly to the Agency, where it went into the IIM (Individual Indian Money) accounts for disbursing to allottees. Had that money been divided up equally among the 6,000 allottees whose lands were being leased, each would have realized $29.80. But that money was apparently for the 2,000 allotments for which leases had been executed; nothing could be collected for the other 4,000 until the leases were approved.

The trespass fees that had been promised in lieu of lease money did not take up the slack. Superintendent Tidwell's tardy announcement of the advent of the big leasers stated that "Regular leases will commence November 1st, 1918, but in the meantime, these people will be allowed the use of the land under a trespass fee. Such trespass fee will be paid into this office by these different outfits and then disbursed to the Indians whose lands are being used." It was an empty promise. None of those fees were even collected until the fall of 1918, and then the only fees that were collected were for those lands for which leases had been executed. A year later the situation remained the same; in September 1919, Tidwell reported that "There are a great many cases at the present time where trespass is still due and will be collected by this office for the allottees as soon as the area that he is to lease is determined."[21]

In November, 1920, two years after the expiration of the trespass agreement, and despite Tidwell's assurances, outside cattlemen continued to enjoy free use of a substantial portion of Oglala land on Pine Ridge Reservation. For one thing, there were still "quite a deal of allotted lands where Indians failed or refused to sign lease contracts," and those lands were within the pastures that the government's agreements had reserved for the lessees. Even in cases where leases had been executed, there was no guarantee of payment. Inspector Bale characterized the monies Oglala did realize from leasing as a "pittance," but Agency control over the situation was such in 1920 that there was not even any way to determine how much lease money was being collected.[22] That state of affairs came about as a result of collaboration between cattle interests and the OIA.

In 1919, 7L boss W.D. McKoen floated a proposal with OIA Inspector Linnen to reduce the work load that leasing placed on Agency personnel. Why not have the Oglala collect their lease money directly from the lessees and save a lot of work for the Agency clerks, he suggested? The Indian Department must have thought it was a good idea, because in March 1920, the CIA directed that allottees whose lease amounted to less than $200.00 per annum should collect their lease money directly from the lessees. Thus the OIA, which had proven less than proficient at the task, declared Oglala landowners "competent" for the purpose of collecting their own lease money.[23]

Tidwell surely welcomed the work-saving measure, and did what he could to make his work load, and that of the lessees, even lighter. Although he prepared a letter asking the lessees to forward receipts for lease monies they disbursed to the Agency, he did not send it. Instead, he instructed the lessees to keep their receipts so that "'. . . at any time this office deems it advisable to call on you for information concerning same you can readily furnish it.'" Showing some degree of prescience, he remarked that "'No doubt numerous complaints will be made that these rentals are not paid and if you are not possessed of the above information, this office must hold that same has not been paid by you, AND WILL DEMAND PAYMENT.'" Inspector Bale took a dim view of Tidwell's doings; he doubted ". . . whether the courts will agree with Mr. Tidwell in enforcing a payment on demand if a lessee cannot produce a check or returned receipt . . . and upon hearing the burden would be upon the plaintiff or claimant to show that his lease money was not only due but unpaid. This burden would not be upon the lessee."[24] In addition, Bale noted, some of the lessees were already in default before the Oglalas were declared competent to collect their own lease money. The Brown Cattle Company was $16,000 in arrears, and several smaller lessees were in default to the Agency. As for the monies owed to allottees, Bale concluded that "There is no way of ascertaining how much any lessee leasing from an Indian declared competent to collect his rental is in default with the individual Indian."[25]

The evidence shows that Oglala allottees were no more successful in getting their lease money directly from lessees than they were when the Agency acted as collection agent for leases. Oglala complaints about the failure of lessees to make good their lease payments were legion. A January 18, 1921 petition by 122 Oglalas from Wounded Knee District, for example, pointed out that they had not received their lease money, even though some of them had seen the lessees as many as five times without being able to secure payments. The petitioners recommended that the lessees be instructed to mail the checks to the Agency or to the boss farmers. Finally, in March 1923, three years after declaring all adult allottees competent for purposes of collecting their grazing leases, Tidwell reversed the policy. Once again, he advised, lease checks should be forwarded to his office, as, he artfully put it: "In a great many cases, the lessee overlooked making the payments . . . [or] lessors have forgotten [that they received payment]."[26] Another factor that figured in this situation was the fact that many Oglala men were serving in the U.S. Army; they certainly had no way to try to collect lease money from delinquent ranchers.

In addition, the practice of refusing to pay the trespass fees that were owed to allottees until a lease was signed kept some Oglala landowners from getting any payment at all from outsiders for the use of their land. It was a classic Catch-22 for allottees. If they refused to sign a lease, or if a lease had not been executed for some other reason (such as the alleged clerical bottleneck), the Agency would not release the trespass payment.[27] That practice was a convenient club that the Agency used to pressure allottees to sign a lease, the terms of which they had no control over.

In April 1920, Oglala allottee John White Wolf told his story to the CIA:

> The Superintendent has leased my allotment for five years. He did this without my knowledge or consent. I am a full blood Indian, about 47 years of age, I have a wife and three children. . . . The McKeon Cattle Company cattle destroyed seven stacks of hay for me so that my stock are without feed and I have no hay to sell. They have run over my land for two years feeding on the grass and I have not received any pay for the use of this land, and I have been damaged also. I am living upon this land, my allotment that the Superintendent leased, and the cattlemen and the agency official force have tried to run me off my land by having the cattle run over me, my land, garden, and crops. I want the cattle removed from my land, I want the lease that the agent made cancelled, and I want to be paid for all the damages that they have done to me, my land, garden, grass, stock and hay . . . My son, Charlie White Wolf, is living with me and he has no allotment, so that the only home he has is with me upon my allotment, and that has been given to the cattle company by the Superintendent in charge of the reservation. We are hard up, cold and hungry, in need of clothes and everything to live upon. There is no work because the cattle company has taken all the lands for miles around and they destroyed the meadows which furnished hay, and there is no work of putting up hay, and the pasture land has been overstocked so that it will take years to make the grass good again.[28]

Tidwell did not bother to deny any of what White Wolf told the Commissioner. He merely pointed out that White Wolf had refused to sign the lease he was offered, and that if he would not sign, and did not want his land used by cattlemen, he would have to fence it out at his expense. Once the fence was complete, Tidwell said, White Wolf could collect the trespass fee for the period the land had been used. After all, White Wolf's allotment covered a section of land and it would have been, ". . . unfair to require the Newcastle Company [i.e., McKoen's 7L outfit] to fence out this whole section, requiring four miles of fence. The Indian Office in such cases instructed that we advise the allottee to take steps to fence off his own land to turn the stock belonging to a lessee." Yet the Indian Office exempted lessees themselves from meeting the requirement of fencing off the perimeters of their "agreed on" trespass areas because of the difficulty of obtaining the necessary fencing material in wartime. It was April, 1920 when Tidwell told Assistant CIA Meritt that White Wolf should fence off his own allotment, which required four miles of fence. In a September 1919 letter to Inspector Linnen, Tidwell excused the failure of cattlemen to accomplish the much more modest requirement of fencing out the garden plots of allottees, maintaining that fencing materials were hard to get and labor was scarce. White Wolf, Tidwell implied, should acquiesce: "The quickest way for White Wolf to get this back pay is to come in and sign his leases." White Wolf said he thought the Superintendent had signed a lease, since the land was being used beyond the period of the government enforced trespass period. But because no lease had been executed, there was no lease money – just a de facto transfer of control over White Wolf's land to an outsider. Assistant CIA Meritt's reply to White Wolf essentially repeated Tidwell's message. White Wolf did finally receive $25.00 for the loss of his hay, but that did not cover his loss.[29]

Widespread loss of hay to large herds of stock owned by outside cattle outfits preempted Oglala use of their land base for grazing their own cattle. As John White Wolf's case illustrates, it also deprived them from realizing profit from the hay that they had been in the habit of harvesting. In cases where damages were awarded for loss of hay to lessees cattle, the amounts represented only a fraction of what Oglalas formerly realized for the sale of hay they cut from their lands. In 1919, Manual [sic] Martinez, an Oglala mixed blood, and his wife, Mary Martinez, from Porcupine District, testified that their land had been leased against their will. Lessees' cattle had eaten the hay Mr. Martinez customarily harvested from the 960 acres his family owned (i.e., one and one-half sections of land: probably the 640 acres he was allotted as head of household and the 320 his wife was allotted as spouse of head of household). He had been realizing between $500 and $600 per year through the sale of that hay; he was told that under the terms of the forced lease they should realize $48.00 a year for the 960 acres, but three years had passed and not a cent had ever been paid.[30]

After the takeover of the reservation land base, even when Oglalas were able to cut hay and to safeguard it from the ravages of roaming cattle, they were unable to realize its worth. White traders (nine of the ten traders on the reservation in 1920 were white), who were major purchasers of hay, paid minimal amounts for it. W.D. McKoen, the biggest lessee on the reservation, avoided markups by such middlemen. He managed the Porcupine Trading Post himself and paid just $6.00 a ton for hay.[31]

The cumulative effects of OIA agreements with outside cattlemen for the use of Oglala land, plus regulations and practices that kept Oglala landowners from using their own allotted lands, devastated the mixed subsistence economy of full blood Oglalas, and of mixed bloods like the Martinez'. Even those Oglalas who had capital to invest and who wanted to lease land in addition to their own allotments were cut out by the OIA. According to Fred Badger of Porcupine District, who had been an Agency policeman for 16 years, the Agency ignored the applications of his daughter and of other Oglalas who applied for leases at the going rate.[32] But in the deteriorating economic regime few had any capital at all to invest. Even the many Oglalas who turned to land sales did not realize control over sizeable funds. In 1920, Mrs. Beulah Tidwell, wife of the Superintendent and in control of the Individual Indian Money (IIM) accounts, reported to Inspector Bale that there were 5,859 open accounts, with $3,143,031.91 on hand as of September 30, 1920. The bulk of that sum represented land sales and estates. Oglalas with land sale money on the books were given a monthly allowance of $20. Under the circumstances those funds went for necessaries at inflated rates. None of the ten traders on the reservation were obeying federal regulations that mandated the publication of price lists; merchants in the village of Dewing, about a mile and a half from Pine Ridge Village but too long a trip for people living in the reservation Districts, were selling goods for much lower prices.[33]

When John Red Feather from Wakpamni District needed some money so that he could work some land, he attempted to access the proceeds from his deceased daughter's estate. What he found out, and apparently only after a number of attempts, was that the money, which amounted to $200, had been used to purchase Liberty Bonds. When he complained at a public hearing, OIA Special Agent Lee Ellis explained that he had been

> ... authorized by the Secretary of the Interior to invest in those bonds from the estates of deceased Indians. That is why this $200 was taken. John came to me the other day, and I told him that the $200 was drawing 4 per cent interest – $4 every six months. The records will show that; and Mr. Tidwell has the bond. I could invest my money [sic] at that time and get more interest, but it was our duty to support the Government.[34]

Among the obstacles the OIA erected against Oglala control over their own resources were the regulations and practices surrounding the leasing of allotments of minor children. Allotments of minor children, which some families customarily used for grazing their stock or which were used communally before wholesale leasing of the reservation, were leased at the discretion of the Superintendent. In 1919, when George Bettelyoun, a mixed blood with a patent in fee to his own land and thus a U.S. citizen, asked to control the allotments of his minor children so that he could graze his cattle on them, Assistant CIA Meritt advised him

. . . that the issuance of such a patent [i.e., patent in fee] to you does not authorize you to supervise the interests of your minor children; however, if you desire the privilege of leasing their lands independent of the agency officials, it is suggested that you make application therefor [sic], through the Superintendent on form 5-180C, and the matter of granting you this privilege will then be given proper consideration.[35]

In 1920, when Oglala Council delegates Charles Turning Hawk, Joseph Horn Cloud, Iron Hail Stone and Henry Standing Bear pointed out to Commissioner of Indian Affairs Cato Sells that such practices posed problems for the people and constituted inequitable treatment in comparison with that afforded white men, even in cases where an Oglala had been granted a fee patent to land and U.S. citizenship conferred, Sells responded that:

". . . the Supreme Court of the U.S. has held that citizenship is not inconsistent with wardship, – that is, even though an Indian may be a citizen of the U.S. and of the State [sic] in which he resides, under proper circumstances the relation of guardian and ward between the Government and such citizen Indian still exists so far as may be necessary to protect his interests and welfare, and to this extent, the Government may still exercise control over his person and property.[36]

When Oglala Council member Henry Standing Bear's 1918 request to lease the allotments of his minor children was denied by Superintendent Henry Tidwell, he wrote a letter of protest to Commissioner Sells. The Carlisle-educated, returned student explained that he had already lined up a lessee for his children's land, and that he planned on leasing it one year at a time. That way, he said, the property might eventually bring fifty cents an acre, and be of considerably more help to his children than the flat rate of fifteen cents per acre for five years at a stretch, the terms the Agency had negotiated.

Typically in such cases, the Superintendent was asked to make a reply to the Commissioner, and his office responded in turn to the complainant. Tidwell was adamant that Standing Bear's request should be denied and that he should sign "regular Government leases." He donned his social worker's hat, claiming that Standing Bear just wanted the money from the lease for himself anyway, and that he would not use the money to help out his minor children.[37] Yes, he agreed, allottees should ". . . receive as much for their land as it is reasonably worth," but, he continued, he did ". . . not think it a good plan that one Indian should play a hold-up game," because others would hear of it and try it too, and then to their detriment many pastures would not be leased at all. Tidwell's comments are echoed in Assistant CIA Meritt's reply to Standing Bear. He sent Standing Bear a copy of the regulations governing leasing, noted that even in cases where authority to lease allotments of minor children had been given, it could be revoked "if deemed advisable," and pointed out that leases negotiated by parents or guardians on behalf of minor children could be declined by the Superintendent, "if he thinks it proper to do so."[38]

The formidable array of institutional obstacles limiting Oglala access to their land and to money capital was augmented by the practices of the boss farmers, the sub-agents in the reservation Districts who were essentially colonial administrators at the local level.[39] Even after World War II the boss farmers exercised control over the expenditure of money that was distributed through federal government channels. Freda Apple, an Oglala elder from Medicine Root District, detailed her own experience:

> On my eighteenth birthday I remember that 'I'm free now, I'm free now' I kept saying to myself. And I had $700 [from the Sioux Benefit fund]. I remember that when I was 18 years old that boss farmer system was still there because he decided what I was gonna buy. . . . He was kind of a stern, real sober faced guy. I remember I was scared of him when I was making out my budget, you know, for my $700. We never saw the cash. It was given out in purchase orders. My brother said 'Why don't you buy some cows, so we could maybe raise cows. ' So I told this boss farmer I wanted to buy cows with my $700. He said 'No. In the first place,' he said, 'you wouldn't be able to take care of them because your brother's away and you and your mother are alone. He evidently knew all about our family structure, you know, our family affairs. . . . They didn't understand that Luke [her older brother] is the head of the family for us. . . . 'You could get one cow and you could take care of him,' he said. So I bought one cow and I bought a team of horses and two saddle horses and I bought a saddle and a bridle and a saddle blanket and then I had only about $150 left so I bought a sewing machine for my mother. I didn't tell the boss farmer that but I told him I wanted a sewing machine . . . the rest went into clothing.[40]

Mrs. Apple figured that the boss farmer let her buy horses because they already "had some horses." Though the boss farmer knew "all about their family affairs," he "didn't understand that Luke is the head of the family for us." The boss farmer did not understand (or approve of?) the *tiospaye*; "That's where the breakup [of the *tiospaye*] comes in."[41] At any rate, his practices, were geared toward the patriarchal, nuclear family.[42]

The big leasing era of World War I constituted a virtual confiscation (though temporary) of Pine Ridge Reservation allotted lands by the OIA for outside cattle interests, revealing the depth of oppression on Pine Ridge Reservation. Denying Oglalas control over their own land and capital was a textbook case of the colonial process at work; small wonder that Oglala elders today often sum up the antics of the federal government with the phrase "They don't want to see Mr. Indian get ahead."[43]

LEASING AND THE PLAIN FACTS: A SOCIAL AND
ENVIRONMENTAL CATASTROPHE

"The reservation is covered with cattle like a whole lot of worms on it. I cannot raise any garden and cannot do anything. The Superintendent went as far as to try to put some Indians in jail for driving cattle from their gardens."

James H. Red Cloud

Never before, not even during the 1890's when thousands of outside stock trespassed regularly, had there been so many grazing animals on the reservation as in 1918. Figured at the official stocking rate of one head for each fifteen acres, the total number of outside stock grazing on the 2,000,000 leased acres in 1918 would have been 133,000 plus. Those, in addition to the 15,000 head of hereford cattle bearing the I.D. brand (Indian Department Brand – owned by the Oglala), the majority of which were owned by mixed bloods, would have brought the total number of stock, exclusive of Oglala-owned horses, on reservation lands to 148,000. But that is a conservative estimate. The number was probably substantially higher because some cattle operators, looking to cash in on higher wartime prices, overstocked their leases.[44] The huge influx of grazing animals, and the circumstances under which they were brought in and managed, was a formula for a social and ecological nightmare.

Outside stock destroyed allottees' pastures, ate up and trampled down their crops and gardens, and fed on the wild hay that they had customarily harvested for sale and for overwintering their own stock. Stock owned by Oglala mixed in with outside stock and were lost or shipped off to market. The creeks the people depended on for drinking water and for irrigation were fouled with organic matter.[45] OIA Inspectors investigating the situation on the reservation were deluged with complaints. In 1919 Inspector Linnen reported that "Endless complaints were being made by the numerous Indians about their crops being eaten up and destroyed by the lessees' stock."[46] Inspector Bale reported ". . . innumerable complaints and small claims filed by individual Indians for trespass, loss of gardens, loss of hay, etc."[47] Big leasing was literally eating away the foundation of Oglala self-sufficiency.

So serious was the situation that it had, OIA Inspector H. Traylor concluded, become "impossible for the Indian to attempt cultivation of crops and garden [sic] adjacent to these pastures, so long as they are stocked with range cattle which have no respect for any fence." Day school teachers told him that the cattle completely destroyed their gardens, despite careful watching. The range cattle were unlike the more stolid, heavy-bodied, domestic beef cattle that you are likely to see along a country road in the U.S. today. They were the leggy and rangy descendants of the feral herds of Texas Longhorns that became the staple of the range cattle industry once they were rounded up by enterprising men after the Civil War. According to the cattlemen Inspector Traylor talked with during his October 1919 visit to Pine Ridge, those animals knew ". . . little or nothing about barb wire and fences and pay no attention to it. . . . When they get it into their heads to move, especially in a storm, it is impossible to prevent it." When a storm hit during his visit, Traylor found out he was not being sold a bill of goods. "I personally saw scores of hay stacks which were being destroyed by the cattle having broken the fences, even though the storm was only two or three days old."[48]

Some of the worst damage wrought by outside stock occurred along the creeks, where sub-irrigated and irrigated crop and garden plots were grown and where *tiospaye* settlements had clustered when the land was allotted. Those creeks were a magnet for thirsty stock. Stock drank from the creeks, lingered in nearby areas to graze, ran through and broke down fences allottees erected to protect their gardens, destroyed the gardens, and fouled the vicinity with their wastes. Thus the ravages of outside stock were particularly acute in the areas where Oglala *tiospaye* were located, where the people lived. In some cases the grasses were completely grazed off and the land rendered useless. Inspector Traylor confirmed such conditions for the allotments of "Mousseau and Mrs. Red Willow" in Eagle Nest District; he was outraged. He argued that "Any allottee who must have his grass destroyed and his land trampled as hard as a brickyard, should receive enough compensation from the lessee to justify him in having his allotment thus treated."[49]

Oglala landowners never received monetary awards for the serious, long-term damages their land sustained, but they did occasionally get compensation for losses to property caused by the depredations of outside stock. But even instances of that were few. Moreover, when investigations were done, and damage claims substantiated, the process was slow and the awards paltry. Samuel Red Dog filed one of the successful claims.

In September 1920, Red Dog filed a claim alleging that cattle from the McKoen outfit and from J.J. Linehan's had broken through the fence he had around his 1.5 acres of corn in White Clay District and had destroyed his crop. He lined up six witnesses to support him and filed a complaint with the boss farmer. The farmer investigated immediately, found for Red Dog, and told him to take the matter up with the lessees. He did, asking them for a total of $75.00 in damages, which they refused to pay. Red Dog apparently followed up on the matter, and in February, five months after the complaint was filed, the boss farmer sent McKoen a statement detailing the destruction of Red Dog's corn. Red Dog still had not gotten satisfaction in March when Agency Detective E.L. Rosecrans visited with him and estimated the worth of Red Dog's lost corn at $14.20. Linehan's share was set at $1.20, and McKoen's at $13.00. Linehan agreed to pay but McKoen's outfit initially refused. Only after Superintendent Tidwell wrote to McKoen, closing his letter "very respectfully," did John Glover, McKoen's manager, agree to send a check for $13.00.[50]

Most complainants did not fare as well as Red Dog. Inspector Bale believed that in "quite a few of these cases," even where the findings were for the allottees, lessees failed to settle.[51] The circumstances placed Oglala landowners at a distinct disadvantage. Although their land had been leased, it was the federal government that had leased it; it was the government, and not the landowner, that the lessees recognized when it came to claims for damage. Assuming for the sake of argument, that the government's excuse that it lacked the necessary clerical help to execute the needed leases was true, then there were surely not enough government personnel to properly handle the "innumerable and endless complaints" of individual Oglala allottees either. A government that lacked sufficient political will and resources to execute leases certainly would not and could not be expected to fairly and energetically handle voluminous Oglala claims against lessees. (See section titled "Who Or What Was Responsible?" for discussion of other factors that mitigated against a fair and expeditious handling of Oglala complaints.)

Besides undermining the economy and devastating the environment, big leasing precipitated serious public health problems. By 1922, four years after the introduction of outside stock, OIA Inspector Brandon reported that both trachoma (an infectious disease of the eyes that can lead to blindness) and tuberculosis had ". . . almost reached a permanent epidemic stage," affecting 13% of the population. A 1924 U.S. government health report found that "Trachoma is directly traceable to the fact that the Indians are without soap and without pure water. The water supply generally is the creeks or river; such water seldom being clear and free from organic matter."[52] When Oglalas controlled the land livestock did not pose a serious public health threat. In 1910, the year Oglala-owned stock peaked at 60,000 cattle and horses combined, two "old and chronic cases" of trachoma were reported for the entire reservation.

There had never been sufficient medical care on the reservation, but by 1924, under a regime of deteriorating public health, the two Agency physicians that provided services for over 7,000 Oglala had their hands full. The 1924 government health report concluded that "Practically every Indian on the reservation is undernourished."[53] Significantly perhaps, Clark Wissler's careful demographic analysis of a community of about 1,000 Oglalas on Pine Ridge Reservation shows an increase in the death rate/1,000 from 28 for the period 1908–1915, to 37 for the period 1916–1925.[54]

The decline of environmental, economic, and physical health attendant the takeover of the reservation land base had dramatic impacts on Oglala social organization as well. Though data are scarce, Inspector John Bale's 1920 account is suggestive:

... the lease system in force on this reservation has absolutely demor-
alized domestic conditions. It is true the Indian has been getting a pittance for leasing his land, but he has done so to the absolute destruction of home life at the present. It would be far better, if the Indian is
'land poor' that portions of his land be sold, reserving a sufficiency for
his home and building him a home and encouraging him to live on it,
than the policy of encouraging him to lease his land and wander from
place to place.[55]

Big leasing brought an end to the subsistence cattle economy that many
Oglala full bloods had depended on, an economy that had already been
eroded by the combined effects of trespassing, the workings of the reservation system, and OIA corruption.[56] The implementation of CIA Cato Sells'
1917 Policy Declaration, that all Native Americans with one-half or more
white blood should be declared competent and issued fee patents to their
land, was coincident with the heyday of the big leasers on Pine Ridge
Reservation. Once certified as competent, most of those individuals soon
lost their land, either through outright sale, loss to taxes, or under cloudy
circumstances, joining the ranks of a growing number of landless Oglala
mixed bloods. Those two factors, the creation of a large class of landed,
albeit land-poor, Oglala full bloods, and of landless Oglala mixed bloods,
both differentiated and created the symbolic materials that have been
seized upon as one of several factors that Oglalas use to distinguish
between mixed blood and full blood until the present day. In the words of
one Oglala full blood in 1985, "Land, language, culture, history, and roots
are what makes you Lakota. In order to be Lakota you have to have land,
to speak Lakota, to practice culture. You also have to be part of a *tiospaye*
– you have a history as part of the community. You are with your *weuno-
takuye* (relations of my blood)." In the words of an Oglala mixed blood
in 1991, "Full bloods have land but it doesn't mean anything to them. They
don't use it and a lot of them just want to sell it."[57]

But while most Oglala mixed bloods and full bloods suffered losses during the big lease era, some of those who came to the Pine Ridge area with
large herds of cattle in the latter part of the nineteenth century held onto
some of their stock. They were the Oglala who owned the majority of the
Indian-owned cattle on the reservation in 1920 – the 15,000 head of here-
fords Inspector Bale referred to in his report for that year.[58]

OGLALA RESISTANCE AND U.S. RESPONSE

"Innumerable and endless" complaints by individual Oglala did not add up
to a serious challenge to the leasing situation. To paraphrase Vine Deloria
Jr., "You can't take back the Black Hills by asking the enemy for a camping permit."[59] Besides lodging individual claims for damages to their land
and property, the Oglala pursued several collective strategies aimed at
reestablishing Oglala control over the reservation land base. They worked

both inside and outside the system in an effort to influence the Indian Department and to disrupt the operations of the big leasers. Working through the Oglala Omniciye and through reservation districts, they petitioned against leasing, sent delegations to Washington D.C. to register protests with OIA officials, and provided formal testimony about the abuses of cattlemen and government officials. Other actions were aimed directly at the outsiders who were using Oglala land. The Oglala often refused to work for the cattlemen, burned the rangelands they used without Oglala permission, tore down the fences they erected, and rustled their cattle.

The Indian Department dispatched a series of Inspectors to the reservation in those years and conducted several hearings. Eighty-five Oglala, representing each of the reservation's seven districts, testified at the largest of those hearings, at Mission Flats, north of Pine Ridge Village, on August 20 and 22, 1919. The hearing at Mission Flats was convened by the CIA pursuant Oglala requests. OIA Inspector E.B. Linnen presided. Several other OIA officials, including Charles Ellis, the Special Agent who worked hard to facilitate big leasing on the reservation between Agent John Brennan's and Superintendent Henry Tidwell's tenure, and E.L. Rosecrans, the Agency Stock Detective, attended. William Garnett served as the official interpreter.[60] In addition to accounts of property losses similar to those contained in individual damage claims, the speeches Oglala landowners made described their experiences with lessees and government officials, and laid out their analyses of the situation.

White Cow Bull of White Clay District testified that although he had refused to lease his land, McKoen's stock were trespassing on it without his permission. "Two droves or bands of sheep were near my place the last part of June 1919. I told the herders to keep them off my place. They come on – a large number – and when I went to drive them off, the stockman's rider, Thos. Huslde, abused and used me and tried to pull me off my horse and threatened to strike me." The stock that McKoen's drovers herded across White Cow Bull's land had destroyed his hay. He requested a damage payment for the trespass, but received none.[61]

Silas Fills The Pipe reported similar conditions in Wounded Knee District:

> My name is Silas Fills The Pipe, but my father's name is Red Dog [a tiospaye leader in Wounded Knee District]. . . . I have found out that the lessees and the farmers can do anything with this land that they please. I live on a piece of this land and have three quarter sections under fence. One day one of McKoen's men drove a herd of sheep through my fence and they got into what I had inside the fence. Well, I took a stick and started to chase the sheep out of my fence, and the herder made a dash for me on horseback, with a big stick, and spoke in loud angry tones. I was on foot with no means of protection and seeing such a well armed [sic] man charging me, I made up my mind that

my time had come and I was prepared to meet my God (applause and laughter). Of course, you know I am a preacher myself. Well, I kept on going and did not flinch and the herder I guess changed his mind about dispatching me, and just barely missed running over me, only making a menacing motion with the stick. I made up my mind that these people had taken possession and I came back to my house and let the sheep go. The herder kept the sheep inside my fence all day and in the evening he drove them off after they had gotten away with all my hay and destroyed my garden. His attitude towards me was that he dared me to protect my own property . . . I live on the Cheyenne River and there are any number of my people living there who have undergone similar treatment . . . I want my trust patent which I handed you a moment ago, I was going to let you take it back with you so you can have the title changed, but I guess I will take it back (applause and laughter).[62]

Fills the Pipe's use of his trust patent (deeds for trust land are held in Washington D.C.) to dramatize the fact that control over land had been severed from ownership was vintage Oglala humor. Some Oglalas today make a point of injecting humor into their public discourse, often commenting explicitly that "Indian humor" is what helps people overcome the difficulties they face.

Clayton High Wolf, a missionary in Porcupine District for twelve years, also addressed the violent behavior of cattlemen in his summary of problems associated with big leasing:

. . . there has been a great deal of discontent among the Indians on account of this leasing, and this year especially the feeling among them that they are being abused by the stockmen, and not getting proper protection from the Agency officials, has made them more discontented. I now share this same feeling. There are three things I wish to mention. The lessees have been running their cattle on lands which are not leased, and also on Church property. Second, they do not like to pay damages, and third, the Indians do not get their money, and they keep the telephone busy because the lessees do not pay the lease money – sometimes six months overdue . . . The conditions are such that young men have stopped farming, and there is a great deal of suffering.[63]

High Wolf's contention, that the behavior of cattlemen was not being addressed by Agency officials, surfaced repeatedly at the hearing. Short Bull, of White Clay District, suggested that the OIA had abdicated in favor of the cattlemen:

Our country is full of cattle running on land that is not leased . . . We have farmers and other officials to look after our affairs, but they are unable to do anything for the reason that the cattlemen are in control. The lessees seem to have everything their own way, and the Superintendent is powerless, and has no control over the Reservation

... It seems that the majority of the officials at the Agency are in agreement with these cattlemen. We have councils, and talk over these
matters, and have told the Superintendent, but we find him powerless.[64]

Testimony by Oglala mixed blood Thomas Flood, the boss farmer in
White Clay District, and who was a former Secretary of the Oglala
Council, advanced his explanation for the cattlemen's exemption from the
rule of law. The biggest lessee, W.D. McKoen, Flood said, went over the
heads of people in the Agency. "I guess influence is brought to bear through
members of Congress. . . . Indians come to the Farmer to complain; what
can the farmers do?"[65]

But Charles Turning Hawk, former President of the Oglala Council, was
not about to let the local officials abdicate their responsibility for the situation.

> We don't want this Superintendent and don't want Rosecrans [sic],
> Stock Detective. They don't work to our interest. We don't get our
> lease money. Promised same and disappointed and dissatisfied. All of
> the Indians now have bad hearts. We are being fooled and feel bad and
> I speak for my people. Got the young men to work on the roads and
> don't pay they. We are not slaves or in captivity. I talk for the whole
> reservation.[66]

Lawrence Bull Bear spelled out other problems that the Superintendent
and the cattlemen were responsible for. The Superintendent, Bull Bear said,
leased land that the the people refused to lease, and did nothing to insure
that lease agreements were kept. Stockmen, he claimed, were fencing
". . . the land without a lease and turn their cattle and sheep on the land,
and get away with the range." That was what had happened to the allotments of "Jeffery Otaapela, Wallace Henry Pawnee Leggins, Thomas Blue
Bird, Amos Parts His Hair, John Little Soldier, Frog, Peter Chief Eagle,
Peter Red Eagle, Elmore Red Eyes, Yellow Wolf, Red Eyes, Daniel Red
Eyes, and others." McKoen's outfit fenced in those lands in Medicine Root
District, along American Horse Creek, even though no agreement had been
executed. Bull Bear testified that in other cases where the people had not
wanted to lease their land,

> The Agent tells the Indians to fence up their land and of course, hav-
> ing no means to do it with, they give up after all those cattle and sheep
> are turned loose on them, and they go and lease their land since they
> know they have no one to protect them or help them collect damages.
> I had a meadow, but the stock belonging to McKoen got away with it,
> and I have no hay[67]

The August 1919 testimony at Mission Flats distilled the collective dissatisfaction of Oglala landowners, and provided the OIA with a compre-
hensive and damning indictment of big leasing. During the hearing Red
Cloud's grandson, James Red Cloud, in accord with the tradition of per-

sonalizing such exchanges, raised the issue of whether the proceedings were indeed a good faith effort: "Our friend tells us he would look into things that will be of benefit to us. I want to ask you what we are, animals or men?" Inspector Linnen's reply was stiff: "You are people, and I believe the majority of you are good people, whom the Indian Office is duty bound to protect."[68] Duty bound or not, no remedy was forthcoming; it was business as usual for the Indian Department.

In March, 1920, James Red Cloud and other Oglala Council delegates met with Assistant CIA Meritt in Washington D.C., to once again assail the leasing of the reservation land base and to ask that it be stopped. Red Cloud maintained that the federal government ". . . forced us to lease it. Some of us wanted to use it but they stopped us and the Superintendents combined and forced us." Red Cloud rebutted Meritt's retort that "No Indian allottee is forced to lease his land," saying, "The Superintendent there has done it. Some of them didn't know their land was leased." Meritt, who had been in his position since 1917, asked for names claiming it was ". . . very easy to make charges but we find that a number of these charges are without foundation. We want the plain facts."[69]

An October 1994 description of Bureau of Indian Affairs' officials by three Oglalas from Porcupine portrays them as ". . . sometimes listening, and having nice things to say, but not following up their words with actions." One man said, "The Bureau is soft. You can hit it and it just absorbs the punch."[70]

Sometimes the Indian Department's response was just to flatly deny that problems existed. The following exchange is from the meeting that James Red Cloud, Calico, and Joseph Horn Cloud had with Assistant CIA Meritt in Washington, D.C., on March 31, 1920:

Red Cloud:

> We think there is going to be trouble on our reservation. Some are dying. About the time of the war you wanted us to lease our lands on account of the war, for beef to be used to provide for the soldiers that was at war. At the end of the war that lease ought to be ended. Old and young want more, and old women and children have money in that Office and it is held there. We can't get it. Some are hard up for clothing and eatables. Some are starving and some almost naked.

Meritt:

> I was on the Pine Ridge Reservation last summer and saw a number of Indians and I did not meet up with the conditions that you speak of.

Red Cloud:

> I heard that you was there and I came there and you was already gone. You didn't stay long.

Meritt:

> I was on the Pine Ridge Reservation for over a day – spent the night there. We will look into the matter of holding back the individual funds of the Indians.[71]

On the occasion of another meeting, this time at the Pine Ridge Agency one month later, Meritt seemed a changed man:

> We sympathize deeply with the Indians on the Pine Ridge Reservation because of the conditions that have existed on that Reservation as a result of leasing to cattle men. Now that the war is over, however, we are endeavoring to the limit of our power to see that the contracts are complied with, and to see that the money due the Indians is paid. As I have said before, we are sending an Inspector there . . . we think within the next three months conditions will be very materially improved and the Indians will have no unusual grounds for complaint. Those leases are all going to be checked up and the terms complied with – strictly.[72]

But whose terms? When John White Wolf wanted to exclude his allotment from lease he was told that he needed to fence it off himself. Tidwell, it will be recalled, claimed that he had been so directed by the Indian Department. But when CIA Cato Sells replied to complaints expressed at the April 1920 hearing at Pine Ridge Agency, in a letter to Charles Turning Hawk, Joseph Horn Cloud, Iron Hail Stone, and Henry Standing Bear, and dated the same day as Tidwell's letter to the CIA regarding White Wolf's complaint, he contradicted that statement saying "The Indians should not be disrupted by cattle of outside stockmen, who should recognize the rights of the Indians and keep their cattle off land that is not leased."[73] But his underling, Assistant CIA E.B. Meritt, was supporting Tidwell's version in his own letter to White Wolf on June 11, 1920.[74] This kind of confusion, or "softness" is part of what some Oglalas today refer to as the "Indian Run Around."[75]

The fact that Oglalas from every reservation District participated in the Mission Flats hearing is suggestive of the ongoing Oglala capacity to organize around reservation-wide issues. The choice of Mission Flats as a meeting ground, instead of Pine Ridge Agency, is significant. Mission Flats, several miles north of Pine Ridge Agency, had been used as a meeting place by the Oglala Council in the past. The Oglala Council itself was involved in the effort to marshall information and to designate speakers. This recognition came despite the fact Superintendent Henry Tidwell, acting with CIA concurrence, had outlawed the Oglala Council in 1918, replacing it with an elected council of 21 delegates. The new council was meant to be a paper organization only, and the infrequent meetings were called only at Superintendent Henry Tidwell's discretion. It must have rankled Tidwell that Thomas Flood of White Clay District, Clayton High Wolf of

Porcupine District, and Clarence Three Stars of LaCreek District, three of the 28 Oglala who spoke at the hearing, were members of the council he created. Three Stars, in fact, had been designated its President. The Mission Flats hearing gave them a forum that Tidwell's Council, which had only been allowed to meet once since the election of March 19, 1918, did not.[76]

The Oglala Council had proven itself a tenacious foe of outside interests intent on taking over reservation land in its struggle against the leasing proposals pushed by Agent John Brennan in the first decade of the century. More recently, at what was apparently a joint meeting between the Oglala Council and the Rosebud Council, held at White River on the Rosebud Reservation, which adjoins Pine Ridge Reservation on its eastern boundary, it was resolved that certain leasing provisions should be enforced in regard to leases made to "white men and cattle companies." Such leases were, the Council contended, ". . . troublesome all the way through for the farmers [i.e., boss farmers], Superintendent and the stock Inspector, and after all the owners of the land don't get much money and his or her allotment remains without any fences or improvements." Therefore, the Council concluded in its written report addressed to the Indian Office through the Pine Ridge Superintendent, all such leases should ". . . be fenced with a good substantial fence."[77] The Oglala Council's unswerving resolve to insure that the reservation land base serve the needs of the Oglala people may be what moved Brennan's successor, Superintendent Henry Tidwell, to move against it. In February, 1918, oblivious to Brennan's 1909 assessment that even if the Oglala Council were disbanded, it would continue to meet in some other guise, he obtained permission from the CIA to eliminate it, and to proceed with his plan to replace it with a new Council that would have three elected delegates from each reservation district.[78]

Tidwell claimed that his action was taken in the interests of Oglala unity. Different factions, he said, were representing themselves as leaders of the Oglala Council. With quintessential paternalism, in a letter ironically addressed to "Citizens of the OST," Tidwell explained himself: "Realizing that it was to the best interest of the Indians themselves that these factions be united if possible, I immediately began a study of the situation to determine, if possible, what in my opinion, was best for them."[79] Tidwell's research showed him that the best thing for the Oglala was a puppet council that would meet at his pleasure, and under his supervision, or not at all.[80] 532 ballots were cast in the March 19, 1918 election; the first meeting was held four months later. For the next fourteen months, at least, the Council was dormant because, Tidwell explained, ". . . no matters of a tribal nature have arisen that I felt would justify me in assembling this council. . . ."[81]

The outlawed Oglala Council made requests for OIA sanction and recognition for its meetings and constitution but those were denied, both by Superintendent Tidwell and by CIA Charles Burke. But, unlike the elected Council, which was obedient to Tidwell's control, the outlawed Oglala Council continued to meet.[82] Its long-standing position against the wholesale leasing of reservation land to outsiders continued to be articulated by Oglala leaders who supported the outlawed Council. Among the business the outlawed Oglala Council took up at its February 17, 1920, meeting was the denial of tribal rights for three mixed bloods from LaCreek District, and a decision to send seven delegates to Washington to lobby against leasing. Collections made in the various districts provided $425.86 for the trip. Such actions helped insure that the voices of prominent Oglala leaders, including those of James Red Cloud, William Spotted Crow, Charles Turning Hawk, Henry Standing Bear, and Joseph Horn Cloud, all of whom had been active with the outlawed Council, would continue to be raised against the regime of big leasing at hearings on the reservation and in Washington, D.C.[83] (See the following chapter for more details about the evolution of the Oglala Council and about the role of the U.S. government in manipulating Oglala political organization.)

One of the ways Oglalas protested big leasing was through petitions.[84] Petitions were filed against leasing in protest of the lack of payment for leases and for the removal of Superintendent Tidwell. One petition was addressed to the Secretary of the Interior on behalf of the people of Medicine Root District shortly after the advent of outside stock in April, 1918:

> We the undersigned delegates of Kyle, S.D. authorized by the people to protest against leasing of Medicine Root District to five persons from Wyoming for the following reasons: including preventing Indian stock raisers from getting water and grass in future; That many of the Indians utilize the Streams for drinking purposes and fear spreading of disease from the animals on account of no water available . . . The charge per acre for trespass being the same as that of leasing price per acre is a secondhanded price and is not a benefit to the Indians. That, stock will damage young trees and wild berries and prevent the Indians from utilizing this food for future use . . . Leaseholders dishonest not doing straight things with the Indian people and no administrator has ever been look after the interests of the Indian people during the past. We therefore oppose the leasing of the people from the State of Wyoming.[85]

The petition was addressed to the Secretary of the Interior through Tidwell and transmitted to Tidwell under a cover letter from the Medicine Root District boss farmer, L.L. Smith. Smith received the petition from Otto Chief Eagle. Chief Eagle had long been active with the Oglala Council and served as President in 1916.

Tidwell likely felt kinship with Smith upon reading his depiction of Chief Eagle: "Otto is one of our Oglala Council or as Mr. Bates [Charles Bates, the Chief Allotting Agent for Pine Ridge Reservation] used to say our Oglala kickers." In the eyes of the OIA, of course, the Oglala Council no longer had any legal right to exist, having been outlawed in March. The petition probably never made it to the Secretary of the Interior. Another, which Chief Eagle sent through Tidwell in 1919, protesting both Tidwell and the continued leasing, was simply answered by Tidwell himself "as though he, Tidwell, were the Secretary of the Interior," Chief Eagle said.[86] Chief Eagle and others bypassed Tidwell in February 1922, submitting a petition directly to the Commissioner of Indian Affairs:

> We, the undersigned Indians of Medicine Root District Pine Ridge Reservation South Dakota, Hereby respectfully "Petition" your honor for justice on the following grievances, Our lands have been leased at the instance [sic] of your Office to the white cattle people, who have violated their contracts on the leases in various manners hereby Indians suffered loss of money and damages of various kinds, Therefore, we earnestly pray and request that all these cases be placed immediately in the hands of the United States District Attorney for the purpose of suing for damages and for nonpayments arising from this lease and Trespasses on our lands.[87]

Commissioner Charles Burke did reply, suggesting to Chief Eagle that he talk with Tidwell, and noting for Tidwell that, "Various inspectors who have visited Pine Ridge have recommended that the practice of leasing so many allotments be discontinued so far as possible and that the Indians be encouraged to make use of the land themselves. What if anything, do you think can be done along this line [sic]." Tidwell's four page, single-spaced answer apparently satisfied Burke (or brought the bureaucratic dictum of CYA [cover your action] to completion). Of the 101 persons from Medicine Root District who signed the petition, Tidwell told Burke, "I believe it is safe to say that very few, if any, of the individuals who signed the petition have any real trouble. . . ." Chief Eagle, he said, was just making the most of the difficult economic situation, which gave ". . . additional opportunity for agitators and elements . . . who are working for personal ends as well as to work dissatisfaction among the Indians."[88]

The petitioning efforts during the big lease era represented activity at the district and community (sub-district) level. There is no record or indication of efforts comparable in scale to those of the large, reservation-wide petition drives that the Oglala Council mustered against outside leasing schemes in the first decade of the century. One reason may be that Tidwell's regime was particularly repressive. The written record indicates that he threatened to use force to stop meetings of the Oglala Council; oral accounts recount the use of the Indian Police to break up meetings. Tidwell also directed the boss farmers to prohibit Oglalas who were trying to raise money for lobbying efforts from engaging in public assembly.[89]

Some Oglalas used direct action to combat big leasing. Fire, evidently aimed at destroying the subsistence base for cattle, was the most dramatic weapon used. The Bennett County Board of Commissioners were concerned or frightened enough by the situation to resolve ". . . that the Indian Department be and is hereby requested to take drastic action to remove the peril by causing the removal of the ground of grievances." (Bennett County, on the eastern end of the Pine Ridge Reservation, contains a sizeable amount of farming land, and by the 1920s it was heavily settled by non-Indians.) The Commissioners believed that ". . . a large number of Indians on the Pine Ridge Reservation have widespread grievances against local Agency for failure to make distribution of annual lease money, and are menacing the reservation with devastation by fire, and many fires during the present autumn have occurred on the Reservation, all of which are of suspected of [sic] incendiary origin."[90] W.D. McKoen, manager of the 7L outfit, blamed the fires on ". . . a few mixed blood agitators who stir up friction, trouble and dissension."[91]

Less dramatic than fire, but more troublesome to cattlemen, was the widespread destruction of those fences that they did actually erect. In July of 1922 Tidwell expressed concern that ". . . fences erected by lessees in accord with provisions of their leases are being seriously damaged and in many cases removed by various Indians and others." The problem was not new. In 1919 McKoen claimed that of the 200 miles of fence that his outfit had erected, half had been torn down.[92] One possible explanation for the destruction of the fencing is that the fences kept lessees cattle in the huge pastures they had taken over under trespass agreements negotiated with the OIA, pastures that included many allotments that Oglala allottees did not want leased; another is that Oglalas were availing themselves of the materials they needed to fence their gardens and homes off against the ravages of stock.

In spite of Oglala resistance, the leasing situation did not improve. In April, 1922, the CIA agreed with Otto Chief Eagle that there were many delinquencies on leases and assured him that work was being done to collect them. In August, 1923, OIA Livestock Supervisor J.B. Wingfield reported "quite a lot of agitation" in Medicine Root District by Oglalas who were against both new leases and extensions of existing leases. Wingfield did not say what he made of that but a year earlier he had expressed concern that ". . . full blood Indians only have approximately one thousand head of cattle" and recommended ". . . keeping after the Indians with a sharp stick so they could be induced to raise lots of wheat." Exhibiting the instrumental and ahistorical view so common among technocrats and extension agents,[93] he concluded his letter to the CIA with: "If they can't or won't raise cattle it means farm, starve or leave the Reservation."

In 1925, their source of livelihood denied them, Iron Whiteman and Calico petitioned the CIA, noting that Treaty provisions had not been met and asking for increased rations because of the economic situation. Then

Pine Ridge Superintendent Jermark labeled them as "two of our older Indians whose point of view is usually reactionary." The CIA concurred, telling them that "It becomes necessary as time goes on for the Indians to adopt in a larger degree the kind of life lived by the white people. The amount of money that can be allowed to buy rations is so limited that only the very old and needy can be furnished with any rations at all, and it is not possible to allow them very much."[94]

WHO OR WHAT WAS RESPONSIBLE?

Oglala analyses of the problems they were experiencing with big leasing often turned on the role of local OIA officials. Much of the responsibility was placed on Superintendent Henry Tidwell, who was viewed as an ally of the cattle outfits. In 1918, George Holy Dance wrote to U.S. Senator Johnson, noting that he had travelled to the Agency on three separate occasions to see Tidwell about problems he was having with Fowler and Bailey, the cattle outfit that had leased his land. He said he had not seen any lease money for eighty acres they used, and that the same thing was happening to "every Indian." He wanted his eighty acres taken out of lease but Tidwell "don't want to have nothing to do with it."[95] During a meeting with Assistant Commissioner E.B. Meritt in Washington D.C., in March 1920, Calico, one of several Oglala Council delegates there to address reservation conditions, testified that Tidwell ". . . helps the stock men instead of us. When the Indians go there to have a talk with him he tells them he hasn't got the time and shuts the door. Lots of Indians are not satisfied with him. They want you to take him back where you got him from."[96] In April, testifying before the House Commission on Indian Affairs, Joseph Horn Cloud described how he had twice ridden 50 miles to Pine Ridge Agency to complain about non-payment of a farm lease but on each occasion Tidwell refused to talk with him.

> We go to the Superintendent's office to have a talk with him, and he tells us to get out; that he does not have time to talk to us. He wants to talk to white men there. I would like to ask you one question, and that is this, whether this office is there for the Indians, or for the white men?

Tidwell kept his interactions with tribal members to a minimum. He restricted Oglala access to the Agency Office to the hours of 11 to noon and 1 to 2 p.m., which perhaps afforded him something of a buffer, but certainly posed a definite hardship on those who were forced to travel long distances in order to address concerns about their land, their leases, their damage claims, their IIM (Individual Indian Money) accounts, and other matters.[97]

When Tidwell was around he got low marks from the Oglala for his public comportment. *Younihan* (respect) is an important Lakota value. Strong Talk singled out Tidwell's lack of respect in his testimony at Mission

Flats. "This summer our agent came back from a trip to Washington, and I went up to him and said 'How do you do Father?' and put out my hand to shake his hand, and he knocked my hand away and made some unpleasant remark. He hurt me to my heart. . . . If he keeps on that way there is going to be serious trouble some day."[98] And there was. An Oglala woman in one of my classes at Oglala Lakota College shared a story of how her grandfather, fed up with Tidwell's behavior, took action of his own. As her family tells it, her grandfather, a big man and slow to anger, went to Tidwell's office, bodily removed him, and escorted him to the reservation line.[99] Tidwell finally went too far. When he saw a young man running by the Pine Ridge Village cafe where he was taking supper, he jumped up, went outside, and yelled at him to stop. When the youth kept running Tidwell fired his pistol. He missed, but several eye witnesses said he had fired at the youth; Tidwell maintained he fired in the air, and argued that the failure of the youth to stop suggested to him that he may have been guilty of something.[100] Tidwell's lack of respect for Oglalas probably derived in part from his unabashed racism. In a 1921 letter to the Commissioner he complained about the work that ". . . the full-blood class of Indians, which of course includes the less intelligent. . . .," were doing on the Black Hills Claim.[101]

The shooting incident precipitated Tidwell's transfer to the Agency at Pawnee, Oklahoma, on April 1, 1924. That, plus his indebtedness, which had been a cause for concern in the Indian Department, and which had grown worse over the years, moved the CIA to act.[102] Tidwell was in arrears with several merchants, off of the reservation and on. Among his creditors were J.D. Corder and H.A. Dawson, white ranchers who owned stores in Pine Ridge Village.[103] Such conflicts of interest were the order of the day on Pine Ridge Reservation.

Among the grievances on an undated Oglala petition asking for the removal of Superintendent Tidwell was the following complaint against the Agency Stock Detective: "Our claims against cattlemen don't help us. Superintendent lets Rosecrans investigate them. He is president of the cattlemens association and he is against us. He sides in with the cattlemen every time and we have hard time to collect any damages. Rosecrans is stock detective but he don't work for us works for the cattlemen."[104] The reference to E.L. Rosecrans' presidency may have referred to a local cattlemen's association. James Craig, a white rancher, was the Western South Dakota Stock Grower's Association (WSDSGA) president at the time, but Rosecrans, the Agency Stock Detective who was charged with investigating complaints about trespassing stock, was a member of that organization's Executive Committee from 1919–1926. W.D. McKoen, the 7L boss, served on that Committee in 1920; Tom Arnold, who had a big spread on Pine Ridge Reservation, served from 1920–1924; and Tom Jones, who had earlier leased the entire Lower Brule Reservation with Scotty Phillips, served from 1914–1921. Of course Pine Ridge Agent John Brennan himself had served on the Executive Committee from 1915–1918. Overall, many WSDSGA members were running reservation leases.[105] It is certainly conceivable that Detective Rosecrans might have been influenced to serve interests other than those of the Oglala allottees who depended on him to investigate their claims against fellow Executive Board members like W.D. McKoen and Tom Arnold. Complaints against Rosecrans neither dislodged him nor improved his job performance. In 1925 OIA Special Inspector L.B. Roberts, Sr., noted that "When at Pine Ridge two years ago making an investigation, I had occasion to call on him [Rosecrans] for help, but he did not help me a particle and I thought then he was traveling under a misnomer, when called a Detective."[106]

Because local officials at Pine Ridge Agency were unwilling to vigorously pursue, or for that matter to seriously entertain, Oglala complaints about big leasing, they proved useful to cattle interests and to the OIA. They played important roles by taking up for outside interests against those of the Oglala, by carrying out OIA policies that disenfranchised Oglala landowners, by influencing the details of policy implementation in order to insure favorable outcomes for cattlemen, by their passive resistance to Oglala requests for assistance, and by merely being inept. The OIA certainly had no interest in insuring that its local officials were attentive to the rights of the Oglala. OIA inaction considered against the backdrop of the overlap, indeed, the congruence, between the reports of OIA Inspectors like John Bale and E.B. Linnen, and the testimony and complaints of the Oglala attested to that. In 1920, in the face of the voluminous evidence of gross mismanagement at Pine Ridge, Assistant C.I.A. E.B. Meritt could still testify to the Committee on Indian Affairs of the U.S. House of Representatives that Superintendent Tidwell was doing the best he could for the Oglala, and that the Indian Department had given him as much help as it could.[107]

That, of course, was to cover the OIA's role in events on the reservation. Tidwell was ostensibly removed because of his embarrassing personal misconduct, not for his incompetence or, for example, for his failure to protect the rights of Oglala allottees who he had insured through his willful mishandling of the record keeping attendant on lease collections and who would not be able to press for payments of delinquent lease money after they were declared competent to collect lease money. Tidwell's personal misconduct gave the OIA a convenient way to rid themselves of Tidwell – a chance to guard against further embarrassment over the big leasing fiasco. In the overall leasing drama, men like Agent Henry Tidwell and Stock Detective E.L. Rosecrans were minor players. They helped keep the system in place and were directly responsible for much of its repressive character, but their roles were essentially those of functionaries. Much of what led to the takeover of the reservation land base was already in place before they came on stage.

Just parallel to the decline of the subsistence cattle raising enterprise on Pine Ridge Reservation between 1915 and 1917, the cattle market was depressed. There was some recovery by 1917, and by 1918, South Dakota steers marketed in Chicago averaged $130.13 and cows averaged $64.75, increases of 60 and 21 percent, respectively, over 1914 prices[108] The upturn in the market and the under-stocked ranges on the reservation made for an irresistible combination for investors. The Interior Department began to ease the access of outside stock interests to reservation lands. In February, 1917, the Secretary of the Interior approved a request, originating with Agent John Brennan on behalf of John Riemers, for a waiver of the time limit on grazing regulations, so that lands could be leased for five years.[109] The April, 1917 edition of the *Oglala Light* exalted that "Leasing on Pine Ridge is on the boom. W.D. McKeon and John E. Mead [Meade] of New Castle, Wyo., and G.A. Brown and H.G. Weare, of Buffalo Gap, S.D., were at the agency office in March, making application for lease of three hundred thousand acres of Indian grazing land." In early May, Meade withdrew his offer of ten cents an acre for 100,000 acres, as he could not secure the consent of sufficient Oglala allottees to insure his stock a supply of water from the White River. Allottees in that vicinity were demanding from thirty to fifty cents an acre.[110]

But with President Woodrow Wilson's delivery of his war message to Congress on April 2, 1917, the leasing situation heated up rapidly.[111] On April 9, at a mass meeting at the YMCA hall in Pine Ridge Village, Inspector Linnen held forth about ". . . the part the Indians of the Reservation could play in the coming campaign in greater farming activities . . . Patriotic songs assisted in arousing the enthusiasm of those present, all feeling that tho' [sic] they may not be called to the colors, each can assist in some capacity in the struggle in which our country is entering."[112] In May, when Walter Scott expressed an interest in the lease Meade had wanted and encountered the same demands for higher rent from allottees, the Indian Office got involved on Scott's behalf. On May 24, 1917, the CIA telegrammed Agent Brennan, putting him on notice that the Indian Office was taking an interest in the case: "'Confer with Scott and secure definite response as quickly as possible relative to taking application Meade lease. Advise particulars relative to Indians advancing price for grazing on allotments.'" Brennan advised the CIA that if allottees refused to sign at the price offered, and that if lessees would not pay the price demanded, no lease could be entered into. He concluded with pointed sarcasm: "The consent, I am sure, of each allottee is essential and necessary to the proper completion of any lease."[113] Brennan's compunction about private property may be what led to led to the end of his long tenure in Pine Ridge. In August, just two months after Brennan made his position clear to the CIA, he was replaced by Special Agent C.L. Ellis, a man who shared none of Brennan's sensibilities about Oglala property rights.[114]

Special Agent Ellis got the leasing of Oglala allotments into high gear. On August 7, 1917, he informed the CIA that the Brown and Weare outfit, represented by Walter Scott, had ". . . accepted the entire 100,000 acres originally applied for by Mr. Meade . . . quite a few of Messrs. Brown and Weare leases have already been transmitted to your office." Meade reentered the picture several months later, signing an agreement for a large lease on December 19, 1917.[115] In a few short months Ellis had orchestrated the leasing of 950,000 acres and, in addition, obtained agreements for the leasing of "nearly a million acres." He estimated the nearly 2,000,000 acres would produce $220,000 in lease revenue. Even if all of that money had been collected, it would have yielded an average return of $36.67 to each Oglala allottee. Meanwhile, with grass-fed steers bringing $12.00 per CWT on the Omaha market in 1917, cattlemen were realizing windfall profits.[116] At the official stocking rate of one head per 15 acres, the allotment of an Oglala man, who had been allotted 640 acres as head of household, was being grazed by 42 head of cattle. Say, conservatively, that the owner shipped 15 steers to market in 1917, and if those steers weighed 900 pounds, he would have realized a gross profit of $1,620, just from the lease of the one allotment. At an average leasing fee of ten cents per acre, the allottee could theoretically have expected $64.00. Consider, too, that just a few years earlier, Oglala owned cattle were being sold for a song; now that the prices were high, most Oglalas had none to sell.

Soon after the first large herds of white-owned cattle were brought onto the reservation in 1917, Oglalas registered many complaints. OIA officials made all the right noises. After McKoen applied for the first of his large leases, Ellis cautioned him about living up to the fencing provisions of his lease arrangements, noting that "All of yesterday afternoon and part of today I listened to complaints from many Indians over the reservation of stock trespassing on their hay meadows, and destroying gardens they have planted, all because the tract was not properly fenced out as should have been done by the lessee."[117] In January 1918 C.I.A. Cato Sells cautioned Tidwell that although he was ". . . very desirous that all the grass on your reservation, as well as every other reservation, should be utilized to its fullest possible extent, but in doing this the interests of the Indians must not be disregarded. . . . " Tidwell calmed Sells' fears, telling him that the arrangements would not cause problems for the Oglala, as they lived along the creeks and rivers, and the cattlemen would fence as much land off as each allottee needed for his or her own use.[118]

After the damage was done the OIA used patriotism as a rationale. Inspector Bales' report contains a marvelous example:

> In the fall of 1917 the world was in the throes of war. . . .Millions of men were called from fields, shops and marts of trade to the colors. They had to be fed and clothed. . . .The eyes of the eastern world turned pleadingly to America with her fertile fields and vast prairies.

The patriotic cry went up from every heart and every throat, 'Make productive every acre of land in America.' It was as essential and as patriotic to produce food to sustain those who fought as it was to fight. In the midst of these circumstances and conditions, with every patriotic citizen of America doing all in his or her power to render available every resource of America, some of the cattle men of Wyoming, Montana, and elsewhere, having suffered from drought and lack of grass for their herds during previous years, and knowing of the splendid range on the Pine ridge Reservation, brought to bear with tremendous force and weight justifying the argument 'the world demands food production, and the grassy prairies on the Pine Ridge Reservation should be used for grazing purposes and production of beef cattle, rather than a training ground for Indians in various lines of husbandry and agricultural pursuits.' With conditions as they were at the time, the weight of the argument for utilizing all possible available land for production must be admitted.[119]

Superintendent Tidwell proffered a less sweeping rationale in his 1918 Annual Report:

> In the past, the vast possibilities of the reservation as a grazing country have never been utilized. . . . The scarcity of grass upon the western ranges and the diminishing territory, brought about by the land being homesteaded, has caused cattlemen to seek the necessary pasturage for his stock, and as the result the past year has seen practically this entire reservation leased by both large and small ranchers. For the first time therefore all of the grass on the reservation will be utilized in the production of beef and mutton so very much needed.[120]

Needed in the interests of national security or not, the Indian Department denied that it ever used Oglala land against the wishes of Oglala allottees. In April, 1920, when Congressman Homer P. Snyder, Chair of the House Committee on Indian Affairs, asked Assistant C.I.A. E.B. Meritt "Were those leases made with the consent of the Indians?", he replied "Those leases covering allotted lands are made with the consent of the individual allottee, except in the case of minors, when the Superintendent signs the lease."[121] In his response to the testimony of Charles Turning Hawk, Joseph Horn Cloud, Iron Hail Stone, Henry Standing Bear, and others at that Congressional hearing, C.I.A. Cato Sells fell back on the standard line, that the "Superintendent was not able to get enough clerical help to handle 6,000 leases promptly," and had the gall to say "I hope that the Pine Ridge Indians will use their land to the very limit of their ability as I would much rather have the Indians utilize it themselves than to lease it to outside people."[122] The Indian Department was in denial, suffering from collective amnesia.

At a recent seminar on reservation economic development, Mohawk educator Mike Myers remarked that there is sometimes a tendency to see reservations as laboratories, as "under glass."[123] The special relationship with the federal government and the presence of an overweening bureaucracy are perhaps partly responsible. But the Pine Ridge Reservation was anything but a closed system, as this story about how outside interests, with the willing assistance of the Office of Indian Affairs (OIA), took control of the land base during World War I demonstrates.[124]

A combination of the robust market for beef, the availability of investment capital, and the OIA drive to harness reservation resources, ostensibly for the war effort, all played a role in the takeover of Oglala allotted land for white interests in World War I. Oglalas resisted the takeover of their allotted land, and they forcefully brought the problems that big leasing created to the attention of U.S. authorities. But even though Oglala testimony was corroborated by the reports of OIA Inspectors, the OIA falsely represented the actions of its officials to the U.S. Congress in 1920.[125] The OIA bureaucracy was not self-regulating – even though it had the information that could have enabled it to be so – and there was no effective oversight. The U.S. colonial system, of which the OIA was a part, served white interests well, at Oglala expense. The takeover crushed the local economy, devastated the environment, and alienated the Oglala people from their land.

The World War I takeover of Pine Ridge Reservation land by U.S. government supported corporate interests devastated the economy and the environment and alienated the majority of Oglalas from their resources. Oglala full bloods and most mixed bloods never again enjoyed the degree of control over and access to the land that they did before the big lease era. The environmental degradation wrought by the severe overgrazing that was ushered in with the takeover continues to this day.

The takeover of the reservation land base signaled a change in the political equation on Pine Ridge Reservation too. The power of the Oglala Council was tied in large part to control over land. Allotment of most tribal land between 1904–1915 eroded its power. Allotment gave control of land putatively owned by over 8,000 allottees to the OIA, voiding the Council's legal authority to regulate land use. The U.S. would no longer heed the wishes of the Oglala's own Council regarding reservation land use as it had in earlier years when the Council's steadfast refusal to submit to wholesale leasing of land so frustrated Agent John Brennan. In the face of the Council's continued attempt to protect the land base, Superintendent Henry Tidwell simply outlawed it. He created a puppet government, presaging subsequent OIA meddling in Oglala political organization in the 1920s and 1930s, a subject detailed in the next chapter.

Despite the oppressive conditions they faced, Oglala leaders were unflagging in their resistance to the federal government's agenda. Joseph

Horn Cloud, James Red Cloud, Henry Standing Bear, Charles Turning Hawk, Lawrence Bull Bear, Otto Chief Eagle, and many others worked diligently to protect the interests of the Oglala people from the OIA and other outside interests.[126] Popular resistance was widespread and took many forms. Many, like John White Wolf, refused to sign lease papers. Others engaged in direct action, destroying assets of white ranchers by tearing down hundreds of miles of fences and burning the range of the expropriators.

This story of the takeover of the reservation land base in World War I points to the necessity of digging deeply into the archives and of heeding the oral histories of the people. Accounts of Oglala oral historians like Johnson Holy Rock, who heard from his ancestors that meager lease monies from the huge cattle outfits were often not even paid, are supported by the archival research that forms the basis for this chapter. Oral history offers a guide past the deliberate misrepresentations that typify official government versions of events.[127]

William Horn Cloud's oral account of Oglala resistance to big leasing is strongly supported by the documentary evidence as is Russell Loud Hawk's claim that the U.S. government helped create an opportunity for "cattle interests [that] wanted to get the land."

Published accounts of the leasing of Oglala land, on the other hand, underplay the role of the OIA and overlook the phenomenon of Oglala resistance. George Hyde and Thomas Biolsi's contention that Oglalas willingly leased their land, Hyde's report that Oglalas sat down to live on their rents, and Biolsi's claim that it was more profitable for Oglalas to lease their land than to work are not supported by the evidence.[128]

The takeover of Oglala land is analogous to the near universal history of land theft that peoples of Africa, Asia, and Latin America suffered at the hands of European colonizers.[129] Dependency theories' postulation that colonialism was responsible for the "development of underdevelopment" fits the takeover of the reservation land base well. Outsiders prospered at the expense of Oglala landowners who, in Joseph Jorgensen's homely but apt phrase, were reduced to "the super-exploited underconsumers of the periphery."[130] The U.S. colonial regime on reservations regularly acted to separate Indian people from their land and resources and continues to put the interests of outside economic interests first and those of the people whose trust it is charged with last.[131]

Notes

1. RCIA 1913; RCIA 1919, M1011, Roll 106; Report of E.B. Linnen, Chief Inspector, September 23, 1919, Pine Ridge c1909–363 to Pipestone c1909–238, BIA Inspector Division – Inspection Reports 1908–1940, RG 75 NA; Report of Inspector John W. Bale, November 30, 1920, 75-33-053 to 80965-22-054, 1907–1939, PR, CCF; Annual Report for 1917, File 051, MDF-PR. The significance of cattle raising in the Oglala economy is detailed in Chapter 3. In addition to Oglala mixed bloods, white men married to Oglala women continued to engage in stock raising. The mechanisms and the conditions that resulted in the sale of some of the stock owned by full blood Oglala, to mixed bloods and white men married to Oglala women, and to boss farmers and others, are described in Chapter 4. By 1920, those Oglala classified as competent were much more likely to be engaged in farming or stock raising than those classified as restricted. Restricted Oglala were more likely to be full blood in 1920, as those with one-half or more white blood had been declared competent in 1918, pursuant CIA Cato Sell's 1917 Policy Declaration. Cf. Report of Inspector John W. Bale, November 30, 1920, 75-33-053 to 80965-22-054, 1907–1939, PR, CCF.

2. Annual Report to the Commissioner of Indian Affairs 1911, p. 134: Quoted in Johnston, Sr. Mary 1948, p. 115.

3. Hyde, George 1956, p. ix–x.

4. Hyde, George 1956, p. ix–x.

5. DeMallie, Raymond 1978, p. 257.

6. Utley, Robert 1963, p. 25.

7. Biolsi, Thomas 1992, p. 13.

8. Biolsi, Thomas 1992, p. 30.

9. Author's notes.

10. Jorgensen, Joseph 1978.

11. H.M. Tidwell, 1918 Annual Report, June 30, 1918, File 051, MDF-PR; Leasing Agreements, December 19, 1917, File 300, Box 342, MDF-PR.

12. H.M. Tidwell to Mr. L.L. Smith, Farmer, Kyle, S.D. (with copies to the other Farmers), April 12, 1918, File 321, Lists, Notices, Miscellaneous Inquiries, MDF-PR. It is noteworthy that the current situation on the reservation today is marked by the deliberate refusal of Bureau of Indian Affairs (BIA) officials to provide reservation residents with needed information about development projects in their communities. Typically, those who are going to be affected by such projects are among the last to know about them. That is the case, for example, with proposals to dump solid waste, with the siting of sewage lagoons for housing projects, and with proposals to do surface mining on tribal lands. Cf. *Kiwitaya O Kinanjin* (Coming Together and Taking a Stand), July, 1991.

13. A "Township" is a block of land six sections square. A section is one square mile, or 640 acres. Thus a township covers 36 sections of land, which is 36 square miles, or 23,040 acres.

14. In 1918, South Dakota steers marketed in Chicago averaged $130.13, and cows averaged $64.75, increases of 60, and 21 percent, respectively, over 1914 prices. Lee, Bob and Dick Williams 1964, p. 265.

15. John W., Bale, Inspection Report, November 30, 1920, 75-33-053 to 80965-22-054, 1907–1939, Pine Ridge, CCF; Memo by C.L. Ellis, Special Indian Agent, December 15, 1917, File 155, Box 208, Complaints 1918–1921, 1922, MDF-PR; Report of E.B. Linnen, Chief Inspector, September 23, 1919, Pine Ridge c1909–363 to Pipestone c1909–238, Inspector Division -Inspection Reports 1908–1940, RG 75 NA. BIA Classified Files 48079-18-321 to 99311-18-321.1, 1907–1939 Pine Ridge, contains several linear feet of grazing leases dated between 1918–1921.

16. H.M. Tidwell to CIA, January 4, 1918, Box 130, "Leasing of Allotments," KC.

17. Big Foot Historical Society, 1968, p. 72.

18. Report of E.B. Linnen, Chief Inspector, September 23, 1919, Pine Ridge c1909–363 to Pipestone c1909–238, Inspector Division -Inspection Reports 1908–1940, RG 75 NA.

19. Report of E.B. Linnen, Chief Inspector, September 23, 1919, Pine Ridge c1909–363 to Pipestone c1909–238, Inspector Division -Inspection Reports 1908–1940, RG 75 NA.

20. Report of E.B. Linnen, Chief Inspector, September 23, 1919, Pine Ridge c1909–363 to Pipestone c1909–238, Inspector Division -Inspection Reports 1908–1940, RG 75 NA.

21. H.M. Tidwell to E.B. Linnen, September 6, 1919, Box 130, "Leasing of Allotments," KC.

22. John W., Bale, Inspection Report, November 30, 1920, 75-33-053 to 80965-22-054, 1907–1939, Pine Ridge, CCF.

23. Henry Tidwell to Lessees of Pine Ridge Reservation, March 20, 1920, File 320.7, MDF-PR. See also testimony of Assistant CIA E.B. Meritt, in Complaint of the Pine Ridge Sioux, 1920.

24. John W., Bale, Inspection Report, November 30, 1920, 75-33-053 to 80965-22-054, 1907–1939, Pine Ridge, CCF.

25. John W., Bale, Inspection Report, November 30, 1920, 75-33-053 to 80965-22-054, 1907–1939, Pine Ridge, CCF.

26. John W., Bale, Inspection Report, November 30, 1920, 75-33-053 to 80965-22-054, 1907–1939, Pine Ridge, CCF; Report of E.B. Linnen, Chief Inspector, September 23, 1919, Pine Ridge c1909–363 to Pipestone c1909–238, Inspector Division – Inspection Reports 1908–1940, RG 75 NA; Tidwell to lessees of Pine Ridge Reservation, March 20, 1920; and Tidwell to allottees and lessees, March 31, 1923, File 320.7, MDF-PR; Petition dated January 18, 1921, File 321, Lists, Notices, Miscellaneous Inquiries, MDF-PR.

27. John W., Bale, Inspection Report, November 30, 1920, 75-33-053 to 80965-22-054, 1907–1939, Pine Ridge, CCF.

28. John White Wolf to CIA, April 7, 1920, 95661-13-320 to 38355-20-320, 1907–1939, Pine Ridge, CCF.

29. John White Wolf to CIA, April 7, 1920; H.M. Tidwell to CIA, April 26, 1920; E.B. Meritt to White Wolf, June 11, 1920; Hauke to Tidwell, January 4, 1921,

95661-13-320 to 38355-20-320, 1907–1939, Pine Ridge, CCF; Superintendent Henry Tidwell to Chief Inspector E.B. Linnen, September 6, 1919, Box 130, "Leasing of Allotments," KC; Superintendent Henry Tidwell, undated, Pine Ridge Agency's responses to charges made by Oglalas on August 20 and 22, 1919 at Mission Flats Hearing, File 155, MDF-PR.

30. Proceedings of the Council of the Pine Ridge Indians with E.B. Linnen, Inspector, on August 20, 1919.

31. "Proceedings of the Council of the Pine Ridge Indians with E.B. Linnen, Inspector on August 20, 1919; Report of Inspector John W. Bale, November 30, 1920, 75-33-053 to 80965-22-054, 1907–1939, PR, CCF.

32. Proceedings of the Council of the Pine Ridge Indians with E.B. Linnen, Inspector, August 20, 22, 1919, File 155, Box 208, Complaints 1918–21, 1922, MDF-PR.

33. Report of Inspector John W. Bale, November 30, 1920, 75-33-053 to 80965-22-054, 1907–1939, PR, CCF.

34. Proceedings of the Council of the Pine Ridge Indians with E.B. Linnen, Inspector, August 20, 22, 1919, File 155, Box 208, Complaints 1918–21, 1922, MDF-PR.

35. E.B. Meritt to George Bettelyoun, October 18, 1919, 95661-13-3230 to 38355-20-320, 1907–1939, Pine Ridge, CCF. The leasing regulations for 1924 still held that the lands of minors were to be leased by the Superintendent of the Agency unless parents were granted the authority: "Regulations Governing the Execution of Leases of Indian Allotted and Tribal Lands." Washington: Government Printing Office, 1924, p. 3, sec. 4.

36. CIA Cato Sells to Turning Hawk, Joseph Horn Cloud, Iron Hail Stone, Henry Standing Bear, April 26, 1920, 9514-37-054 to 7406-30-056, 1907–1939, Pine Ridge, CCF.

37. CIA Cato Sells' ruling that the lease money of minors could be used to purchase Liberty Bonds showed just how much interest the OIA really had in the welfare of those children. Proceedings of the Council of the Pine Ridge Indians with E.B. Linnen, Inspector, August 20, 22, 1919, File 155, Box 208, Complaints 1918–21, 1922, MDF-PR.

38. Henry Standing Bear to Cato Sells, July 18, 1918; H.M. Tidwell to CIA, August 21, 1918; E.B. Meritt to Henry Standing Bear, September 14, 1918, 48079-18-321 to 99311-18-321 pt. 1, 1907–1939, Pine Ridge, CCF.

39. The activities of boss farmers are described in Chapters 3 and 4.

40. Tape recorded interview by author.

41. Tape recorded interview by author.

42. The links among boss farmers, other OIA officials, and traders, described in Chapter 4, may also have been a factor in the decision of the boss farmers to limit access of full bloods to cattle. After World War II, the reservation grasslands were largely controlled by white ranchers and some mixed bloods, though that control was contested by the Bureau of Indian Affairs, and by Indian Reorganization Act programs in the 1930s (See Chapter 6).

43. Author's notes. For more on the takeover of land and capital as part of the colonial process, see Gamer, Robert E. 1988; Stavrianos, L.S. 1981; or Wolf, Eric 1982.
44. H.M. Tidwell to CIA, July 24, 1919, Box 130 "Leasing and Grazing Permits," KC; H. Traylor to CIA, October 30, 1919, Pine Ridge c1909–363 to Pipestone c1909–238, Inspector Division – Inspection Reports 1908–1940, RG 75 NA; Report of Inspector John W. Bale, November 30, 1920, 75-33-053 to 80965-22-054, 1907–1939, PR, CCF.
45. Report of E.B. Linnen, Chief Inspector, September 23, 1919, Pine Ridge c1909–363 to Pipestone c1909–238, Inspector Division – Inspection Reports 1908–1940, RG 75 NA; H. Traylor to CIA, October 30, 1919, Pine Ridge c1909–363 to Pipestone c1909–238, Inspector Division -Inspection Reports 1908–1940, RG 75 NA; Minutes of hearing with E.B. Meritt, Asst. CIA, April 22, 1920, 9514-37-054 to 7406-30-056, 1907–1939, Pine Ridge, CCF; F.E. Brandon, Health Inspection Report, September 15, 1922, 75-33-053 to 80965-22-054, 1907–1939, Pine Ridge, CCF.
46. Report of E.B. Linnen, Chief Inspector, September 23, 1919, Pine Ridge c1909–363 to Pipestone c1909–238, Inspector Division -Inspection Reports 1908–1940, RG 75 NA.
47. Report of Inspector John W. Bale, November 30, 1920, 75-33-053 to 80965-22-054, 1907–1939, PR, CCF.
48. H. Traylor to CIA, October 30, 1919, Pine Ridge c1909–363 to Pipestone c1909–238, Inspector Division - Inspection Reports 1908–1940, RG 75 NA.
49. H. Traylor to CIA, October 30, 1919, Pine Ridge c1909–363 to Pipestone c1909–238, Inspector Division - Inspection Reports 1908–1940, RG 75 NA.
50. Farmer (name illegible) to W.D. McKoen (with relevant handwritten comments added to the typed copy), Feb 2, 1921, Box 810, Pine Ridge Legal and Legislative Records, KC; H.M. Tidwell to Newcastle Land and Live Stock Company, March 16, 1921, Box 810, Pine Ridge Legal and Legislative Records, KC.
51. Report of Inspector John W. Bale, November 30, 1920, 75-33-053 to 80965-22-054, 1907–1939, PR, CCF.
52. Health Inspection Report by F.E. Brandon, September 15, 1922, 75-33-053 to 80965-22-054, 1907–1939, PR, CCF; Narrative Report on Health, 1924; Annual Report 1924, File 051 MDF-PR; RCIA 1910, M1011, Roll 106. Trachoma is caused by a chronic bacterial infection and is the world's leading cause of preventable blindness. It continues to be a problem in areas of the formerly colonized world where antibiotics are not available and water supplies and sanitation are problematic. See *www.CarterCenter.org/trachoma.html* for more information.
53. Annual Report 1924, File 051 MDF-PR; RCIA 1910, M1011, Roll 106.
54. Wissler, Clark, 1936, p. 59.
55. Report of Inspector John W. Bale, November 30, 1920, 75-33-053 to 80965-22-054, 1907–1939, PR, CCF.
56. The circumstances surrounding the decline of Oglala cattle raising are detailed in chapter 4.
57. Quote from full blood Oglala transcribed from tape in possession of author. Quote from mixed blood Oglala from author's notes.

58. John W., Bale, Inspection Report, November 30, 1920, 75-33-053 to 80965-22-054, 1907–1939, Pine Ridge, CCF.

59. Vine Deloria Jr., April 1994, Presentation at a meeting on the 1851 Fort Laramie Treaty at the Howard Johnson Hotel in Rapid City, South Dakota, author's notes. Dakota American Indian Movement (AIM) leader Russell Means submitted a request to the U.S. Forest Service for a camping permit for Yellow Thunder Camp, in the Black Hills. Yellow Thunder Camp was founded by AIM.

60. Proceedings of the Council of the Pine Ridge Indians with E.B. Linnen, Inspector, August 20, 22, 1919, File 155, Box 208, Complaints 1918–21, 1922, MDF-PR.

61. Ibid.

62. Ibid.

63. Ibid.

64. Ibid.

65. Ibid.

66. Ibid.

67. Ibid.

68. Ibid.

69. Hearing before Meritt, Assistant CIA, March 31, 1920, 9514-37-054 to 7406-30-056, 1907–1939, Pine Ridge, CCF.

70. Author's notes.

71. Minutes of hearing with Meritt, Washington, D.C., Assistant CIA, March 31, 1920, 9514-37-054 to 7406-30-056, 1907–1939, PR, CCF.

72. Minutes of hearing with E.B. Meritt, Pine Ridge Agency, Assistant CIA, April 22, 1920, 9514-37-054 to 7406-30-056, 1907–1939, PR, CCF.

73. CIA Cato Sells to Charles Turning Hawk, Joseph Horn Cloud, Iron Hail Stone, and Henry Standing Bear, April 26, 1920, 9514-37-054 to 7406-30-056, 1907–1939, PR, CCF.

74. E.B. Meritt to White Wolf, June 11, 192095661-13-320 to 38355-20-320, 1907–1939, Pine Ridge, CCF.

75. The humorous reference "Indian Run Around," is sometimes used to refer to the IRA government as well. The IRA government is the Oglala Sioux Tribal Government, organized under the auspices of the Indian Reorganization Act of 1934.

76. H.M. Tidwell to Citizens of the OST, March 9, 1918, File 064, Box 118, MDF-PR; H.M. Tidwell to OST members, September 6, 1919, File 064, Box 118, MDF-PR; Names of Members of the Oglala Council, Pine Ridge Reservation, Elected March 19,1918, *Oglala Light*, February–March 1918, No. 6 & 7, OLC.

77. Charles Giroux to Indian Office through Pine Ridge Agency Superintendent, November 10, 1916, File 064, Box 118, MDF-PR. The Oglala Council's fight against outside leasing is described in chapter 4.

78. Brennan to CIA, June 24, 1909, 75-33-053 to 80965-22-054, 1907–1939, CCF; H.M. Tidwell to Citizens of the OST, March 9, 1918; H.M. Tidwell to OST members, September 6, 1919, File 064, Box 118, MDF-PR.

79. H.M. Tidwell to Citizens of the OST, March 9, 1918, File 064, Box 118, MDF-PR. Interestingly, Tidwell's use of the acronym "OST," which refers to "Oglala Sioux Tribe," is the only such use I have come across from those pre-IRA (i.e., pre-Indian Reorganization Act of 1934) years.

80. H.M. Tidwell to OST members, September 6, 1919, File 064, Box 118, MDF-PR; H.M. Tidwell to Ivan Star Comes Out and James Walks Out, n.d., File 064, Box 118, MDF-PR.

81. H.M. Tidwell to OST members, September 6, 1919, File 064, Box 118, MDF-PR; Information on ballots cast from the *Oglala Light*, February–March, 1918, No. 6 & 7, OLC.

82. Burke to James Red Cloud, August 1, 1921, File 064, MDF-PR; Tidwell to Ivan Star Comes Out and James Walks Out, n.d., File 064, Box 118, MDF-PR; Red Willow et al. to CIA Charles Burke, June 20, 1921; Tidwell to Burke, July 28, 1921, 75-33-053 to 80965-22-054, 1907–39, PR, CCF; Sam Rock to Tidwell, March 16, 1921, File 155, Box 208, MDF-PR.

83. Minutes of Hearing with E.B. Meritt, Assistant CIA, in Washington, D.C., March 31, 1920; Minutes of Hearing with E.B. Meritt, at Pine Ridge Agency, April 22, 1920, 9514-37-054 to 7406-30-056, 1907–39, PR, CCF; Complaint of the Pine Ridge Sioux, April 6, 1920.

84. The use of petitions was, and is to this day, a common means of registering political sentiment on Pine Ridge Reservation.

85. L.L. Smith, Farmer, to Tidwell, April 22, 1918, with copy of petition from Otto Chief Eagle, Box 131, "Miscellaneous Correspondence," KC.

86. Otto Chief Eagle to C.I.A., February 1, 1922, File 155, Box 208, MDF-PR.

87. Petition to Charles H. Burk [sic] from Indians of Medicine Root District, February 1, 1922, File 155, Box 208, MDF-PR; see also petition from Wakpamni District, December 6, 1919, File 155, Box 208, MDF-PR.

88. Petition to Charles H. Burk [sic] from Indians of Medicine Root District, February 1, 1922, File 155, Box 208, MDF-PR; Burke to Chief Eagle, March 23, 1922; Burke to Tidwell, March 23, 1922; Tidwell to Burke, April 6, 1922, File 155, Box 208, MDF-PR.

89. Oral account from Severt Young Bear Sr., author's notes. Tidwell to All Farmers, n.d., File 062, MDF-PR; Hon. Wm. Williamson, U.S. House of Representatives to C.I.A., February 28, 1923, File 064, Box 118, MDF-PR.

90. Howard A. Wilkinson, Bennett County Auditor, to U.S. Senator Thomas Sterling, August 23, 1919, File 155, Complaint File, 1914–1917, MDF-PR.

91. Report of E.B. Linnen, Chief Inspector, September 23, 1919, Pine Ridge c1909–363 to Pipestone c1909–238, RG 75 NA.

92. Henry Tidwell to Farmers, July 20, 1922, File 320.7, MDF-PR; Report of E.B. Linnen, Chief Inspector, September 23, 1919, Pine Ridge c1909–363 to Pipestone c1909–238, RG 75 NA.

93. See Friere, Paulo, 1986, p. 91–110, for discussion of the problems associated with the practice of extension, and agents of extension.

94. CIA to Otto Chief Eagle, April 24, 1922; Petition to CIA from Iron Whiteman and Calico, June 1925; Jermark to Burke, June 9, 1925; Burke to Iron Whiteman

and Abraham Calico, June 26, 1925, 14081-13-059 to 37426-35-062, PR, CCF; J.B. Wingfield, August 18, 1922; J.B. Wingfield to CIA, August 20, 1923, 75-33-053 to 80965-22-054, 1907–1939, PR, CCF.

95. George Holy Dance to Senator Johnson, September 11, 1918, 48079-18-321 to 99311-18-321 pt. 1, 1907–1939, Pine Ridge, CCF.

96. Hearing before Meritt, Assistant CIA, March 31, 1920, 9514-37-054 to 7406-30-056, 1907–1939, Pine Ridge, CCF.

97. Proceedings of the Council of the Pine Ridge Indians with E.B. Linnen, Inspector, August 20, 22, 1919, File 155, Box 208, Complaints 1918–21, 1922, MDF-PR.

98. Proceedings of the Council of the Pine Ridge Indians with E.B. Linnen, Inspector, August 20, 22, 1919, File 155, Box 208, Complaints 1918–21, 1922, MDF-PR.

99. Author's notes.

100. Tidwell to CIA Burke, January 17, 1924; CIA Burke to Tidwell, February 13, 1924, 14081-13-059 to 37426-35-062, Pine Ridge, CCF.

101. Tidwell to CIA, September 13, 1921, File 062, MDF-PR.

102. Burke to Tidwell, February 13, 1924, 14081-13-059 to 37426-35-062, Pine Ridge, CCF.

103. Inspector James McLaughlin to CIA Burke, October 20, 1921, 14081-13-059 to 37476-35-062, 1907–1939, Pine Ridge, CCF.

104. Petition against Tidwell, n.d., 14081-13-059 to 37426-35-062, Pine Ridge, CCF.

105. Lee and Williams 1964, p. 186, 258, 263, 278, 454.

106. L.B. Roberts Sr. to Commissioner of Indian Affairs, June 8, 1925, 75-33-053 to 80965-22-054, 1907–1939, PR, CCF.

107. Complaint of the Pine Ridge Sioux, 1920.

108. Lee and Williams 1964, p. 265.

109. E.B. Meritt to Brennan, February 13, 1917, Box 130, Leasing of Allotments, KC.

110. John E. Mead to Brennan, March 27, 1917, and John E. Mead to Brennan May 4, 1917, Box 130, Leasing of Allotments, KC.

111. Smith, Page 1985, p. 517.

112. *Oglala Light*, April, 1917, No. 8, OLC.

113. Office telegram of May 24, 1917, quoted in letter of Brennan to CIA, May 25, 1917, Box 130 Leasing of Allotments, KC.

114. Memorandum of Special Indian Agent C.L. Ellis, December 15, 1917, "Complaints 1918–21, 1922," File 155, Box 208, MDF-PR 155.

115. C.L. Ellis to C.I.A., August 7, 1917, Box 130, Leasing of Allotments, KC; Lease Agreement with John E. Mead, December 19, 1917, File 300, Box 342, Lands, MDF-PR.

116. Memorandum of Special Indian Agent C.L. Ellis, December 15, 1917, File 155, Box 208, Complaints 1918–21, 1922, MDF-PR; Cook and Cahow, Great Western Commission Co. to Tidwell, August 30, 1917, File 530, Box 631, A Bunch of Miscellaneous Stock Stuff 1912–1914, MDF-PR.

117. C.L. Ellis to W.D. McKoen, October 2, 1917, Leasing of Allotments, Box 130, KC.
118. Cato Sells to Tidwell, January 14, 1918; Tidwell to Cato Sells, February 11, 1918, "Leasing of Allotments," Box 130, KC.
119. Report of Inspector John W. Bale, November 30, 1920, 75-33-053 to 80965-22-054, 1907–1939, PR, CCF.
120. Annual Report 1918, Pine Ridge Agency, File 051, MDF-PR.
121. Complaint of the Pine Ridge Sioux, 1920.
122. C.I.A. Cato Sells to Charles Turning Hawk, Joseph Horn Cloud, Iron Hail Stone, Henry Standing Bear, and Pine Ridge Indians, April 26, 1920, File 155, Box 208, MDF-PR.
123. Myers, Mike 1991, author's notes.
124. If the reservation provided a buffer for anything, it was a buffer for the stock interests so they could be insulated from political and market forces that had brought their former ways to an end outside of the reservation: the practices they pursued outside the reservation were inimical to the interests of homesteaders and to the notion of development being pursued in South Dakota, but they could still get away with such things on the reservation, could still get free grass and water; the interests of Indian residents were of little consequence to them or to the OIA. In fact it was said to be beneficial to Indians to get the lease money, but somehow detrimental to homesteaders – essentially a double standard, institutional racism, to put a name to it.
125. Testimony of Assistant CIA, E.B. Meritt in Complaint of the Pine Ridge Sioux, 1920.
126. Raymond DeMallie's contention (1978, p. 297, 301) that there is a gap in effective Oglala leadership from the late nineteenth century to the present, and an ". . . obvious lack of unity and common goal orientation on the part of the Oglala [which] simply fostered an ever-more paternalistic attitude on the part of the Bureau," is overdrawn and oversimplified.
127. George Hyde used both oral accounts and archival records. He was particularly interested in the question of what happened to Oglala cattle, but because of infirmity he was unable to travel to Pine Ridge to gather information on what had happened. He thus had to rely on correspondence with Bureau of Indian Affairs' officials, who misled him, hence his account in *A Sioux Chronicle*. Re. Hyde's attempt to gather information about the loss of Indian owned cattle see Hyde to CIA Rhoads, January 4, 1932, File 051.5-054, 1928, Box 172, Historical Data 1927–1932, MDF-PR.
128. Hyde, George 1956, p. ix–x; Biolsi, Thomas 1992, p. 13, 30.
129. Cf. Frank 1966, Stavrianos 1981, Wallerstein 1974, Wolf, Eric 1982, Worsley 1984.
130. Jorgensen, Joseph 1978.
131. Richmond Clow documents a situation analogous to the World War I takeover on Pine Ridge Reservation for the Standing Rock Reservation, where 788,480 acres of tribal land were leased for three cents an acre in 1902, yielding a per capita payment of about $7.00 per year. Once the door to outside control opened, tribal cat-

tle herds declined in size. (Clow, Richmond 1987a, p. 23, 26, 30.) The disposition of the U.S. government to favor outside interests has continued with predictable results. Nancy Owens' 1979 study of the economic effects of reservation border towns and energy exploitation on reservation economic development concludes that ". . . white control and development of reservation resources will result in the economic betterment of whites, not Indians." (Owens, Nancy 1979, p. 326. Cf. also LaDuke, Winona 1990.)

CHAPTER 6

Representative Democracy and the Politics of Exclusion

Allotment gave feckless federal authorities in the OIA carte blanche to do what they would with the reservation land base. It was the politico-legal underpinning for the big leasing debacle in the first place and it unleashed a process that has lent itself to land loss and to virtual disenfranchisement of putative landowners wherever it has been implemented. The application of allotment and allotment era policies on the Pine Ridge Reservation contributed to the growth and reinforcement of ethnic difference between mixed blood and full blood Oglala that came to play a crucial role in Oglala politics.

The disenfranchisement of mixed bloods created hurtful divisions between them and full bloods who retained their land. The notion of landless mixed bloods and landed full bloods became an enduring element in the representation of ethnic difference. In the words of Vine Deloria, Jr., "... if you had kept your allotment while others sold theirs, you had kept the faith with the old people who had signed the treaties and later the allotment agreements, and therefore you were a recognized member of the tribe."[1] To this day, some full blood Oglalas argue that mixed bloods who were issued fee patents should not be eligible for tribal membership, arguing frequently that "mixed-bloods sold their birth-right." The fact that fee patents were forced on most of their recipients against their will is overshadowed by ideology. Similarly, mixed blood Oglala sometimes say Oglala full bloods do not use the land base because they lack the requisite skills and the ambition.[2] Ideology obscures the facts of history, contributing to ongoing conflict.

By 1918, the U.S. government had issued fee patents to 1,530 Oglalas. Most of them were mixed bloods and most were issued those patents against their will. In November, 1918, U.S. Special Agent Lee Ellis, the same that had proven himself so efficient at drawing up leases of reservation land for outside cattle interests, drew up a list of 463 Oglalas and rec-

ommended that they should be issued fee patents to their land. They made
the list because the government considered them to be one-half or more
white blood. In the eyes of the government, that much "white blood" made
them "competent" to handle their own affairs. The fee patents freed them
up from the restrictions placed on land taxation and sale inherent in the
trust stipulations surrounding land allotted under the Dawes Act. Ninety-
two percent, or 425 of those 463 fee patents, were issued without the consent of the mixed blood landowners. Once the land was patented, taken
out of the trust status that protected it from taxation and from unscrupu-
lous land sharks, most of those that were fee patented, including some full
bloods, lost their land. By 1922, Superintendent Henry Tidwell reported
that 95% of all Oglalas who had been fee-patented had lost their land,
mostly to whites.[3]

Most Oglalas determined to have "1/2 or more white blood" were the
unwilling beneficiaries of a package deal. By becoming bona fide landowners (their deeds were no longer held in trust by the federal government) they
were automatically made U.S. citizens. Within three years most were landless citizens. Taxes on their fee lands mounted up quickly. Many lacked the
wherewithal to pay and their lands were sold for taxes. Sheriffs in Martin
and Hot Springs stood on the steps of the courthouses auctioning off their
holdings to the highest bidder – usually a non-Indian. So corrupt was the
practice of forced fee patenting that some Oglalas who served in the armed
forces in World War I returned home from overseas to find their land had
been patented and sold for taxes in their absence.[4]

The population of mixed blood Oglalas had grown significantly through
recent immigration.[5] Many had become involved in the affairs of county
and state government and some had been catalysts in the organization of
Bennett County. Those demographic and political developments, side by
side with an alienating ideology, further separated them from full bloods
and helped set the stage for a novel development in Oglala politics. That
development, which saw ethnic difference rise to the fore as a dimension in
Oglala politics for the first time, in turn fed back into and sharpened the
underlying contradiction. This chapter examines the early development of
representative government on Pine Ridge Reservation and land use and
control patterns in the 1920s and 1930s in order to assess the validity of
those contentions.

The first section is an attempt to understand conflicts that swirled
around the controversial 21 Council, a kind of precursor to the longer lived
representative tribal government established under the Indian
Reorganization Act of 1934 (IRA). The second examines the controversial
first IRA administration. The third and fourth sections examine land tenure
arrangements and the reservation economy before and after the IRA. The
IRA, a watershed in federal-Indian relations in the U.S., had vast implications for Indian land.

THE 21 COUNCIL AND THE CHANGING TERRAIN OF OGLALA POLITICS

During the nineteenth century, the U.S. government employed a combination of military force and peace making delegations in an attempt to impose its will on Oglalas and other groups on the northern plains. Army officers and peace negotiators alike were confounded and frustrated by a political system they did not understand and by their failed efforts to make it conform to their expectations. In particular, they wanted Oglalas and other bands to negotiate through a single leader, a notion far removed from the reality of Oglala political organization and a source of mirth and anger among Oglalas to this day. Oglala leaders they met were often perceived as being at the pinnacle of a fixed hierarchical system rather than as leaders among others in a complex and fluid array.[6]

Valentine McGillycuddy, first and most infamous Indian Agent at the Pine Ridge Agency, tried to break the power of Oglala leaders through the mechanism of ration distribution. Agent John Brennan tried to override the Oglala Council's practice of limiting grazing by outsiders by strong-arming people to sign a petition supporting it. Superintendent Henry Tidwell, with the concurrence of the CIA, outlawed the Oglala Council and created a puppet council. All those efforts to shape Oglala politics were clumsy and mostly unsuccessful.[7]

Tidwell's successor Ernest Jermark seemed bent on undermining the Oglala Council. He disparaged its designated leader Otto Chief Eagle, complained that meetings were overly frequent, notified CIA Charles Burke that he wanted to ban it entirely. Burke advised him to allow meetings but to stipulate only those called by the Superintendent would be recognized.[8]

In 1928, after some Oglalas apparently suggested changing the Oglala Council's constitution and bylaws, Jermark called a "General Council of the Oglala band of Sioux Indians" to "consider and adopt rules, regulations and by-laws governing the Oglala Business Council." On November 30, 1928, at "Red Cloud's Hall" in Pine Ridge Village the Council voted 27–2 to adopt a constitution and bylaws that the Commissioner's office had helped draft, thereby establishing the "21 Council" or "Business Council."[9]

The 21 member Council was elected on December 31, 1928, in a regulatory vacuum. The results and the process were roundly criticized; several newly members were alleged to have collected ballots prior to the election. The behavior of the 21 Council soon made it the object of more concerted attack by members of the older Oglala Council and its supporters. The most frequent charge was that the 21 Council, or the "Business Council" as it was commonly called, represented only a narrow constituency and was out of touch with the people.[10]

Opponents maintained that 21 Council delegates met in secret, failed to consult elders, acted in haste, took shortcuts, and ignored treaty matters.

There were also charges that the new council met criticism with threats and was disrespectful, a serious cultural breach of Lakota meeting protocol which places a premium on respect. Critics also charged that 21 Council members were "fee patent men" [i.e., mixed bloods who had received fee patents to their land] and charged that they "did not take up with the tribe in general anything they want to put before the Department, or the Superintendent, and then they do not return to their districts, and explain at an open meeting, or in any other way, what they have been doing."[11]

The 21 Council lashed back at its critics. At a February 19, 1931 meeting in Porcupine, one representative warned that anyone who spoke out against the 21 Council would be arrested, jailed, and tried before the Court of Indian Offenses.[12] A March 10, 1931 letter to the CIA signed by the Council's mixed blood Secretary James La Pointe and 17 other members attacked the full blood controlled Oglala Council in terms as vituperative as anything penned by the Indian Agents who had impugned it in the past. They characterized their detractors as "elderly, illiterate gentlemen," who were "Ignorant and illiterate" and claimed the "only emotion they seemed to have developed was a sense of self-importance and cheap ostentation." They railed against their perceived backwardness, comparing them to a "1910 model automobile" and attacked them saying "All that the old fellows like to do is feast and sleep." In a backhanded compliment to the elders they added that "in due justice to some real nice old people on this reservation I'll admit that there are some real sensible, broad-minded and reliable old Indians who realize the importance and the necessity of education in tribal affairs." But lest they give them too much credence, they concluded "as a whole, the old people would just as soon keep this reservation steeped in ignorance if they can have enough control to be called 'chiefs.'"[13]

21 Council members used some of their strongest language to denounce the operation of the Oglala Council and its integration of Lakota cultural practices in the conduct of its affairs: "They danced, feasted, slept and danced some more; their councils were replete with traditional ceremonies which called for plenty of eating and sleeping but no heavy brain action." One passage in the letter illustrated the radical disconnection they had from the Oglala past. In the past, they contended, "Their [sic] weren't any problems to speak of in those days with which the Indians were confronted. The government was feeding the Indians in those days . . . and they didn't have a thing to worry about but to hitch up their ponies and drive to the government stations to get their provisions."[14]

The one charge the 21 Council chose to respond to was that it failed to work on treaty issues. Actually, the 21 Council leaders had no interest in pursuing the Black Hills Claim and other treaty claims that were of such overriding importance to the older Oglala Council. In fact, they rejected the importance of working on them at all, contending that treaties ". . . aren't worth the paper they are printed on" since the U.S. never intended on keeping the treaties anyway. Besides, they wrote, "these old Indians are less informed on these treaty matters than anyone." In another letter, 21 Council member Hermus Merrival ridiculed "illiterate old men's" oral knowledge of the treaties, claiming the 21 knew much more about treaties because they had a "full volume of Kappler's Indian Laws and Treaties."[15]

Merrival's letter evinced nothing but scorn for the Oglala Council and Oglala customs:

> They are illiterate, many of them depending on the government for rations. The meetings called by the old Oglala Tribual [sic] Council are usually conducted in a haphazard way and culminate in a dance and feast, with no beneficial results to the Tribe as a whole and to the disgust and embarrassment of the civilized members of the Tribe.

In contrast, he argued, the Business Council would ". . . bring the Tribe a step closer to their goal – civilization and a final recognition from the government of the competence and good citizenship of the Tribe as a whole."[16]

The 21 Council leaders believed they represented the future – a future shorn of Lakota culture and tradition, disabused of treaty claims, marked by "civilization" and integration into the mainstream of equal opportunity for all Americans. In a revealing passage 21 Council members claimed the Indian Citizenship Act of 1924 had given the people ". . . equal advantages with the most despotic old chief." Disparaging references to "chiefs" were clearly aimed at the older Oglala pattern of politics, where leaders were drawn from tiospaye in contrast to the eight or more mixed blood members of the 21 Council who did not have that foundation.[17]

In May 1930, 53 mixed blood tribal members petitioned Jermark seeking his permission to hold a mixed blood council in Martin, the county seat of Bennett County. The petition was submitted under the signature of John Monroe, the appointed "Chief" of the "Organization of Mixed Blood Sioux Indians of Bennett County." Its stated purpose was ". . . to aid, cooperate with and be a part of the Pine Ridge Ogallalla [sic] Council, with which Ogallalla Council [the 21 Council in this context] the said Mixed-blood Organization will closely co-operate." Outspoken 21 Council member Hermus Merrival signed along with four more of the eight or more mixed blood members of the 21 Council. Edward Amiotte, who was listed as one of the principal mixed blood ranchers on the reservation by 1934, was temporary Chairman of the organization; Emery Amiotte, who ranched in nearby Long Valley, was the Secretary.[18]

The actions and inaction of the 21 Council generated strong opposition from the older Oglala Council leadership. In February 1931, the older Oglala Council met for three days in the Council Hall on Porcupine Creek to consider their options. Hobart White Plume's motion that the "tribal Council previously known as Oglala Council shall now be and stand as the tribal council of our reservation" carried 48–0. Dog Chief's motion to base the reorganized council "on the authority of three-fourths (3/4) of the members of this tribe," also passed 48–0. William Spotted Crow's motion to discontinue the 21 Council passed 45–1. Charles Red Cloud was elected Temporary Chairman and Henry Standing Bear as Acting Secretary of the reorganized Oglala Council. Both men were descendants of chiefs and were part of what the Oglala Council referred to in English as the "Tribunal of Chiefs."[19]

Oglala Council leaders, who signed off on the meeting minutes as "chiefs," knew that in the face of OIA support for the 21 Council, their vote alone would not be a satisfactory remedy. What was needed, they decided, was an "expression of the will, the consent, and authority of the tribe . . . by a petition signed by a majority of the adult members of the tribe." That, they concluded, would "establish properly the true authority of the tribe as the base of the former tribal council now reorganized."[20]

The success of that petition drive is a testament to the enduring organizational capacity of the Oglala Council and to the continued broad support among the Oglala people for a form of government that rested on the authority of the Treaty of 1868 and on the leadership of the "Tribunal of Chiefs." More than two-thirds of the Oglala people, both men and women, signed the petition by April 1931 – less than two months after the meeting in Porcupine! The accomplishment, at a time when communication was face to face and travel was primarily on foot or horseback, and after years of OIA attempts to manipulate or eliminate the Oglala Council, was phenomenal. The petition:

> We, the undersigned, adult members of the Oglala Sioux Tribe of the Pine Ridge Reservation of South Dakota, hereby repeal the Constitution and By-laws adopted November 30th, 1928, for the Business Council, which had run the last two years on trial; and declare the said Business Council ended and discontinued. And we hereby approve and confirm the former tribal Council as reorganized on February 19, 20, 21, 1931, at Porcupine, South Dakota, based on the authority of three-fourths (3/4) of the adult members of the tribe.

The petition was submitted to Commissioner Charles Rhoads and U.S. Vice President Charles Curtis in April 1931.[21] William Spotted Crow's letter to Curtis prompted him to query Rhoads. Acting CIA B.S. Garber wrote back to Curtis in defense of the 21 Council. Apparently ignorant of the conflict that the 21 Council had generated and unable to grasp the import of the petition, he simply argued that the 21 Council was created to "establish harmony and better cooperation and overcome these factional differences which have existed for some time." The problem lay with the people's own form of government, and the solution in adopting the representative model of the "advanced civilization":

> In order to encourage the Indians to take a greater part in their affairs and to encourage the adoption of the advanced civilization, it has not been our policy to formally recognize Indian chiefs. We believe all

Indians should have a voice in the selection of their tribal representatives or business organization and at present we see no need for making any change in the plan in effect at Pine Ridge [emphasis added].[22]

The 21 Council sought outside support as well. Progressive Indian activist Gertrude Bonnin, a well-known crusader for Indian rights and President of the National Council of American Indians, weighed in on their side. She wrote to CIA Rhoads from her Washington D.C. office noting that "It appears there is a dissenting element against the present form of the Business Council." She disparaged the "dissenters" for favoring a Council composed of "so-called Chiefs," touting the western principle of democratic representation and observing that "Chiefs are not barred from running for Office on the present council."[23] Like the OIA and the 21 Council, she promoted western style governance over the long-standing Lakota model.

Local resistance to the 21 Council did not let up. At a joint meeting of the Oglala Council and 21 Council at Mission Flats Hall on September 4, 1931, Peter Dillon's motion that the Business or 21 Council be discontinued carried 67–10.[24] The Oglala Council met again in December and approved a new constitution and bylaws. Jermark was gone. Superintendent James McGregor declared his office neutral in the dispute and recommended that the CIA approve the new constitution with several changes.[25]

The new constitution emphasized the continuing importance of treaty, culture, and sovereignty to the Oglala people. Unlike the 21 Council's constitution, the new one emphasized the role of the Tribunal of Chiefs. Under Article Three the officers of the council were to be elected by a General Council that would be arranged for by the Tribunal. Article One provided that the council would be called the Oglala Treaty Council. The word Treaty was subsequently dropped but its initial inclusion in the constitution was a reminder that treaty rights were important and should not be ignored as they were under the 21 Council.[26] The new constitution provided increased scope for tribal authority, omitting the clauses in the 21 Council constitution that provided for increased U.S. government control over tribal affairs. The 21 Council constitution provided that changes made by the Council would not be final until after the CIA approved them in writing, and stipulated that the superintendent would call special council meetings.[27]

Elective politics provided an opportunity for landless mixed bloods and a small group of mixed blood ranchers to compete in the arena of Oglala politics, something the older Oglala Council did not. Conflict over the 21 Council illustrated the emergent role of ethnic difference in Oglala politics. For the first time, mixed blood and full blood Oglalas with opposing interests and different values competed directly for the reins of formal power. Bitter discourse and a high level of conflict marked that competition. The

21 Council disparaged the Oglala Council and the "Tribunal of Chiefs" and trumpeted the virtues of a "strictly representative body," [28] while the Oglala Council charged that the 21 did not communicate with the people and violated Lakota canons of respect. Although the overwhelming success of the Oglala Council's 1931 petition drive would seem to have closed off the avenue of western style governance to an increasingly politicized minority, events on the national stage soon overshadowed more local sensibilities.

IRA GOVERNMENT AND THE INSTITUTIONALIZATION OF CONFLICT

On October 27, 1934, Oglalas voted 1,169 to 1,095 to support the Indian Reorganization Act the U.S. Congress enacted earlier that year. Slightly more than half, or 55%, of 4,075 eligible voters went to the polls. While other federal legislation subject to local referenda usually required the votes of a majority of eligible voters, the IRA was applied to Pine Ridge Reservation on the strength of a little more than one-fourth of the electorate – 28.8% voted for ratification. Many Oglala full bloods boycotted the IRA referendum.[29] But CIA John Collier, the chief architect and proponent of the Act, had anticipated the boycott strategy. He had successfully lobbied to insert a provision that the IRA would apply to reservations "unless a majority of the adult Indians, members of the tribe or reservation, voted to *exclude* themselves from the provisions of the Act [emphasis in original]."[30]

On Pine Ridge Reservation the "Old Dealers," largely full bloods and proponents of the old way of choosing leadership from families and tiospaye, denounced the IRA before and after the ratification election. "New Dealers" who supported it argued that the "New Deal for Indians" was the key to a better future. Differences over the IRA and especially between mixed bloods and full bloods surfaced "frequently throughout many of the Indian conferences," (essentially field hearings on the legislation), that were held before the referenda in Indian Country.[31]

Support for the IRA was particularly strong in Pass Creek and Martin, Eagle Nest, and Medicine Root, where mixed blood populations were high. The strongest opposition was in Wounded Knee, where full bloods had been particularly active in opposition (see vote tallies in Table 5). When the results are broken down by areas within districts the pattern is even stronger. Rockyford in Porcupine District is and was predominantly a mixed blood community. The vote there was 56 to 18 in support of the IRA. Long Valley, a sparsely populated area where mixed blood ranchers predominated, went 15–2 for ratification. The town of Martin, where the effort to organize Bennett County had been led by mixed bloods, supported it 45–12. It was a different story in Wounded Knee Village, where the predominantly full blood settlement, part of Wounded Knee District, voted 93–9 to reject the IRA. [32]

The IRA brought many welcome changes to Indian Country. It signaled the intent of some in the Indian Bureau and in the U.S. Congress to end the devastating assimilative thrust of the allotment era and to put a new regime of programs and policies in place. The IRA ended allotment, extended the trust period for Indian land indefinitely, provided federal money for education and business development, estblished Indian preference in the Bureau of Indian Affairs (formerly OIA), made funds available to purchase additional land that could be placed into trust, and extended federal recognition to tribal governments organized under it. [33]

Table 5: IRA Referendum and Charter Election Results[34]

IRA Ratification Vote, October 27, 1934			Charter Election, March 16, 1939	
District	Yes	No	Yes	No
Porcupine	143	156	126	179
Wakpamnee	257	223	179	357
Eagle Nest	128	43	153	72
Medicine Root	180	109	158	203
White Clay	152	181	110	222
Wounded Knee	88	296	56	369
Pass Creek & Martin	214	87	242	114
Absentee	7	0	68	8
Totals	**1169**	**1095**	**1092**	**1524**

The first Oglala Sioux Tribal Council (OST) organized under the IRA was seated in April 1936, and soon provoked as much indignation as the 21 Council had. In 1938, 1,061 Oglalas signed a petition to revoke the OST Constitution and by-laws that had been approved by a January 15, 1936 election.[35] The ultimately unsuccessful effort was spearheaded by the influential Henry Standing Bear. The effort grew out of widespread discontent with the actions of the first OST President, Frank G. Wilson.[36] Wilson, a mixed blood tribal member, was active in Republican politics in Bennett County and had opposed the New Deal at first, but after the IRA vote on Pine Ridge Reservation he jettisoned that baggage and mounted a whirlwind campaign for the presidency, netting fewer than 900 votes in an election many full bloods boycotted.[37]

Complaints about the first IRA government turned on complaints that it served mixed blood interests. Although full bloods far outnumbered mixed bloods in that first OST Council under President Frank G. Wilson, complainants alleged that he and the predominantly mixed blood Executive Committee controlled it.[38] Superintendent William O. Roberts contended that Wilson ". . . arbitrarily assumed authority that never was intended in the first place and in the appointment of his committees and in other ways he has seen fit to use only mixed blood people." Standing Bear, a representative on that first IRA Council, complained to Collier about

". . . arbitrary actions of the President and also to [sic] the Executive Committee."[39] The President's abrasive style compounded the situation. According to Roberts, his "loud, officious and arbitrary" behavior added to the "uneasiness of the full blood people."[40]

Besides alleging discrimination against full bloods, many Oglalas complained that Frank G. Wilson's administration was violating their civil rights. A delegation of leading full blood Oglala Old Dealers met with Assistant CIA Zimmerman in Washington D.C. in 1939 to discuss repealing the IRA, and to lodge complaints that the OST government was violating the civil rights of Oglala full bloods. Zimmerman reported that "They were strong in their statements that the present officers of the Council and the police and judges set up under the code were oppressive and they stated that they were afraid to hold meetings to discuss their problems because they might be arrested and thrown in jail."[41]

Although attempts to overturn the IRA failed, the degree of support for such an initiative was evidenced in the resounding defeat of the Charter of Incorporation. The Charter election vote was to determine whether the OST should establish a corporation that could engage in business and apply for loans from the revolving credit fund authorized in the legislation.[42] But on Pine Ridge Reservation, IRA opponents apparently widely viewed the Charter election as another referendum. Some who had boycotted earlier elections turned out to cast their votes against incorporation. On March 6, 1937, Oglalas defeated the Charter 1,524 to 1,092 (Table 5). It was hailed by opponents as a great victory and by supporters as evidence of betrayal. (Over time the provisions of incorporation were extended to tribes that voted against Incorporation.)

Wilson was livid about the defeat.[43] He submitted an angry letter addressed to Roberts from the OST Executive Committee alleging that he, Roberts, had worked with "known reactionary factions" on the reservation against adoption of the Charter. Besides Wilson, the Executive Committee included Vice-President Harry Conroy, Secretary Charles Little Hawk, and Treasurer Ted C. Craven. Conroy also blamed the previous Superintendent, James McGregor, for the Charter defeat, claiming he had worked through ". . . his old Indian lieutenants" to achieve it."[44] The Executive Committee's letter also expressed outrage that Roberts had apparently recommended that the federal government bear the cost of transporting the "Old Unofficial reactionary Chiefs Council" to Washington, D.C.

> We also object to ration Indians take the liberty of representing non ration, progressive, intelligent members of the Oglala Sioux Tribe in matters of vital tribal importance. The New Council has never and does not intend to surrender its right to speak and act in behalf of the Indian people of this reservation.[45]

The perspective on Oglala society and culture in the OST Executive Committee's letter was nearly identical to that 21 Council members had expressed when they were under heavy criticism several years earlier, and not unlike those OIA officials expressed about Oglalas in the early part of the century. [46] The lines were drawn between them and the majority of the Oglala people. In a revealing letter to Collier, Wilson left little doubt about who he considered to be the "progressive, intelligent members" of the tribe that he believed should represent the rest.

> The Indians living on the reservation consist of many types and class-
> es, from the most primitive to those that are educated. The educated
> ones form the class that is now landless. They are the younger genera-
> tion and for the most part, are making their own way. . . . The Indians
> who have inherited large tracts of land are mostly old Indians who
> already have land of their own and they are antagonistic toward any
> progressive movement on the part of the educated, landless, class. . . .
> The Indians who opposed the acceptance of the charter are peyote
> users, those who receive pensions and those who receive rations. They
> are afoot, do not own stock and are not earning their own living. The
> Indians who want the charter are those who are cultivating their own
> allotments, or rented land, stockraisers and those who are working at
> various trades to make a living and are doing so by their own efforts. [47]

In Wilson's view, the class that should lead was constituted primarily by landless mixed bloods, mixed blood ranchers, and others who had suffi-cient formal education. For Wilson and his supporters, the IRA govern-ment represented an opportunity to advance the interests and the agendas of a largely mixed blood constituency. Mixed bloods, he reportedly argued, ". . . should not be tied down to the level of the full bloods." [48]

Differences between Wilson's interests and those of Oglala full bloods were evident in relations between the Council and communities in the reservation districts. In a detailed, thoughtful report on the reasons for the defeat of the Charter, Charles Brooks, a mixed blood Oglala and the Head Community Worker from Pine Ridge Agency, emphasized the important role of tiospaye on Pine Ridge Reservation. He argued, as had anthropolo-gist Haviland Scudder Mekeel who had campaigned for the adoption of the IRA government alongside Ben Riefel, a mixed blood OIA employee and tribal member from the neighboring Rosebud Sioux Reservation, that the "tiyospaye or natural groups should be given special emphasis" in the trib-al constitution, and that the failure to recognize those groups was central to the discontent being expressed with the IRA. Brooks' analysis was the defeat of the Charter reflected fallout over the representation issue. [49]

Cultural differences over tiospaye, more loosely referred to as "commu-nities" in Article VI of the OST Constitution, had political consequences. Article VI makes provision for the recognition of organized communities. In 1937, the eight communities that asked for recognition received "scant

attention" from the OST. Wilson, Brooks reported, had "Time and again
. . . stated in the council that the community idea [natural groups or
tiospaye] is based on communism. . . ."[50] At stake was the question of the
growth of central authority versus community control, of "representative
democracy" along the lines of the U.S. model, versus a continuation of
Oglala modes of organization that were rooted in community, in tiospaye,
in kinship. Mixed blood control over the OST militated against those elements of Oglala society that were associated with Oglala full bloods.
Whereas the older Oglala Omniciye was controlled by full bloods and represented the interests of tiospaye and community, the Oglala Sioux Tribe
had fallen under the sway of Oglala mixed bloods and naturally tended to
represent their interests, which were not dissimilar from those of the white
ranchers, businessmen, and homesteaders they ultimately sought to
replace.

OIA AS BROKER AND OPPRESSOR IN THE 1920S AND 1930S

When the artificially high prices created by wartime conditions plummeted
and the bottom fell out of the cattle market in 1920, the huge cattle outfits
that had taken over the Pine Ridge Reservation land base with the support
of the Office of Indian Affairs (OIA) lost big. Brown and Weare, Newcastle
Land and Stock Company, and the rest defaulted on their lease payments
and left behind a legacy of overgrazed cow pasture in place of the once
diverse prairie ecosystem.[51] Though the exodus of the big cattle outfits and
the depressed market for cattle might otherwise have finally allowed Oglala
landowners more control over their own land it was not to be. The colonial bureaucracy scampered to fill the breach with outsiders.
Superintendent Henry Tidwell, erstwhile champion of big cattle, busied
himself recruiting smaller white-owned outfits, continuing the U.S. colonial
regimes predilection for brokering Oglala resources to non-Indian interests[52]

White ranchers soon occupied the 2,000,000 acres plus of reservation
range land. Many were absentee operators from reservation border towns.
They lived in Gordon, Rushville, Cody, White Clay and Chadron Nebraska
and Buffalo Gap, Rapid City, Belvidere, Kadoka, Vetal, Interior, Scenic,
and LaCreek South Dakota. Some of them had leased reservation land
before the influx of the larger corporate cattlemen and were probably
thrilled to have the opportunity their departure created. Still others, like
Newcastle's 7L manager John Glover, stayed behind after the exodus and
became successful ranchers in their own right.[53]

The cattle herds many Oglala families had just a decade earlier, when
Indian-owned stock on the reservation tallied over 60,000 head, were gone.
The subsistence herds that many full blood families once owned had been
reduced to scattered remnants. Many of the larger commercial herds of sev-

eral hundred head that a fair number of mixed bloods owned before the advent of corporate cattle outfits were gone as well. But a significant few mixed blood ranchers had weathered the onslaught and they owned the majority of the 15,000 head of Indian-owned Hereford cattle on the reservation; Oglala full bloods owned about 1,000 head.[54] Some mixed blood ranchers were successful enough to compete directly with whites for the leasing of reservation land. By 1934, Superintendent McGregor reported that Oglala ranchers, most of whom were mixed bloods, leased 52,000 acres.[55]

In keeping with the pattern set by their corporate predecessors, many off-reservation ranchers secured leases but did not trouble themselves to pay for them. They violated contracts, illegally trespassed their stock on land that was not leased, and destroyed the people's crops and gardens in the process. Oglalas continued their practice of petitioning the OIA to remove trespassing cattle and to make wrongs right; the OIA continued its practice of ignoring their pleas and working against their interests.

In 1925, when Oglala Council leader James Red Cloud, grandson of the famous Chief Red Cloud, traveled to Washington D.C. to testify about the abuses directly to Assistant CIA E.B. Meritt, the latter did not even deign to respond.[56] It was the same Meritt who had lied to congress about the depredations of the corporate cattle industry on the reservation.[57] The World War I takeover of Oglala land, facilitated through the creation of putative Oglala landowners through allotment, had put the OIA firmly in the seat of middleman currying favor with outside interests and had the effect of denying the Oglala Council an effective role in controlling the most important material resource Oglalas had. In the 1920s and early 1930s, the OIA functioned primarily as a broker, simply abrogating its trust responsibility. Leases for individually owned trust land were arranged but in many cases little or nothing was done to administer them. Many white outsiders and some Oglala mixed blood ranchers used allotted and tribal land at will. Many did not pay the allottees or the tribe a cent and the OIA did nothing. By the OIA's own reckoning, Oglala landowners lost an estimated $50,000 a year in lease income as a result.[58]

Some landowners bypassed the OIA and leased their lands directly to white ranchers and farmers. That gave rise to a kind of reverse patron-client system, with landowners client to white land users. Remnants of the system still exist. The pattern was reinforced in the depression years when many lessees unable to pay their leases ". . . settled with trade in lieu of cash."[58] The reputation of individual ranchers turned on their behavior as patrons. Some were seen as beneficent, helping out with a beef when there was a death in the family or in times of crisis. Others ran roughshod over their "clients," abusing the land by overgrazing and illegal subleasing. A number of the more disliked were known to shoot the dogs of Oglala landowners, and some were widely believed to be rustlers, "slicking" cat-

tle and horses from Oglala people.[60] Patron-client relations further differentiated full blood and mixed blood Oglalas. Recall that by the 1920s,
mixed blood Oglalas, who had been declared competent, had mostly lost
their land. Full blood landowners, whose land had remained in trust
because the federal government did not deem them competent to handle
their own affairs, were the clients.

Needs of Oglala families in the 1920s and 1930s far outstripped any
returns they realized from patron-client relations and land lease. The negligible amount of rations issued by the OIA added little to the larder. Times
were already bad before the onset of the Great Depression. In the winter of
1926, Oglalas were eating their horses, something they were loath to do.
Lakota culture accords sunkawakan – "mysterious" or "sacred dogs" – a
special place of respect.[61] During those hard times, the earlier pattern of
seasonal work and migrant labor in the potato and sugar beet fields of
Nebraska and other states in the region intensified. Oglala elders recall that
whole communities were nearly abandoned when families trekked to the
fields and lived in tents while they brought in the harvest. Landless mixed
bloods and landed full bloods labored side by side. Civilian Conservation
Corps and Works Project Administration projects were a godsend for
mixed blood and full blood alike in the depression years.

Depression era drought on the northern plains drove out many homesteading whites from the region, including those who had come to Pine
Ridge Reservation to break the dense prairie sod for their crops of wheat
and flax.[62] The drought squeezed cattlemen too. Once again, as they had in
the World War I era, they sought access to the grasslands on Pine Ridge
Reservation for their stock, and once again trespassing cattle flooded reservation grasslands. In 1934, Pine Ridge Agency Superintendent McGregor
reported that "Drouth [sic] and grasshoppers to the east and west of us has
brought an influx of cattle men such as we have never known."[63] The short-
age of grass in the drought-stricken country west of the Missouri had
fueled an ". . . unprecedented influx of cattle and sheep men who, during
the past 3 or 4 weeks, have simply swamped the Lease Department with
applications for permits and farm pastures, ranging in size all the way of
one or two sections [1280 acres] up to a half township [11,520 acres], and
more."[64] Applications for lease of reservation land by outsiders did not
slow during the depression era years. Between 1,500 and 2,000 allotments
under grazing permits for which the paperwork had not been fully completed.[65]

Government accommodation of outside interests was facilitated through
the creation of grazing units that combined individual trust land holdings
(allotments) and tribal land into large contiguous parcels ranging in size
from thousands to tens of thousands of acres. Grazing units, or range units,
were the governments answer to heirship fractionation. When landowners
die intestate, their holdings pass equally to all their offspring and over sev-

eral generations once large tracts often come to be owned by hundreds, and eventually even thousands, of heirs. Grazing units were a boon to the lessee who could bypass numerous individual owners to deal solely with the OIA, but Oglala landowners regarded them as a scourge.[66]

In October 1933, a delegation of Oglalas angered by the problem confronted Superintendent James McGregor. He agreed with their complaints, translated for him by his interpreter, and wrote a summary for Collier:

> In regard to the present grazing units, the Indians came to find that it is a detriment on their behalf . . . the lessee is not obliged to fence his unit, but that his cattle are allowed to range outside of the unit, but when an Indian makes any complaint about it, he is a bad Indian, and is told to fence his allotment. And furthermore that the Indian is being threatened that the lessee has the authority to round up the Indian horses and auction the said horses at sale regardless to whether the Indian wants to or not, and this is a detriment. According to the regulations of the units, it is stated that, if we don't want to lease our land within the boundary of the unit that we are instructed to fence our allotments, but times are hard at present and we have no money whereby we could get barbed wire fence to fence around our allotments, but it seems that we have no representation in regards to the grazing units.[67]

Regulations governing range units favored the cattlemen and made it difficult or impossible for small holders who wanted to use their own land to do so. Requirements that landowners fence their land if they did not want their land permitted as part of a range unit constituted virtual theft. The practice started even before the advent of the grazing unit system. In 1919, when Kills on Horse Back of Manderson sought to remove his land from the huge 7L spread headed by McKoen and was rebuffed, he took his case to US Senator Thomas Sterling who inquired to Commissioner of Indian Affairs Cato Sells on his behalf. Sells' reply left no doubt about OIA priorities:

> Respecting the inquiry of Kills on Horse Back, as to whether he would be requested to fence any of his land contained in the lease of Mr. McKeon, which he might desire for his own use, you are advised that if he wishes to retain all of his allotment he would be required to fence *it as it would hardly be fair to the lessee to require him to fence all of an allotment not leased or which he could not use.* However, if he desires only a small portion, say not more than 10 acres for his own use, the lessee would be required to erect a good fence around such tract [emphasis added].[68]

Today, Oglala landowners who want to remove their land from a grazing unit still have to fence it off at their expense, something most cannot afford to do. They can remove their land from a unit but unless they fence it off the permittee holding the grazing unit is within his rights to allow cattle to graze on it.

The grazing situation on the reservation in the 1930s was a less dramatic rerun of the takeover of the land base Oglalas experienced two decades earlier. Some Oglalas were forced to abandon their homes because range unit boundaries circumscribed their home sites on their own private land. The influx of cattle and sheep put so much pressure on the areas along the creeks where the people lived and gardened that conditions were intolerable.[69] In some cases, Indian homes had been included within grazing units and "Indians within the units were forced to move out and seek another abode." Regional Forester George Nyce's 1939 review of OIA land management practices up to 1934 concluded that application of the grazing unit system resulted in a "chaotic state of affairs." [70]

While OIA extension agents worked to secure land for outside cattlemen, they urged Oglalas to plant gardens, dig root cellars, and make use of the mobile canning kitchens that made the rounds through the reservation districts in the fall. Between 1925–1929, the government formed farm chapters and enlisted women's auxiliaries and 4H clubs to carry out Superintendent Ernest Jermark's "Five-Year Industrial Program." That Program's publicity speaks volumes about OIA perceptions of Oglala people and about its studied refusal to acknowledge its role in shaping the political economy of the reservation. It also provides an instructive window onto the colonial attitudes and ideologies of the OIA.

One piece of OIA propaganda that must have been "mind blowing" to Oglalas at the time depicts the "Trail of Today" as a straight furrow made by a moldboard plow, and, naively or cruelly given the recent history, depicted the trail of yesterday as closed, marking it with an "X" formed by crossed branding irons bearing the "FoF" and "ID" brands of the Indian Department (Figure 3).[71] The imagery evokes the potato famine in Ireland. While the English shipped food out of Ireland the people starved because the only crop they could grow in sufficient quantities to feed them on the small plots left to them after their lands had been stolen had succumbed to the potato blight. Had the OIA forgotten, or did they think the people had forgotten, how their land had been delivered up to outsiders and how their gardens had been and still were being trampled by trespassing stock?

A drawing of a smiling Oglala farm family busily working the land while a rabbit sheds tears outside a boarded up community dance hall captures a favorite OIA theme (Figure 4). Indian Agents and other officials never tired of the thesis that the culture kept people down. The weeping rabbit represents the people who are hopelessly wedded to the rabbit dance, and to Lakota ways in general. Rabbit dances are lively couple's dances that are still popular today. The OIA proscribed them, boarded up dance halls, and outlawed dancing. The prosperous farm family – nuclear, industrious, and assimilated – was the OIA ideal.

Figure 3: "Trail of Yesterday, Trail of Today"

Figure 4: Business Before Pleasure

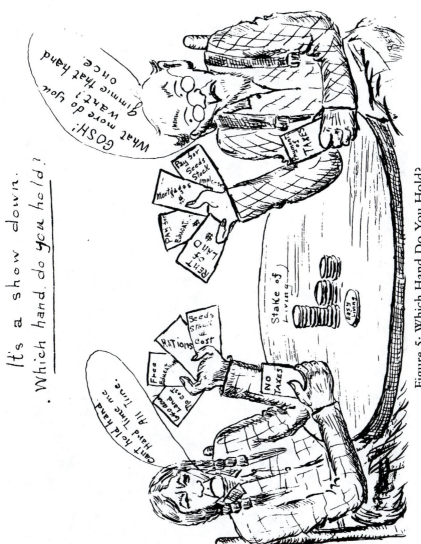

Figure 5: Which Hand Do You Hold?

Figure 6: Uncle Sam Is Watching You!

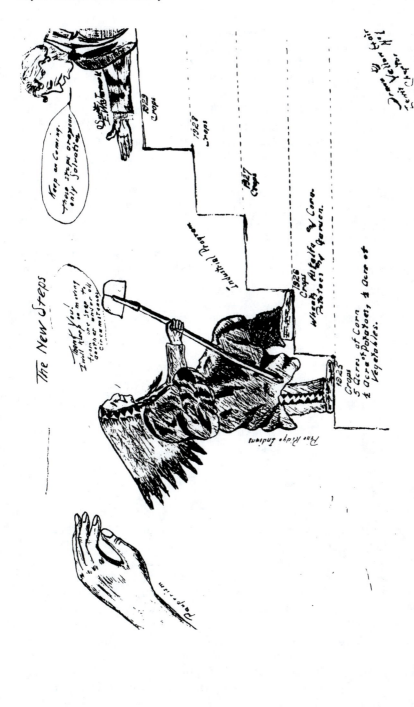

Figure 7: Five Year Plan, or "Superintendent Ernest Jermark as Savior, and the Five Year Plan as the Path to Salvation"

In the ideology of the colonizer there was more than culture that kept people down. The dependency discourse averred that Oglalas, like spoiled children, were unappreciative of the breaks the government bequeathed them, lazily squandering them all. Whites, on the other hand, could succeed without the supposed advantages the reservation system conferred (Figure 5). Consider the irony of the Indian player's hand: rations, free education, 640 acres of land at no cost! How do you calculate the benefits of rations, often consisting of spoiled meat?[72] How do you measure the benefits of forced acculturation through boarding schools where children regularly ran away because of beatings and sexual abuse? And what do you make of the "gifted" 640 acres of land allotted to heads of households, land that was theirs to start with that represented a tiny fraction of what they once held, and that was a product of the disastrous allotment policy? The consternation of the white farmer at the supposed good fortune of the Indian captures a foundation belief in the stereotypes that feed racist notions toward Indian people to this day: "They have it made because of all the federal government does for them. Too bad they are so lazy." It is right out of the best of the European imperial tradition. These lines by Britain's premier literary apologist for imperialism, Rudyard Kipling, from his 1899 poem "White Man's Burden," are apropos:

> Take up the white man's burden-
> The savage wars of peace-
> Fill full the mouth of Famine
> And bid the sickness cease;
> And when your goal is nearest
> The end for others sought,
> Watch sloth and heathen Folly
> Bring all your hopes to naught.

In the event that Oglalas did not willingly avail themselves of the "opportunities" the white man presented, the colonizer could always fall back on force or the threat of force to deal with "sloth and heathen folly." In Figure 6, Uncle Sam interrogates and threatens, his pointing finger a cultural faux pas. "Are you farming? Are you trying? I'm going to find out. Get Busy!" Sometimes the government did "find out," serving as a tool for some to report about others. The consequent erosion of trust is a factor in the "lateral violence" that finds fertile soil in colonial situations.[73]

Figure 7 is a fanciful depiction of the OIA's Five Year Plan and is a ministudy of the colonizer's sense of the relations of domination that characterize the federal-Indian relationship. It features a stereotyped plains Indian leader ascending the steps of progress, closely pursued by the grasping hand of pauperism and beckoned by the open palm of the beneficent Superintendent Jermark, who exhorts his charge to "Keep on coming.

These steps are your only salvation." The white man's way purports to be the people's only hope. Progress up the ladder away from poverty, a condition for which the people themselves are blamed, depends on their willingness to follow the government's imposed plan. That requires humility, and above all deference to the white man and his solutions. The Indian man wears the headdress of a Lakota leader, but instead of pride and defiance, he is abject before the great white father's representative and grateful for the chance to put aside his staff and lance for a hoe. In the words of Frantz Fanon, "In the colonial context the settler only ends his work of breaking in the native when the latter admits loudly and intelligibly the supremacy of the white man's values."[74]

INDIAN BUREAU'S LAND REFORM INITIATIVE FOUNDERS ON SHOALS OF ITS OWN MAKING

A new wind was blowing in the Indian Service in the 1930s. Under the extraordinary stewardship of reform-minded CIA John Collier, attempts were made to turn the land situation around.[75] At a 1935 meeting in Pass Creek District, Collier deplored the fact that the reservation land base was leased principally to whites, attributing it to the fact that Oglalas lacked "the capital with which to put stock on the land . . ."[76] Collier's land reform goals went directly to the heart of the control issue. He summed up his agenda in an address to Department of Agriculture and OIA officials at the Land-Use Conference at Glacier Park, Montana in August, 1938: "The Indian Service must manage in the allotted and unallotted areas to find some scheme of tenure or management that will enable the Indians to use their resources, or everything else is in vain."[77] Like-minded officials on Pine Ridge Reservation, including reform-minded Superintendent W.O. Roberts, knew the problems BIA mismanagement had caused and were committed to solving them.

Roberts noted that white use of reservation land led to ". . . tremendous over-grazing, plowing of lands that should not be plowed, domination of water ways and the like." He judged the situation of Oglalas on Pine Ridge Reservation ". . . so desperate as to rate disaster proportions," and said that he regarded ". . . as our most important immediate step the procedure of land use and range management *based on the needs of Indians and not the convenience of white men* [emphasis in original]."[78]

In 1937, Roberts embarked on an ambitious program that excluded from lease the home sites and surrounding lands of around 1,200 Oglala families, affecting around two-thirds of the families on the reservation. Under the "blue land plan," so named because the parcels singled out for Indian use were outlined in blue on a map, the land those homes were situated on would be exempted from lease by whites and reserved for Oglalas.

In 1937, whites were using an estimated seven-eighths of the grazing land on the reservation to pasture about 50,000 of their cattle and about the same number of sheep. The blue land plan was designed to empty the reservation of those white-owned stock so that the land could be secured for the use of the people who would get stock from a heifer replacement herd the Bureau had in order to help make Indian use of Indian land possible.[79]

Extension agents held meetings with the landowners about the plan, and Roberts claimed that most Oglalas were supportive and enthusiastic. "The attempt was made," he wrote, "to bring the Indians into groups and talk to them about this matter, putting the situation before them and allowing the democratic principle to work."[80] Communities decided by popular vote whether they would be involved in the plan. Of the 1,200 or so affected families, not more than 20 opposed the plan.[81]

Oglalas supported the blue land plan, but white ranchers whose interests it threatened were outraged. In a January 1937 letter to the Secretary of the Interior, Fred Hans of Gordon, Nebraska, a border town about 18 miles from the southern border of Pine Ridge Reservation, complained directly to the Secretary of the Interior. Roberts responded to Hans, quoting a revealing passage from the latter's own letter to Interior:

> 'The reason for this [i.e., withdrawing land from lease] is that they claim they desire to make a more self supporting Indian which all sounds sweet and possibly would be so had they any practical material to work with. I think the Department at Washington is aware of the fact that give an Indian 25 head of good white face cows and plenty of land for them to run on, dig him a good well, put a good pump on it, build him a nice new house, build him some nice new barns and fence it all nice, and give him some rations and a few clothes and some medicine and in six weeks he will be out of every thing and back to Uncle Sam for the same thing over again.'[82]

Hans' remarks, Roberts said, typified prevailing white opinion in the area. He cited the example of Tom Arnold, a prosperous white lessee on the Rosebud Reservation, (the same individual who secured trespass authority for a large operation on Pine Ridge Reservation in 1917), who, in a recent presentation before the State Planning Board, had developed ". . . the thesis that a lease hold on the reservation constitutes a *vested right* [emphasis in original]." In his discussions with leading ranchers, stockmen, and businessmen in the area Roberts' found that ". . . they view Indians as a worthless lot, undependable, unindustrious, thriftless. They feel that the way to remedy this condition is for the white man to use his [sic] land."[83]

Racist white ranchers – who had up to that time been actively courted by the Indian Bureau – were not alone in their opposition to the blue lands plan. Though the Oglala Sioux Tribal Council (OST) generally supported it, two influential mixed blood residents of Bennett County found serious fault with the initiative.[84] OST President Frank G. Wilson, and OST Vice-President Harry Conroy charged that by setting aside the blue lands from lease Roberts' office had helped send the Charter down to defeat in the 1937 election. Conroy claimed that hundreds of white men had taken to the "Indian field spreading propaganda telling the Indians that the Indian Service, under the Reorganization Act, was exercising powers over their properties and denying them due process rights. Under the circumstances it was not hard for the Indians to swallow this poison." Wilson claimed that ". . . the unlettered tribesmen generally construed this plan [i.e., blue lands plan] as a part of the intended new deal. . . . Whether this arrangement was purposely designed to discourage the Indians from incorporating we have as yet no positive proof."[85]

Roberts defended the blue land plan to the CIA, maintaining that ". . . neither community or individual gardens, to speak of, would have been possible because of the use or occupation of the land by white owned stock." The people, he said, expressed a lively interest in the plan, a plan Roberts contended corresponded ". . . to the needs and desires of Indians as well as a sound administrative range supervision." [86]

The gulf between Wilson and his supporters on the one hand, and Oglala landowners on the other, was starkly demarcated by their disagreement over a small parcel of land in Corn Creek Community in the northeast portion of Pine Ridge Reservation. At issue was the future expansion of the Corn Creek Cattle Association, a cooperative enterprise involving about 20 largely full blood families. The families had pooled their allotted lands, husbanded their own cattle, obtained a loan from the OIA's reimbursable fund (made possible by the Indian Reorganization Act), and were cooperatively raising a herd of 760 cattle. A range management plan developed in concert with Association members and Roberts' staff made provisions for expansion of the Association's range through the lease of a portion of the adjacent Allen Timber Reserve [unallotted trust land].[79]

When Corn Creek Association members applied to the OST Council for use of the Allen Reserve in November, 1939, Wilson blocked their application with bureaucratic red tape. Nothing could be done, he said, until their Association drafted a constitution and had it approved by the OST Council. What he failed to tell them or the Council was that he had already promised use of the timber reserve to his friend, Emery Amiotte. Amiotte ranched in Long Valley, some 40 miles from the timber reserve. He was the Secretary of the "Organization of Mixed Blood Sioux Indians of Bennett County," and was used to having his way with reservation land. Several years earlier when the OIA called him on his practice of running stock on allotted land without landowner permission, he maintained he did not need a lease and that it was his right to use the land free of charge.[88]

Roberts' support for the Corn Creek Association landed him in a running battle with Wilson. When a Civilian Conservation Core crew started fencing off the timber reserve area for the Association, Wilson personally told the crew's foreman to stop, whereupon Roberts advised the CCC foreman to continue the work.[89] Wilson also tried to get rid of the OIA's Extension Department head Russell Coulter because of his support for the Corn Creek Association. He asked U.S. Representative Francis Case to help, invoking the tribe's right to control the land: "We have enough tribal lands being used by the government now. . . . We want them to pay or release what they are using."[90] But the lands in question were being used by Indian families, not the government. Their right to use the land was actually protected by the OST Constitution and Wilson was violating it by denying the Corn Creek Association's request. Article X states that "In the leasing of tribal lands preference shall be given first, to Indian communities or cooperative associations, and secondly, to individual Indians who are members of the Oglala Sioux Tribe."[91]

On October 1, 1938, OST Council member Peter Dillon, and 23 other mixed bloods and full bloods, petitioned the OIA protesting the permitting of a range unit to the mixed blood rancher, Joseph Livermont, Jr. Petitioners stated that they owned the allotted land adjacent the range unit and that permitting the unit to Livermont would deny them their customary access to that land. They charged that the OST Executive Committee acted alone to award the range unit to Livermont, that the whole council should have been involved, and characterized the decision as made by a "Dictatorship." In fact, President Wilson and OST Secretary Charles Little Hawk did act alone to seal the deal. With no Agency supported initiative at stake, Roberts supported the Council's decision on behalf of Livermont, suggesting that the petition merely reflected the interests of Dillon and two other mixed bloods.[92]

The unit system was an opportunity for some OST politicians to use the grazing permit power to benefit certain constituencies, especially if the interests they represented were those of commercial ranchers and not subsistence users. The constituencies that benefited were definitely the ranching class, whose use of units would bring money to the tribal coffers insofar as those units included tribal lands, and not a broader category of "mixed bloods." Dillon himself was a mixed blood, but unlike Wilson's rancher friend or Livermont, he had long been allied with the pre-IRA Oglala Council that was dominated by full bloods.

The Indian Bureau supported numerous cattle cooperatives on the reservation in the 1930s and into the late 1940s. An important factor leading to their demise was the pressure on them from ranchers, including mixed blood ranchers, and from the IRA government that developed the practice of allowing certain individuals, usually the President and one or two others, or the Executive Committee, to handle the allocation of range units.[93]

Frank Wilson used the power over grazing unit allocation to support individual ranchers and to shut out those who used allotted lands in common. Representative government under the IRA had the potential to be a tool for supporting commercial ranching interests against cooperatives and subsistence use. Bringing money into tribal coffers for the use of politicians like Wilson through support for a small constituency of ranchers was a 180 degree turnabout from the goal of the older Oglala Omniciye, which had always been to secure land for the use of larger numbers of Oglala people and tiospaye.

With the advent of representative government on Pine Ridge Reservation, contradictions in Oglala society that had been relatively tangential came to the fore and were reflected in competition for political leadership, the likes of which had not been seen before. Those contradictions were partially determined by changing relations with the land, and in the new arena of political struggle they in turn fed back into the competition over it, changing the nature of the struggle.

Competition for leadership over the 21 Council and the conflict attendant on the adoption of IRA government on Pine Ridge Reservation bore no resemblance to a two party political system like that in the United States today, where both parties share fundamental assumptions. Representative government under the IRA reflected the cultural, political, and economic chasm that differentiated a relatively small group of mixed bloods and the rest of Oglala society. Older Oglala notions about leadership growing out of tiospaye, and of sovereignty resting on the Treaty, ran directly counter to elective leadership that had its roots in narrow local interests informed by ideologies mirroring those of the colonizer and white society.[94] Once those competing tendencies found an outlet in representative government, the relative unity of purpose that the Oglala had forged in the reservation era was reduced to a thing of memory and yearning. Where the Oglala Omniciye advocated for people's use of land against commercial interests, the new IRA government, the OST, advocated for commercial interests in much the same way the Indian Bureau had done throughout the reservation period.

The role of the Indian Bureau in integrating the reservation economy into the market system came to a brief halt after the adoption of the IRA, but as the Collier vision faded its functionaries retreated back to reclaim their preferred niche as broker of the people's interests to others. Collier's vision of land reform, of Indian people reclaiming the reservation land base, ultimately foundered on the rocks of the IRA government. In the years to come, the small group whose interests were served by Frank G. Wilson and similarly situated politicians who reached out to control the disposition of grazing land through the range unit system in that first IRA government, would consolidate its control over the reservation land base. In the era of the IRA, the OST picked up the mantle of defender and promulgator of commercial interests the Indian Bureau had temporarily abandoned. When Collier and company turned a corner, the new IRA leadership kept on going. The role of the IRA government as land rights advocate for the privileged few would have important implications for the Oglala people in the years to come.

Notes

1. Deloria, Vine Jr. and Clifford Lytle, 1984, p. 121.

2. Author's notes.

3. "A Report on the Bureau of Indian Affairs Fee Patenting and Canceling Policies, 1900–1942," June 1, 1981. Tidwell to Burke, April 6, 1922, 14081-13-059 to 37426-35-062, PR, CCF. Copy of November 21, 1917 letter from Ellis and attached list in author's possession.

4. Richmond Clow, Personal communication, June 2000. Clow is an Assistant Professor in the Indian Studies Department at the University of Montana in Missoula. He has done extensive research on the forced fee patenting issue.

5. See Chapter 3.

6. Price, Catherine, p. 33–42.

7. See chapters 4 and 5.

8. Charles H. Burke to Ernest W. Jermark, Feb. 28, 1927. 1131-24-054 pt. 1 to 3 39497-31-054, 1907–1939, CCF.

9. E.W. Jermark, Election announcement, December 3, 1928; B.G. Courtright, Field Agent in Charge to CIA, April 15, 1931 and May 8, 1931, 11131-24-054 pt. 1 to 3 39497-31-054, 1907–1939, CCF.

10. B.G. Courtright, Field Agent in Charge to CIA, April 15, 1931 and May 8, 1931, 11131-24-054 pt. 1 to 3 39497-31-054, 1907–1939, CCF.

11. Ibid.

12. Ibid.

13. James LaPointe, 21 Council Secretary, plus 17 other members of the 21 Council to the CIA, stamped received March 13, 1931. 1131-24-054 pt. 1 to 39497-31-054, 1907–1939, Pine Ridge, CCF.

14. Ibid.

15. Hermus Merrival to CIA, forwarded from Pine Ridge Agency on March 10, 1931. 1131-24-054 pt. 1 to 39497-31-054, 1907–1939, Pine Ridge, CCF.

16. Ibid.

17. James LaPointe, 21 Council Secretary, plus 17 other members of the 21 Council to the CIA, stamped received March 13, 1931. 1131-24-054 pt. 1 to 39497-31-054, 1907–1939, Pine Ridge, CCF.

18. Petition from Mixed-Blood Sioux Indians of Bennett County, n.d.; John Monroe to Jermark, May 29, 1930; E.W. Jermark to John Monroe, June 2, 1930. 1131-24-054 pt. 1 to 39497-31-054, 1907–39, CCF. James H. McGregor to John Collier, October 23, 1934, File 321, Miscellaneous, MDF-PR.

19. Minutes of the Oglala Council for February 19–21, 1931. 1131-24-054 pt. 1 to 39497-31-054, 1907–39, Pine Ridge, CCF.

20. Ibid.

21. BG. Courtright (Field Agent in Charge) to CIA, April 15, 1931; Petition to the CIA to discontinue the 21 Council, n.d.; William Spotted Crow to Honorable William Williamson, stamped received April 16, 1931. 1131-24-054 pt. 1 to 3 39497-31-054 1907–39, CCF.

22. B.S. Garber to Vice President Charles Curtis, May 6, 1931. 1131-24-054 pt. 1 to 39497-31-054, 1907–39, Pine Ridge, CCF.

23. Gertrude Bonnin to Charles Rhoads, CIA, April 4, 1931. 1131-24-054 pt. 1 to 39497-31-054, 1907–39, Pine Ridge, CCF.

24. Minutes of joint meeting of Oglala Tribal Council and 21 Council, September 4, 1931. 42953-31-054 to 12021-34-054, 1907–39 Pine Ridge, CCF.

25. James H. McGregor to CIA February 28, 1931; James McGregor to CIA Rhoads, January 14, 1932. 1131-24-054 pt. 1 to 3 39497-31-054 1907–39, CCF.

26. Constitution of the Oglala Treaty Council, December 1931. 1131-24-054 pt. 1 to 3 39497-31-054 1907–39, CCF. Clow, Richmond L., 1987b.

27. Clow, Richmond L., 1987b, p. 128.

28. James LaPointe, 21 Council Secretary, plus 17 other members of the 21 Council to the CIA, stamped received March 13, 1931, 1131-24-054 pt. 1 to 39497-31-054, 1907–39, Pine Ridge, CCF.

29. Memorandum of Charles Brooks, Head Community Worker, Pine Ridge Agency, n.d., E1012 PR 057-9684 to 068-9684 RG 75 NA. James H. McGregor, Superindent Pine Ridge Agency to CIA John Collier, October 29, 1934. E1012 PR 057-9684 to 068-9684, RG 75 NA. Elders on Pine Ridge Reservation also maintain that many persons boycotted the IRA elections.

30. Deloria, Vine Jr., and Clifford Lytle, p. 151.

31. Deloria, Vine Jr., and Clifford Lytle, 1984, p. 105.

32. List of votes for and against the IRA by poling place. E1012 Pine Ridge 057-9684 to 068-9684, RG 75 NA.

33. Useful references on the IRA include Deloria, Vine Jr. and Clifford Lytle, 1984; Biolsi, Thomas, 1992; Taylor, Graham D., 1980; Cornell, Stephen, 1988.

34. IRA referendum results in E1012 Pine Ridge 057-9684 to 068-9684, RG 75 NA. Charter election results in File 020, Box 150, Legislation: Wheeler Howard Act, MDF-PR.

35. W.O. Roberts to Asst. CIA Zimmerman, April 17, 1939, File 064, Councils, 1937–1941 KC.

36. Collier to Standing Bear, November 14, 1938, E1012 PR 057-9684 to 068-9684 RG 75 NA.

37. W.O. Roberts to Collier, January 8, 1937; W.O. Roberts to CIA, March 20, 1937, E1012 Pine Ridge 057-9684 to 068-9684, RG 75 NA.

38. Blood quanta of OST Council members are noted in "List of OST Council members elected on April 4, 1936," E1012 Pine Ridge 057-9684 to 068-9684, RG 75 NA.

39. Henry Standing Bear to John Collier, June 12, 1937, E1012 Pine Ridge 057-9684 to 068-9684, RG 75 NA. W.O. Roberts to John Collier, January 8, 1937. E1012 Pine Ridge 057-9684 to 068-9684, RG 75 NA.

40. W.O. Roberts to CIA John Collier, January 8, 1937, E1012 PR 057-9684 to 068-9684, RG 75 NA.

41. Assistant CIA William Zimmerman to W.O. Roberts, February 17, 1939, E1012 Pine Ridge 057-9684 to 068-9684, RG 75 NA.

42. Deloria, Vine, Jr. and Clifford Lytle, 1984, p. 78–9.

43. List of OST Council members elected on April 4, 1936, E1012 PR 057-9684 to 068-9684, RG 75 NA.

44. Harry Conroy to Collier, n.d., E1012 PR 057-9684 to 068-9684, RG 75 NA;

45. OST Executive Committee to W.O. Roberts , March 27, 1937, E1012 PR 057-9684 to 068-9684, RG 75 NA.

46. See, for example, the section "Ethnic structure of colonial administration" in chapter 2, Agent John Brennan's views of Oglalas (1901–1917) in Chapter 4, or Superintendent Henry Tidwell's views in Chapter 5.

47. Frank G. Wilson to John Collier, n.d., E1012 PR 057-9684 to 068-9684, RG 75 NA.

48. W.O. Roberts to CIA, March 20, 1937, E1012 Pine Ridge 057-9684 to 068-9684, RG 75 NA

49. Memorandum of Charles Brooks, Head Community Worker, Pine Ridge Agency, n.d., E1012 Pine Ridge 057-9684 to 068-9684, RG 75 NA.

50. Ibid.

51. Cf. Report of Inspector John W. Bale, November 30, 1920, 75-33-053 to 80965-22-054, 1907–1939, PR, CCF for information about defaulting lessees on Pine Ridge Reservation. Lee, Bob and Dick Williams 1964, p. 266, report on the large drop in prices for cattle on the Chicago market for 1920.

52. The famous Matador Cattle Company was willing to try its luck on the reservation and took over the 7L lease from McKoen's Newcastle Land and Livestock Company. But it pulled out several years later.

53. Names of Lessees, Pine Ridge Reservation, 1917, Series: Trust responsibilities, File: List of lessees, 1917, Box 872, Pine Ridge, KC.

54. J.B. Wingfield to CIA, August 18, 1922, 75-33-053 to 80965-22-054, 1907–1939, PR, CCF. Report of Inspector John W. Bale, November 30, 1920, 75-33-053 to 80965-22-054, 1907–1939, PR, CCF.

55. McGregor to Collier, October 23, 1934, File 321, Miscellaneous, MDF-PR.

56. Petition from Pass Creek to CIA, January 22, 1922, 14081-13-059 to 37426-35-062, PR, CCF. Record of Hearing before E.B. Meritt, Assistant CIA, May 7, 1925, File 064, MDF-PR.

57. See previous chapter.

58. The Local Situation, 1931, File 304.3, Box 352, MDF-PR.

59. Notes from Pine Ridge Lease Dept., initialed W.W.T., n.d., File 321, Box 369, Farming and Grazing Lease Matters 1932–1937, MDF-PR; Author's notes. Cf. also OIA report titled "The Local Situation," 1931, File 304.3, Box 352, MDF-PR.

60. Author's notes.
61. Clow, Richmond 1989, p. 366.
62. William G. Pugh to Mr. A.W. Simington, September 16, 1935, File 304.1, MDF-PR. (Pugh was the publisher of the *Shannon County News*, and an Oglala Sioux Tribal member.)
63. McGregor to Collier, May 28, 1934, File 321, Box 369, Miscellaneous, MDF-PR.
64. McGregor to CIA Collier, May 14, 1934, File 321, Box 369, Miscellaneous, MDF-PR.
65. Notes from Pine Ridge Lease Dept., initialed W.W.T., n.d., File 321, Box 369, Farming and Grazing Lease Matters 1932–1937, MDF-PR.
66. Superintendent James H. McGregor, Circular, May 4, 1933, File 308.1, Box 354, Submarginal land use – trespasses or settlement, MDF-PR.
67. Superintendent McGregor to CIA Collier, October 10, 1933, File 031.0, Box 152, Dept. Relations Forest Service Department of Agriculture, 1930–36, MDF-PR.
68. Cato Sells to US Senator Thomas Sterling, July 16, 1919. RG 75 BIA Classified Files 1907–1939 Pine Ridge 95661-13-320 to 38355-20-320.
69. McGregor to Collier, May 14, 1934, File 321, Box 369, Miscellaneous, MDF-PR; The Local Situation, 1931, File 304.3, Box 352, MDF-PR; George Nyce to W.O. Roberts, May 16, 1939, File 320.7, Box 366, General Range Advertisements, 1938–1940, MDF-PR.
70. George Nyce to W.O. Roberts, May 16, 1939, File 320.7, Box 366, General Range Advertisements, 1938–1940, MDF-PR.
71. Figures 3–7 in Industrial Program Publicity Material, File 103.81, Box 194, MDF-PR.
72. Cf. Chapter 3.
73. Cf. Fanon, Frantz 1963, p. 54 and more generally, first section "Concerning Violence." Reports of unauthorized dancing and unauthorized meetings made to Indian Agents are reported in earlier chapters.
74. Fanon, Frantz 1963, p. 43.
75. The crowning piece of legislation during the Collier era was the Indian Reorganization Act of 1934. Although it was changed a great deal before passage, important elements affecting land tenure were incorporated into the Act: The allotment policy was terminated and the trust period on allotted lands was indefinitely extended; surplus lands previously opened for sale were returned to tribal control; and funds could be appropriated for the purchase of additional land for reservations. Deloria, Vine Jr., and Clifford Lytle 1984, p. 269.
76. Notes of "Meeting held by Mr. John Collier, Commissioner of Indian Affairs at Allen, South Dakota, November 19, 1935," RG 75 BIA Classified Files, Pine Ridge, 1907–1939, 9684-E-36-054, pts. 1 to 3.
77. Minutes of the Land-Use Conference held at Glacier Park, Montana, August 14–17, 1938, OLC.
78. W.O. Roberts to CIA, February 12, 1937, 51062-20-320 to 14039-13-321, 1907–39, CCF.

79. W.O. Roberts to CIA, February 12, 1937, CCF; W.O. Roberts to Fred Hans, February 12, 1937; Asst. CIA William Zimmerman to OST delegation, September 23, 1937, 51062-20-320 to 14039-13-321, 1907–39, CCF.
80. W.O. Roberts to Hon. Francis Case, Member of Congress, September 22, 1937, File 321, Box 369, Farm and grazing lease matters – general correspondence, MDF-PR; cf. also Roberts to CIA, August 31, 1937, File 308, Box 353, Tribal Lands, MDF-PR.
81. W.O. Roberts to Peter Red Elk, October 6, 1937, 9514-37-054 to 7406-30-056, 1907–39, Pine Ridge, CCF.
82. W.O. Roberts to Fred Hans, February 12, 1937, 51062-20-320 to 14039-13-321, 1907–39, CCF.
83. W.O. Roberts to CIA, February 12, 1937, 51062-20-320 to 14039-13-321, 1907–39, CCF.
84. W.O. Roberts to CIA, August 31, 1937, File 308, Box 353, Tribal Lands, MDF-PR. The OST was established under the Indian Reorganization Act of 1934, and was recognized as the official governing body in 1936.
85. Frank Wilson to W.O. Roberts, March 27, 1937, E1012 Pine Ridge 057-9684 to 068-9684, RG 75 NA; Harry Conroy to Collier, n.d., E1012 PR 057-9684 to 068-9684, RG 75 NA. Note how the term "Indians" is used as a distancing mode.
86. Roberts to CIA, August 31, 1937, File 308, Box 353, Tribal Lands, MDF-PR.
87. W.O. Roberts to CIA, December 7, 1939, 51062-20-320 to 14039-13-321, Pine Ridge, CCF; Untitled, handwritten description of Corn Creek Association organization and plan, January 4, (no year), 7 pages, 51062-20-320 to 14039-13-321, Pine Ridge, CCF.
88. James H. McGregor to Collier, June 24, 1935, 24891-34-301 to 2651-26-302, 1907–39, Pine Ridge, CCF. Petition from Mixed-Blood Sioux Indians of Bennett County, n.d., 1131-24-054 pt. 1 to 39497-31-054, 1907–39, CCF.
89. W.O. Roberts to CIA, December 7, 1939, 51062-20-320 to 14039-13-321, Pine Ridge, CCF.
90. Frank G. Wilson to Francis Case, November 12, 1939, File 308, Box 353, Tribal land, MDF-PR.
91. OST Constitution, copy in author's possession.
92. Petition from Peter Dillon, et al. to CIA, October 1, 1938, 14081-13-059 to 37426-35-062, Pine Ridge, CCF; W.O. Roberts to CIA, November 2, 1938, 14081-13-059 to 37426-35-062, Pine Ridge, CCF; List of OST Council members elected on April 4, 1936, E1012 Pine Ridge 057-9684 to 068-9684, RG 75 NA.
93. OST Resolution of February 6, 1941, File 300.9, MDF-PR; OST Resolution 222, July 12, 1944, File 061, Box 177, OST Council 1940-44, MDF-PR; author's notes.
94. Steven Feraca attributed Oglala full blood opposition to the IRA to traditionalism and mixed blood support to greater acculturation. See Feraca, Steven 1964, p. 31–37, and 1966, p. 7. Raymond DeMallie cited the opposition between "more acculturated mixed-bloods" and "traditionally oriented" full bloods but he also emphasized that Oglala beliefs about government, leadership, and nationhood, are

at odds with the IRA as it evolved on Pine Ridge Reservation, noting that "Oglala living in the various district communities, do not as a whole believe in a representative form of government. They do not identify with the tribe as a political group and would prefer to run their own affairs at the local level, under the direction of local leaders whose support comes from community faith in their abilities." Quotation is from DeMallie, Raymond 1978, p. 274; see also p. 260–261,307, 309.

CHAPTER 7

Land and Power in the Era of the IRA

"Makasitomini lakol wicohan kin lila tehi yelo."
"All around the world the Lakota way is very hard"
Title of Sissy Good House Song

On January 16, 2000, the Grass Roots Oyate (people) occupied the Red Cloud Building in Pine Ridge Village. The small group put out a call for support over KILI Radio and by late afternoon the building was jammed with supporters calling for an end to IRA government and condemning it for corruption and failure to address land and treaty rights. The Red Cloud Building was the administrative headquarters for the Oglala Sioux Tribal government (OST) but the occupiers, who remain in the building as of April, 2001, have designated it the *Oyate tipi* or "people's house," and increasingly refer to it as the "Lakota embassy." *"Oyate tipi"* signifies the occupiers' belief that governance belongs to the people, not to a group of elected politicians that they charge with lining their own pockets and serving the interests of a privileged few at the expense of the 80% who are unemployed. They believe that they could turn that situation around by establishing a "traditional Lakota government" based on Lakota *tiospaye,* and they reject the "white man's western style" government that provides for the election of Council members from each of the nine reservation districts every two years. The more recent designation of the building as the "Lakota embassy" underscores the widely shared aspiration for "nation to nation" relations with other countries, and reflects the appraisal that the current "government to government" relation with U.S. federal authorities is high sounding rhetoric – a disguise for domination and continuing colonial oppression.[1]

Oglala Sioux Tribal government, organized under the Indian Reorganization Act of 1934 (IRA), and often scornfully referred to simply as the "IRA government" has been under fire by its own people since it was created in 1936.[2] Oglalas, and many other groups, have a 60 year plus tradition of contesting the legitimacy of tribal governments that critics argue are akin to the British model of indirect rule, falling far short of the goals of the visionary architect of the New Deal for Indians, John Collier.

199

Resistance to the IRA has been particularly stiff on Pine Ridge Reservation where the American Indian Movement (AIM) answered the call of elders and others whose freedom to assemble and basic civil rights had been eroded under the controversial and U.S. supported tenure of OST President Richard "Dick" Wilson, who served two consecutive terms from 1972–1976. The 1973 Wounded Knee Occupation at the site of the Wounded Knee Massacre grabbed headlines around the world after the U.S. government deployed federal marshals and the military against the popular movement that advocated replacement of the IRA government with one based on Lakota tradition and the authority of the 1868 Fort Laramie Treaty. The current standoff is peaceful and much less well known, but both share the underlying and enduring aim of establishing a sovereign government based on a Lakota foundation.[3]

Scholarly opinions about the IRA experiment run the gamut from wholesale approval to outright condemnation. Noted anthropologist Fred Eggan claimed that because of the IRA ". . . Indians are in a much better position in almost all respects."[4] Widely cited historian of Indian affairs Wilcomb Washburn offered a more specific but similarly optimistic appraisal, declaring IRA governments to be ". . . autonomous, functioning political organisms, capable of maintaining themselves against the power of their white neighbors and against the power of the states and the federal government."[5] Noted Native American scholar Vine Deloria, Jr., whose writings pricked the conscience of anthropologists and moved some to rethink their discipline in the 1970s, called the IRA a "giant step forward in the development of the Indian communities" and credited Collier with engineering U.S. Congressional support for "a form of self-government that was suitable for the conditions under which Indians then lived."[6]Cahuilla historian Robert Costo, on the other hand, charged that Collier was vindictive and manipulative and that IRA governments were pushed down the throats of tribes, many of which favored their traditional arrangements over the IRA's western style electoral democracy.[7] Anthropologist Karl Schlesier vigorously denounced IRA governments, contending that they ". . . are maintained only through the BIA bureaucracy and Indian lackeys operating against their own people," and asserting that the "Oglala are a case in point."[8]

Anthropologist Thomas Biolsi studied the IRA on Pine Ridge and neighboring Rosebud Reservations, and concluded they had been disempowered by the OIA. That kept them from controlling "the critical resources in the artificial reservation economies or from truly representing the people or guaranteeing civil liberties." The resulting ineffectiveness of tribal governments made them an object of dissatisfaction, and they appeared to be "oppressive and parasitic to their would-be constituents in ways that the OIA [federal government] did not."[9]

But if the sanguine assessments of Eggan and Washburn seem unwarranted, so does the bleak appraisal of Schlesier. Broad generalizations about the IRA and tribal governments, at least in their evolved state, do not hold up under scrutiny. Case studies carried out by Harvard's Kennedy School of government reveal a highly mixed record. Some tribal governments, like White Mountain Apache in Arizona, Flathead in Montana, and Cochiti Pueblo in New Mexico have secured political stability and a measure of economic success for their people. Others, like the Crow in Montana, and the Oglala Sioux Tribe on the Pine Ridge Reservation, where tribal officials estimate the unemployment rate 80%, have failed to deliver.[10] Steven Cornell and Joseph Kalt found that successful tribal governments have developed solid institutions, instituted separation of powers, and have solved basic problems of governance, including the establishment of mechanisms to safeguard the people's resources. Some, like Cochiti Pueblo, achieved success by building on traditional foundations; others, like Flathead, achieved it by building on a western model. One characteristic successful tribal governments do share is that they have ". . . aggressively made the tribe itself the effective decision-maker in reservation affairs."[11]

Undoing the damage caused by a century or more of solutions imposed by the federal government and creating a viable polity is possible but it presupposes the exercise of sovereignty. But why do some tribes take the necessary steps to build effective institutions of governance while others fail? Are there factors that militate against assertion of sovereignty by the IRA government on Pine Ridge Reservation? Does the federal government disempower the OST and render it ineffective? Is the OST in league with the BIA against its own people? Why is the history of IRA government on the reservation marked by conflict and crises of legitimacy?

Partial answers to those questions were suggested by the presentation on the 21 Council and the discussion of the advent of the IRA in the previous chapter. This one follows the thread of the struggle for the land, and of the evolving political economy in the era of the IRA in the search for fuller understanding. An overview of people's movement over and off of the reservation land base offers a window into the role that federal legislation and local implementation by the OST and the BIA have played in alienating people from their land since the 1950s, and of the significance of that development for the Oglala people and for ranching interests. An examination of changing land ownership, use, and control patterns shows how a small group of mixed blood ranchers were able to capitalize on their identities and use the OST and their connections in the BIA in a successful bid to take control over the reservation land base. A somewhat detailed account of the recent struggle of the Lakota Landowner Association to influence tribal grazing legislation illumines connections between the local BIA and certain elements in the OST that seek to hold those who seek to reestablish ties with the land in check. A brief look at the controversial administration of OST President Richard "Dick" Wilson draws attention to an important new dimension in reservation political economy.

AN OGLALA DIASPORA

The right of Oglalas to choose where they want to live has been contested on Pine Ridge Reservation for over one hundred years. In 1885, after Agent McGillycuddy stopped issuing canvas so that the people could no longer use tipis and would have no choice but to build log cabins, he had several hundred of the cabins torn down because he wanted the people to live in dispersed settlements, not in the tiospaye settlements they preferred.[12]

The huge influx of outside cattle during the era of big leasing in World War I so degraded the environment around some people's homes that they had no choice but to move. In the late teens and early 1920s, pursuant Cato Sells' racist 1917 Policy Declaration that forced a fee patent on those Indian persons possessed of one-half or more white blood, and who were otherwise deemed "competent," hundreds of mixed blood families were taxed off their lands and moved off reservation or to neighboring towns.[13]

Some of the newly landless Oglala mixed bloods settled down around Pine Ridge Agency, adding to the nucleus of the colonial town and helping make Pine Ridge Village what it is today – a largely mixed blood settlement that grew up around the Bureau of Indian Affairs. James Red Cloud complained about that development and asked that the new settlers be moved out onto the land to farm.[14] But they were landless, Pine Ridge Superintendent Ernest Jermark replied, and they had already ". . . built small houses, or acquired houses from others on the agency and school reserve within the town of Pine Ridge."[15]

In 1942, the war provided an excuse for the U.S. government to usurp some 400 square miles of Oglala land. On September 8, 1942, the U.S. government filed suit in federal court for condemnation of the individually owned lands in a strip of land 40 miles long and 10 miles wide along the northern reservation border. By October 24, 1942, over 300 mixed blood and full blood Oglalas in 125 families were evacuated from the area so that the U.S. government could use it for target practice. In their 1981 study, Women of All Red Nations (WARN was an AIM affiliated organization of Indian women) decried the fact that the people "were moved out of their homes almost overnight." At the time of the expropriation the OIA, ever the guardian of Indian rights and well being, "'warned'" Superintendent W.O. Roberts to keep payments for the land it was expropriating "'down to the lowest possible level.'" Two years after the families were summarily relieved of their homes and their land they were destitute. Roberts commented on their predicament:

almost all of the 125 families so dispossessed and who were making their own living prior to the action of dispossession are now either living on the money which they got for their lands, or have exhausted it and now are on relief. Only about a dozen families have been satisfactorily re-established.[16]

OST tribal member and AIM leader Ted Means estimated that a much more ambitious government project was responsible for removal of "nearly half the Indian population" to urban areas in the 1950s and 1960s.[17] Operation Relocation was introduced in 1952, during President Eisenhower's administration, to solve the "Indian problem" by moving Indian people off reservations to jobs in cities. CIA Dillon Myer, the architect of the solution, apprenticed for the job at the helm of the War Relocation Authority in World War II. That agency carried out "the removal, incarceration, and relocation of Japanese-Americans and Japanese aliens in the U.S. . . ."[18] Myer surrounded himself with cronies from the Relocation Authority and moved quickly to develop his plan. At the end of his first year as Commissioner, ". . . former Secretary of the Interior Harold L. Ickes characterized him as '"a Hitler and Mussolini rolled into one . . ."'[19]

Many Oglalas who relocated in the 1950s and 1960s had been living on their own land. Some grazed cattle and raised gardens. Some would not have relocated had their livelihood not been cut out from under them by the application of the grazing unit system. Oglala families who made a living through communal sharing arrangements or through individual lease agreements, despite heirship fractionation, were seen as an impediment to sound use of the land. Their own methods for coping with the problems the government had wrought were of no consequence to the government. According to government calculation, they used too much land for the number of animals they kept and were not efficient. Once the government put land people owned and used into a range unit, their subsistence operations were finished.

One Lakota elder recalled the chaos his family suffered because of the unit system:

> In 1955 we were forced, around '54 we had a fight of trying to get units. And this is where, again, a Bureau official sitting down and getting a ruler and a red ink pencil and drawing lines. 'This will be a unit and this will be.' So finally, we couldn't borrow any money, my father, my uncles, they went all over trying to get, borrow money to [get the unit]. So we had to sell out, October of '55. Boss farmer went out there, land operations. They rounded up all the cows and horses and they put spray paint on their back and they shaved the brand and semis came and they drove them up. . . . So I stayed drunk for about November and December. I went into service 1956. And that kind of, my dad got mad and burned down all the haystacks, all the corrals, sheds, hay racks.[20]

The white rancher who took over the range unit that included the families' allotments still uses that land. The Lakota *tiospaye* that used it in the 1950s is spread out to different reservation districts and to Rapid City and Minneapolis.

Oglalas relocated to Cleveland, Minneapolis, Denver, Chicago, Los Angeles, and other urban areas. The displacements affected mixed blood and full blood alike. Many who have returned from relocation would like to access the land they once lived on but cannot. Relocation and forced removal from the land have left a legacy of anger and sorrow. It is part of what Lakota elder and former OST President Johnson Holy Rock calls "a long history of injustice that goes back to the Wounded Knee Massacre and beyond."[21]

Some argue that Relocation was a conspiracy to benefit ranchers. Conspiracy or not, the conjunction of Relocation and BIA land use policies were part of a long-term process that served to prop up commercial ranching and extensive land use at the expense of subsistence tenure and the associated cultural pattern of *tiospaye* living. Some oral accounts implicate the South Dakota Stock Grower's Association (SDSGA, formerly the Western South Dakota Stock Grower's Association) in the land dealings of those years. Interestingly, one SDSGA director during that period was longtime Porcupine resident and rancher Mert Glover. His father, John Glover, managed the Newcastle Land and Livestock Company's 7L spread, the same that in December, 1917, was given legalized trespass authority over more than 400,000 acres of land belonging to Oglala allottees on Pine Ridge Reservation. He stayed behind after the 7L pulled out in the 1920s. His son eventually owned 10,000 acres of fee land in Porcupine.[22]

Oglala residence patterns were dramatically altered again in the late 1960s and 1970s by yet another government program. Cluster housing projects paid for by HUD (Housing and Urban Development) are the most visual reminder that Oglalas have been progressively separated from their land. One or more such projects were built in every reservation district in the late 1960s and 1970s. Many families had come back from relocation and the population was growing fast. The need for housing was acute and federal dollars were plentiful. More than 1,000 units were built. Sunrise, Sharps, Cherry Hill, East Ridge, and Upper Crazy Horse housing clusters filled an immediate need for low-rent affordable housing, but they were not what the people wanted and they had become a flash point for controversy even before they were completed.

Severt Young Bear Sr. recalled that the Porcupine District Council voted against cluster housing many times. According to Wounded Knee Legal Defense Offense Committee (WKLDOC) records:

> In the Porcupine District alone, the district council voted 13 times against the cluster housing and in favor of homes being built on an individual's land. The tribal gov't [sic] ignored all of these resolutions

and went ahead and built cluster housing in the Porcupine District . . .
Since they have been opened there has been constant trouble as there
has been in all of the housing projects . . . The trouble reached a peak
again on Christmas eve when several people were stabbed resulting in
the death of one. The houses are cheaply built, there is no grass or
trees, and people are not used to living so close together. . . . This is just
another example of how the wishes of the people in the districts are
constantly ignored by the tribal government.[23]

No one disputed that housing was needed. They just wanted some control
over the planning. Why? Because people want to live in their own communities, with their own *tiospaye*, and on their own land, Young Bear said.

Resistance to cluster housing was widespread. Reservation wide surveys
conducted by Community Health Representative (CHR) Director and tribal member Geraldine Janis showed that Oglalas "were over-whelmingly
against" cluster housing.[24] Participants at a November 23, 1971, Porcupine
District meeting voted unanimously for individual home sites on their land
and against cluster housing. Lakota elder Ike Iron Cloud expressly tied the
cluster housing initiative to removal from the land: ". . . if the Bureau and
Tribe go along with it, the individual houses would be ideal, because, the
stockgrowers and Bureau wants you to forget your land, because then they
can use it, it would be better for us to build individual houses."[25] Meeting
minutes include the following exchange between unnamed persons: "Will
we get houses if we hold out for individual houses? Yes, if we stand together for what we want."[26] Despite the consensus of the people, Porcupine
District's OST Council representative voted with the majority of OST
Council members to put cluster housing in Porcupine. Families started
moving into the 68 unit "Evergreen" cluster in Porcupine District in the
summer of 1974. It is a source of small satisfaction for some that in suc-
cessive runs for public office he has never received more than a handful of
votes.[27]

Iron Cloud's 1971 contention that stockgrowers and the BIA wanted the
people off the land and into cluster housing so they could have the land to
themselves is still a standard explanation that Oglalas give for cluster housing in 2001. Lakota landowners applied the same interpretation to a recent
proposal by two OST Council members to confine home sites to designated tracts in each district. Cluster housing, relocation, and grazing units
have pushed people off the land.

Where there were once entire communities living on the land, there may
be only a few homes today. Many, but not all, of the communities recognized as sub-units of the reservations nine districts have their antecedents
in Lakota *tiospaye*. No Water's *tiospaye* settled in White Clay District after
Pine Ridge Agency was established in 1879. The area now known as No
Water Community is nearly depopulated today. But people still identify
themselves as members of No Water Community and continue to have

standing as a district sub-unit. Today, members live in clustered HUD housing, or in other communities, or have moved away from the reservation. Some dream of returning and reestablishing their connections with the land.

Dreams of reviving ties with the land are strong. The tug of land that has been in the family is compelling. The old hand-hewn cabins elders were born in still stand on some of the allotments. Usually there is a well or a spring on the site. Often the family has pictures, and there are always the memories. Stories tell of hardship but of self-sufficiency, of a time when people visited more often, and followed the Lakota ways more faithfully. Gerald One Feather, a visionary leader who served as the youngest elected OST President from 1970–1972, is working with the American Friends Service Committee and with Treaty organizations from other reservations to develop a plan to help people move back to the land and reconstitute their *tiospaye*. "*Tiospaye* exist today partly as relationships and partly as ideas," he says, and "To fully realize *tiospaye* the people have to move back to the land."[28] During the past few years, some Oglalas have begun to move back to the land, though most are confined to narrow ribbons along the paved roads. Some have come back from urban areas and others have been moving out of the over-crowded HUD housing projects that were built during the late 1960s and 1970s. In a few instances they are creating extended family and tiospaye settlements on the land. Getting back to ancestral land or finding another suitable home site in a rural area where land seems so plentiful and appraised values are low, might seem to be a relatively easy proposition, but there are plenty of obstacles.

For years, says one Oglala man in his fifties, "It has been my dream to live on my own land with my children." He worked for years to save enough for a down payment to a modular house he planned to move onto the five acres he inherited from his father. But he was unprepared for the institutional resistance he encountered when he tried to make the necessary arrangements to access his land. The OST Land Committee directed him to the OST Housing Authority, where he was sent to BIA Land Operations, where he was given a form and sent to get a signature from the rancher who has a permit to the range unit his five acres are in. When the rancher refused to sign the waiver that would allow him to take the land out of the unit before the lease expired, he went to Plains Legal Aid in Pine Ridge Village where a legal aid attorney advised him that the "BIA has its protocols." Now he has a house but no place to put it.

Merely following the procedures to secure a home site is no guarantee of results, even for someone who "knows the system." One longtime tribal employee with a college degree, and more important perhaps, a car that enabled her to follow up the interminable referrals from one office to another that people call the "Indian Run Around," (a reference to IRA government), accomplished the task in two years. "I know the system and look how hard it was for me. Just think how hard it would be for someone else, who doesn't have my advantages," she said. Another woman, not so lucky, tried to get a suitable home site for seven years. After her story was printed in the *Mila Yatapika Eyapaha*, *(Knife Chief Community News)* others contacted her to share their own frustrating experiences.[29]

If home sites can be difficult to acquire, finding housing can be tougher yet. The double scarcity creates painful dilemmas. There are around 1,500 persons on the waiting list for government housing on Pine Ridge Reservation, but less than 100 new units are available each year.[30] When people do reach the top of the eligibility list after years of waiting, unless they have connections, they are under time pressure to find a suitable home site lest they miss the opportunity. Families often settle for sites that are very close to the highway, sites they would never have selected except that they were turned away again and again by ranchers who refused to sign waivers. They could opt to wait for the next year's housing allocations, but imagine passing up a chance to a house knowing that the system works there is no guarantee that they would actually get the house or a more suitable site for it. A 1993 OST Council resolution that would have made it easier to get a home site never made it out of committee, indicative of the influence of the ranching lobby on the OST.

Ranchers are worried about the prospect of increasing numbers of people moving out onto their land beyond a narrow ribbon close to the major roads. Cattle get out of pastures when gates are left open. Easements and home sites take land cattle could graze on. Beyond such practical concerns, ideology clouds the issue. One mixed blood rancher, flatly opposed to liberalizing the home site provisions of the grazing ordinance, put it this way: "The full bloods don't understand the ranchers. If they go back out on the land to live, you don't know what kind of people you will get out there. They will shoot everything in sight, and the deer population will suffer." Earlier the same day he had an almost identical conversation with an Oglala woman. He was apparently unaware that her family lives out on her land several miles away from the main road and oblivious to the fact that she considers herself a full blood. She retorted that ranchers are the ones to watch out for, the ones with reputations for "shooting everything in sight, especially people's dogs, and the wild game."[31]

Under rules established by the OST in 1990, no home sites are authorized where there are "existing dams, dugouts, wells or running streams" if the land is permitted to ranchers, and most grazing land on the reservation is permitted to ranchers. The regulations in effect from 1980–1985 contained no such restriction. Grazing regulations increasingly favor ranchers over landowners and help keep the people off the land.[32]

AN UNHOLY ALLIANCE

Outside cattle interests have longtime connections with reservation-based white and mixed blood ranchers who front for them through the practice of illegal subleasing. As far back as the early 1900s, full blood Oglalas complained that mixed bloods and whites were illegally running outside cattle on reservation land. Superintendent Henry Tidwell, who was probably being solicitous of the big cattle interests he helped bring to the reservation, threatened cancellation of leases if the practice of taking in outside stock without OIA approval continued.[33] In 1934, Superintendent James McGregor reported that some of the ranchers who secured leases that year had practically no stock of their own and were fronting for others.[34] In 1976, BIA Superintendent and tribal member Anthony Whirlwind Horse notified a mixed blood rancher that it had come to his attention that the latter was illegally running 243 head of cattle belonging to "a white man" on his range unit. He did not, however, suggest that anything would be done about it. An investigation done that year found that there was no mechanism in place to stop illegal subleasing.[35]

Evidence for the continuing vitality of illegal subleasing comes from some of the ranchers themselves, who are concerned about the threat it poses to their legally pastured herds. In a complaint she filed with the BIA, one mixed blood rancher detailed the practice of illegal sub-leasing by another mixed blood rancher and argued flatly that outside cattle should not be allowed in. She was concerned by the risk of infection that unregulated unvaccinated animals from outside posed to the health of her own herd.[36]

Lakota landowners know illegal subleasing is short-changing them and hurting the land. They are angry at a system that denies them control of their own land and delivers it up to white and mixed blood ranchers who are often running other people's cattle. Mixed blood ranchers, who are positioned to act as "middlemen in a real estate game" stand to gain the most. Allocation of range units to ranchers who are tribal members guarantees them lower prices for leases and shields them from competitive bidding and market fluctuations. Ranchers effectively turn their leases into de facto ownership, subleasing land for much more than the rent they pay. They can realize a fat profit with limited investment and without any residuals to the landowner whose lands are overgrazed in the process.[37]

A popular perception on the reservation is that white cattle ranchers control most of the reservation's grazing land, but mixed blood Oglala ranchers displaced white cattlemen as the predominant users of the reservation land base over thirty years ago. Already in 1969, 62% of the acreage in grazing units was leased by tribal members and that figure rose to 72% in 1972 when 230 tribal members were grazing stock on 1,030,000 acres of allotted and tribal land. By 1994, 297 of 364, or 82% of all the range units on Pine Ridge Reservation were permitted to tribal members, almost all of whom were mixed bloods. OST Land and Allocation Committees take credit for the displacement of the white ranchers, citing it as evidence that they have accomplished their objective, which long-time Allocation Committee member Melvin Cummings summed up at a 1995 OST Council meeting as "Indian land for Indian use."[38]

The grazing unit system and the allocation process figure largely in the development of the grossly inequitable land tenure pattern on the reservation. A 1974 study of land use and purchase patterns on Pine Ridge Reservation conducted on the watch of mixed blood tribal member and Agency Superintendent Al Trimble, who went on to be the OST President from 1976–78, created a furor upon its release. The controversy stemmed from the finding that blood quantum and land use and purchase patterns on Pine Ridge Reservation were inversely related. There was a "singular absence" of full blood ranchers, and almost "90% of all the Indian-owned land was used by ranchers of less than 1/2 degree of Indian blood." Of all of the "Indian land in Indian use," only 12% was used by those of 1/2 or more blood quantum, while 25% was being used by those of less than 1/8.[39]

Land ownership patterns were becoming similarly skewed. Over 80% of all land sales were being made to individuals of less than 1/2 degree of Indian blood. Ranchers of more than 1/8, but less than 1/4, degree of Indian blood accounted for almost 43% of such sales. Of 164 land sales reviewed, only 19 were to non-ranchers. Most of those sales were of small tracts, probably for residential use, and most of the buyers had jobs. The study concluded that if the trends in land use and purchase continued, ". . . within a short span of time Oglala land will be overwhelmingly controlled and owned by Indians who are less than 1/32 degree of Indian blood."[40]

Discriminatory lending practices of border town banks contributed to the skewed ownership and control patterns. Those ". . . people of lesser degrees of Indian blood are least handicapped by their Indianness. They are more readily served by banks and lending institutions." Non-Indians married to Indian women were doubly favored. They had access to capital and could use their spouses to claim Indian preference. They held 13% of the grazing permits. Land ownership was being skewed toward mixed bloods because of access to capital and an OST policy that gave ranchers first option to buy parcels that came up for sale in range units they held.[41] Today, informal BIA practices favor the same group. Some BIA Realty personnel function as real estate brokers for relatives and ranchers. When parcels come up for sale they notify their connections. Others are purposely kept in the dark about potential sales. Oglalas who expressly desire to sell land to their own relatives or friends are often thwarted by Bureau personnel. Mixed blood tribal member and current Pine Ridge Agency Superintendent Robert Ecoffey, Jr., sometimes arbitrarily denies land sales to non-ranchers. The appeals process is a difficult one and on appeal the Great Plains Regional Office reflexively backs the Superintendent.[42]

Mixed blood ascendancy in grazing hinged on their BIA connections and their control over the allocation of grazing units through the OST Allocation Committee.[43] The Committee allocates grazing permits for hundreds of thousands of acres of reservation land. Eligible tribal members have preference for allocated units at a fixed rate established by BIA appraisal. That keeps rates down considerably, sometimes by a factor of two or three vis-a-vis units that are competitively bid. Over the years, mixed blood ranchers served with little turnover and dominated the Committee. The OST Council appointed Committee members until 1995, but did not exercise oversight over its operation. There is very little public understanding of its makeup or role. Inter-generational connections within the Bureau were apparently critical factors in mixed blood success. Mixed blood tribal member Tom Conroy headed the BIA Realty Branch for many years. His son, Tom Jr., has been a member of the OST Council and Land Committee, and worked in the BIA land division as well. The OST Council gave Conroy, Sr., a vote of confidence, asking that he be transferred to the position of Branch Chief of BIA Realty in Pine Ridge in 1963. He had been heading up the OST Land Consolidation Program at the time.[44]

A 1976 report concluded that "The entire process of issuing and administering grazing permits followed by the Pine Ridge Agency and the Allocation Board is loose and unstructured." No one checked to see if ranchers awarded Indian preference were actually tribal members. There was ". . . absolutely no effort to ensure that applicants for grazing permits by allocation or Indian preference bidding comply [with eligibility criteria specified in the Grazing Ordinance]." The Ordinance clearly placed the responsibility on the BIA, but the head of the Land Operations Office said he was leaving it up to the OST Allocation Committee. And the OST Allocation Committee ". . . scrupulously avoided involvement in such determinations."[45]

The BIA and the Allocation Committee likewise avoided enforcing proof of ownership requirements that made Indian preference contingent on proof that the economic head of family owned the livestock that would be grazed on a unit. Non-enforcement provided a sweet opportunity for ranchers and illegal subleasers in the short run and a sour deal for the environment in the long run. It was a negative sum game and the temptation in such a game is to reap short term gain without regard to long term consequences – that is precisely what has happened. Ranchers intent on profit maximization massively overgraze the land, extending the habitual mismanagement of reservation land begun by the U.S. in the 1890s when it refused to enforce trespass regulations that would have kept white-owned stock out.

   Where the creeks once ran clear, they are muddy. Where children and fish used to swim, the water is polluted. Where springs once bubbled up, they are clogged up or stopped up entirely by the action of too many cattle. Where ground-nesting birds once made their nests in the prairie grasses, there are few to be found. Where nutritious perennial prairie grasses once covered the land, there are thistles in abundance. Where many kinds of herbal medicines once were plentiful, traditional healers can find only a few. Where cherry trees flourished, in many places there are only remnants.

   Non-enforcement of grazing regulations opened the door for non-Indian ranchers married to tribal members, Indians with small degrees of Indian blood who were not enrolled tribal members, and even non-Indians, to use Indian preference. That situation underlies the characterization of many of the ranchers who use the land as "the real *ieskas,*" the "blue eyed Indians" who "look and act white," and have only "a drop of Indian blood." Their cowboy trappings set some of them off from others. Some wear big hats, cowboy boots, tight-fitting jeans, and most drive pickups. Sometimes humorously and sometimes not, Lakota landowners compare themselves to the ranchers using the phrase "cowboys and Indians."

   Oglalas who want to break into the ranching business, or who want to run a few horses on the land, or move out onto the land are often thwarted by ranching interests supported by the BIA and some elements in the OST government. One young Lakota man, who had a few head of cattle and wanted a little more land for them, was repeatedly rebuffed by BIA officials and the OST Allocation Committee when he asked them to subdivide the unit of a neighboring white rancher to help him out. The authorities told him repeatedly that subdividing the unit was contrary to good management practices. Eventually a mixed blood rancher who had a sizable herd already was awarded the land he had been denied. It is a familiar story. The mixed blood rancher had a relative on the OST Allocation Committee who in turn had a connection in the BIA.

   Oglala's often attribute differential access to the reservation land base to a network of cattle interests with connections in the BIA. One young man laid out a typical analysis at a large gathering of landowners in 1995:

> The lessees [i.e., ranchers, permittees] are making a lot of money. The lease rate is cheap. They especially make a lot of money when they sublease, and lots are doing it. They are all tight, are all related. The ones running cattle in Medicine Root District are related and those in Porcupine District are related and they are related to the ones in the Bureau. If they wanted to do something about it [the sub-leasing] they could, but they won't. They are all related. They give you the runaround on this reservation when you're Indian [i.e., full blood]. . . This is discrimination from your own people. When you try to get your uncle and auntie's land out [i.e. out of a range unit] you can't, even when you have the papers signed. They give you the runaround. It is hard.[46]

Limited access to capital plus mixed blood control of grazing units equals very limited opportunities for Oglala full bloods who want to break into the ranching business. Mixed blood control over the Allocation Committee plus their kinship and business connections with key personnel in the BIA Land Operations and Realty offices give them the edge.

THE FACE OF POWER UNVEILED: THE GRASSROOTS STRUGGLE FOR THE LAND

"This is our land. It belongs to us, not [to] the ranchers. We should stand firm. We don't need their lease money. This is our land."
Guy White Thunder, Oglala Lakota elder, 1995

Lakota woman: "Who is more important, the landowner or the rancher?

OST Land Committee member: "The rancher is more important."
In Porcupine, Pine Ridge Indian Reservation, 1992

In September, 1994, a group of landowners, frustrated by the failure of the BIA and their own tribal government to do anything about their complaints of misuse of land and failure to receive their lease money, established a Lakota Landowner Association in Medicine Root District.[47] One of the founders had repeatedly reported that cattle were trespassing on her land but neither the BIA's Land Operations Office, nor the OST Land Committee, a standing committee of the OST Council, had taken any action. Another was outraged that the rancher who leased her land was mining and selling gravel deposits from her land without her consent.[48]Grazing permits authorize use of grass and water on a grazing unit – nothing else. They do not confer any right to take wood, wild fruit, or minerals, or anything else from the land, but violations are widespread. She made a formal complaint to the BIA and followed it up, but nothing was done. A third woman had determined that overgrazing was destroying her land, which was in a grazing unit that was allocated to the mixed blood rancher. He was overstocking it with cattle owned by off-reservation whites. She calculated his illicit profit in the tens of thousands of dollars. She lodged complaints with the BIA and her elected representatives to the OST Council to no avail. Later, reservation-wide testimony gathered by Association members at public forums showed that the pattern of official non-response was reservation-wide and decades deep. When the women discovered their shared problems, they enlisted the support of Guy White Thunder, an Oglala elder who had recent experience fighting against strip mining and toxic dumping on Pine Ridge Reservation. He worked with several others, including Vincent Black Feather, to establish the Association.

The first major task the new Association set itself was to provide input into development of the OST Grazing Ordinance. In October 1994, the

OST Land and Allocation Committees were working with the BIA to revise the Ordinance that was due to expire on April 1, 1995.[49] The Ordinance stipulates grazing rates for tribal land, regulates hay cutting, wood gathering, and hunting and fishing on range units. It also sets Indian preference priorities for bidding on range units, establishes eligibility requirements for allocation of range units (tribal members with less than 300 head of cattle, or equivalent, are eligible for allocation of range units at the minimum established rate, i.e., without competitive bidding), and establishes the rules for removal of land from range units, including for home site purposes. Association members saw the revision of the far ranging Ordinance as an opportunity to address a number of their concerns at once.

When Association members heard that Ada Deer, the Assistant Secretary for Indian Affairs, planned to meet with tribes in a Rapid City hotel on October 28, they made plans to be there. They were angered and hurt when BIA officials at the door told them they would not be admitted into the meeting room unless they could pay an admission of $75.00 each. They refused to pay – most were elders and their pockets were not that deep anyway – and simply walked into the meeting.[50] OST Land and Allocation Committee members were there too, piggybacking the session with one to revise the OST Grazing Ordinance.[51s]

Association members including Guy White Thunder, Lucy Bull Bear, and Lucille Fire Thunder described several items they wanted to see in the grazing ordinance and pressed OST Land and Allocation Committee members to give them further opportunity to participate in the revision process. Gerald "Jump" Big Crow, Pine Ridge Village representative to the OST Council and a member of the Allocation Committee, said the ordinance should "go back to the districts." Other Land Committee members agreed. Referring an issue "back to the Districts," is theoretically a method of getting the people's input through District Councils in each of the reservation's nine districts, but in most cases the actual objective is to defer discussion and to deflect input.[52]

When several weeks passed without any indication that the grazing ordinance would be referred back to the districts, Association members pressed their OST Council representatives for an opportunity to have their say. But the OST Land and Allocation Committees continued to work on grazing ordinance revisions, and there were no signs that they would welcome any input. In November, when OST Tribal Attorney Marvin Amiotte forwarded a revised version of the ordinance to the Land and Allocation Committees, it was clear the promise to refer the ordinance back to the districts was a subterfuge.[53] The only concession to the input the landowners gave in Rapid City was a welcome change making range unit permittees responsible for fencing off cemeteries from their livestock, a responsibility the current ordinance placed on relatives of the deceased. After reviewing

Amiotte's draft at a December meeting, Association members styled it a "cattleman's ordinance, made by cattlemen for cattlemen."

The Association sent a letter to all 16 OST Council members, noting that revising the grazing ordinance should not be the job of "one man," a reference to mixed blood attorney Marvin Amiotte, and asked again for an opportunity to give their input. Soon after that, OST Council representatives Pete Richards and Manuel Fool Head informed Association members that the OST Land Committee had decided not to honor the request for input, "because the request was not accompanied by the organization's constitution and by-laws."

The Association did not have a constitution and by-laws and members wanted it that way. Nevertheless, the stipulation was repeated frequently by various OST Council representatives over a period of several weeks. Members asked tribal attorney Russell Zephier for his opinion about the legality of such a stipulation. He waffled, saying that "If they asked for one those, then there must be a serious issue at stake." Pressed, he agreed that he had never heard that tribal members needed to produce a constitution and by-laws in order to give input on legislation, but he refused to give an official opinion. Landowners were not surprised. One remarked that "Tribal attorneys work for the IRA, not for the oyate [people]."

Debbie Garland, a non-Indian attorney doing pro bono work for the Association, assured members that there was no legal basis for requiring groups wanting to give input to their elected representatives to have a constitution and bylaws. Although most Association members were certain that they did not legally need a constitution and by-laws, some felt that they would never be given a voice without them. Serious consideration was given to drafting the documents, but most were against it. Some felt it would play into the hands of the IRA, that the documents would somehow be used against them. Some maintained that because the Association was a Lakota organization, it did not need such documents. The absurdity of the situation was frustrating and a cause for humor too. Pressured by the Association, the OST Council hosted a special meeting in February to inform the public about the grazing ordinance. The meeting was broadcast live over KILI Radio. When one Association member joked that soon he would "need a constitution and by-laws to drive down the street," Land Committee Chair David Pourier announced that he wanted it "on record that the Land Committee was not standing in the way of input from the landowners."[54]

Some of the tactics that elements in the IRA government used to preclude input from the people were applied against its own elected representatives. At a January, 1995 Association meeting, OST Council representative Manuel Fool Head, a close relative of an elder who was a very active member, provided some insight into just how secretive and exclusive the process of drafting the grazing ordinance had become. Quizzed about the refusal of the Land Committee to meet with the Lakota Landowner's, Fool Head said he disagreed with the OST Land Committee's constitution and bylaws ploy. When one member reminded him that he had been elected to represent the people and urged him to bring his influence to bear so that the people's concerns could be addressed, he became very agitated, stood up, made a fist, and said in a loud voice full of emotion`:

> It's a Mafia. They stick together and it's like a Mafia. I went to a Land Committee meeting to talk about this, [grazing ordinance] but they decided to have an Allocation Committee meeting instead, and they shut the door on me and kept me out. It's like a Mafia. They run it like a Mafia.[55]

Fool Head had been shut out too. In light of that revelation, some argued it was futile to try to give input to the OST Council. If they would not listen to their fellow elected representatives, why would they listen to the Association? It would be better, Anthony "Buzzy" Black Feather and another man said, to work with the United Nations.[56] The Association stuck with it but the encounter with Fool Head convinced even the most optimistic members that it would be very difficult to provide input, let alone influence, the Council. Several weeks later, two more OST Council members, who had cautiously supported the Association by providing information and encouragement, reported that they too had been purposefully excluded from participation in some of the grazing ordinance meetings held by the OST Land and Allocation Committees at the BIA offices and in Rapid City.

Since the OST Land Committee had no interest allowing input, Association members decided to draft their own version of the grazing ordinance. They met weekly, sometimes several times a week, in community buildings and homes across the reservation in order to get input and support for the effort. They spent long hours pouring over the current ordinance, dissecting, discussing, recommending, and writing. They came from across the Pine Ridge Reservation to meet in facilities that were sometimes so cold they had to keep their heavy coats on. But there was always food, usually soup and sandwiches, sometimes fry bread and *wojapi* (berry pudding) and the ever present coffee pot. Meetings were most often held in the evenings and lasted from four to six hours. At one meeting on a Saturday in February, members came from 70 miles away during a heavy snowstorm to participate at the White Clay District Community Action Program office. The younger people wondered at the stamina and determination of their elders who could meet for hours and hours on end without losing interest in a subject that sometimes turned on arcane legalisms.

Once Association's first draft was readied, they held meetings in the various districts, explained the contents over KILI radio, sent copies to OST Council members and to the other elected officials, made and distributed numerous flyers, and asked the Land Committee for a chance to discuss

their version of the ordinance. By mid-February public support was building. Association members from Medicine Root District presented a resolution at their District Council asking for support for their ordinance. The
vote was 30 for and none against. The District directed its two OST
Council representatives to vote for the proposal when it came to the OST
Council. White Clay, Porcupine, Pass Creek, and Wounded Knee Districts
did the same. The populace was clearly in support of the landowner's initiative. In the face of that support, and at the urging of Association members, OST Vice-President Mel Lone Hill agreed to put the Lakota
Landowner's version of the grazing ordinance on the OST Council's
February 22, 1995 agenda, along with the version the Land Committee and
BIA officials had been working on. It had been a tough campaign. An
Association of Lakota elders and grassroots people, most of whom were
unemployed, and one of whom was physically attacked by a white rancher for her role in the Association, had successfully roused the people behind
a piece of legislation that held the promise of significant change in land
management on the Pine Ridge Reservation (see Table 6). They savored the
moment.

**Table 6: Lakota Landowner Association Grazing Proposal Compared to
OST Grazing Ordinance 90-01***

Lakota Landowner Association Proposal	OST Grazing Ordinance for 1990-1995
Eliminates sub-leasing	Allows sub-leasing of up to 50% of livestock depending on total number of stock
Affirms OST Constitution clause giving communities and districts first preference for bidding and range unit allocation	Gives individual ranchers first preference, even though OST Constitution gives first preference to communities.
Require the BIA to publish a map of all range units and note the number of stock authorized for each unit.	No requirement for publication of maps or for providing information about range units.
Requires that natural features, including springs and features such as sacred sites be protected by the permittee.	Silent on the issue
Provides provision to provide for tribal members who need small parcels of land for their use. Allows people with a few head of stock to get started without having to rent an entire range unit.	Makes provision for allocation of units for those with up to 300 head of stock and for competitive bidding for those with over 300 head. Those who need some land, but who cannot afford an entire unit, are left out.
Establishes land use fund to assist communities and districts wanting to enter livestock business. Money for fund to come from "Land Use Tax" and from penalties levied against those who fail to comply with provisions of grazing ordinance.	Provides for collection of "Land Use Tax" with revenues going to OST government.
Provides for strict application of Indian preference guidelines.	Vague provisions for enforcing Indian preference guidelines.
Emphasizes right of Lakota landowners to hunt and gather traditional foods, medicines, and firewood	Requires that tribal members who want to use land hunting and gathering contact permittees before entering a range unit.

*Comparison based on provisions of OST Ordinance 90-01 and Lakota
Landowner Association's proposed grazing ordinance, 1995. There are many differences not included in this table.

On the eve of the Council meeting, Association members tried to get a copy of the grazing ordinance that the OST Land Committee planned to present to the OST Council for adoption the following day but were told it was not available. A Lakota Landowner Association flyer documented the situation for the public:

> Between 4:00 and 4:30 p.m. on Tuesday, February 21, when we asked for a copy of the Grazing Ordinance that the Land Committee was scheduled to present to the Council on February 22, we were told that it was not yet available, that changes had been made during a meeting with the BIA earlier in the day, and that a clerk in the BIA Land Operations Office was typing the Grazing Ordinance. We were told that the Land Operations Office would deliver the Grazing Ordinance to the OST Land Office on the morning of February 22. The Grazing Ordinance that the Land Committee planned to present to the OST Council on February 22 was still not available as of 4:30 p.m., close of business, on February 21, 1995.[57]

On the morning of February 22, about 30 Association members and supporters attended the OST Council meeting at Wakpamnee CAP Office. The OST Land Committee Chair produced the Grazing Ordinance that Association members had been unable to access the previous day. OST Councilman and Land Committee Chair David Pourier, and Council members Tom Conroy, Jr., and Donovan Youngman spent more than one and one-half hours reading the ordinance over the radio. Conroy was virtually yelling into the microphone when he read his portion. The tension in the meeting room was high. The presence of several Oglala Lakota College students prompted Conroy to complain to the college president who in turn admonished the instructor not to take any more students to Council meetings as part of a class. Conroy was a member of the college's Board of Trustees. Like a number of other prominent mixed bloods on the reservation, he was a member of a number of Boards, another important source of influence and control. Once the ordinance was read, there was a motion to approve and a second and the Council was going to proceed with a vote before even mentioning the Association's version of the ordinance.

Before that could happen, Lucille Fire Thunder asked her Wounded Knee District Council representative to give her the floor and asked why the Council was not even considering the Lakota Landowner Association version of the Ordinance. It was, after all, on the agenda. Others, including Mary Locke Iron Cloud, Edward Iron Cloud, Jr., Guy White Thunder, and Verlene Ice were also recognized. They spoke of the people who gave input, who wanted to have some say over their own land. And they warned the Councilmen that if they did not listen they could be recalled and would find themselves out of office. After a lengthy and heated debate, the Council voted thirteen to two that the OST Land Committee, OST Allocation Committee, BIA Superintendent, and BIA Land Operations

Director needed to sit down and negotiate differences with the Lakota
Landowner Association.

If Association members had not pushed hard, the OST Council would
not even have considered the draft ordinance they had worked so diligently on, that reflected the input of people across the reservation, and that had
the support of a majority of the nine district councils. During the debate
following the reading of the Land Committee's version of the Ordinance,
OST Councilman Tom Conroy, Jr., apparently thinking he had been out
maneuvered, addressed OST Vice-President Lone Hill in a loud angry voice
saying

> You said the landowner's was just on the agenda for informational pur-
> poses. Their ordinance has never even come to the Land Committee
> and so we can't consider it [sic!] . . . In each district you have the same
> people. These groups of people are the landowners of each district but
> they are a small voice of all the 20,000 landowners throughout the
> reservation. This grazing ordinance, in my opinion, does not hurt or tie
> any landowner's hands. We have tried to listen to the individuals who
> have come forward to us. They didn't really quite touch the surface of
> what the ordinance is about. . . . I don't see myself where we have dam-
> aged, held up, stepped on, any landowner's rights. The tribe is trying
> to protect the landowners. This ordinance will do it [emphasis added].

Earlier in the proceedings, OST Land Committee members Conroy and
Melvin Cummings amazed Association members with the preposterous
claim that they had already taken into account all of the landowner rec-
ommendations. Such claims, in the face of obvious evidence to the contrary, had the effect of angering and exasperating Association members.

Cummings, one of four mixed blood ranchers on the seven-person Land
Committee, was clearly upset by the turn of events himself, and delivered
an impassioned defense of reservation ranchers.

> There was also a little group of individuals out there who never come
> to the Council and they have a right too and they are landowners. I am
> a landowner. I own five sections of ground. Was I asked to join the
> Association? No . . . I could have had all the cowboys on this reserva-
> tion [here] too, but all they want is a fair shot . . . When we set down
> to work on that ordinance there isn't one person on that committee
> that didn't have the landowner at heart. When you look at landown-
> ers, don't forget the land user. I know individuals who own as many as
> ten sections yet they keep it in trust . . . I know what it is to have noth-
> ing and I know that to get something you have to pay for it [emphasis
> added].[58]

Cummings' statement spoke eloquently to the gulf between Lakota
landowners and Indian cowboys. The cowboys and their representatives on
the OST Land Committee had the landowners "at heart" when they

obstructed their efforts to provide input into it. The Indian cowboys are the big landowners, keeping five sections of ground, or maybe ten sections – anywhere from 3,200 to 6,400 acres – in trust. They were the ones, Cummings said, that kept the land base together, but his intimation that cowboys were making a sacrifice by keeping it in trust for the benefit of the tribe was disingenuous. It certainly is better for the society if land stays in trust because it insures tribal jurisdiction, but it also benefits the Indian cowboys by keeping their large holdings free of county tax obligations. Subsequent attempts by Association members to access land ownership records from the BIA have been rebuffed. Even Freedom of Information Act (FOIA) requests for the kind of information that is public nationwide do not produce results. Guy White Thunder's submitted a request for land ownership information for the Pine Ridge Reservation on September 11, 1998 on behalf of the Lakota Landowner Association. On September 22, Senate Minority Leader Tom Daschle (D,SD) contacted the BIA's Director of Congressional and Legislative Affairs on White Thunder's behalf. The Bureau's Washington office referred Daschle's inquiry to the Aberdeen Area Office, Aberdeen, South Dakota. Alice A. Harwood, the Acting Area Director, responded to Daschle on October 27, claiming that the information White Thunder requested "may fall under provisions of the Privacy Act." She claimed the "Field Solicitor is currently reviewing this request as it pertains to the Privacy Act and Freedom of Information Act," and went on to say that after the Field Solicitor responded "we will establish policy. A formal written response will be provided to you and Mr. White Thunder at that time." It must have been a tough assignment because as of April, 2001, there has been no response.[59]

Ranchers, for the most part, move in different circles than Lakota landowners and Lakota full bloods. They are separate societies, with separate cultural practices, and very different and often conflicting economic interests. Only rarely will you find the Indian cowboys Cummings referred to at Lakota Landowner Association meetings, Treaty meetings, or ad hoc gatherings grassroots people regularly call to work on a myriad of issues and problems they face. With few exceptions they are also absent from other events that are an integral part of the life of the Lakota communities on Pine Ridge Reservation.

Several Association members at the Wakpamnee meeting charged that "*ieskas*" and "*ieska* ranchers" (using *ieska* in the sense of "mixed bloods") had more support from the Council than the Lakotas (meaning, in that context, "full bloods"). One Councilman, whose ethnic identity is ambiguous – he is full blood according to some Association members and a mixed blood according to others – but whose political position in support of ranching interests is clear, lectured Association members about the upcoming meeting: ". . . I hope we leave the mixed blood, full blood behind us.

That is in the past. We all have relatives who are mixed bloods. We have to leave that home."[60]

The promised meeting with OST and BIA officials was held at the Piya Wiconi (New Beginning) conference room at Oglala Lakota College on March 7, 1995. Lakota Landowner Association members were hopeful that they would at last have a meaningful session with their Council representatives and the BIA. In an attempt to insure that the meeting would be run fairly they drafted a twelve-point protocol for the negotiations and got OST President Wilbur Between Lodges to endorse it several days before the meeting.[61] The protocol stipulated that negotiations would be co-chaired by a Council representative and an Association spokesperson, and that each side would have five negotiators. Before the meeting they went live over KILI Radio to explain its purpose and to encourage the public to attend.

Among the first arrivals at the meeting was a group of about 25 of the "Indian cowboys" that Cummings referred to at the Wakpamnee meeting. They sat down together in the front row seats. Their attire set them off sharply from the Association members and other Lakotas. The younger ones wore tight jeans and cowboy boots. A good number sported large black cowboy hats that they kept on throughout the meeting. Several had blue eyes; most were very light skinned and "looked white."

Association members and other Lakota landowners filtered into the meeting gradually and took seats in the rear and along the sides of the round conference room. There were no cowboy hats or boots among them. A few of the men wore their hair long, tied back in ponytails. They greeted each other with the traditional Lakota handshake and distributed flyers and tables comparing the two competing versions of the grazing ordinance.

The atmosphere was electric. Association members and their supporters had never laid eyes on a number of the ranchers, and the reverse was probably true as well. The cowboys were clearly concerned about the challenge from the Association and they had prepared for the moment. They distributed a position paper rejecting the Association's version of the ordinance outright. It would hurt them economically, they argued, suggesting that Association members knew nothing about ranching. They rejected the Association's proposal for small-scale subsistence herds, maintaining that a 300 head minimum was needed to have a viable operation.

The position paper was addressed to the OST Council from the "Oglala Lakota ranchers" and was prepared for them with the assistance of Lakota Fund Director Elsie Meeks.[62] Association supporters were concerned about Elsie Meeks' role in support of ranching interests. The Fund had become well known for its interest and work in Circle Banking, based on the Grameen model so successful in Bangladesh. The Circle Banking concept entailed no-collateral micro-loans that relied on peer pressure for repayment. But many locals felt, deservedly or not, that the Fund's main function was to provide larger traditional loans to people with collateral, i.e., to mixed bloods and ranchers, while full bloods got the lions share of micro-loans. And now the Fund's Director was supporting large-scale ranching and trying to undermine more traditional, small-scale use of the land. Meeks' husband, a mixed blood rancher himself, spoke in defense of the Indian cowboys that day. The ranchers' self-reference as "Oglala Lakota" was also troubling to some Association members. They do not consider them to be Lakota and said the ranchers generally did not refer to themselves in that way either, but were using the term for their own advantage. It was not an auspicious beginning to the long awaited meeting.

About 50 persons were assembled when OST Vice-President Mel Lone Hill opened the meeting. KILI Radio's station manager broadcast the meeting live at the Association's request. The proceedings caught the public's interest and the audience grew throughout the day. Among the officials present were OST Land Committee members, Allocation Committee members, and BIA Superintendent Delbert Brewer and Land Operations Director Jim Glade. Lone Hill set the deferential tone toward the Oglala Lakota Ranchers that marked the behavior of BIA officials and some OST Council members toward them that day. He announced that the ranchers would be giving input at the meeting, and then, over the objections of Association members, who pointed out that the ranchers had had "input" throughout the process, read their entire position paper over the airwaves. After that he instructed OST Land Committee members to decide if they wanted to go along with the twelve-point negotiation protocol that OST President Wilbur Between Lodges had already approved. That move caused a veritable uproar. While Land and Allocation Committee members left the room with several Association members to discuss the matter, Lone Hill asked for "a representative from the Lakota ranchers." The cowboys looked back and forth at each other for a moment, apparently unsure who would represent them. Lone Hill's attempt to reconfigure the meeting was brazen enough but Association members were not prepared for what happened next. To their continuing dismay and disgust, the BIA Superintendent and mixed blood OST tribal member Delbert Brewer stood up and spoke on behalf of the Oglala Lakota Ranchers. If there had been any doubt about where the Department of Interior stood on the grazing ordinance issue, Brewer's action erased it.

Meanwhile, the informal caucus on the meeting protocol was over, and everyone returned to the room. OST Councilman Gerald "Jump" Big Crow announced that everything had changed, that the deal made at the OST Council meeting in Wakpamnee was off: "We came to hear concerns of landowners and Lakota ranchers. We'll not discuss this paper at all [i.e. the 12 point plan for negotiation that OST President Wilbur Between Lodges had approved]. There is not gonna be no negotiation." Council representative Tom Conroy, Jr., followed Big Crow, rejecting the protocol and trying to dictate new terms for the meeting: "Out of respect for the OST Land

Committee, the two co-chairs for the meeting will be Chairman David Pourier and Ruth Brown. We will not discuss this paper at all."

Eileen Iron Cloud, a past OST Council representative herself, and a veteran of a number of grassroots campaigns, was the Association's choice to co-chair the meeting. Disregarding Conroy's announcement, she seized one of the two microphones over the objections of Lone Hill and Conroy and would not give it up: "We'd like to be treated with dignity and respect. This is not a Council meeting. I will be co-chair of this meeting," and she was. Association Secretary Edward Starr, speaking in Lakota and English, expressed the sense of outrage Association members had about the treatment they had experienced all along from the BIA and their IRA government representatives:

> Our relatives experienced oppression in the past. Oppression. We see it today again. Our children will be growing up and soon some will be coming. We're being denied today, here, as Lakota Landowners. We're being oppressed as going on for the past 100 years. You're ruining the land, unci maka [grandmother earth]. This ordinance from the Tribe is their ordinance [i.e., ranchers]. This is a tribal ordinance and doesn't mention Lakota Landowners. We can see oppression that is taking place today.

Association negotiator Myrna Young Bear, well known for her efforts against toxic waste proposals, followed up: "Our greatest interest is the Lakota people. Our government is respect, bravery, generosity. This is based on human rights, human pleas. We want to be part of this grazing ordinance. This [OST draft grazing ordinance] represents only a select few."

Collins Clifford, Allocation Committee member and mixed blood rancher, responded to Young Bear, saying "I try to hire guys that won't work for me because they get relief, commodities." One of the mixed blood ranchers yelled out, loud enough to be heard over KILI Radio, listeners later reported: "They can sure borrow your gas all the time. They borrow money but you can't get them to drive a stake." Association members later said he was referring to the full bloods, the Lakota landowners.

Association Vice-President Guy White Thunder echoed the sentiments of many who spoke later on in the meeting:

> This land is our land. . . . The Land Committee and Allocation Committee, they have no right to our land. This is our land. This belongs to us. This is what we're talking about. The tribal council and Land Committee is not listening to us. . . . We are not gonna stop here. We're gonna keep pushing. We're not gonna let it die.

Pass Creek District Council Representative Pete Richards, one of the Council members who had been shut out of grazing ordinance meetings by the ranching clique, spoke in support of the Lakota landowners. He encouraged them saying "You have the power. It is good you did this. I see no problem with negotiation. I see no problem at all. I am happy with that."[63] Richards underscored his point by speaking only in Lakota, not bothering to translate for the ranchers. Association members and supporters gave him a round of applause.

Tom Conroy, Jr. had the last word before the break for lunch: "All we're doing is going around in circles. The landowners out there forget who pays the bills. They forget who pays those bills. The ranchers work 24 hours a day, seven days a week. They are Indian."

During the afternoon session, Association members went over the provisions of their proposed grazing ordinance point by point. There was no indication from Lone Hill or the Council that anything they said would be considered. OST Land and Allocation Committee members vigorously opposed even seemingly non-controversial provisions in the Association's version. Provisions calling for permittees to protect sacred sites and springs from the action of cattle, and for the BIA to provide the public with maps of grazing units were rejected out of hand.[64] At one juncture, Lone Hill referred to the OST version of the Ordinance as the "BIA version," a slip that told the tale the people already knew – in their support for the ranchers the BIA and the OST Land and Allocation Committees were one. Among the informative nuggets that surfaced that day: Jim Glade, the BIA Land Operations Director was a voting member of the OST Allocation Committee! The lines between the BIA and the small ranching clique on the Council had blurred that much. . .

Although the promised negotiation never materialized, Association members felt they had achieved much that day. They had a full day over KILI Radio to educate the public about the issues, were able to give a good accounting of themselves, and spoke strongly to the issues. The public was more interested than ever and the ranchers, whose influence was usually hidden, had come out as "Oglala Lakota Ranchers."

The OST Council chose to avoid further discussion of the grazing ordinance until September 26, 1995, when it enacted the OST/BIA version by an 8–6 vote. The issue was hotly contested on the floor and Association members did gain one potentially important concession. Allocation Committee members would no longer be appointed by the Council and would be elected from each of the nine districts. The Association wanted to stipulate that Committee members should not be OST Council members nor ranchers but that was rejected. Some of the ranchers rarely seen on such occasions ventured into the public arena again. Several others who had held high office in the OST weighed in for the status quo.

But the struggle for the land continues. In May 2000, a new Council, feeling the pressure of the continuing occupation of its tribal headquarters, adopted most of the Lakota Landowner Association's major provisions. As of April 2001, neither the OST Council nor the BIA had implemented them, but the people persevere. A Lakota Landowner Association initiative inspired by Johnson Holy Rock has resulted in an OST Resolution mandating a land audit of the BIA and OST Land offices. So far though, the BIA has steadfastly refused to cooperate and attempts to get even manifestly public information from out of the offices have come up short. The BIA has not even deigned to respond to the latest FOIA requests filed by landowner advocate Darwin Apple.

Though the BIA collaborates with ranching interests and key members of OST Council committees against the interests of the majority of Oglalas, OST government and the BIA are frequently at odds. In 1980, frustrated with BIA failure to keep adequate land records and to enforce land lease collections, an OST task force detailed problems that BIA non-compliance was causing tribal government. Upon the OST"s request, the Bureau agreed to conduct a management review of its Pine Ridge Agency. But in June of 1981, OST Land and Natural Resource Agency Chair Dennis White Shield complained to Secretary of the Interior James Watt that the Bureau did a review of the OST instead. White Shield asked Watt to intervene, but the latter, infamous in Indian Country for his quip that Indian reservations were examples of "failed socialism," never responded.[65]

In the colonial milieu of Pine Ridge Indian Reservation decisions are often unilaterally imposed. Pleas to be heard on substantive issues like land and constitutional reform go unheard – *nuge wanice* (no ears) the people say. A small coterie in tribal government and the BIA resist people's input and impose solutions of their own making. The BIA sometimes supports and other times thwarts requests from the OST.

In 1995, when Ada Deer directed BIA offices nationwide to collect input on a proposal to address heirship fractionation through escheatment, the Bureau went through the motions and conducted meetings in all nine districts. The Indian Land Consolidation Act of 1983 and its later versions essentially provided that estates of heirs dying intestate and that represented 2% or less of a given tract of land would escheat to the tribe. The U.S. Supreme Court later declared escheatment unconstitutional because it represented an illegal taking under the Fifth Amendment. On Pine Ridge Reservation, the only person who spoke publicly in favor of the Bureau's dogged determination to pursue a variant of the already discredited solution to the breaking up of land into smaller and smaller pieces through inheritance was a retired BIA Superintendent. None of the hours of testimony given in Lakota and English none was ever forwarded to the BIA's Washington D.C. office. When Association members asked BIA officials in Pine Ridge for copies of the testimony, they claimed everything had been forwarded through channels. But the BIA's Area Office and Claricy Smith of the BIA's Trust Division in Washington D.C. reported that the only testimony from the 48–50 meetings attended by about 4,000 tribal members from the 16 tribes in the Aberdeen Area Office that reached Washington was from Winnebago. Nothing was received from the Pine Ridge Agency. A Freedom of Information Act (FOIA) request to the BIA turned up three pages of notes that bore no resemblance to the testimony that was given.[66] About 4,000 tribal members spoke, mostly against against Deer's proposal, but almost none of them were heard.[67]

The BIA and the Department of Interior are simply not responsive to the people they are allegedly carrying out the trust responsibility for. Land information that is public in jurisdictions throughout the country is kept secret in Indian Country. In 1998, at the Indian Land Working Group's annual meeting in Polson, Montana, representatives from 41 tribes, including members of the Lakota Landowner Association and a number of other landowner organizations from tribes in the southwest, the northern plains, and the northwest, had a chance to show their collective disgust with the Bureau's abrogation of trust responsibility. When the Acting Director of the BIA's Portland Area Office responded to a question from one of the delegates about why basic information on land ownership was not made available in Bureau offices, he claimed there was no such problem. The audience's scornful reaction was so strong he quit the microphone.[68] A recent high-profile case filed by Native American Rights Fund (NARF) attorneys against the Department of Interior shows that the intransigence of the Bureau at the local level is mirrored by behavior at the top echelons of the United States government.

In 1996, NARF attorneys filed a class action lawsuit charging the Departments of Interior and Treasury with failure to manage Indian trust fund accounts of 500,000 Indian persons living and dead. A low estimate puts the dollar amount lost to the plaintiffs at an estimated seven billions of dollars ($7,000,000,000). The objectives of *Cobell v. Babbitt* are to fix the system, get a complete and accurate accounting, and to restate the accounts of beneficiaries. The U.S. does not deny that it lost or otherwise mismanaged money due to Indian people for grazing leases, oil and gas production, and timber sales on allotted land. During the June 1999 proceedings, Assistant Secretary of Indian Affairs Kevin Gover labeled the trust management system "broken," and Interior Secretary Bruce Babbitt allowed that the U.S. was "not fulfilling its fiduciary responsibilities." Yet during the course of the litigation, the U.S. has tried mightily to avoid that responsibility and through a combination of shameful foot-dragging and legal maneuvering has tried, albeit unsuccessfully, to outlast the NARF effort. Its agents have also taken patently illegal steps, even destroying evidence in an apparent attempt to undermine the case.

In May, 1999, Court appointed Special Master Alan Balaran toured BIA field offices and discovered that thousands of Indian trust records were still being kept in barns and condemned buildings across the country, several years after the case had been filed. He also learned that the Department of the Interior was continuing to destroy Individual Indian Money account documents relevant to the case, the contempt ruling against such actions notwithstanding. A December 6, 1999 report released by the U.S. District Court revealed that lawyers for the U.S. Department of Treasury destroyed 162 boxes of documents relevant to the trust funds case between 1993–1998, and then proceeded to cover it up. On February 22, 1999, Secretary of the Interior Bruce Babbitt, Secretary of the Treasury Robert Rubin, and Assistant Secretary of Indian Affairs Kevin Gover were found guilty of civil contempt of court for their failure to produce records as the court had ordered in 1996 and 1998. The struggle between Department of Justice and Treasury lawyers and NARF is a classic David and Goliath match-up but justice may yet be done. An important court ruling, but by no means the end of the legal battles, was issued on February 23, 2001, by the U.S. Court of Appeals, D.C. Circuit, affirming that the federal government has "a legally-enforceable duty to properly manage and account for Indian trust assets."[69]

PARTNERS IN A DANCE – A WATERSHED IN OGLALA POLITICS

In discussions after the tumultuous meeting with OST Council and BIA officials on the grazing ordinance at Piya Wiconi, Lakota Landowner Association members and supporters were quick to draw parallels with the Wounded Knee era of the 1970s. Disparaging remarks by ranchers about Lakotas, brazen public support by the Bureau for the inequitable status quo, loud and angry words spoken against landowners by several mixed blood Council members, and anger by Lakota Landowner Association members at the attempt to marginalize them were symptoms of enduring contradictions in Oglala society. "That's how Wounded Knee was. It's like it's happening all over again with the ranchers and the BIA," Myrna Young Bear marveled. Debra White Plume, surprised by the behavior of the Council and BIA officials, recalled "That's how it was around the time of the Knee! Those are the same dynamics!"

Land ownership and control was a high profile campaign issue in the 1973–74 OST presidential race between Russell Means and Richard "Dick" Wilson. American Indian Movement (AIM) leader Means championed a treaty-based, traditional government over the IRA, the same goal that helped catalyze local support for the 1973 Occupation of Wounded Knee.[70] Under his plan, the BIA would have to go, and so would the ranchers who leased the land, because the land would be used to support the people as a whole and would not be rented out.[71] One of his campaign promises was to help people out of clustered housing settlements and back to the land. Treaties and sovereignty figured strongly in the nationalist platform of Means but were essentially a non-issues for Wilson. Means' strongest support came from Treaty Councils, influential Lakota full bloods and elders, Lakota landowners, and people that had fallen out of favor with the tribal government and had consequently suffered the loss of tribally controlled jobs during Wilson's 1972–1974 administration.

Wilson was a controversial figure. His supporters were avid and his detractors more so. He was a staunch supporter of the status quo on land issues, earning him high marks and a strong backing from ranchers and the Bureau. He posed no challenge Bureau policy nor to the control over the reservation land base that mixed blood and white ranchers had consolidated, arguing it was not feasible for the people to ranch and farm the land themselves because it was fractionated into small parcels by heirship.[72] He also pushed cluster housing hard, despite the resistance of the people in the districts who saw it as a move to further sever their ties with the land. He was a cheerleader for the IRA government and had no inclination to push treaty rights – and apparently no understanding if his claim that they were isomorphic with tribal government can be taken at face value. He made the outlandish claim, which Collier must have smiled at from the grave, that ". . . the treaties in their entirety are incorporated right into our Constitution, in that we're allowed to deal directly with the Federal, State or any other Government on behalf of Indian people."[73] That must have put people in western South Dakota at ease. Wilson, at least, would not be pushing the Black Hills Claim as Means, AIM, Lakota Treaty Councils, and highly respected leaders like Frank Kills Enemy, Matthew King, and Frank Fools Crow were wont to do.

Wilson's position on land use was in line with his blood ties to important ranching interests. His uncle on his father's side had a very sizeable ranching operation on the west side of the reservation for many years. Mixed blood rancher Frank D. Wilson was a thorn in the side of Superintendent W.O. Roberts in the 1940s. Roberts blamed him for undermining the Red Shirt Table Cooperative, a model cooperative land tenure venture favored in the early years of the IRA and organized by Roberts. For a time at least, the Red Shirt Cooperative had provided the economic means for both mixed blood and full blood families to make a living from the land.[74] Such cooperative ventures, with a strong subsistence component, took land away from those who saw their future as inextricably linked to commercial grazing and agriculture and who continually needed to expand in order to remain competitive in the market system. Wilson's descendants continue to be involved in the cattle industry on Pine Ridge Reservation. One of them was recently the head of the SDSGA.

Control over federal programs that began coming into the reservation during the Great Society era represented a new, and potentially vital base of support for the IRA government. Wilson operated a spoils system that plugged hundreds of people into the resource pipeline from Washington D.C. By his own reckoning, the OST employee roster jumped from 14 to 752 during his first administration. Political appointments were the rule of the day. Wilson said he did not use the merit system because "he would be unable to place enough of his people in key positions in Tribal operations."[75] Control over hundreds of jobs in the economically poorest county in the United States was a veritable political windfall.

The federal pipeline offered a number of possibilities for an ambitious politician and Wilson was quick to tap into them. During his first administration his Executive Committee simply ignored the eight member Housing Board the Council had appointed, replacing it with five hand-picked people. Wilson was widely alleged to use the Housing Board to allocate housing to his supporters and to have secured lucrative construction projects for his connections in Rapid City, who in turn along with ranchers reportedly helped bankroll his re-election campaign against Means.[76] The numerous boards that sprung up during those years and since were, and remain, an important mechanism of control over resources in an economically poor environment, and are frequently subject to interference, suspension, or removal by tribal government. In April 2001, the OST Council that was seated in December 2000 removed the OST Parks Board, Housing Board, Empowerment Zone Board, and the nine member Personnel Board whose delegates were elected by the people in the districts.

Wilson augmented his circle of support by drawing on the talent of educated mixed blood Oglalas who had been living and working off the reservation. He needed educated people to run tribal programs and was able to place some in important positions in the BIA and tribal government as well. Among them were G. Wayne Tapio who had worked for years in Arizona. He later became an influential OST Council member who served for many terms as a representative from Pine Ridge Village. Pat Lee, a trained attorney, came back from eight years in Arizona to head the newly created OST legal office. In 2001, Lee is the Chief Judge of the OST Court, and has been for the past decade. Leo Vocu, the former director of the influential Washington D.C. based National Congress of American Indians, returned to fill the position of OST Business Manager during Wilson's administration. Dr. Jim Wilson, who had six years experience as Director of the Office of Economic Opportunity's Indian Desk in Washington, D.C. came back as Director of the OST's Planning Center and has been active in economic development committees and projects ever since. Besides recruiting talented tribal members for important posts administrative posts, Wilson claimed that he secured important BIA positions for tribal members too. Among those were Nelson Witt who filled the BIA's Administrative Manger position and Al Trimble who was appointed BIA Superintendent. Wilson's campaign literature for his second term emphasized his ability to secure the talents of those who previously had been "forced to work in other areas because there was no place for them to work on their own reservation." Not surprisingly perhaps, the campaign literature used a military metaphor to characterize his leadership style: "Yes, it takes a true leader to know that

Lieutenants make the General's plans come true and that the troops will follow dedicated, fair, and hard working lieutenants: Simply put – it takes a leader to lead other leaders."[77]

Means won the primary election despite Wilson's formidable political base. But Wilson took the general in an election marred by well-documented and widespread irregularities. There was little doubt in the minds of many Oglalas and outside observers that the election had been rigged. But even after the U.S. Commission on Civil Rights substantiated "massive irregularities" the BIA ignored charges of election fraud, and exercised its preferential option not to act in cases where doing so might serve the general welfare. Oglalas familiar with the situation say that the Bureau picks and chooses when to intervene, using the doctrine of tribal sovereignty to suit its purposes – tribes are sovereign when the Bureau chooses not to intervene. The commissioners had no explanation for the BIA's refusal to act: "The reasons why the BIA chose not to act on the allegations of massive irregularities are not yet clear. . . ." The Bureau had intervened in similar situations elsewhere. Why not then? Why not even an investigation?

One of many violations, in an election where it was determined that one-third of the votes cast were improper, was that persons who were not tribal members were allowed to vote. The Wounded Knee Legal Defense Offense Committee (WKLDOC), an organization of attorneys who represented the American Indian Movement in court and helped gather evidence of corruption and oppression on the reservation, determined that some of the non-Indian voters were white ranchers.[78] Local observers who remember the Wilson administrations (1972–1976) cite connections with hate groups and ranchers as evidence for a "ring" they say represents the real power on Pine Ridge Reservation, and that mobilized to support his administration's agenda against the AIM supported insurgency of people who wanted no less than a revolutionary change in the political and economic arrangements on Pine Ridge Reservation.

Organizations of ranchers and hate groups surfaced on Pine Ridge Reservation during the 1973 Occupation of Wounded Knee and throughout Wilson's administration. The "Liberty Group," an organization of white ranchers who supported Wilson and who were openly anti-AIM operated out of the community of Batesland.[79] Hate groups including the John Birch Society and Posse Commitatis worked actively with ranchers. Armed groups called "goons" who gave their allegiance to Wilson terrorized reservation residents in support of his administration. Goons were trained and apparently even armed by U.S. federal agents. A recent revelation by mixed blood tribal member and goon squad leader Duane Brewer corroborates AIM's longtime contention that the Federal Bureau of Investigation supplied Wilson's goon squads with ammunition for use against the Lakota people.[80]

Wilson's ability to mobilize violence in support of an agenda that was very unpopular with so many, and to secure a significant level of federal support for that agenda, was a watershed in the landscape of Oglala politics. Elements in the IRA government had reached a kind of informal rapprochement with federal authorities wherein they would support the IRA against its own people, even if support meant subjecting tribal members who were U.S. citizens to violence. Perhaps there was a quid pro quo – if the IRA would support the status quo in land and treaty matters, the federal government would support repressive regimes on Pine Ridge Reservation. That might not be the speculative stretch it may appear to be. It would plausibly fit with IRA architect John Collier's own assessment that the IRA was a form of indirect rule.

"There is room for everyone at the rendezvous of victory."
                                                            Aime Cesaire

"Liberation is much more than becoming a mirror image of the white man whom we've thrown out and just replacing him and using his authority."
                                                            Edward W. Said

The Lakota Landowner Association's struggle unveiled the hidden face of power, illuminating underlying fault lines and contradictions in Oglala society. The BIA and a coterie on the OST Land and Allocation Committees were aligned with ranching interests against those of the disenfranchised majority. In the IRA government, a small elite element seized on an instrument it wielded with notable success to forward its own self-interest. A small group of mixed bloods, some of whose roots in the ranching business reached back to days along the North Platte River before the 1868 Fort Laramie Treaty, had shown that they could use the IRA and their connections in the BIA to achieve the objective of "Indian land for Indian use."

The contention that resistance to the IRA on Pine Ridge Reservation stems from its disempowerment and subsequent failure to deliver for the people[81] is partially right but for the wrong reason. OST government does exercise real power, albeit with the consent and/or complicity of the federal government. It wields that power on behalf of a select few, both with regard to ownership and control over land and the federal resource pipeline. It is that selective effectiveness, in addition to the sometimes federally sanctioned use of coercive power against its own people, that catalyzes discontent and fuels recurrent crises of legitimacy. The OST is increasingly effective in providing support for a small and relatively privileged constituency of ranchers, politicians, and certain jobholders on a reservation where unemployment runs around 80%.

The assertion that IRA government on Pine Ridge is run by "Indian lackeys operating against their own people" gives the federal government too much credit and local politicians too little.[82] Local politicians, epitomized by the late Richard "Dick" Wilson, can rely on federal support to move their own agendas, even against an aroused populace, but there is no mistaking the fact that those agendas are their own.

Some research on other reservations has linked tribal governments to elites and social class. Patricia Albers reported that even on the relatively tiny Devils Lake Sioux Reservation of North Dakota, anti-poverty programs created ". . . incipient forms of internal stratification [and] a moneyed tribal elite. . . ."[83] Louise Lamphere and Lorraine Ruffing linked the Navajo Nation's representative government to the growth of an elite class of Navajo whose interests may tie them more closely to outsiders intent on exploitation of Navajo resources than to their own people.[84]

The incipient class relations on Pine Ridge Reservation resemble a stratified ethnic system, where some mixed blood Oglala, a small percentage of mixed bloods overall, enjoy relative power and influence. Their actions are, in effect, like those of a comprador group that shows more allegiance to outside interests than to those of the Oglala people. They are intent on using power for their own ends and shun the urgent project of decolonization and the crying need to effectively wield sovereignty to build a nation.[85]

Where grassroots people, Treaty Councils, and descendants of non-Treaty signers affirm their sovereignty and seek to aggressively assert it, the IRA government most often seeks to defend the status quo. Where grassroots people seek to implement guidelines that would protect the interests of the disenfranchised majority and the health of the land, the federal government and the IRA meet them with secrecy and oppression. Where leaders of the Oglala Omniciye sprung from *tiospaye* and served at great personal hardship to preserve land and treaty rights against outsiders, some – by no means all – New Deal IRA politicians use IRA machinery to further their own ends against the wishes and interests of the people. Ambition, not vision, rules the day.

Underlying contradictions on Pine Ridge Reservation are often obscured by a divisive ideology that undercuts the potential for unifying around a nationalist agenda. Emotionally laden notions about "mixed bloods" and "full bloods" help shore up inequitable social and economic arrangements. While Oglalas sometimes argue that a small segment of mixed bloods and supporters have inordinate influence over reservation affairs, and sometimes characterize local power arrangements as a "ring centered in Pine Ridge Village," more purely ideological interpretations are commonplace. Over and over again, blame is placed on "mixed bloods" in general, and the obverse is also true. Essentialist beliefs about the other often preclude clear vision. The vertical intra-ethnic split between mixed blood and full blood Oglala exists in dynamic tension with a horizontal split between a small, elite group of Oglala mixed bloods and the majority of the Oglala people. The interaction of the two generates an ideological curtain that obscures the nature of the political and economic forces that are generating the inequities in wealth and power that have become such important considerations on Pine Ridge Reservation today.

Mutually beneficial alliances among local ranchers, BIA officials, and OST Council members suggest the metaphor of a dance, where the partners bear responsibility for the outcome. When Pulitzer prize winning author Wole Soyinka returned home to Nigeria in 1998, he delivered a ringing challenge to his fellow countrymen in a speech called "Redesigning a Nation." "It is about time," he said, "that we decided, in a forthright manner, whether it is the structure itself that is at fault, or it is the conduct and protocols of its internal relationship that govern its occupancy. Again, we should recognise the real possibility that it may prove to be an interactive combination of both."[86]

There are signs of movement on Pine Ridge Reservation. There are signs that the "wind from below" that is blowing in Chiapas and in indigenous communities in Mexico is beginning to blow on Pine Ridge Reservation and in the Fort Laramie Treaty and aboriginal lands as well.[87] People are increasingly on the move and determined to make changes. As the late Edward Iron Cloud, Jr., descendant of Knife Chief who rode with Crazy Horse, put it:

> All along I say that people power is our hope. . . The BIA workers only come because they want land, our land. Small lands will be made into tribe land. . . . Since Columbus came we had hard time. We are shy, wisteca, and bashful. We listen to what the BIA want us to do. . . . Each district needs to support the few landowners remaining on the reservation. We have land but we are unable to use it for our own use. This government is over 50 years old. Is it time to change it? IRA placed all this as it is today. We can say we don't want the IRA. Go to the radio and talk because people need to hear these things.[88]

Notes

1. Much of the information about recent events in this chapter, especially the information on the struggle of the Lakota Landowner Association, is based on the author's notes. Readers should be aware of my involvement, along with my wife Eileen Iron Cloud, my late father in law Edward Iron Cloud, Jr., and some others mentioned in the text in addressing some of the issues discussed in this chapter. My wife and I and her family attended meetings, helped organize meetings, talked about the issues over KILI Radio, helped gather testimony from the people, and were otherwise involved on behalf of the Association.

2. Conflicts over IRA governments, which were adopted by over 200 different tribes, are frequent on many reservations. Conflicts over the legitimacy of those governments have plagued the Hopi, the Sicangu Sioux of Rosebud Reservation, the Flathead and the Blackfoot, the Sac and Fox, the Pueblo of Santa Clara, the Oglala, and many other groups. (See Clow, Richmond 1977, p. 245–6; Jorgensen, Joseph and Richard Clemmer 1980, p. 87; Mekeel, H. Scudder 1944, p. 214; Nagata, Shuichi 1977, p. 146; Taylor, Graham 1974, p.136, and 1980 p. 46.) Some groups appear to have avoided the conflicts that mark the experience of the Oglala and other groups. On some reservations, where representative IRA governments and the notion of allegiance to a central government are certainly as alien as they are to the Oglala, they have somehow been integrated with traditional notions about leadership and with traditional organizational principles. Loretta Fowler's ethnohistorical account of Arapahoe politics, for example, shows that the Arapahoe were able to adapt the IRA to their traditional age-grade system, and they have avoided the conflicts and schisms characteristic of the experience on many other reservations. She reports that at Northern Cheyenne, where there is a mixed blood, full blood split, full bloods control the IRA government, and have applied traditional Cheyenne notions about the "good man" to the role of elected IRA leaders, perhaps helping to explain the relative lack of conflict over the IRA on that reservation. (Fowler, Loretta 1982, p. 308.)

3. Author's notes. See Deloria, Vine, Jr., 1984 for more on the Wounded Knee Occupation.

4. Eggan, Fred 1981, p. 285.

5. Washburn, Wilcomb 1984, p. 287.

6. Deloria, Vine, Jr. 1999, p. 195; Deloria, Vine, Jr.1984, p. 188.

7. Robbins, Rebecca L. 1992, p. 95–6.

8. Schlesier, Karl 1980, p. 561.

9. Biolsi, Thomas 1992, p. 183, cf. also p. 175–178.

10. The U.S. Department of the Interior, Bureau of Indian Affairs, 1997 Labor Market Information on the Indian Labor Force put unemployment at 73% in 1997.

11. Cornell, Stephen and Joseph Kalt 1989, p.33.

12. See chapter 3.

13. Cf. McCurdy, James R., 1981.

14. James Red Cloud to CIA, January 13, 1930, 9514-37-054 to 7406-30-056, 1907–1939, PR, CCF

15. Jermark to CIA February 3, 1930, 9514-37-054 to 7406-30-056, 1907–1939, PR, CCF.

16. Huber, Jacqueline et al., 1981, p. 2–4.

17. Testimony of Ted Means at the Sioux Treaty Hearing, December, 1974, In Ortiz, Roxanne 1977, p. 182.

18. Owada, Patricia, 1979, p. 293.

19. Ibid.

20. Interview tape recorded by author.

21. Johnson Holy Rock, December 16, 1994, speech at Oglala Lakota College, during a presentation by Frank Pommersheim on "Native American Testimony and the Black Hills Claim."

22. See chapter 4 for information about Newcastle Land and Livestock's activities on Pine Ridge Reservation. Information on land ownership from the Office of the Director of Equalization, Fall River Court House, Hot Springs, S.D.

23. Report titled "Cluster Housing," 1974, Subject files, No. 11, "Cluster housing," Boxes 4–6, WKLDOC.

24. Report titled "Cluster Housing," 1974, Subject files, No. 11, "Cluster housing," Boxes 4–6, WKLDOC.

25. Minutes of Special District Meeting, November 23, 1971, Subject files, No. 11, Cluster housing, Boxes 4–6, WKLDOC.

26. Minutes of Special District Meeting, November 23, 1971, Subject files, No. 11, Cluster housing, Boxes 4–6, WKLDOC.

27. Author's notes.

28. Discussion with Gerald One Feather, April 7, 1994.

29. Author's notes; *Mila Yatapika Eyapaha*, February, 1995, Knife Chief Community, Porcupine, S.D., copy in author's possession.

30. Figure cited by OST Housing Authority Director over KILI Radio in February, 1995.

31. These encounters on March, 7, 1995, Author's notes.

32. OST Ordinance 90-01, March 27, 1990; OST Resolution 80-34, March 25, 1980, copies in author's possession; OST Resolution 75-23, excerpted in Rogers, C. Bryant 1976.

33. Tidwell's threat in Henry M. Tidwell to Lessees, February 8, 1919, File 321, Lists, Notices, Miscellaneous Inquiries, MDF-PR. The history of subleasing on the reservation is discussed in chapter 3.

34. James McGregor to Collier, May 14, 1934, File 321, Miscellaneous, MDF-PR.

35. Anthony Whirlwind Horse, Superintendent, to rancher (name withheld), October 29, 1976, OLC. Rogers, C. Bryant 1976.

36. Name withheld. 1995 letter in author's possession.

37. Land Use and Purchase Patterns on the Pine Ridge Reservation, 1974.

38. Ibid.; Pine Ridge Agency "Grazing Rental" report, Fiscal year 1994, copy in author's possession. The BIA report shows 67 range units permitted to non-members out of a total of 364 . Melvin Cummings' statement was made at an OST Council meeting on February 22, 1995.

39. Land Use and Purchase Patterns on the Pine Ridge Reservation, 1974, p. 1, 9, 10.
40. Land Use and Purchase Patterns on the Pine Ridge Reservation, 1974, p. 10, 11, 13.
41. Ibid., p. 11, 12.
42. Based on testimony gathered at meetings by the Lakota Landowners Association.
43. Defining who is an "Indian" enters into the grazing issue and into other areas involving tribal preference. One mixed blood Oglala, who served on the OST Council a number of times and as Chair of the Allocation Committee for many years, maintains that his successful case before the OST Court in the 1970s insured for himself and others that blood quantum would not be a consideration for tribal membership. Unlike many other tribes the OST chose lineal descent as its criterion for membership. The lineal descent guideline allowed some persons to become tribal members regardless of their degree of Indian ancestry. Persons of 1/64 or 1/256 degree of Indian blood or even less could still apply for enrollment under. It has been a controversial policy that has led some Oglalas to openly question whether certain individuals should actually be accorded status as a tribal member. Some maintain that application of the rule has resulted in non-Indians becoming tribal members. If an individual can get someone to vouch that she or he is a blood relative they could be enrolled, a scenario that does occur. The high profile case of Richard Erie, who became the Attorney General for the OST during the conflict-ridden1998–2000 administration, caused an uproar over enrollment. Erie had several persons vouch that he was a family member. Others who knew the family totally rejected their claims. Erie was a very controversial figure. Those who supported his claim to be a lineal descendant were related to Council member Manuel Fool Head who was indicted by federal authorities for actions he took as an OST Council member and who was one of the more unpopular figures in an unpopular administration. As of this writing, no decision has been made on Erie's enrollment application. Author's notes.
44. OST Resolution 63-27, January 25, 1963, MDF, Box 177, File 061, OST Council 1940–44, KC.
45. Rogers, C. Bryant, 1976 and author's notes.
46. Author's notes.
47. "Lakota Landowner Associations" (LLA) have been a regular fixture on Pine Ridge Reservation since the 1960s. Most members own allotted land, identify as full blood Oglala or simply as "Lakota," and speak the Lakota language. They identify as "Lakota landowners" and are quick to distinguish themselves from *ieskas* (literally, "interpreters," but used in this context as a referent for "mixed blood") who, some members say, "sold their birthright," a reference to the loss of land that mixed blood Oglala suffered after the U.S. forced them to take patents to their land in the first two decades of the century. Like the various Lakota Treaty Councils, they view the 1851 and 1868 Treaties as the foundation of their relationship with the federal government, and the legal basis for tribal sovereignty. Many members hold that the Oglala Sioux Tribe (OST), organized under the IRA

(Indian Reorganization Act of 1934) is not a legitimate government and does not represent their interests. Members are keenly aware of the losses of land they have experienced as a people in the pre-reservation era, and interpret the decline in land ownership by individual Oglalas and the diminishing reservation land base as evidence for a continuing process of colonization and disenfranchisement. Associations generally work to protect the environment and to secure control over that which is rightfully theirs.

48. The Code of Federal Regulations, and the current OST Grazing Ordinance, 90-01, of the OST, stipulate that tribal and individually owned trust land that is suitable for grazing will be placed in tracts called range units. Through a system of allocation and competitive bidding, those range units are permitted to Indian and non-Indian ranchers. On Pine Ridge Reservation allocations are awarded to tribal members at a minimum rate, if their herds are smaller than 300 animal units (one cow and a calf of less than six months of age), or through a competitive bidding process if they have larger herds, or are non-members. OST Ordinance 90-01, Ordinance of the Oglala Sioux Tribal Council, March 27, 1990, Copy in author's possession.

49. Six OST Council members served on the OST Land Committee in 1995. It is one of several standing committees. The Allocation Committee is a group of seven persons appointed by the OST Council to administer the Grazing Ordinance. OST Grazing Ordinances have regularly been in effect for a five year period, since their inception in 1970. Grazing permits are also awarded for five year periods. Technically, Ordinances do not "expire," and remain in effect until another Ordinance is adopted in lieu of the existing one.

50. It was especially dismaying to landowners that they would be treated as they were at a meeting featuring Ada Deer. Deer is a Menominee tribal member who has a long record of commitment to Indian causes. She was a very important figure in the drive to regain federal recognition for the Menominee, after they were terminated. But she was one person in a large bureaucracy with deep-seated attitudes and long-standing practices that have often been anything but favorable toward the Indian peoples whose interests it is charged with representing.

51. BIA officials and OST Council committees frequently meet in hotels in Rapid City, a practice that enables them to collect per diem, mileage, and to enjoy other perks, and that enables them to minimize influence from their constituents.

52. The Pine Ridge Reservation is divided up into nine separate political units. Each of the units has a District Council, with officers elected at large within the District. Each District also sends elected representatives to the OST Council.

53. Marvin Amiotte, OST Attorney, to All OST Council Members, November 23, 1994, draft OST Grazing Ordinance. Copy in author's possession.

54. Author's notes.

55. Author's notes.

56. The two individuals do, in fact, work with the United Nations, and have been to Geneva to work on Treaty issues there. They want to take the U.S. to the World Court.

57. Flyer, March, 1995, "History of the Grazing Ordinance Proposal by the Lakota Landowner Association" copy in author's possession.

58. Author's notes.

59. Guy White Thunder to Superintendent Robert Ecoffey et al., September 11, 1998; Senator Tom Daschle to Jacqueline M. Cheek, Director, Congressional and Legislative Affairs, BIA, September 22, 1998; Alice A. Harwood to Senator Tom Daschle, October 27, 1998. Copies of correspondence in author's possession.

60. OST Council Meeting, March 22, 1995, Wakpamnee CAP Office, author's notes.

61. Description of the March 7, 1995 meeting between Lakota Landowner Association and OST and BIA officials based on author's notes and a videotape of the meeting, videotape in author's possession.

62. Lakota Fund Director Meeks attended the Piya Wiconi meeting and was scheduled to go on KILI Radio, on Milo Yellow Hair's show, the following weekend to explain the paper, but did not appear.

63. To "encourage" the people as Richards did is a recurring feature of Lakota culture. At gatherings where people are honored, or where people are troubled, "words of encouragement" are often given by elders, or by others who are recognized by the people as authorities.

64. During a recent conflict over an easement for BIA Highway 27 through Porcupine District, BIA Superintendent Robert Ecoffey, Jr. defended the BIA plan to take down part of a hill for fill dirt, despite the pleas of landowners and a traditional healer, to preserve it because of the medicinal plants growing on it and because oral histories held that a man and the horse he had been riding on had been struck by lightning on the hill and buried on the spot. Ecoffey's response was "There is medicine and graves on all these hills." Recorded by the author.

65. OST Resolution No. 80-104, October 1, 1980; Shirley Plume to Task Force Members, February 5, 1981; and Dennis Bush [White Shield] to Hon. James Watt, Sec. of Interior, June 4, 1981, File: OST Land Office, Box 27/175, OLC.

66. *Mila Yatapika Eyapaha*. May, 1996. FOIA request and BIA response in author's possession.

67. Personal communication with Claricy Smith.

68. Author's notes.

69. Story of the Cobell v. Babbitt suit based on author's notes from Indian Land Working Group meeting in Polson, Montana and case history materials and other documents provided on NARF's website which can be found at www.narf.org.

70. Cf. Talbot, Steve, 1979.

71. Russell Means, Shannon County News, December 28, 1973, OLC.

72. "Heirship land" refers to individually owned trust lands. Those lands were once part of an original allotment. There are approximately 800,000 acres of heirship land on Pine Ridge Reservation today. "Tribal land" refers to trust land that is owned by the Oglala Sioux Tribe. The OST owns over 830,000 acres of tribal land.

73. Dick Wilson, *Shannon County News*, December 28, 1973, OLC.

74. Roberts, William 1943.

75. Wilson's count of tribal employees from *Shannon County News*, December 28, 1973, OLC. Wilson's comment on the merit system in *Occupation of Wounded Knee: Hearings before the Subcommittee on Indian Affairs*, 1974, p. 408.

76. Transcript of taped interview with Richard Little, November 16, 1973; Complaint of OST Council members Hobart Keith, Richard Little, and Birgil Kills Straight, February 7, 1973, 147.I.4.9 (B), WKLDOC.

77. Re-elect Wilson campaign literature, n.d. 147.I.4.9 (B), papers ca. 1960s–1976, WKLDOC.

78. U.S. Commission on Civil Rights, 1974, p. 2, 3, 20, 24; Reports of white ranchers voting include oral reports, and *Wounded Knee Legal Defense/Offense Committee Newsletter*, V. II, No. 12, May 27, 1974, OLC. In 1983, when Means put his hat in the ring for the presidency a second time, he made the land an issue again. As in his previous campaign, he stressed that people needed to take control of their land base, to take control away from ranchers and the BIA. The OST Council put a stop to Means' second presidential bid, passing Ordinance 83-19, which declared that no one ever convicted of a felony could run for political office. Means and others filed suit against the OST for not placing his name on the ballot, claiming that 83–19 was illegal because it amended the qualifications for office stipulated in the OST Constitution, and amendments require popular elections. OST Chief Judge, Jerry Matthews, a white, ruled against the plaintiffs arguing that since the OST Constitution contains a provision mandating that those who commit felonies while in office must forfeit their office, then Means would have had to step down as soon as he was elected [sic]. Means' supporters maintained that Matthews' decision had to be understood in the context of lack of separation of powers, the fact that judges are elected by OST Council members, that the Bureau picks and chooses when to intervene, using the doctrine of tribal sovereignty to suit its purposes. The local/regional power structure was likely a player as well.

79. *Crazy Horse News*. March, 1975, OLC; Author's notes.

80. In the recent documentary, "In the Spirit of Crazy Horse," Duane Brewer, currently serving as an OST Council member from Pine Ridge Village , (1994–1996), and goon leader during the Richard Wilson administration, reported that he was supplied with armor piercing ammunition by the FBI during the period following the Occupation of Wounded Knee in 1973. In explanation for why he might want the ammunition, he said that they, the goons, were fighting "a war."

81. Biolsi, Thomas 1992, p. 183. Cf. also p. 175–178.

82. Schlesier, Karl 1980, p. 561.

83. Albers, Patricia 1982, p. 257.

84. Lamphere, Louise 1976; Ruffing, Lorraine 1979, p. 36.

85. "Nation" is a controversial word. Some Oglalas use it to symbolize sovereignty and their desire for a nation to nation relationship with other countries. Some, in particular some elders, prefer to refer to the Oglala as a "band" and suggest the term nation would be better used to refer to the collective bands of the Sioux Nation that were signatory to the 1868 Fort Laramie Treaty.

86. Soyinka, Wole 1998.

87. Subcommandante Marcos refers to the Zapatista and the indigenous movements in Mexico as the "wind from below."

88. Iron Cloud did not go past the sixth grade, but he read widely, practiced the traditions, and worked tirelessly for change as his ancestors did. He was also the Treasurer of the Lakota Landowner Association during the recent struggle.

CHAPTER 8

A Nation in Crisis, Poised for Change

"I have made the recommendation time and time again – let us have a referendum on IRA, which is designed to obliterate the Lakota people."
Johnson Holy Rock, Lakota elder and former OST President, January 17, 2000.[1]

This is who we are. We are a sovereign nation. We are the Lakota people. We have had all these laws and this paperwork built over us to suppress us. But we [are] the Lakota nation, not that Tribal Council. We are abolishing that IRA government.
Marie Randall, Lakota elder and activist, March 22, 2000.[2]

The January 2000 takeover of OST Headquarters by the Grass Roots Oyate (people) in protest of the OST Council's alleged corruption quickly drew widespread support from across Pine Ridge Reservation. The evening of the takeover, the number of supporters swelled to well over 200. Larger gatherings of up to 800 supporters turned out to show their support for the effort in the days and months that followed. Members of the *tokala* societies (Kit Fox warrior societies) provided around the clock security, manning posts inside the building and on top of it. Supporters furnished cameras, radios, food, and other necessaries. Canned goods, sleeping bags, blankets, and warm clothing streamed in from supporters on and off the reservation. Volunteers cooked huge pots of soup to feed the people that kept vigil at the building and for the large numbers of supporters that turned out for the frequent strategy meetings.[3]

The takeover was accompanied by an upsurge in public pronouncements about the importance of Lakota culture and traditions and by a deepening sense of a collective experience of oppression.

> Sacred dreams shared by women in the Red Cloud Building reveal aht this event is meant to be and is guided by the strength of and truth of our sacred *cannupa*. Prayers are made daily in front of the altar which holds the sacred pipes, staffs and the offerings. The altar is located in the Council chambers, jokingly referred to as the 'torture chamber.' Now the round room is filled with an air of peace and prayer. At night the room is filled with women, elders and children, sleeping under the security and safety of the *cannupa*. During the day we are reeducated in the ways of the Lakota culture through dialogue with the old people. We listen respectfully, we laugh and we cry when we hear the stories of those left broken-hearted by the IRA system, the Bureau of

Indian Affairs and those individuals who have taken on the role of the oppressor.[4]

When OST Council members threatened to take the building back, supporters rallied to the building in large numbers. Many went on KILI Radio to protest the Council's threats. The *cannupa* was regularly invoked to remind the people that the push for change was grounded in Lakota ways and in nonviolence. Other traditions of nonviolent resistance, including Gandhi and Martin Luther King were cited as examples of strong leaders who accomplished much through nonviolent means. Some men took oaths to support the occupation until the demands for financial accountability and removal of offending officials were met.

Women organized the *Wico On Cage Winyan Okolakiciye* (Lifegiver's Society) and met separately to plan strategies to support the aims of the occupation. Youth formed their own society and soon young people in high schools were voicing support for the effort, wondering aloud what tribal officials had done with the people's money and asking why their elected leaders were not providing for the needs of the future generations. Elders weighed in strongly with their support. Several stayed at the building day after day, providing guidance for the effort.

On the third day of the occupation, the OST Executive Committee resolved to support the protestors demand that records of the OST General Fund should be audited in order to show definitively whether the Council was indeed corrupt.[5] On the strength of the Executive Committee's Resolution the BIA agreed to pay for an audit of Fiscal Year 1999 General Fund records and the FBI came in and removed them, transferring them to the Federal Building in Rapid City for safe keeping until the audit could be done. Pass Creek District records were also removed at the request of another group of Oglalas who had surrounded the district headquarters and refused entry to district officials they claimed had misused the people's resources.

OST Council members condemned the occupation and chided the Oyate and the OST Executive Committee for asking for federal assistance with an audit. "If they are for sovereignty as they claim," they argued, then "why invite the feds in?" Meanwhile, by a 13–1 vote, the OST Council adopted OST Resolution 00-15, "requesting technical assistance and manpower from the Bureau of Indian Affairs, Federal Bureau of Investigation, U.S. Marshal's Office, Alcohol, Tobacco and Firearms, Drug Enforcement Agency, Department of Justice, and the U.S. Attorney's Office for the arrests [sic] and prosecution of federal crimes and offenses and prosecution therein for crimes committed on or about the Pine Ridge Indian Reservation."[6] The OST Council could not rely on its own Public Safety Division which was split over the takeover. Officers had refused to carry out orders by the OST Judiciary Committee to remove the protestors.

When the OST Council met at Billy Mills Hall in Pine Ridge Village on January 31, between 400–500 Oyate supporters jammed the old gymnasium there, while several hundred more assembled for strategy meetings down the street at the Red Cloud Building. In a heated meeting, Oyate spokespersons repeatedly asked the Council to call for a five year audit of General Fund records and called for the suspension of the unpopular Treasurer, Wesley "Chuck" Jacobs. The Council complied with the people's wishes that day but soon rolled those actions back, reinstating Jacobs and suspending the popular OST President Harold Dean Salway on February 25. Salway had expressed sympathy for the Oyate allegation of massive corruption and had issued a temporary suspension of all OST Council members the previous day. The Council's unpopular moves further infuriated an aroused public.

District Councils met in Medicine Root, Wakpamnee, and Wounded Knee Districts and voted for removal of their representatives to the OST Council, but like other actions welling up from the people, the Council steadfastly ignored them, effectively closing off the main channel of communication the OST Constitution provided for. The Council was in no mood to listen to the people at all, and began to meet at the Prairie Winds Casino on the far west side of the reservation and in other locales without announcing their plans in advance. But each time the people found out where they were meeting and showed up in significant numbers to air their grievances. Between mid-March and August 2000, the Council took the further step of fleeing the reservation all together, meeting at the Rapid City Civic Center and various hotels. That made it physically difficult for large numbers of people to attend Council meetings because they lacked necessary transportation and gas money to make the 80–100 mile trip from the reservation. The cost of the meetings further angered the people who had heard the claims of Jacobs and Finance Committee Chair Michael Her Many Horses that an $8 million bond was needed to pay off debts from previous administrations and to cover the heavy spending they claimed individual Council members had made on behalf of TANF (Temporary Assistance to Needy Families) recipients who had been taken off the rolls by South Dakota Department of Social Services. They claimed that they simply could not help themselves from helping the people out because they were practicing the Lakota virtue of generosity. But how then, the people asked, could they justify meeting Rapid City? Weren't they eating up a lot of resources by drawing per diem, paying for hotel rooms and meals, and claiming gas mileage? Furor over finances increased in intensity after a thick printout of credits and debits from the OST General Fund was leaked out and distributed across the reservation.

People were amazed at what the reports contained, and just as amazed that they actually had some real information to base their longstanding concerns on. They took the financial ledgers to District Council meetings, excerpted reports from them, read their findings at the meetings and over the radio, and renewed the call for the removal of Council members. Some, including the Grass Roots Oyate, called for wholesale sacking of all seventeen OST Council representatives. Council members' claims that the reports were corrupted, fake, and had been manufactured were contradicted by their own actions. While they directed scathing attacks against "whoever had leaked them out," claiming that whoever was responsible was "guilty of criminal behavior," they simultaneously increased controls at the Financial Accounting Office in order to preclude more public information from surfacing.

The record of debits and credits from the OST General Fund for the period December 1, 1998 through November 18, 1999, and the preliminary audit of the General Fund, corroborated the charges of corruption and gross mismanagement that were being leveled against the OST Council, Treasurer, and Finance Committee. The audit showed that financial controls were virtually nil,[7] despite the fact that the non-Indian accountant John Dunham had been working for the OST for 16 years and it was his job to implement such a system. Donham was late on audits as well. He had the Council support though and they were loath to replace him. A number of revelations damaging to the OST Council and to individual Council members grew out of the analyses of the ledger books that Grass Roots Oyate supporters made and distributed. Those analyses were lent credence when Jaime Arobba, the accountant the BIA contracted with to audit the OST General Fund, announced that the ledger book copies they were based on were indeed authentic.

Among the damaging revelations that the analyses brought out was the fact that each Council member was receiving a vehicle maintenance payment of $500 per month on top of mileage and their $32,000 per year salaries. Jacobs and the OST Finance Committee had arranged for them to receive the vehicle maintenance payments from indirect cost accounts and then allowed several of them to draw from those line items for over a year in advance, even beyond the period for which they had been elected to serve.[8] People were angry about the vehicle maintenance money but they were outraged by what the ledgers revealed about the use Council representatives made of their financial assistance line item.

OST Council members each had a $6,000 line item to provide financial assistance to tribal members, but they had grossly overspent them. The ledgers showed that between December 1998 and November 1999, seventeen Council representatives overspent their financial assistance line items by more than $700,000. Breakdown of the records showed a pattern of Council members lining their own pockets, providing inordinate amounts of assistance to their own family members, and to tribal employees. Porcupine District Representatives gave themselves and their immediate families more than $11,000 in financial assistance. Medicine Root representative Manuel Fool Head gave more than $41,000 to himself, his wife, and other family members. Many of the Council members gave money to tribal employees, especially in the Financial Accounting Office (FAO) office. Various Council members provided FAO employees with $31,796 in assistance. In addition, the Council and the Treasurer hd authorized $459,000 in interest free loans drawn on the General Fund. Most of the loans were to people with jobs, many of whom were tribal employees. Furthermore, it turned out, those "loans" were in effect grants because, as the audit showed, there was no tracking system in place and most were aware of that and did not feel the need to pay them back.[9]

In light of the revelations of unbridled corruption, President Salway declared a state of emergency on March 8. He argued that he had to do it because the Council conducted business without a quorum at the February 25 meeting where they suspended him and reinstated Jacobs, and were otherwise in violation of the OST Constitution. Meanwhile, the *tokalas* physically escorted Richard Erie off the reservation, once on the strength of an OST Public Safety Commission order and another time because they felt he was a lynchpin in the Council's continued lawlessness.

Erie was a newly appointed OST Attorney General who had written a number of unpopular Ordinances the Council passed in order to strengthen its position against the Oyate. He was brought in after the takeover. The *tokalas* actions and Salways declaration of emergency brought a strong response from the U.S. government. U.S. Attorney Ted McBride threatened the people with federal kidnapping charges if they took matters into their own hands again, although as Lakota elder Marie Randall pointed out "We didn't kidnap Erie." After *tokala* society members asked him to leave the reservation "He got in his car and left, but the people followed him in their cars" in order to make sure he left.[10] The Interior Department's Assistant Secretary for Indian Affairs, Kevin Gover, did not mince words in his March 23 letter to Salway, threatening him and his supporters with civil and criminal liability "for any wrongs they may commit . . . under the laws of the Tribe and of the United States." He also threatened to withdraw funds for the OST Public Safety if they did not follow the "chain of command established by the Tribal Council." With consummate irony in light of the history of the BIA, Gover wrote that ". . . as the trustee of the Oglala Sioux people [sic], the United States will not stand by and watch you and your supporters violate the rights of tribal and American citizens."[11] Soon after, on March 29, the Council enacted OST Ordinance 00-06, appointing the Judiciary Committee and "other interested Council members" as the governing board of Public Safety. That same session they voted 10–3 to retrocede the Criminal Investigator division of Public Safety to the Bureau of Indian Affairs, thereby giving up an important aspect of tribal sovereignty.

The Oyate tried to address some of their grievances through the tribal court. Chief Judge Patrick Lee, who came on the scene in Pine Ridge Reservation during Dick Wilson's first administration, was unceremoniously dubbed "flipper" as he issued orders seeming to support one side or the other only to change them hours or days later. There is no separation of powers and the Court leans the way the wind blows in times like those. The lesson the people learned with a vengeance is that they have no recourse within their own system, that there are no local checks and balances on actions the IRA might choose to take that infringe on the rights of the people. The Council flees from input. The Court will not exercise oversight and cannot. The U.S. government ultimately supports the IRA/OST government because it is in many ways, as the people point out, "an arm of the federal government."

The people's persistence in bringing out abuses and in pushing the U.S. Attorney's office in Rapid City to take action have produced some results. One Council member has been indicted on charges related to those exposed by the leaked ledger. Another has been indicted on fraud charges connected with defrauding the OST Housing Authority. Other indictments are pending. But indictments will not address the problem of a system that is fundamentally unaccountable to the people.

The OST government serves certain interests very well. Its priority is to serve the Council members themselves, their kin networks, ranchers, and some of the employed. The tendencies that were manifest during the administration of Richard Wilson in the 1970s have essentially become institutionalized. Instead of moving to build strong institutions of governance, the OST government flees from the people and from the task of nation building. The results leave the people without an infrastructure they can depend on.

Nowhere are those results more apparent than in the Court system, where five prosecutors rarely present a case for prosecution, with the result that crimes committed against each other are not addressed in a predictable way unless they are serious felonies that fall under the Major Crimes Act and that are reported to the U.S. Attorney.[12] The criminal justice system on the reservation is in a state of virtual collapse and the government is powerless or unwilling to improve it.

During the 1996–1998 administration, a crusading Attorney General who had been brought in by President John Yellow Bird Steele and who aimed to make a difference ran into stiff resistance from OST Council members and finally left. His spot was filled by another who made the mistake of issuing a pickup order for Treasurer Jacobs for alleged infractions of the OST criminal code. She was immediately removed and replaced with the compliant Richard Erie. Similar difficulties face many of the nearly 60 tribal programs funded by the federal government. Fifty percent of OST Council members' salaries are paid out of the indirect cost account, giving them, they say, the prerogative to manage those programs. The results have been disastrous. Employees report harassment, arbitrary removal, and micromanaging by Council members and standing committees.

Though most of the Council members from the administration that was in power when the takeover of the Red Cloud Building occurred decided not to run or were turned out of office by the electorate in November 2000, many people are arguing the new Council is going down the same road as the one it replaced. In the first four months of the new administration, the Council has hired back, through the mechanism of political appointments, many of those who did not get reelected – a recurring practice that insures that many of the same people stay close to the reins of government year after year, administration after administration. The new Council has also removed several governing Boards, including the powerful Personnel and Housing Boards, despite the fact that those board members were elected by the people in the districts. Once it removed the Housing Board, the Council placed some of its own members on the Board.

After the reservation was created, there was a brief period of ration-dependency but Oglalas made use of the land and the live cattle issue to build sizeable herds they could rely on. Those herds reached their zenith in 1910. Although that period of relative self-reliance was soon eclipsed by corporate ranching, it showed that oral accounts of Oglala elders wre correct and illustrated the capacity of the Oglala people to creatively and innovatively use their resources when they had access to them.

Difference between mixed blood and full blood Oglalas originated in the period before the 1868 Treaty. Distinct differences that existed at that time, including differences in cultural style and economic pursuits, were reinforced and elaborated after the establishment of Pine Ridge Agency in 1879. Mixed bloods preferred commercial ranching and an entrepreneurial lifestyle to that of the full blood majority who pursued the remaining buffalo herds as long as they could, later opting for communal pursuits on the reservation in the early twentieth century.

The U.S. colonial regime used the mixed blood/full blood ethnic split in order to help carry out its agenda of assimilation and control. Full blood resistance to allotment was ignored and mixed blood support was used to advance the process. Mixed blood teachers were preferentially used as adjuncts to the assimilation process. Full bloods were tapped for the Indian Police, which were used against their own people and served to undermine traditional authority structures. The federal government further divided the people through the mechanism of Blood Quantum, arbitrarily adopting the racist standard that said that anyone of 1/2 or more white blood should be declared competent and issued a fee patent to their land. Most Oglala mixed bloods quickly lost their land and became a landless group on the margins of Oglala society. But a few short years later they reemerged to challenge full bloods for political power through the mechanism of representative government.

Conflicts between mixed blood and full blood groups were apparent in the first decade of the century as mixed bloods sought to expand their purchase on the land base by fencing off the commons that full bloods depended on for their subsistence herds. The notion that the reservation acted as a buffer to outside economic forces was put to rest by the evidence of the U.S. led takeover of Oglala allotted land by outside cattle interests during World War I. During that period, mixed bloods and full bloods alike were largely denied the use of their land by the influx of white-owned corporate cattle outfits that flooded the reservation with stock at the behest of U.S. colonial officials in the OIA. The federal government abrogated its trust responsibility in those years as it did not collect lease money from the ranchers and allowed the reservation to be taken over by lawless elements, much as it had in the 1890s when it refused to stop trespassing stock from the large ranching operations that had come in to the Dakotas to fill the breech left by the calculated destruction of the buffalo herds. The so-called "trust responsibility" of the BIA is a smoke screen masking its real agenda. That agenda has been to service outside interests at the expense of the Oglala Lakota people, and so it remains.

After Congress enacted the Indian Reorganization Act of 1934 and pursuant its adoption on Pine Ridge Reservation, progressive New Deal bureaucrats initiated projects that emphasized cooperative ranching and worked to reclaim the reservation land base for the people their predecessors had helped alienate from it. But entrenched ranching interests aided by the newly formed IRA government eventually displaced those communal experiments.

Representative government in the form of Superintendent Henry Tidwell's puppet council, the later 21 Council, and the IRA government itself were a far cry from earlier Lakota based governmental forms, including those expressed during the reservation period through the Oglala Omniciye (Oglala Council). The 21 Council and the IRA afforded mixed blood Oglala a novel opportunity to challenge the full blood dominated Oglala Omniciye for control over the reins of tribal government. That gave rise to a new set of contradictions in Oglala society and catalyzed the sustained conflict that has marked OST government ever since.

On Pine Ridge Reservation, the IRA has been a vehicle for the advancement of the interests of a small group of Oglalas, primarily mixed blood ranchers, as the actions of the first OST Council under Frank G. Wilson's administration in the 1930s demonstrated. In the 1960s and 1970s, mixed blood Oglalas were able to leverage the power of the IRA government and with BIA support were able to secure the majority of the land base for themselves. That situation continued to benefit outside interests as well. Outsiders subleased their cattle to mixed blood and white ranchers while the BIA and OST overlooked the practice despite the dangers it posed to the environment and in spite of complaints by largely full blood landowners. The system was nearly impervious to complaints even when they were advanced by an organized and determined group of landowners organized under the banner of the Lakota Landowner Association.

A small group of mixed blood ranchers is able to effectively carry out an agenda, which is often at odds with the expressed wishes of the majority of Oglala landowners because of its economic and political power. Newly emerging elites control the largesse of transfer payments and tribal revenues. They work alongside older ranching interests and together they effectively control the major resources on the reservation, and use that control to advance their own narrow interests against those of the majority. In that sense, Oglala society on Pine Ridge Reservation is a class society that resembles in striking ways those societies that are characteristic of many areas of the world that were colonized by Europeans, societies where small self-interested elites concern themselves with their own gain at the expense of the project of nation building.[13]

The current unrest on the Pine Ridge Reservation is the outcome of more than a century of U.S. colonial rule. The IRA government has evolved into a patronage system that rewards the older ranching class and an emerging elite of politicians and their supporters. The system provides no accountability to the people, whose only real avenue to redress collective grievances is to do what the Oyate did when they occupied tribal headquarters in January 2000.

The hope for the future is in the continuing struggle and resistance of the Oglala Lakota people. In the words of Emily Iron Cloud-Koenen, "The wise Chiefs, elders, grandfathers and grandmothers continue to encourage the people to *blihiciya pi*, have courage. The spirits of Crazy Horse, Red Cloud and other wise ones still live in us! We will overcome!"[14]

Notes

1. Author's notes.
2. CPT Pine Ridge: Lessons in Listening to Grandmothers," by Carl Meyer in Mila Yatapika Eyapaha, May 2000.
3. Author's notes. N.B., Much of the information on the takeover of the Red Cloud Building by the Grass Roots Oyate is based on the author's notes and is not footnoted.
4. Iron Cloud-Miller, Alberta "To Rebuild, Rehumanize and Retribalize the Oglala Oyate," by Alberta Iron Cloud-Miller in *Mila Yatapika Eyapaha,* January 2000.
5. The OST General Fund is tribal money that can be used at the discretion of the OST. About $ 10 million per year from casino revenue and tribal land lease and other sources flows through the General Fund each year.
6. OST Resolution 00-15, dated March 12, 2000.
7. OST General Fund Audit Draft, March 7, 2000.
8. Oglala Sioux Tribe Cash/General Fund General Ledger for December 1, 1998 through November 18, 1999. Copy in author's possession.
9. OST General Fund Audit Draft, March 7, 2000.
10. Minutes of "General Council" meeting held in support of the Grass Roots Oyate at Red Cloud Building on April 22, 2000. Copy in author's possession.
11. Assistant Secretary of Indian Affairs Kevin Gover to OST President Harold Dean Salway, March 23, 2000. Copy in author's possession.
12. Oglala Sioux Tribe Department of Public Safety Assessment and Review, February 2001.
13. Cf. for example Harvey, Neil 1998; Frank, Andre Gundre 1966; Stavrianos, L.S. 1981; Wallerstein, Immanuel 1983; Worsley, Peter 1984.
14. Iron Cloud-Koenen, Emily, "Traditional chiefs lead the occupation," *Mila Yatapika Eyapahai* editorial, January 2000.

Abbreviations Used in Footnotes

CCF: Bureau of Indian Affairs Records, Record Group 75, Central Classified Files, National Archives, Washington, D.C.

IRAP: Indian Rights Association Papers, 1868–1968 (1974) Glen Rock, New Jersey: Microfilming Corporation of America.

KC: Bureau of Indian Affairs Records, Record Group 75, National Archives, Kansas City, Missouri.

M1011: Superintendent's Annual Narrative and Statistical Reports from Field Jurisdiction of the Bureau of Indian Affairs, 1907–1938. National Archives Microfilm Publications.

MDF-PR: Main Decimal Files, Pine Ridge Records, Record Group 75, National Archives, Kansas City, Missouri.

NL: Newberry Library, Chicago.

OLC: Oglala Lakota College Archives, Oglala Lakota College, Pine Ridge Reservation, Kyle, S.D.

RCIA: Reports to the Commissioner of Indian Affairs.

RG 75 NA: Bureau of Indian Affairs Records, Record Group 75, National Archives, Washington, D.C.

RI: Reports of Inspection of the OIA, 1873–1900, Record Group 75, National Archives, Microfilm Publication M1070.

WKLDOC: Wounded Knee Legal Defense Offense Committee papers. File T76-9004, Wounded Knee Trial Documents, Minnesota State Historical Society Collection, Minneapolis, Minnesota.

Bibliography

Books, articles, government reports, manuscripts

Albers, Patricia C. 1982. "Sioux Kinship in a Colonial Setting." *Dialectical Anthropology.* V. 6, p. 253–269.

Anderson, Harry H.. n.d. *Before the Indian Claims Commission.* Docket No. 74, *Sioux Nation, et al. v. United States of America.*

Balandier, Georges. 1961. "The Colonial Situation: A Theoretical Approach." In Wallerstein, Immanuel, ed., *Social Change: The Colonial Situation.* New York: John Wiley and Sons. p. 34–61.

Barsh, Russel Lawrence. 1991a "Are We Stuck in the Slime of History?" *The American Indian Quarterly.* Vol. XV, No. 1, Winter, 1991, p. 59–64.

_____. 1991b "Progressive-Era Bureaucrats and the Unity of Twentieth-Century Indian Policy." *The American Indian Quarterly.* Vol. XV, No. 1, Winter, 1991, p. 1–17.

Batchelder, George Alexander. 1870 *A Sketch of the History and Resources of Dakota Territory.* Yankton: Press Steam Power Printing Company. Newberry Library.

Big Foot Historical Society. 1968 *Reservation Round-Up.* Shannon County, South Dakota: Big Foot Historical Society. Copy in possession of the author.

Biolsi, Thomas. 1992 *Organizing the Lakota: The Political Economy of the New Deal on the Pine Ridge and Rosebud Reservations.* Tucson & London: The University of Arizona Press.

Bromert, Roger. 1980 *The Sioux and the Indian New Deal, 1933–1944.* Ph.D. diss. in History. University of Toledo.

Brophy, William A. and Sophie D. Aberle. 1956 *The Indian: America's Unfinished Business.* Norman: University of Oklahoma Press.

Burawaoy, Michael. 2000 *Global Ethnography: Forces, Connections, and Imaginations in a Postmodern World*. Berkeley: University of California Press.

Cahn, Edgar S. and David Hearne, eds. 1969 *Our Brother's Keeper: The Indian in White America*. New York: New American Library.

Chittenden, Hiram Martin. 1902 *History of the American Fur Trade of the Far West*. New York: Francis P. Harper, Volume 2.

Clow, Richmond L. 1987a "Cattlemen and Tribal Rights: The Standing Rock Leasing Conflict of 1902." *North Dakota History* V. 54, No.2, p. 23–30.

Clow, Richmond L. 1987b "The Indian Reorganization Act and the Loss of Tribal Sovereignty: Constitutions on the Rosebud and Pine Ridge Reservations." *Great Plains Quarterly.* V. 7, Spring 1987, p. 125–134.

_____. 1989 "Tribal Populations in Transition: Sioux Reservations and Federal Policy, 1934–1965." *South Dakota History.* V. 19, No. 3, p. 362–391.

Cohen, Felix S. 1942 *Handbook of Federal Indian Law*. New York: AMS Press.

Comaroff, Jean. 1985 *Body of Power Spirit of Resistance: The Culture and History of a South African People*. Chicago: University of Chicago Press.

Complaint of the Pine Ridge Sioux. 1920 Hearings before the Committee On Indian Affairs, House of Representatives, Sixty-sixth Congress, Second Session, April 6, 1920. Washington D.C.: Government Printing Office, 1920.

Constitution and By-Laws of the Oglala Sioux Tribe. 1969 "Constitution and By-Laws of the Oglala Sioux Tribe of the Pine Ridge Reservation, South Dakota." U.S. Dept. of the Interior, Office of Indian Affairs.

Cornell, Stephen. 1988 *The Return of the Native: American Indian Political Resurgence*. New York: Oxford University Press.

Cornell, Stephen and Joseph P. Kalt. 1989 "Pathways from Poverty: Economic Development and Institution-Building on American Indian Reservations. Boston, Mass.: The Harvard Project on American Indian Economic Development, Kennedy School of Government. 47 pp.

Deloria, Vine, Jr. 1970 *Custer Died for Your Sins.* New York: Avon Books.

Deloria, Vine, Jr. 1999 "Indian Affairs 1973: Hebrews 13:8," in *Spirit and Reason: The Vine Deloria, Jr., Reader*, Barbara Deloria, et al., eds. Golden, Colorado: Fulcrum Publishing.

Deloria, Vine, Jr. and Clifford Lytle. 1984 *The Nations Within: The Past and Future of American Indian Sovereignty.* New York: Pantheon Books.

Deloria, Vine, Jr. and Raymond Demallie, eds. 1975 *Proceedings of the Great Peace Commission of 1867–1868.* Washington, D.C.: Institute for the Development of Indian Law.

DeMallie, Raymond J. 1978 "Pine Ridge Economy: Cultural and Historical Perspectives." Sam Stanley, ed., *American Indian Economic Development.* The Hague: Mouton. p. 237–312.

Densmore, Francis. 1918 *Teton Sioux Music.* Bulletin 61. Washington, D.C.: Bureau of American Ethnology.

Eckholm, Erik. 1979 "The Dispossessed of the Earth: Land Reform and Sustainable Development." *Background papers for the United States Delegation, World Conference on Agrarian Reform and Rural Development*, FAO Rome 1979. Worldwatch Paper 30, June 1979. Worldwatch Institute.

Eggan, Fred. 1981 "The Politics of Power: Indian-White Relations in a Changing World." Ernest L. Schusky, ed., *Political Organization of Native North Americans.* p. 283–297.

Eicher, Carl K. 1960 *Constraints on Economic Progress on the Rosebud Sioux Indian Reservation.* Unpublished Ph.D. diss., Harvard University.

Fals-Borda, Orlando. 1991 "Some Basic Ingredients." in *Action and Knowledge: Breaking the Monopoly with Participatory Action Research*. New York: Apex Press.

Fanon, Franz. 1963 *The Wretched of the Earth*. New York: Grove Press.

Feraca, Stephen E. 1964 "The history and Development of Oglala Sioux Tribal Government." Unpublished Manuscript. 97 pages.

_____. 1966 "The Political Status of the Early Bands and Modern Communities of the Oglala Dakota." *Museum News* 27:1–19.

Fort Laramie Treaty of 1868. 1869 "Treaty with the Sioux - Brule, Oglala, Miniconjou, Yanktonai, Hunkpapa, Blackfeet, Cuthead, Two Kettle, Sans Arcs, and Santee - and Arapaho, 1868." 15 Stats., 635, Ratified February 16, 1869, Proclaimed February 24, 1869.

Fowler, Loretta. 1982 *Araphoe Politics, 1851–1978: Symbols in Crises of Authority*. Lincoln: University of Nebraska Press.

Frank, Andre Gunder. 1966 "The Development of Underdevelopment." *Monthly Review*. V. 18, p. 17–31.

Gamer, Robert E. 1988 *The Developing Nations: A Comparative Perspective*. Dubuque, Iowa: Wm. C. Brown, Publishers.

Gay, Robert J. 1984 "The Crook(ed) Commission of 1889 at Pine Ridge." Unpublished manuscript. Copy in possession of the author.

_____. 1987 "The 1910 Theft of Bennett County." Paper presented at the 19th South Dakota History Conference on April 10, 19, 1987. Copy in possession of the author.

Geertz, Clifford. 1973 *The Interpretation of Cultures*. New York: Basic Books.

Gilbert, Hila. 1968 *Big Bat Pourier*. Sheridan, Wyo.: The Mills Company.

Goffman, Erving. 1961 *Asylums: Essays on the Social Situation of Mental Patients and Other Inmates*. Garden City, NY: Anchor Books.

Gonzalez, Mario and Elizabeth Cook-Lynn. 1999 *The Politics of Hallowed Ground: Wounded Knee and the Struggle for Indian Sovereignty*. Urbana and Chicago: University of Illinois Press.

Harvey, Neil. 1998 *The Chiapas Rebellion: The Struggle for Land and Democracy.* Durham: Duke University Press.

Hassrick, Royal B. 1964 *The Sioux: Life and Customs of a Warrior Society.* Norman: University of Oklahoma Press.

Hoxie, Frederick E. 1992a "Crow Leadership Amidst Reservation Oppression." Castile, George Pierre and Robert L. Bee, eds. *State and Reservation: New Perspectives on Federal Indian Policy.* Tucson and London: University of Arizona Press. p. 38–60.

Hoxie, Frederick E. 1992b "From Prison to Homeland: The Cheyenne River Indian Reservation Before World War I." Nichols, Roger L., ed., *The American Indian: Past and Present,* 4th edition. New York: McGraw-Hill, Inc. p. 210–222.

Hodel, Secretary of the Interior, et al. v. Irving, et al. 1987 No. 85–637 (U.S. Sup. Ct., May 18, 1987), *Indian Law Reporter,* June, 1987, p. 1037–45.

Huizer, Gerrit. 1979 "Toward a View from Below." Gerrit Huizer, and Bruce Mannheim, eds., *The Politics of Anthropology: From Colonialism and Sexism Toward a View from Below.* The Hague: Mouton Publishers.

Huber, Jacqueline et al. 1981 *The Gunnery Range Report.* Pine Ridge, S. Dak.: Oglala Sioux Tribe.

Hyde, George E. 1956 *A Sioux Chronicle.* Norman: University of Oklahoma Press.

_____. 1976 *Red Cloud's Folk: A History of the Oglala Sioux.* Norman: University of Oklahoma Press.

Indian Rights Association Report. 1886 "The Honorable Commissioner of Indian Affairs and the Census at Pine Ridge Indian Agency, Dakota." Philadelphia: Indian Rights Association. Newberry Library.

Johnston, Sr. Mary A. 1948 *Federal Relations with the Great Sioux Indians of South Dakota, 1887–1933, with Particular Reference to the Land Policy Under the Dawes Act.* Washington, D.C.: Ph.D. diss. published by Catholic University of America.

Jorgensen, Joseph. 1978 "A Century of Political Economic Effects on American Indian Society 1880–1980." *Journal of Ethnic Studies.* V. 6, No, 3, p. 1–82.

Jorgensen, Joseph and Richard Clemmer. 1980 "On Washburn's 'On the Trail of the Activist Anthropologist', A Rejoinder to a Reply." *Journal of Ethnic Studies.* V. 8, No. 2, p. 85–94.

Klein, Alan. 1983 "The Political Economy of Gender: A 19th Century Plains Indian Case Study." Patricia Albers and medicine, Beatrice, eds., *The Hidden Half: Studies of Plains Indian Women.* Washington, D.C.: University Press.

Kvasnicka, Robert M. and Herman J. Viola, eds. 1979 *The Commissioners of Indian Affairs, 1824–1977.* Lincoln: University of Nebraska Press.

LaDuke, Winona. 1990 "White Earth" *Z Magazine.* V. 3, No. 10, October, p. 39–40.

Lamphere, Louise. 1976 "The Internal Colonization of the Navajo People." *Southwest Economy and Society.* V. 1, No. 1, p. 6–14.

Land Use and Purchase Patterns on the Pine Ridge Reservation. Author unknown. 1974 Bureau of Indian Affairs, mimeograph, October 1974. Copy in possession of the author.

Lee, Bob and Dick Williams. 1964 *Last Grass Frontier: The South Dakota Stock Grower Heritage.* Sturgis, S. Dak.: Black Hills Publishers, Inc.

Lewis, Oscar. 1942 *The Effects of White Contact Upon Blackfoot Culture; With Special Reference to the Role of the Fur Trade.* American Ethnological Society, Monograph No. 6. New York: J.J. Augustin

MacGregor, Gordon. 1946 *Warriors Without Weapons: A Study of the Society and Personality of the Pine Ridge Sioux.* Chicago: University of Chicago Press.

Malan, Vernon D. 1958 *The Dakota Indian Family.* Bulletin 470, May 1958. Brookings, S. Dak.: Rural Sociology Department, Agricultural Experiment Station, South Dakota State College.

Matthiessen, Peter. 1983 *In the Spirit of Crazy Horse.* New York: Viking Press.

Maynard, Eileen and Gayla Twiss. 1970 *That These People May Live.* Washington, D.C.: Department of Health, Education, and Welfare Pub. No. HSM 72–508.

McCurdy, James R. 1981 *Forced Fee Patenting.* 2415 Claims Process Contract No. A))C 14200567. Copy in possession of author.

Mekeel, H. Scudder. 1936 "The Economy of a Modern Teton Dakota Community." *Yale University Publications in Anthropology.* No. 6, New Haven: Yale University Press.

_____. 1944 "An Appraisal of the Indian Reorganization Act." *American Anthropologist.* V. 46, p. 209–217.

Menchu, Rigoberta. 1986 *I... Rigoberta Menchu: An Indian Woman in Guatemala.* Elisabeth Burgos-Debray, ed. London: Verso.

Messerschmidt, Jim. 1983 *The Trial of Leonard Peltier.* Boston: South End Press.

Mooney, James. 1976 *The Ghost-Dance Religion and the Sioux Outbreak of 1890.* Chicago and London: University of Chicago Press.

Mowat, Farley. 1984 *Sea of Slaughter.* Boston: The Atlantic Monthly Press.

Nagata, Shuichi. 1977 "Opposition and Freedom in Hopi Factionalism." M. Silverman and R.F. Salisbury, eds., *A House Divided? Anthropological Studies of Factionalism.* Institute of Social and Economic Research, Memorial University of New Foundland, Social and Economic Papers, No. 9, p. 146–169.

Occupation of Wounded Knee: Hearings before the Subcommittee on Indian Affairs of the Committee on Interior and Insular Affairs, United States Senate, Ninety-third Congress First Session on the Causes and Aftermath of the Wounded Knee Takeover. 1974 Washington, D.C.: U.S. Government Printing Office.

Oglala Sioux Tribe General Fund Audit Draft. 2000   "General Fund Financial Statements and Independent Auditor's Report, January 1, 1999 to December 31, 1999." Jaime Arobba, CPA, author, March 7, 2000. Copy in author's possession.

Oglala Sioux Tribe Department of Public Safety Assessment and Review. 2001   Oglala Sioux Tribe Department of Public Safety, February 2001. Copy in author's possession.

One Feather, Vivian. 1976   "Agricultural Development and Resources on the Pine Ridge Indian Reservation." Unpublished manuscript.

Ortiz, Roxanne Dunbar, ed. 1977   *The Great Sioux Nation: Sitting in Judgement on America.* New York, New York: American Treaty Council Information Center and Berkeley, California: Moon Books. (Based on and containing testimony at the "Sioux Treaty Hearing," December 1974, Federal District Court, Lincoln, Nebraska.)

Ortner, Sherry B. 1984   "Theory in Anthropology Since the Sixties." *Comparative Studies in Society and History.* p. 126–166.

Osgood, Ernest Staples. 1929   *The Day of the Cattleman.* Minneapolis: The University of Minnesota Press.

Owada, Patricia K. 1979 "Dillon Seymor Myer 1950–53." In Kvasnicka, Robert M. and Herman J. Viola, eds., *The Commissioners of Indian Affairs, 1824–1977.* Lincoln: University of Nebraska Press. p. 293–299.

Owens, Nancy J. 1979   "The Effects of Reservation Bordertowns and Energy Exploitation on American Indian Economic Development." In *Research in Economic Anthropology,* Vol. 2., p. 303–337, JAI Press.

Phillips, Paul C. 1961   *The Fur Trade.* (Two volumes.) Norman: University of Oklahoma Press.

Pommersheim, Frank. 1993   "Making All the Difference: Native American Testimony and the Black Hills (A Review Essay)." *North Dakota Law Review.* V. 69, p. 337–359.

Powers, William K. 1975   *Oglala Religion.* Lincoln: University of Nebraska Press.

Proceedings of the Council of the Pine Ridge Indians with E.B. Linnen, Inspector, on August 20, 1919. 1920 Printed in Hearings before the Committee On Indian Affairs, House of Representatives, Sixth-sixth Congress, Second Session, April 6, 1920. Washington, D.C.: Government Printing Office, 1920.

Proceedings of the Great Peace Commission of 1867–1868. 1975 Washington, D.C.: Institute for the Development of Indian Law. Deloria, Vine Jr., and Raymond Demallie, eds.

Report of proceedings of 1903 Council. 1903 "Report of the proceedings of the council held at Pine Ridge Agency, S.D., September 21st and 22nd, 1903: between Congressman E.W. Martin and the delegates of five different tribes of Indians, relative to the Treaty of 1876, known as the Black Hills Treaty." 32 pages. Copy in possession of the author.

Report of Proceedings of the Council of Indians Effecting Agreement of 1889. 1889 "Proceedings of the Council of Indians effecting Agreement of 1889. Chas. Foster, Wm. Warner, and Geo. Crook Commission." RG 75 NA, Box 779, KC.

Report of the Special Commission Appointed to Investigate the Affairs of the Red Cloud Agency, 1875 Ayer Collection, Newberry Library.

Report on the Bureau of Indian Affairs Fee Patenting and Canceling Policies, 1900–1942. 1981 Prepared for the Aberdeen Area Office Rights Protection Branch in Compliance with the Bureau of Indian Affiars [sic] 2415 Claims Program, June 1, 1981. Copy in possession of the author.

Reno, Philip. 1981 *Navajo Resources and Economic Development.* Albuquerque: University of New Mexico Press.

Robbins, Rebecca L. 1992 "Self-Determination and Subordination: The Past, Present, and Future of American Indian Governance." M. Annette Jaimes, ed., *The State of Native America: Genocide, Colonization, and Resistance.* Boston: South End Press.

Roberts, William O. 1943 "Successful Agriculture within the Reservation Framework." *Applied Anthropology,* Volume 2, April-June, 1943.

Robinson, Doane. 1904 *A History of the Dakota or Sioux Indians: From their earliest traditions and first contact with white men to the final settlement of the last of them upon reservations and the consequent abandonment of the old tribal life.* Aberdeen, S. Dak.: News Printing Co. Newberry Library.

Rogers, C. Bryant. 1976 "The Award of Grazing Permits on the Pine Ridge Reservation by Allocation and Indian preference Bidding." Copy in possession of the author.

Roos, Philip D., Dowell H. Smith, *et al.* 1980 "The Impact of the American Indian Movement on the Pine Ridge Indian Reservation." *Phylon.*

Roosevelt, Theodore. 1893 "Report of Honorable Theodore Roosevelt Made to the United States Civis Service Commission, Upon a Visit to Certain indian Reservations and Indian Schools in South Dakota, Nebraska, and Kansas." *Some Indian Reservations and Agencies.* Philadelphia: The Indian Rights Association. p. 3–23. Newberry Library.

Ross, John. 1995 *Rebellion from the Roots: Indian Uprising in Chiapas.* Monroe, Maine: Common Courage Press.

Ruffing, Lorraine Turner. 1979 "The Navajo Nation: A History of Dependence and Underdevelopment." *Review of Radical Political Economics.* V. 11, No. 2, p. 25–37.

Rydberg, Per Oxel. 1965 *Flora of the Prairies and plains of Central North America.* New York and London: Hofner Publishing Co.

Said, Edward W. 1993 *Culture and Imperialism.* New York: Vintage Books.

Said, Edward W. 1994 *The Pen and the Sword.* Monroe, Maine: Common Courage Press.

Schell, Herbert S.. 1968 *History of South Dakota.* Lincoln: University of Nebraska Press.

Schlesier, Karl H. 1980 "Reply to Deloria, DeMallie, Hill, and Washburn." *American Anthropologist.* 82:561–563.

Schuler, Harold H. 1990 *Fort Pierre Chouteau*. Vermillion, S. Dak.: University of South Dakota Press.

Secoy, Frank Raymond. 1971 *Changing Military Patterns on the Great Plains: 17th Century through Early 19th Century*. American Ethnological Society Monograph No. 21. Seattle: University of Washington Press.

Sioux Act. 1889 "An Act to Divide a Portion of the Reservation of the Sioux Nation of Indians in Dakota into Separate Reservations and to Secure the Relinquishment of the Indian Title to the Remainder, and for Other Purposes." March 2, 1889, 25 Statute, 888–899.

Sklair, Leslie. 1991 *Sociology of the Global System*. Baltimore: The Johns Hopkins University Press.

Smith, Carol. 1978 "Beyond Dependency Theory: National and Regional Patterns of Underdevelopment in Guatemala." *American Ethnologist*. V. 5, No. 3, p. 574–617.

_____. 1984 "Local History in Global Context: Social and Economic Transitions in Western Guatemala." *Comparative Studies in Society and History*. V. 26, No. 2, p. 193–228.

Smith, Page. 1985 *America Enters the World: A People's History of the Progressive Era and World War I*, Vol. 7, New York: McGraw Hill Book Co.

Sniffen, M.K. 1906 "Observations Among the Sioux." *Indian Rights Association, Twenty-third Annual Report*. Philadelphia, Pennsylvania: Office of the Indian Rights Association. Newberry Library.

Soyinka, Wole. 1998 "Redesigning a Nation." Public lecture given at the Nigerian Law School, Lagos, Nigeria, October 16, 1998

Sutton, Imre. 1975 *Indian Land Tenure: Bibliographical Essays and a Guide to the Literature*. New York.: Clearwater Publishing Co., Inc.

Stavrianos, L.S. 1981 *Global Rift: The Third World Comes of Age*. New York: William Morrow and Company, Inc.

Takaki, Ronald. 1993 *A Different Mirror: A History of Multicultural America.* Boston: Little, Brown and Company.

Talbot, Steve. 1979 "The Meaning of Wounded Knee, 1973: Indian Self-Government and the Role of Anthropology." Huizer, Gerrit and Bruce Mannheim, eds., *The Politics of Anthropology: From Colonialism and Sexism Toward a View From Below.* The Hague: Mouton Publishers. p. 227–258.

Tanner, Helen Hornbeck. 1982 *A Review of Federal Government Dealings With the Sioux.* Unpublished Manuscript, 136 pages plus list of exhibits. Copy in possession of the Author.

Taylor, Graham D. 1974 "The Tribal Alternative to Bureaucracy: The Indian's New Deal, 1933–1945." *Journal of the West.* V 13, p. 128–142.

_____. 1980 *The New Deal and American Indian Tribalism: The Administration of the Indian Reorganization Act, 1934–45.* Lincoln and London: University of Nebraska Press.

Thompson, E.P. 1978 "Outside the Whale." in *The Poverty of Theory and other Essays.* New York and London: Monthly Review Press. p. 211–243.

U.S. Commission on Civil Rights. 1974 (October) *Report of Investigation: Oglala Sioux Tribe, General Election, 1974.* Washington, D.C.: U.S. Commission on Civil Rights. Copy in possession of the author.

Utley, Robert M. 1963 *The Last Days of the Sioux Nation.* New Haven and London: Yale University Press.

Van den Berghe, Pierre. 1967 *Race and Racism.* New York: John Wiley and Sons.

Wahrhaftig, Albert L. and Robert K. Thomas. 1972 "Renaissance and Repression: The Oklahoma Cherokee." Bahr, Howard M., Bruce Chadwick, and Robert C. Day, eds., *Native Americans Today: Sociolgoical Perspectives.* New York: Harper and Row. p. 80–89.

Wallace, Anthony F.C. 1972 *The Death and Rebirth of the Seneca.* New York: Vintage Books.

Walker, James R. 1982 *Lakota Society.* Raymond J. DeMallie, ed., Lincoln: University of Nebraska Press.

Wallerstein, Immanuel. 1983 *Historical Capitalism.* London: Verso.

Washburn, Wilcomb E. 1984 "A Fifty-Year Perspective on the Indian Reorganization Act." *American Anthropologist.* V. 86, No. 2, p. 279–289.

Webb, Walter Prescott. 1981 *The Great Plains.* Lincoln and London: University of Nebraska Press.

Welsh, Herbert. 1883 *Report of a Visit to the Great Sioux Reserve, Dakota, made durikng the months of May and June, 1883, In Behalf of the Indian Rights Association.* Philadelphia, Pennsylvania: Indian Rights Association. Newberry Library.

Weltfish, Gene. 1971 "The Plains Indians: Their Continuity in History and Their Indian Identity." Leacock, Eleanor Burke and Nancy Oestreich Lurie, eds. *North American Indians in Historical Perspective.* New York: Random House. p. 201–227

White, Richard. 1983 *The Roots of Dependency: subsistence, Environment, and Social Change among the Choctaws, Pawnees, and Navajos.* Lincoln and London: University of Nebraska Press.

Wissler, Clark. 1936 *Changes in Population Profiles Among the Northern Plains Indians.* New York: Anthropological Papers of the American Museum of Natural History. V. XXXVI, Pt. 1. NL.

Wolf, Eric. 1982 *Europe and the People without History.* Berkeley: University of California Press.

Worsley, Peter. 1984 *The Three Worlds.* Chicago: University of Chicago Press.

Zinn, Howard. 1993 *Failure to Quit: Reflections of an Optomistic Historian.* Monroe, Maine: Common Courage Press.

Newspapers, newsletters, and maps

Bennett County Booster, October 4, 1911 to September 25, 1912. Roll 11730. Springfield, South Dakota: State of South Dakota State Archives Microfilm Unit. Oglala Lakota College Archives.

Crazy Horse News. Wisconsin State Historical Society Microfilm. Oglala Lakota College Archives.

Intertribal Agriculture Council Newsletter. Intertribal Agriculture Council, 100 North 27th Street, Suite 500, Billings, Montana 59101

Kiwitaya O Kinanjin (Coming Together and Taking a Stand). One-time newspaper publication, Oglala Lakota College, Human Services Department, July, 1991. Copy in possession of the author.

Mila Yatapika Eyapaha. (Knife Chief Crier). Published by members of Knife Chief Community, Porcupine, Pine Ridge Reservation, South Dakota. Copies in author's possession.

Oglala Light. U.S. Indian School, Pine Ridge, S.D. Oglala Lakota College Archives.

Shannon County News. Oglala Lakota College Archives.

Wounded Knee Legal Defense/Offense Committee Newsletter. Oglala Lakota College Archives.

Washington County, South Dakota, 1915. Map compiled by Bates and Brown, Surveyors, Gordon Nebraska and Martin, South Dakota. Copy in author's possession.

Archival and rare sources

Minnesota State Historical Society, Minneapolis, Minnesota

Wounded Knee Legal Defense Offense Committee (WKLDOC) papers. File T76-9004, Wounded Knee Trial Documents.

Newberry Library, Chicago, Illinois.

Ayer Collection of rare published books and unpublished manuscripts.

Ayer Photo, Siouan II, Alexander Gardiner Photographs.

Indian Rights Association Papers, 1868–1968 (1974) Glen Rock, New Jersey: Microfilming Corporation of America.

National Archives, Kansas City, Missouri.

Records of the Pine Ridge Agency, Main Decimal Files, RG 75 NA. This collection contains over 800 linear feet of records from the Pine Ridge Agency, dating from ca. 1900 to 1960.

Pine Ridge Agency, General Records: Land, RG 75 NA.

Pine Ridge Agency, Letter Books (correspondence of Allotting Agent Charles Bates), RG 75 NA.

National Archives, Washington, D.C.

Central Classified Files, 1907–1939, Pine Ridge, RG 75 NA.

Special Case 191 Leasing, Pine Ridge, 1900–1907, RG 75 NA.

Oglala Lakota College Archives, Pine Ridge Reservation, Kyle, South Dakota.

McGillycuddy Collection

Oglala Sioux Tribal Records

Reports of Inspection of the OIA, 1873–1900, RG 75 NA Microfilm Publication M1070.

Superintendent's Annual Narrative and Statistical Reports from Field Jurisdiction of the Bureau of Indian Affairs, 1907–1938. National Archives Microfilm Publications, M1011.

Index

Indian Reorganization Act (IRA):
    attempts to overturn fail, 174
    Charter defeated, 174
    "New Dealers," "Old Dealers,"
        172
    support for by community and
        ethnicity, 172, 173
    vote on, 172, 173
    and welcome changes, 173
    See also Indian Reorganization Act
        Government; Indian
        Reorganization Act and land
        reform
Indian Rights Association, 29, 53, 106
    and support of allotment, 114
Indian Reorganization Act (IRA) and
        land reform:
    blocked by OST, 189–90
    "blue land plan," 187–9
    blue land plan support, 188
    cattle cooperatives, 190–1
    Collier's assessment of land situa-
        tion, 187
    Corn Creek Cattle Association
    OST leadership opposed, 188–91
    W.O. Roberts on BIA mismanage-
        ment, 187
    removal of white-owned stock,
        188
Indian Reorganization Act (IRA) gov-
        ernment:
    central authority vs. community
        control, 176
    conflicts over among other tribes,
        233n.2
    mixed reviews of effectiveness,
        201
    questions to answer, 201
    scholars disagree on, 200–1
    "under fire" for 60 years, 199
    "white man's western style," 199
    See also Oglala Sioux Tribe

Iron Cloud, Edward, Jr., 232
    on self-sufficiency, 45
Iron Cloud, Eileen, 222
Iron Cloud, Ike:
    on cluster housing, 205
Iron Cloud-Koenen, Emily, 249
Iron Cloud-Miller, Alberta, 241

J
Jacobs, Wesley "Chuck," 243
Janis, Geraldine, 205
Jermark, Ernest, 47
Jorgensen, Joseph, 155
Jumping Bull, Calvin, 79n.85

K
KILI Radio, 214, 215
Kills Enemy, Frank, 227
Kipling, Rudyard, 186
Knife Chief, 232

L
Lakota:
    on being Lakota, 11
    defining who is Lakota, 11–13
    and Oglala usage, 7n.2
    See also ethnicity.
Lakota culture:
    and economic situation, 68
    give-away, 65, 68
    hand shaking, 149
    maza sala, 67–8
    values, 36, 37
    wacipi, 65
    wateca, 68
    yuonihan, 148
Lakota Fund:
    support for commercial ranching,
        220
Lakota Landowner Association, 2
    concern of members, 212
    history of, 235–6n.47

meet on grazing ordinance, 215
public support for, 216
Lakota language:
and gestures, 1
use of at Treaty meetings, 3
land:
differential access to, 211
dreams of return to, 206
94% grazing, 76n.11
land base:
as basis for nation, 108–9
as homeland, 3
integration into market, 4
Oglala Council and communal
ownership, 101
people alienated from, 45
struggle over in 1990s, 212–224
See also takeover of land base
land speculators:
and fee land, 34
land ownership:
BIA role in land sales, 209
increasing inequity in, 209
and "Indian cowboys," 219
land tenure:
inequitable pattern, 209
"unholy alliance," 208–212
LaPointe, James, 168
leasing:
economics of in 1917, 152
explanations for rise in, 123–5
illegal subleasing, 208
See also big leasing
Lee, Pat, 228, 246
Little Wound, George, 105
loafers:
definition of, 40n.18
and 1868 Treaty negotiations, 16
Lone Hill, Mel, 216, 221
Loud Hawk, Russell, 124, 125

M
Macgregor, Gordon, 48
Man Afraid of His Horses, 17
Man That Walks Under the Ground:
railroads disturb buffalo, 16
Martinez, Manuel, 131
Martinez, Mary, 131
mass media:
"Tragedy at Pine Ridge," 47
Matador Cattle Company, 194n.52
Means, Ted, 203
Meeks, Elsie, 220
Mekeel, Haviland Scudder, 175
Meritt, E.B., 34, 131, 133, 142–3, 150,
177
Merrival, Hermus, 169
migrant labor:
economic significance of, 68–9
of Oglalas out of state, 46
compared to government work
projects, 72
See also economy
mixed blood, 11–13
disenfranchisement contributes to
conflict, 165
and 1868 Treaty, 17
families taxed off land, 202
population trends, 63
settlement on North Platte River,
16
success in business, 20
values associated with, 13, 18
See also ethnic difference
Monroe, John, 169
Mooney, James, 33
Myer, Dillon, 203
McBride, Ted, 245
McGaa, W.D., 59
McGillycuddy, Valentine:
establishes Indian Police, 29
on John Brennan, 91
McGregor, James, 178

McKoen, W.D., 128, 129, 131, 137, 139, 147, 179
McLaughlin, James:
  trespass report, 89–90
Newcastle Land and Livestock Company, 125, 127, 128
Northwestern Fur Company, 18
  See also hide trade
Means, Russell:
  and second presidential candidacy, 238n.78
  campaign platform of, 226
  wins 1973 primary, 229
missionaries:
  complain about dancing, 65

N
Native American Rights Fund (NARF), 225
  See also Cobell v. Babbit
No Flesh, 21
non-progressive:
  use of term by Agents, 120–121n.129

O
Office of Indian Affairs (OIA):
  brokers of Oglala resources, 176, 177, 178
  "Five Year Plan" of, 180, 186
  limitations of surveillance by, 79n.82
  ignores trespass law, 90
  See also Bureau of Indian Affairs; colonial administration
Oglala:
  and Oglala usage of term, 7n.2
  See also Lakota; Oglala Lakota
Oglala Council (Oglala Omniciye):
  Asa Kills A Hundred on, 93
  and allotment eligibility, 19
  argument against allotment, 109

  effect of allotment on, 154
  effectiveness of, 112, 113
  established, 92
  role of mixed bloods in, 114
  lobbying in Washington, D.C., 34
  organizes against leasing, 99
  outlawed in 1918, 143, 144
  OIA views of, 94, 95
  critiques OIA practices, 133
  and protection of land base, 95–6, 97
  argument against leasing, 101
  representative nature of, 92–3, 94
  and trespass penalty, 91
  and "Tribunal of Chiefs," 170, 171
  draws on outside support, 100
  See also traditional government.
Oglala Lakota:
  contested linguistic marker, 221
  and Oglala usage, 7n.2
  See also Oglala
Oglala Lakota College:
  M.A. in tribal leadership, 2
  Tatanka Iyacin (in the manner of a buffalo) Conference, 46
Oglala Omniciye. *See* Oglala Council
Oglala politics:
  and demographic and political developments, 166
  ethnic difference and, 166
Oglala Sioux Tribal Council:
  and commercial ranching, 191, 192
  alleged discrimination against full bloods, 174
  early criticism of, 173–4
  early support for ranchers 189, 190–1
  established, 173
  and rapprochement with federal government, 230

leadership style, 191
mixed blood control of, 176
narrow constituency of, 246
and tiospaye representation, 175
See also Indian Reorganization Act
government; OST Allocation
Committee; OST Land
Committee
Oglala Sioux Tribe (OST), 2
and selective effectiveness of, 230
See also takeover of OST headquarters
OST Allocation Committee:
role of, 210
OST Land Committee, 212, 213, 214
avoids input, 214
One Feather, Gerald, 206
oppression:
collective sense of, 241–2
depth of, 134
Ortiz, Alfonso, 47
overgrazing:
and BIA/OST responsibility, 210
effects of on land, 211
See also depredations

P
participatory research, 6, 233n.1
patriotism:
as rationale for leasing, 152–3
and takeover of land base, 151
patron-client system, 177–8
petitions:
against allotment in 1894, 108
against big leasing, 145
against leasing in 1900, 95
against leasing in 1905, 100
for election re. Bennett County,
111
for mixed blood Council, 169
on non-payment of lease in 1921,
129

on nonpayment of lease in 1922,
146
pro-leasing, 98–99
against 21 Council, 170
See also resistance
Plenty Horses, 31
Porcupine Trading Post, 131
Pourier, David, 214, 217
Powers, William, 38

R
racism:
Alfonso Ortiz on stereotypes, 47
"blanket Indian," 76n.26
and denigration of Indian teachers,
30
Henry Standing Bear on, 30, 31
and "shiftless nature," 47
stereotypes and "white man's burden," 186
of Superintendent Henry Tidwell,
149
Randall, Marie, 241
range units, 178–80
allocation of, 208
allocation process, 236n.48
allocation process flawed, 210
favors cattlemen, 179
and people's homes, 180
Oglala delegation on, 179
use of by OST, 189, 190
rations, 68–74
amount of, 70, 71, 72, 73
beef issue figures inflated, 71
drastic cuts in, 70
and General Crook's assurances,
70
reduced by McGillycuddy,
81n.110
857 removed from rolls, 28
myth of dependency on, 68–74
poor quality of, 73